BEAUTIFUL
BOOKBINDINGS

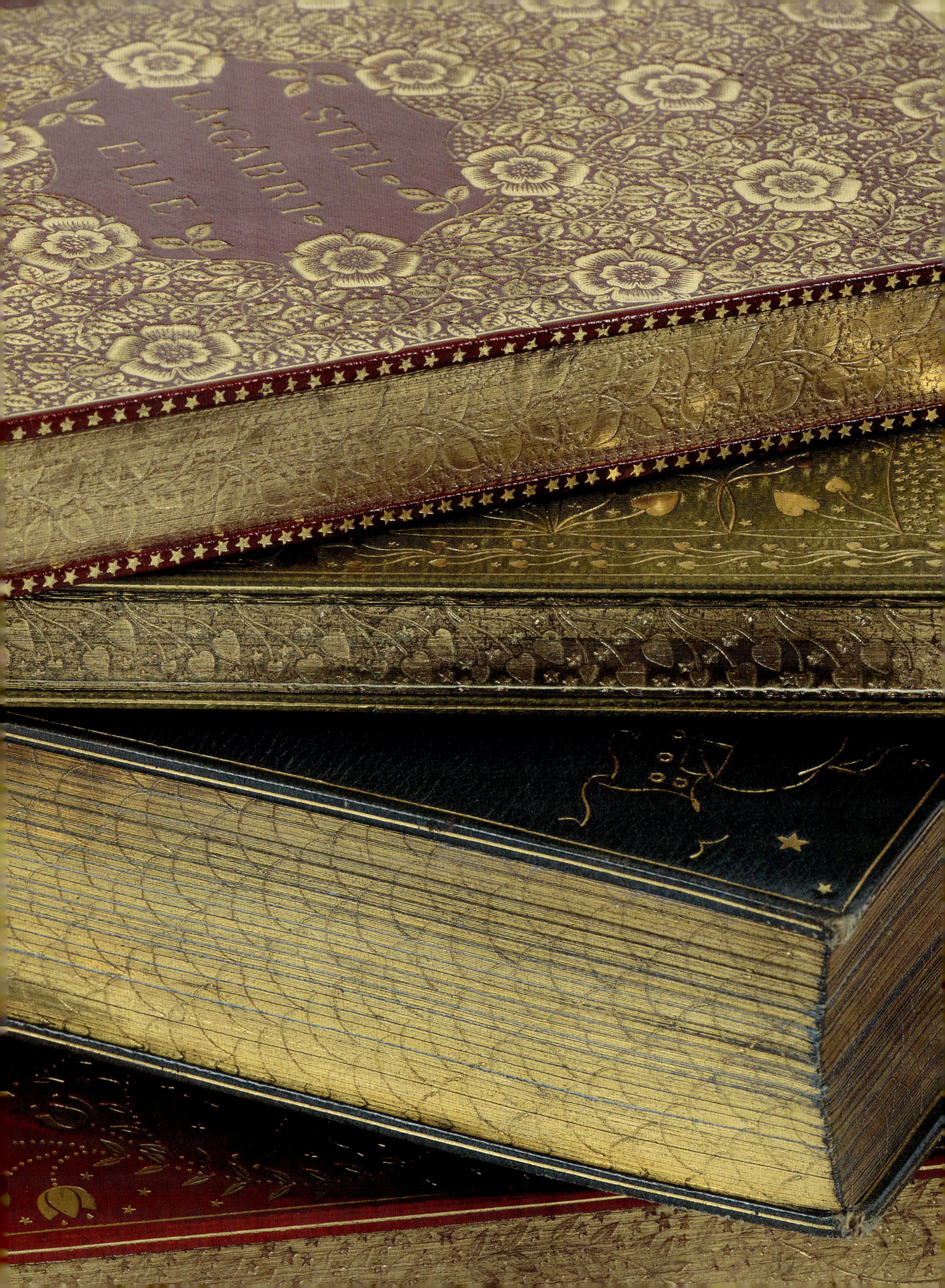
STEL-
LAGABRI-
ELLE

BEAUTIFUL BOOKBINDINGS

A Thousand Years of the Bookbinder's Art

P J M Marks

The British Library
&
Oak Knoll Press

NOTES TO THE READER

The series of numbers and letters given at the end of each entry is the British Library's unique identification code, or shelf mark, for that particular item.

Quotes in the captions are attributed and full bibliographic information for each item is provided at the end of the book.

First published in 2011 by

The British Library
96 Euston Road
London NW1 2DB

and

Oak Knoll Press
310 Delaware Street
New Castle, DE 19720

Cataloguing in Publication Data
A catalogue record for this publication is available from both The British Library and the Library of Congress

ISBN 978-0-7123-5823-1 (British Library)
ISBN 978-1-58456-293-1 (Oak Knoll Press)

Designed by Kate Slotover
Colour reproduction by Dot Gradations Ltd, Essex
Printed in Hong Kong by Great Wall Printing Co. Ltd

Frontispiece: nineteenth/early twentieth-century English gold-tooled leather bindings by Thomas James Cobden-Sanderson.

Below: detail of Jean Grolier's inscription in his copy of *De Medicina libri VIII*, Venice, 1497. BL G.9026.

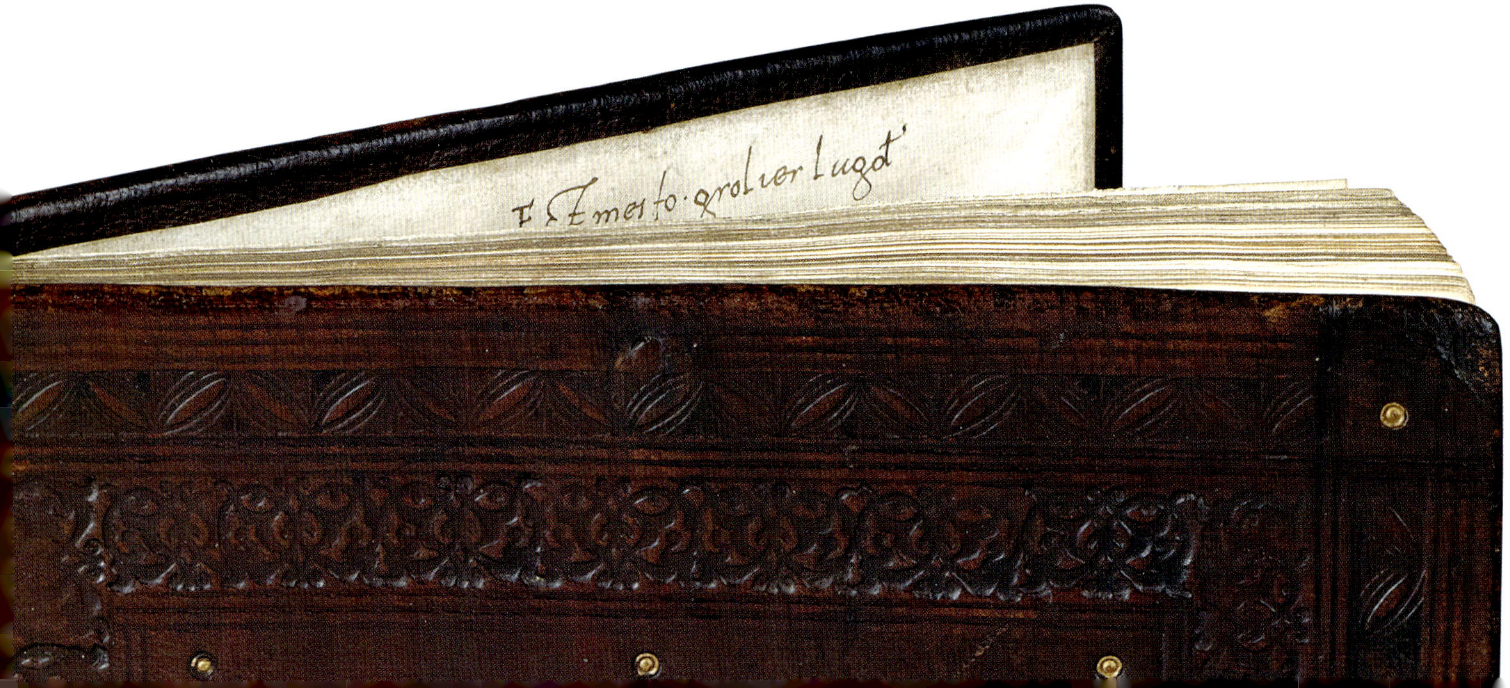

CONTENTS

INTRODUCTION

The great aesthete Oscar Wilde was of the opinion that 'in bookbinding, art expresses primarily not the feeling of the worker but simply itself, its own beauty, its own wonder.'[1] And yet, this form of art for its own sake is so often overlooked, and bindings are often viewed solely for their practical purpose of protecting the pages of a book.

This book seeks to rectify this situation by reconsidering the finest bookbindings as the objects of desire that they were intended to be, and it is hoped that by concentrating on illustrating the art itself their beauty will be revealed to a new and wider audience.

Presented here are around 100 of the most exquisite bookbindings to be found in the British Library's collections. They span more than ten centuries and include books once owned by Francis I and Henry II of France, Jean Grolier, Thomas Mahieu, Elizabeth I of England, the diarist Samuel Pepys, George III of England (who kept his own bindery in Buckingham House) and William Morris. The work of some of the greatest bookbinders, including Mearne, Padeloup, Payne, Simier, Cobden-Sanderson and many unidentified masters, is showcased here, and the beauty and skill of the art form is revealed.

Bookbinding is a craft that is more than 2000 years old, yet it has enjoyed a recent resurgence in popularity. Exhibitions and competitions that attract the interest of amateurs and professionals alike take place throughout the world. These include national and international events run by Designer Bookbinders and the Society of Bookbinders in the UK; the Elizabeth Soutar bookbinding prize in Scotland; the Helen Warren DeGolyer Exhibition and Bookbinding Competition in Texas; the World Biennials of Art Bookbinding in France; and other competitions held in Estonia, Germany, Italy, Spain, Lithuania, New England (US), New South Wales (Australia) and Switzerland amongst many others. A foundation such as the Bibliotheca Wittockiana in Belgium is largely dedicated to book arts, but although institutional collections, for example those in the Folger Library in the United States, the Bibliothèque Nationale de France, the Victoria and Albert Museum and, indeed, the British Library, have long been recognized by specialists, they still await popular discovery. There are a large number of websites and blogs aimed at amateur binders that both instruct and inspire, providing information on everything, from how to make hand-sewn notebooks to recreating historic styles.

The skill is also taught widely in a more formal way. Traditionally, binders took on apprentices, provided board and lodging and trained them in return for an initial payment and their work. In England, this period was seven years and standards were maintained by the trade guild (for example the Company of Stationers, founded in London in 1403). As the apprenticeship system declined, educational institutions took over, although the number teaching bookbinding has recently declined. Today, colleges of art run courses in bookbinding, and some (such as the London College of Communication) offer qualifications in all aspects of the craft, including restoration and design. Evening classes are also available to those who enjoy binding as a hobby. Many binders recognize the necessity of passing on their skills to ensure the vitality of the craft, and run training sessions informally or together with 'friends' organizations.

It is hoped that this book will provide inspiration to those already involved in bookbinding, and encourage more to join in. Today, the internet, with its plethora of instructional sites, has informed and motivated a new generation of amateurs who are taking up the challenge of making their own bookbindings, and reinvigorating an ancient craft. Long may it continue!

SOURCES OF EVIDENCE

Relatively few examples of early bookbindings have survived, the preservation issues being considerable:

covering materials (particularly fabric) are prone to deterioration, colours fade, metal book decoration, such as corner-pieces, and the bosses and tools used for applying decoration have often been melted down, and jewels and ivory panels stolen or re-used. We therefore do not know if the examples that now exist are typical or extraordinary. Fortunately, in more recent times, the number of surviving examples is greater, making the identification of trends easier, though still rather inconsistent in scope. Deliberate efforts have been made to preserve ornate bindings and those commissioned for important people. The significance of bindings covering books that once belonged to the British royal family, for example, was recognized in the Victorian period by staff in the British Museum Library. When books needed repair, efforts were made to retain the decorative covers, but the need to preserve other original features, including the sewing structure, was not realized. Edges of the pages were gilt or stained and, at times, painted motifs were even 'touched up' so the original appearance of the binding was obscured.

The survival of other types of less precious binding is more haphazard, particularly those for plain, inexpensive books used by scholars, tradesmen and commoners. Nineteenth-century survivals are more numerous, but the use of inexpensive machine-made paper adopted by the printing industry – which can be highly acidic and deteriorates rapidly, thus 'infecting' the whole book – has meant that some examples are in poor condition. In spite of these difficulties it is possible to piece together a history of the development of bookbinding, using, where necessary, written sources to fill in the gaps.

Many of these written sources take the form of instructional manuals. Some Arab leaders held the written word in such esteem that they studied calligraphy and book-making, and wrote treatises on the subject. These include the eleventh-century Zirid ruler of North Africa, Tamin ibn al Mu'izz ibn Badis, and the thirteenth-century Rasulid ruler of Yemen, al-Malik al-Muẓaffar. In the West, the Church itself fostered such learning in the monasteries: the twelfth-century handbook *Schedula diversarum artium* was written by a Benedictine monk, Theophilus Presbyter, and included instructions on bookbinding. Such manuals – and there are several other examples – are particularly interesting to the binding historian because they give the binders themselves a voice. The French self-taught binder, Lesné, wrote the first edition of his guide (1820) in verse, and dedicated it to his son, also a binder. Dirk de Bray illustrated his seventeenth-century Dutch book with watercolours of the various workshop operations. In 1776 Silvanus Chirm used his instructional leaflet to criticize the use of stab sewing for school texts, and to promote his own new, sturdier method involving spine bands.[2]

A BRIEF HISTORY OF BOOKBINDING

It is hard to overstate the importance of bookbinding: indeed, it could be argued that, indirectly, the ideas promoted by religion, philosophy, science and literature exist today because of its protective qualities. Right from the beginning of intellectual endeavour, a covering medium helped to ensure the permanence of the written word and this took many forms, from the wax tablets encased in wooden panels used by scribes from Antiquity, to papyrus, parchment or leather rolls (often known as scrolls) protected by wrappers or wound around wooden or bone cores. Another format was developed in the first century BC, whereby Buddhist monks in India copied religious sutras, or verses, onto palm leaves that were then threaded onto twines and enclosed by two wooden boards (see p.23). This method soon spread to Persia, Afghanistan, Iran and China. Scholars sometimes view this Indian practice as the origin of the craft of bookbinding.

Paper, which was being made in China by the second century AD, lent itself to the scroll format perfectly and also proved to be accommodating to new developments. The world's earliest dated printed book (AD 868) is a Chinese paper scroll about sixteen feet long and containing the religious text of the Diamond Sutra.[3] As a continuous roll of material can be difficult to use, alternative methods of producing texts emerged, including the folding of paper into a smaller concertina structure whereby

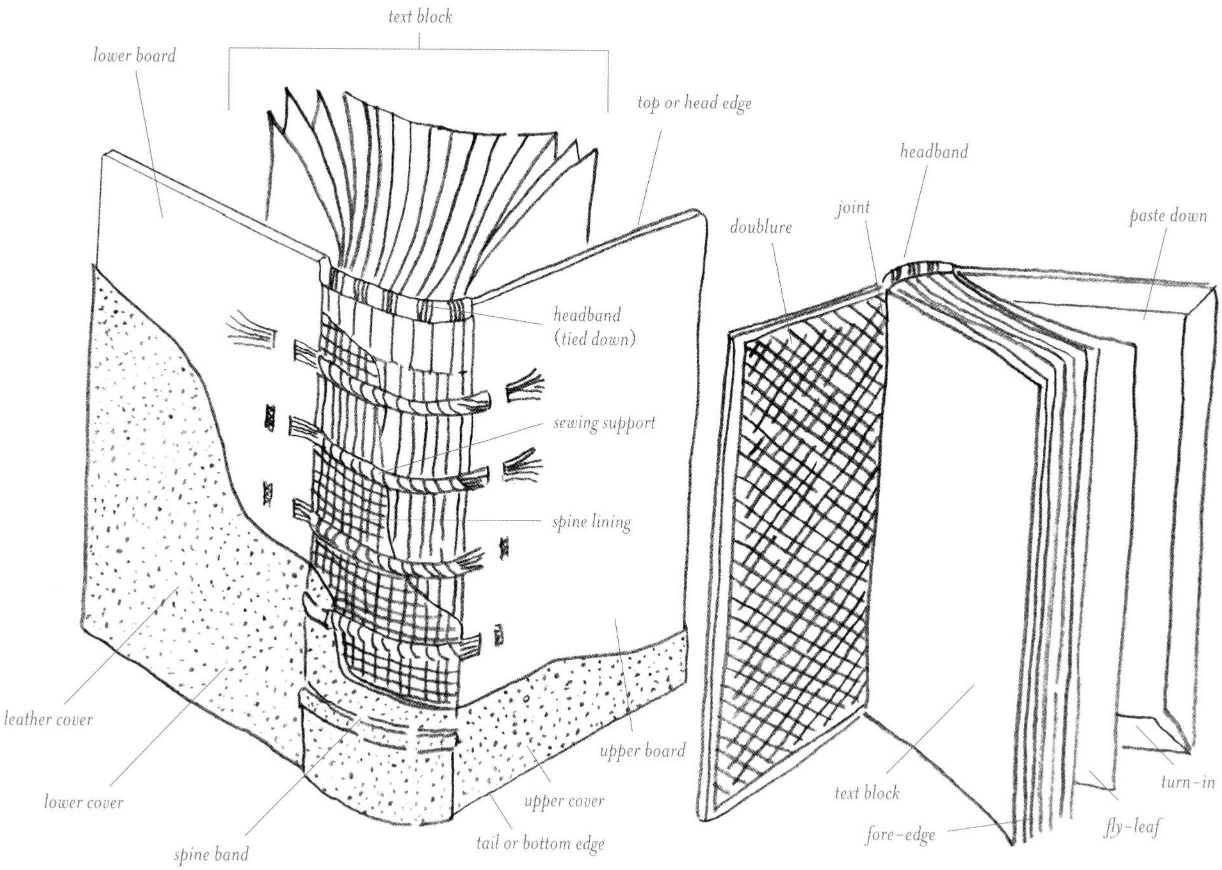

The structure of a Western binding.

pages could be easily turned. A variation became popular during the Song dynasty (960–1279): this was the butterfly binding, involving the application of paste to the folded edges of paper and the addition of a stiff wrapper around the spine and sides. The open leaves resembled butterfly wings.

Stitched bindings, attached by thread, became the predominant Chinese book format late in the Ming dynasty (1368–1644), and represented the last phase in the history of traditional Chinese bookbinding. This involved thread being passed through the sides of the folded paper from top to bottom (rather than linking one separate section to its neighbour). The method was somewhat similar to Western-style 'stab stitching'. Paper or fabric covers or flap cases were added as a further level of protection, and could be easily replaced if damaged. Chinese binding techniques were extremely influential in the East, spreading to Japan and then to much of Asia.

The form of sewing can help ascribe a binding to a particular country. In the West, a different structure called the codex (which consists of folded sheets sewn along one edge or through the fold) emerged. It was initially described in the first century AD by the Roman poet, Martial, and its spread was particularly associated with the rise of Christianity. The codex soon became the norm in Egypt where it was used with a particular style of attachment, called Coptic sewing (see diagram, p.10). Sheets were folded into sections, a thread was passed through each fold, and the folded sheets were linked to their neighbours using a chain stitch, with wooden boards attached at either end. This makes for a very flexible structure. The codex became the preferred format

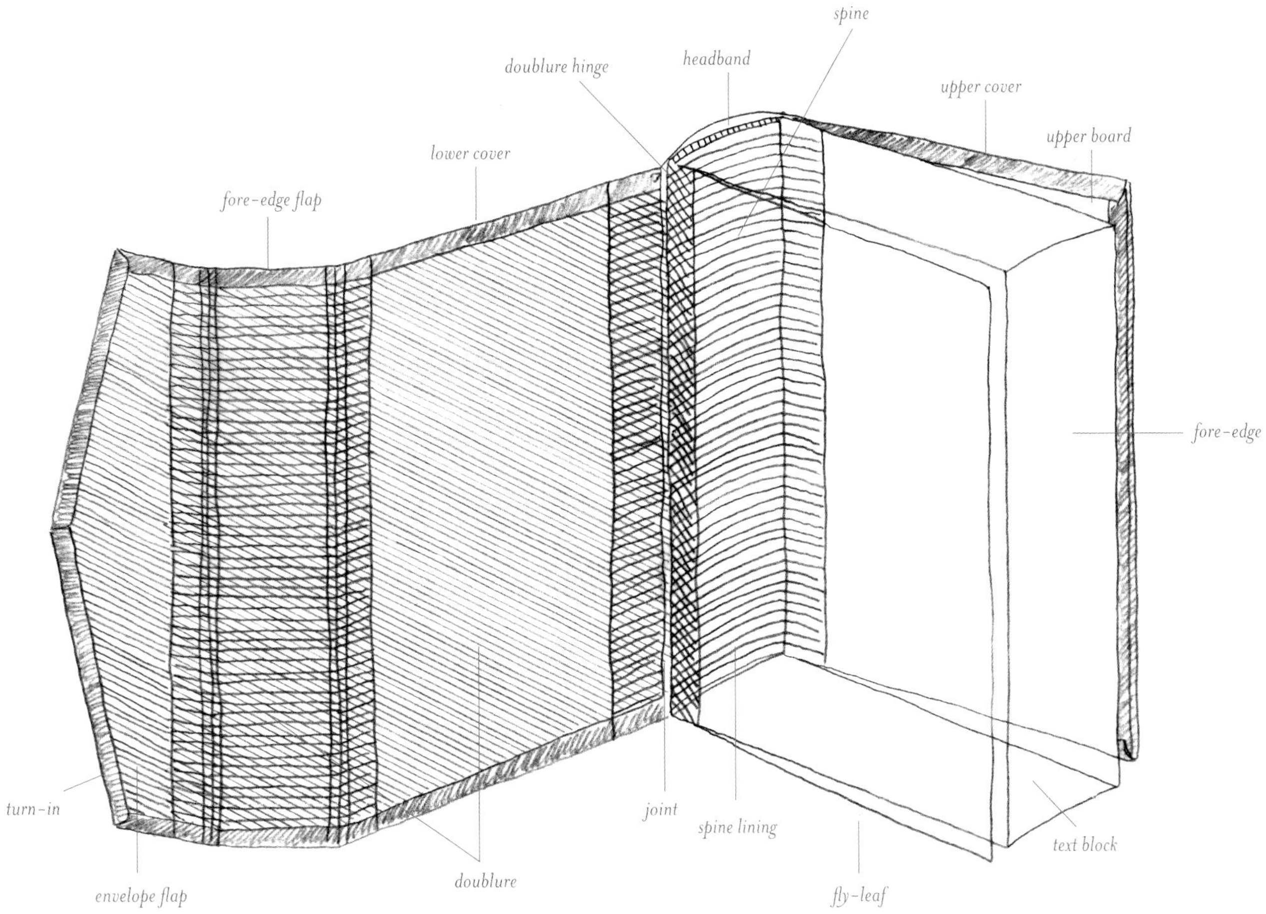

An Islamic book structure.

for protecting literary texts at roughly the same time as the Roman Empire adopted Christianity as its official religion in the late fourth century. Coptic-style sewing was so effective that it spread throughout the eastern Mediterranean (including Constantinople/Byzantium), the Near East and North Africa and Ethiopia. Its popularity continued after the Muslim conquest of much of the area in the seventh century, becoming a characteristic feature of Islamic bindings. Another attribute is that the edges of the pages are always cut flush to the covers (as they are in twelfth and early thirteenth century Western-style Romanesque bindings), in contrast to later Western practices whereby covers project significantly over the text block offering a further element of protection. In an Islamic book the page edges are shielded by a pentagonal envelope flap, which extends from the lower cover (see diagram above, and image on p.24). A less common, earlier Islamic variant was the oblong-box binding with wooden boards and a peg and strap fastening, examples of which can be found in tenth-century Syria and the Yemen. Islamic books always open at the 'back' (to Western eyes) because the Arabic script is read from right to left. The same is also true of Hebrew books.

The current Western sewing tradition in bookbinding developed gradually, but the adoption of the sewing support was an important step. Carolingian bindings (those made during the reign of Charlemagne [d.814], the King of the Franks and Holy Roman Emperor) are the earliest example of this feature.[4] It comprised cords or thongs placed across the spine, around which the sewing thread

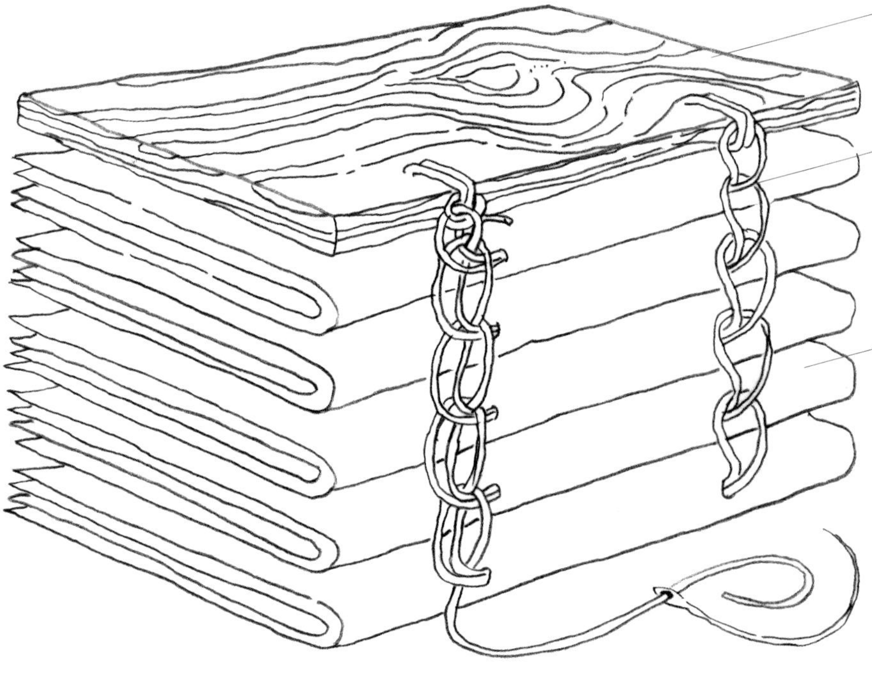

Coptic-style sewing. Note how the sections link together and are then threaded into the board (or cover).

was wound. The thread passed through the fold of the sections, around the sewing supports and then into the neighbouring section. The sections are also attached to each other via the kettle stitch, a small link-stitch at the top and tail. The ends of the sewing supports were channelled into the wooden boards, thus attaching the text block. The focus of this operation was the sewing frame, which was in use by the twelfth century and probably earlier.

Generally speaking, and certainly pre-sixteenth century, Western-style sewing results in raised horizontal spine bands (which accommodate the cords). The number of raised bands can differ and the appearance of the spine was affected by trends: sixteenth-century Italian bindings, for example, frequently featured the addition of thinner half-bands, which are primarily decorative. During this period examples of a smooth spine with no visible bands can also be found. If a particularly strong structure was required, say for large-format or heavy books, a double sewing support was favoured. If a smooth spine was required, cuts were made into the folds of the sections into which the sewing supports would fit, or flat cords were used and the spaces between were lined. The subsequent sewing method was termed 'flexible'. When the covering material was applied, the sewing supports did not protrude.

There was, in fact, a wide variety of stitches available for use and methods could vary in a single workshop, let alone in different regions. Not all Western bindings routinely have sewing supports. Thin and inexpensive books and pamphlets with paper covers can be stab-stitched, which entails stitching through the side of the section, rather than the middle, and there are a variety of such quick and easy techniques.

While temporal rulers also needed books for administrative and auditing purposes, it was the demand for devotional works in the Middle Ages that was the key factor in the early growth of the craft of bookbinding. Many religions emphasize the importance of holy writings, and sacred books could serve much the same purpose as reliquaries (containers which housed items associated with saints), preserving the word and becoming objects of veneration. The bindings of sacred books made of precious metals or ivory were known as treasure bindings. Cassiodorus, a sixth-century Roman nobleman who founded a monastery, was of the opinion that 'the beauty of the sacred writings should have a comely outward appearance imitating, perhaps, the parable of Christ in which those worthy of invitation to the heavenly feast were clothed in fine garments'.[5] He even provided a pattern book with appropriate specimens of different kinds of bindings.[6] Many religious institutions had schools and libraries attached to them, and established workshops where manuscripts were copied and bindings made, to support educational activities.

It is not known precisely when binding workshops emerged from religious institutions and became independent businesses, and the timing of this development varied according to area. Increased student demand for written texts in thirteenth-century Paris is thought to have triggered such a development. Similarly, the growth in commerce in the late Middle Ages stimulated the development of increasingly sophisticated business stationery, especially of account books. Such a book had to open so that the pages lay flat for ease of writing, and intensive use meant that the board attachment had to be particularly strong; therefore, reinforcing strips and supplementary sewing (known as tackets) were frequently added. The format that developed in the West for this purpose had a specific appearance and structure and was known as a stationery, or ledger, binding.

Economic factors had a profound influence on the development of bookbinding. The invention of printing with moveable type in fifteenth-century Mainz meant that texts could be produced quickly and in far greater numbers, and the consequent increase in demand for books meant a similar increase in work for binders, which in turn brought about other technical innovations.

Early techniques for the surface decoration of leather bindings were time-consuming. Simple lines were relatively easy to apply, but as more elaborate hand tools emerged the tool had to be frequently re-applied in order to achieve complete coverage. A larger tool (known as a panel stamp) emerged in fourteenth-century Europe. When the panel stamp was used in a press, it applied a single image to a much larger area, for example the whole of an upper (or front) cover. Decoration could therefore be achieved in a single operation, saving the binder time and money. Similarly, a roll, consisting of an engraved wheel that could be used to create a continuous decorative strip, was employed in continental Europe by the end of the fifteenth century, and was a quick way to make a border or frame.

These tools were used to impress a blind design, but the method was also appropriate when tooling in gold was adopted. Gold-tooling on leather appears to have been an Islamic invention. It was practised in Morocco from the thirteenth century, and by the second half of the fourteenth century it was well established in the Mamluk empire and Iran.[7] It seems to have reached Europe via Italy in the fifteenth century, and was then adopted by Spanish, Hungarian and French craftsmen who rapidly made the skill their own. Some tools incorporate names or initials, for example the German binder, Gregor Bernutz (see p.54). One cannot assume that all such marks denote the binder; it is thought

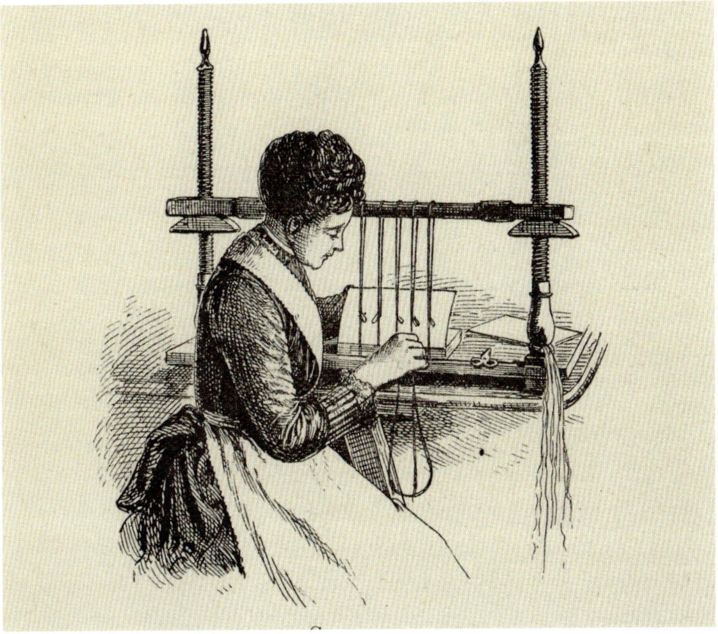

This is a late nineteenth-century English example of the sewing frame traditionally used by bookbinders in the West. The needle passes through the middle of the section and then around the sewing supports. At this time, women were often employed to do the work.

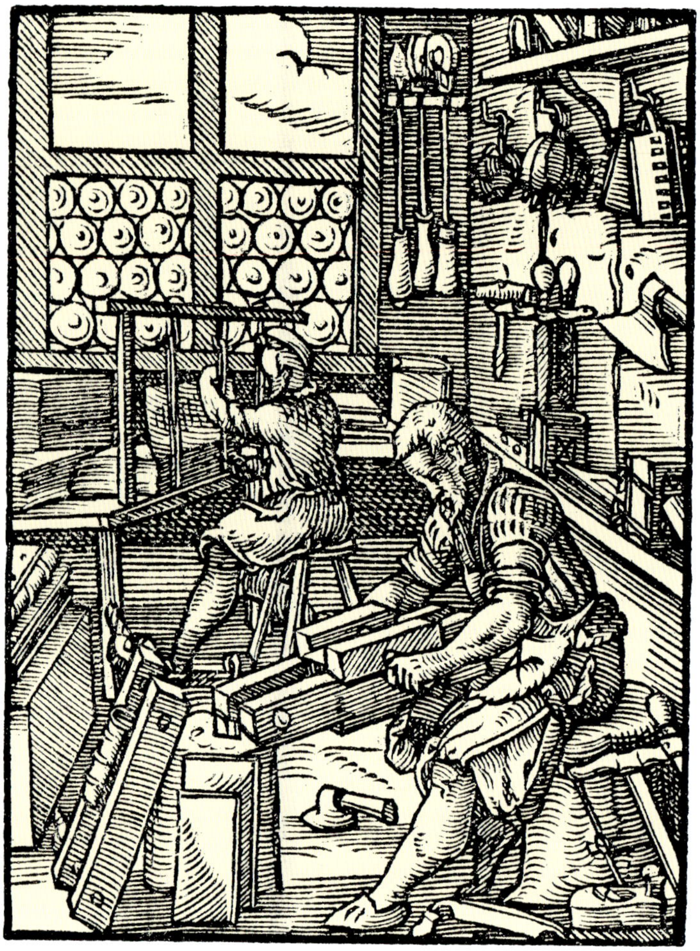

A sixteenth-century German binding workshop showing binders 'forwarding'.

that tool-engravers and publishers may also have incorporated their names in this way.

Until the eighteenth-century Industrial Revolution, each binding was one of a kind, being handmade and crafted according to the personal requirements of the client. Books were usually sold as text blocks (the unbound inside pages of a book) and individual customers then took these to be bound to their tastes and budget. Bibliographer and binding historian, David Pearson, considers that 'all bindings of the hand-press era are essentially unique objects', and this quality tells us a great deal about the purchaser as well as the binder, since so many individual choices as to price, type of decoration and so on were factored in to the final product.[8] Tastes naturally differed from person to person: the English author and book collector, William Beckford (1759–1844), preferred restrained styles, and opted for those, rather than the 'overstated and excessively goldified' bindings made by the 'detestable' Paris bookbinder, Simier, for the Duchess of Berry.[9] A binding by Simier can be seen on p.124.

The nineteenth-century increase in trade and colonialism brought about a rise in the export of Western-style bindings and decoration to the newly adopted lands. During the eighteenth and nineteenth centuries under the Ottomans, Turkish bindings began to lose the typical Islamic flap, and this also occurred in Persia. In the Far East, by contrast, Korea maintained its five-holed, side-stitched bindings until the beginning of the twentieth century, while in Japan, traditional book forms continued to dominate because foreigners were banned during the Edo period (1600–1868). When this policy of exclusion was reversed (from 1868–1912), contact with the West was welcomed and the Western-style bindings format was embraced. During the twentieth century, efforts were made to revitalize traditional regional bindings skills, such as the programme of supporting craftsmen as 'National Living Treasures' in Japan. As for China, it was not until the early twentieth century that the traditional thread-stitched bookbinding was replaced by Western-style bookbinding.

The Industrial Revolution paved the way for the mass production of books, making them more readily available to a wider cross-section of the population. Bookbindings inevitably began to reflect this new market. Increasingly, the covers were made and decorated separately from the printed text (the text block), and the two elements were joined together by means of the endleaves (sometimes known as end papers) and spine lining. Some books were no longer sewn at all. The nineteenth century saw the emergence of the 'perfect' or adhesive binding, where the pages are glued together along the spine. This was, and is, used in mass-produced paperback books and telephone directories. The structure is not long lasting, but is inexpensive.

Progress in technology also led to innovation in decoration. Developments in cloth production during the nineteenth century meant that it could now provide a durable and inexpensive covering material for books. Furthermore, the surface could be grained or embossed with patterns in the same way as leather could (see illustration, right). Paper, too, could be used as a covering material and be embossed and blocked with gold or coloured designs en masse. All this formed the basis for a lucrative market in gift bindings, many of which, like almanacs, were given as presents at New Year. Other texts were produced for special occasions such as christenings or confirmation. Bookbinders in Britain, America and Europe were quick to take advantage of this new niche market and many became rich, thanks to these popular bindings with 'chocolate box' designs. The printing, publishing and binding firm of Mame in Tours, France, (see p.122) produced large quantities of this type of book, as well as more traditional bookbindings. The Report of the Juries of the Great Exhibition in London in 1851 noted: 'France applies binding in boards chiefly to ephemeral books, which must attract the eye by their splendour, and which are intended either to ornament the drawing room tables or to be given as prizes ... The bindings in boards exhibited by M. Mame of Tours display elegance combined with a relative degree of solidity.'[10]

Such developments presented new opportunities for artists to augment their incomes, thanks to publishers who commissioned them to design the covers of whole editions of books. New styles could be applied quickly and easily in response to changes in fashion.

The pre-eminence of these decorative cloth-bound editions did not go unchallenged. William Morris, a founding father of the Arts and Crafts movement in England, believed that industrialization and mass production were destroying the traditional skills and individual talent of the craftsman. Proponents of this philosophy sought to run businesses with this in mind, some also applying the socialist principles advocated by Morris. In 1884 a friend of Morris's, Thomas James Cobden-Sanderson, established the Doves Bindery after having learned to bind books by hand himself,

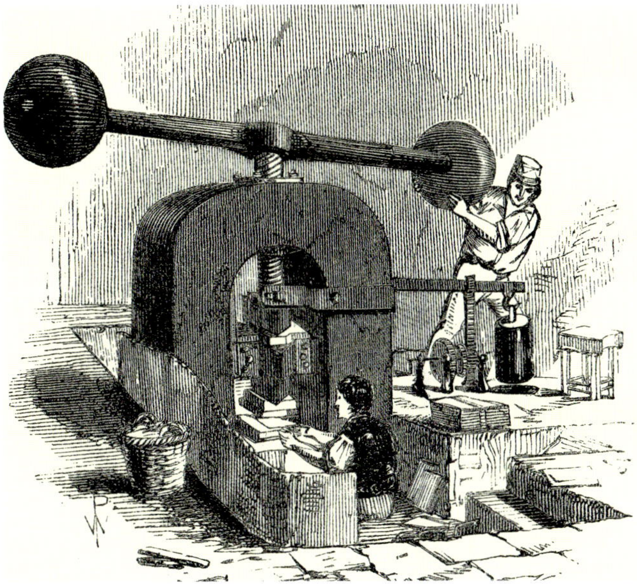

A nineteenth-century English embossing press.

and thus inaugurated a style revolution termed 'the birth of modern bookbinding' by the binding historian, G D Hobson.[11] Students, many of whom were women, travelled from as far as America to learn from Cobden-Sanderson and his binders. One apprentice at the Doves Bindery was Douglas Cockerell (1870–1945), who passed on his knowledge via evening classes, which he gave at the Central School of Arts and Crafts in London, and through his book, *Bookbinding and the Care of Books*, which is still regarded as a standard work on the subject.

Craft bookbinders today, including groups such as the Designer Bookbinders, the Society of Bookbinders, the Guild of Book Workers and Société De La Reliure Originale, stress the importance of individual input and a sound book structure, and owe much to Cobden-Sanderson, although some may not acknowledge the debt! The creators of artists' books have extended this vision further in producing works of art in book form where the primary focus is of the book as artefact, rather than as text.

The craft of bookbinding can be said to have come full circle. We can trace its circular route from the early book structures made by individuals through to the mass production technologies of the

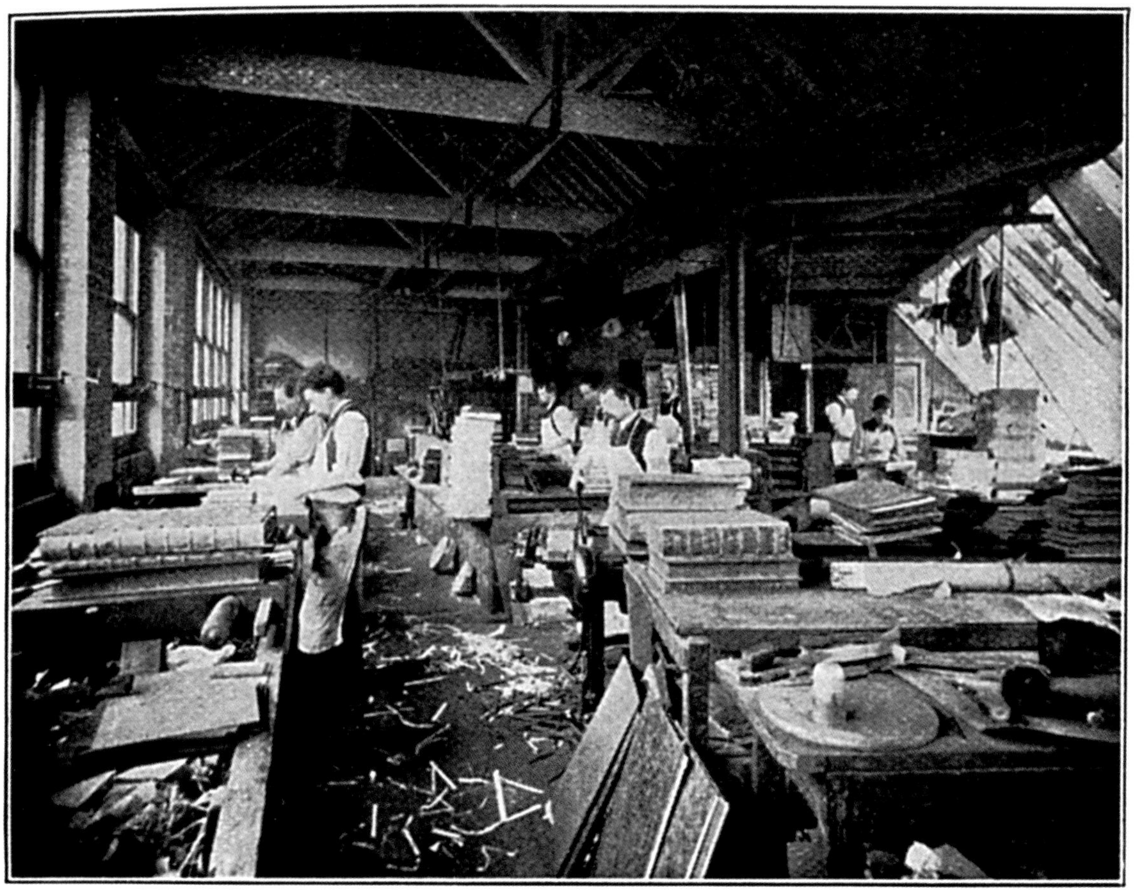

The forwarding department at Zaehnsdorf bookbinders in London at the end of the nineteenth century.

nineteenth century, and thence to the emergence of the professional bookbinder in the twentieth and twenty-first centuries, usually working alone, and seeing him or herself as both an artist and a craftsperson.

WHO WERE THE BOOKBINDERS?

Western binders were relatively poorly paid and tended to rank low in the social scale. Jane Austen reflects this in a conversation in one of her early, lesser-known compositions where the aristocratic Lady Greville asks, 'loud enough to be heard by half the people in the room, "Pray Miss Maria, in what way of business was your Grandfather for Miss Mason and I cannot agree whether he was a grocer or a bookbinder". I saw that she wanted to mortify me.'[12] In fact, many binders took on other tasks, including dealing in pamphlets or patent medicines, to make ends meet.

In many cases we do not even know the name of the individual craftsman, and history may dignify him instead with names descriptive of his work or reference to an important client or bound book. The unknown craftsman responsible for the work on p.55 was given the name 'Dudley binder' after his most important client, Robert Dudley, Earl of Leicester, who was a favoured courtier of Queen Elizabeth I. Similarly, Barlow's 'Aesop binder' was so called because he bound three presentation copies of Aesop's work in 1687 (see p.81). Some binders helpfully 'sign' their work by tooling their names on the binding (see 'Sancha' in the lower frame of the binding on p.108 and 'Simier' on the foot of the spine on p.124). From the late eighteenth century some workshops in Europe pasted trade tickets to the endleaves of their bound books. Details of binders can sometimes be established using official court papers or records issued by town councils or trade bodies.

Even where the names of individual binders are known, it is often difficult to link them with specific examples of their work. This is the case with certain early Arab binders, many of whom formed part of an artistic coterie in the court of an Islamic ruler.[13]

Despite the relatively lowly status of the bookbinding craft as an art form, popular decorative trends were much appreciated and are known to have travelled from workshop to workshop and country to country. Some collectors would even purchase a binding in order to have an example of that particular binder's style. The library of Samuel Pepys contained the work of the finest contemporary London binders, and he wrote in his diary that he purchased some books 'for the love of the binding'.[14]

INFLUENCES ON DESIGN AND STYLE

Bookbindings look the way they do for a variety of reasons, and the nature of the materials available to the craftsman is the most obvious of these. In Germany, pigskin was often used as a covering material because pigs were commonly kept; in Islamic countries the preference was for goatskin, while China favoured paper (although Chinese paper was thinner than that produced in the West). Wood was readily available in Europe to be used as boards, but not, for example, in some regions of Africa, where the humidity would have caused warping.

Technological advances inevitably were an important influence on bookbinding. Less obviously, the vagaries of national politics and economic trends could also have a profound impact: in the 1550s, for example, protectionism aimed at protecting the indigenous workforce limited the influence that foreign binders could have on their English counterparts.[15] The opposite is also true: in the eighteenth century, German craftsmen moved to London to take advantage of the flourishing luxury bindings trade, and left their stamp upon English style.

The content of a book also influenced how and why it was bound. In the West, some categories of books, including devotional works and school texts, could be sold ready bound because there was always a market for them. Specialist books with particular formats, such as atlases, tended to be sold bound because 'contrary to other publications, they were completely unusable unbound'.[16] Less popular works would be sold sewn or unsewn, in plain wrappers or even in sheets, and the owner would decide whether he wanted the work to be bound, and if so, to what effect. Aristocrats often required that their coats of arms should be prominently displayed, and could lend the binders the arms' blocks with which to impress the design (see p.54).

Although the decoration on a book's binding may be regarded as secondary to its primary function of protecting the text within, it is certainly the most conspicuous of the two elements and the one celebrated in this book. Binders soon realized that attractive bindings sold more copies, and although a craftsman might save money undetected by cutting corners in construction, there were good financial reasons to make the covers as attractive as possible. Of course, tastes were more forgiving at some periods than at others: during the early Middle Ages, a hole in a piece of leather would not have prevented it from being patched and then used as a covering material, and this would have been regarded as perfectly acceptable by the purchaser: leather was expensive, and an unblemished piece even more so. Nothing would be wasted, and a superfluous sheet of manuscript or printed paper in the workshop might also be used in the binding.

Today, identification of the contents of the book is an important element of bookbinding design (as is also the case with the much more common book jacket). However, this was not always the case: in an age where books were few, there was less need for each of them to be clearly identified. Storage practices were different too, for books were not stored upright, with their spines outwards as they are now, but often displayed on sloping shelves or lecterns or laid flat with the edge of the pages showing. This meant that authors and titles could be written anywhere on a book cover or on the edge of the pages (see p.62) or not included at all. During the Chinese Ming dynasty (1368–1644), title inscriptions and fascicle (installment) numbers of thread-bound books were frequently inscribed on the tail edges. There is some evidence that Islamic West African manuscripts were stored loose in sturdy leather pouches or satchels, and there are relatively modern examples of these dating from the nineteenth and twentieth centuries.

Most designs on book bindings during the hand-press period (the mid-fifteenth century to the 1830s) were arbitrary, the decorations being 'essentially abstract, and the designs on the covers have[ing] no pictorial or representational relationship with the text of the book'.[17] Christian prayer books and bibles sometimes featured religious motifs, but this was not true of all sacred texts. Figurative illustration is not prevalent in Muslim art, and therefore rarely appears; it does feature, however, in a small number of Persian, Turkish and Indian painted and varnished or lacquered bindings, which were produced in the same tradition as miniatures.

When literacy was not yet universal, manuscripts and books became status symbols of a kind. Some great rulers made a point of acquiring the most attractive and expensive bindings, and the nobility frequently followed suit to the extent that their finances allowed. It was soon realized that an expeditious way of gaining the favour and patronage of an important person was to give them a beautifully bound book, and some were specially bound with the particular recipient in mind. Queen Elizabeth I of England was supposed to prefer embroidered velvet bindings, and must have been delighted with Archbishop Parker's presentation of his book *De antiquitate Ecclesiæ Britannicæ* (London, 1572) in a binding splendidly embroidered with a deer park – a rebus, or wordplay, on Parker's name.

Bookbinders before the nineteenth century were not generally seen as artists, the miniature painters of Islamic lacquered bindings being a notable exception, as were the painters of the covers of the Sienese tax accounts (see pp.136–7). Movements in art did not drive bookbinding decoration as they did in painting. An exception to this was the trend for neo-classical ornaments on English bindings which appeared in the 1760s, promoted by architects Robert Adam and James 'Athenian' Stuart to popularize their own classically inspired designs. Bookbinding tools were expensive, and no binder could afford the outlay on a set of new decorative tools if that style was going to be short-lived. Individual motifs sympathetic to a particular period would often appear, for example palmettes (fan-shaped leaves of a palm tree) in the aforementioned neo-classical style (see p.107). Such motifs could be applied using metal tools, painting or drawing directly onto the binding, or even by sewing in the case of embroidered bindings. A combination of motifs and methods could be employed to build up patterns based on a few simple designs. Mirjam Foot has identified some of these, which are summarized below.[18] Patterns i–iii originated in the Near and Middle East before passing along the trade routes to Europe.

i. Designs involving a regular pattern comprising lines and the repeated use of small motifs, which cover the entire space (see pp.95, 125, 140).

ii. Interlacing ribbons, which compartmentalize the surface (see pp.25, 38, 43, 47).

iii. Centre and corner pieces (see pp.24, 42, 52).

iv. Onlays, whereby thin coloured strips or shapes of leather, paper or other materials, are pasted onto the covering material, and inlays, where such strips or shapes are inserted into the cover, the surface material having been cut away to accommodate them (see pp. 71, 74, 154). Onlays were known in sixth-century Northern Italy and onlays and inlays in eighth-century Egypt.

v. Covers pierced to reveal contrasting material beneath; also used to line the interior of the board (see p.59). This technique can be found in sixth-century Northern Italy (see iv above) and tenth-century Egypt.

CRITERIA FOR SELECTION

Compiling a comprehensive display of world bookbindings spanning over ten centuries might reasonably founder in the face of such an ambitious goal. Since there is no single selection framework that could reasonably be applied to all of the British Library's bookbindings (upon which this selection is based), the main objective is to present items which please the eye. What constitutes a 'beautiful binding' is very much a matter of taste. The bindings that appear in this volume have therefore been chosen by a number of British Library staff, each of them with a different personal favourite. The result is a collection of items with a wide range of appeal, showcasing many of the aesthetic subtleties of the bookbinder's art.

The arrangement is largely chronological, but also included are pages devoted to special themes, including medallions, clasps, embroidered bindings, painted edges, almanacs and gift books, Victorian trade pictorial bindings and the work of the innovatory binder, Thomas James Cobden-Sanderson, who laid the foundations of modern binding in the Western world.

Descriptions are simple, but some bookbinding terms are necessary and are explained in a brief glossary (see p.188). In a book where browsing is encouraged it is inevitable that some of the information is applicable to several bindings and may be repeated. Conventions of vocabulary include the use of the names Spain, Germany and Italy for periods when these countries did not have a diplomatic existence, and the adoption of earlier usage, such as Persia (present-day Iran). The use of such terms as 'Mediterranean', 'Oriental' and 'Asiatic', as well as 'Near', 'Middle' and 'Far East', is problematic since different peoples define them in a variety of ways. Where possible, the name of the country will be specified and where the terms 'eastern' and 'oriental' are included, the broadest definition will be meant, i.e. a world view, East as opposed to West.

The emphasis in this book on Western bookbinding is perhaps misleading. The first binding traditions developed in the East (perhaps due to the early adoption of writing), and because materials including papyrus and parchment (both used by Egyptians in the third-century BC) and paper (made by the Chinese in the second century AD) were readily available. The book in China and Japan developed in a different way from the Western codex, and a greater reliance on less durable materials including paper and cloth have meant that survivals are not in pristine condition and do not photograph to advantage.

In an age where texts are digitized, structural differences between West and East become irrelevant, as the protective function of a binding is redundant. The advantages of the electronic book may be many, but who can deny the visual and tactile appeal of a beautifully bound book?

NOTES

1. Oscar Wilde, 'The beauties of bookbinding' in the *Pall Mall Gazette*, 23 November 1888, p.3.
2. Graham Pollard and Ester Potter, *Early Bookbinding Manuals* (Oxford, 1984), p.1.
3. Frances Wood and Mark Barnard, *The Diamond Sutra* (London, 2010).
4. J A Szirmai, *The Archaeology of Medieval Bookbinding* (Farnham, 1999), p.100.
5. Paul Needham, *Twelve Centuries of Bookbindings, 400–1600* (New York, 1979), p.55.
6. Pollard and Potter, *Early Bookbinding Manuals*, pp. 49, 24, 32.
7. Mirjam M Foot, *The History of Bookbinding as a Mirror of Society. The Panizzi Lectures 1997* (London, 1998), p.13.
8. David Pearson, *English Bookbinding Styles* (London, 2004).
9. Robert J Gemmett, *The Consummate Collector: William Beckford's Letters to his Bookseller* (Michigan, 2000), pp. 17, 67.
10. *Great Britain Royal Commission for the Exhibition of 1851*, Reports by the juries on the subjects in the 30 classes, p.930.
11. G D Hobson quoted in Marianne Tidcombe, *The Bookbindings of TJ Cobden-Sanderson: A study of his work* (London, 1984).
12. Jane Austen *Juvenilia* (Cambridge, 2006) p.200. British Library manuscript shelf mark Add Ms 59874, Jane Austen: 'Volume the Second' comprising later autograph copies of early compositions, dating from *c*.1790–93, p.207.
13. Duncan Haldane, *Islamic Bookbindings* (London, 1983), p.10.
14. Howard M Nixon, Mirjam M Foot, *The History of Decorated Bookbinding in England* (Oxford, 1992), p.74.
15. Mirjam M Foot, 'Netherlandish influences on English Bookbinding' in her *Studies in the History of Bookbinding* (London, 1993), p.161.
16. Jan Storm van Leeuwen, 'Some Observations on Dutch Publishers' Bindings up till 1800' in Dennis E Rhodes (ed), *Bookbindings & other Bibliophily. Essays in honour of Anthony Hobson* (Verona, 1994), p.292.
17. David Pearson, *English Bookbinding Styles 1450–1800: A Handbook* (London, 2005).
18. Foot, *The Mirror of Society*, pp.15–16.

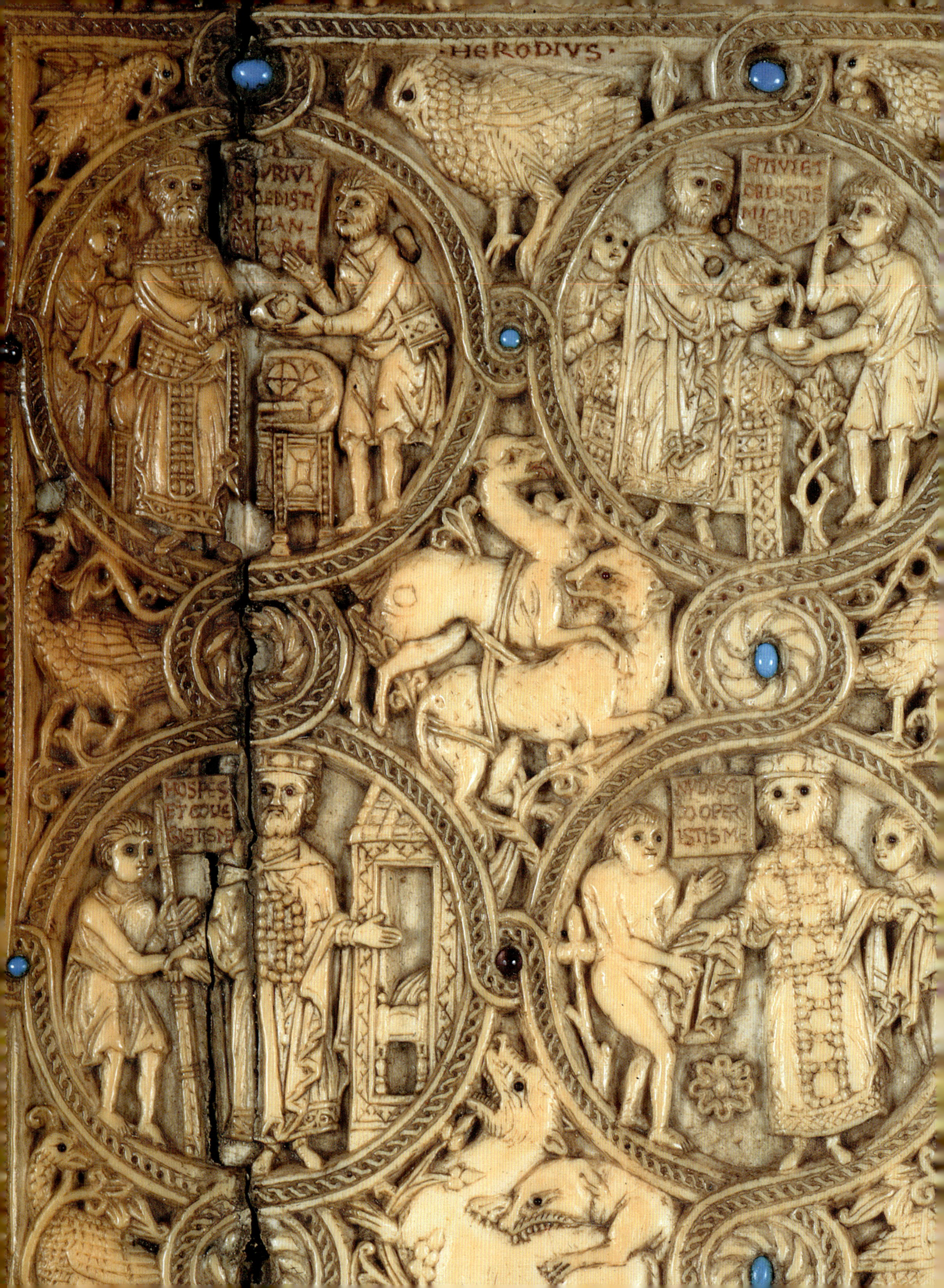
HERODIUS

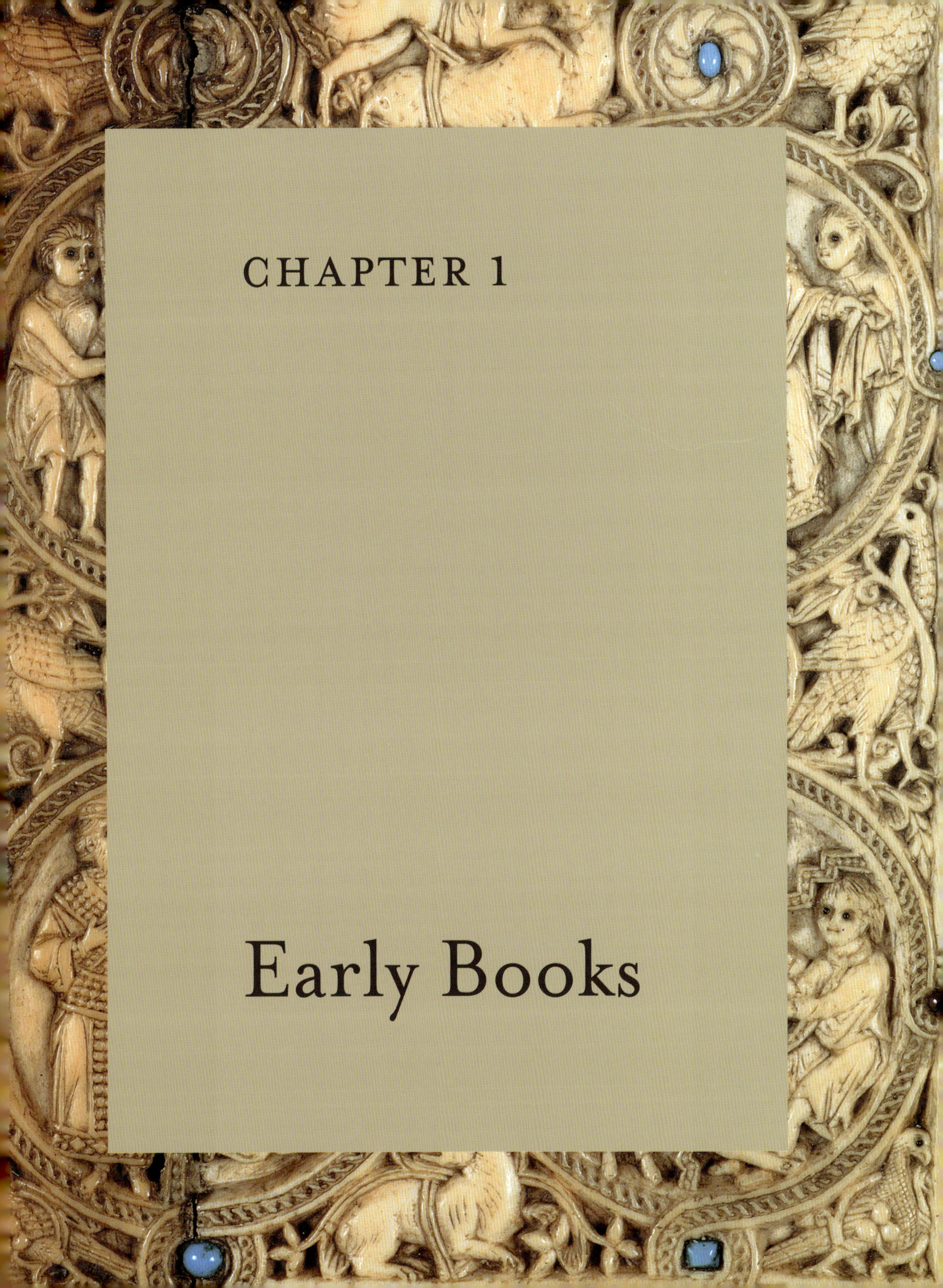

CHAPTER 1

Early Books

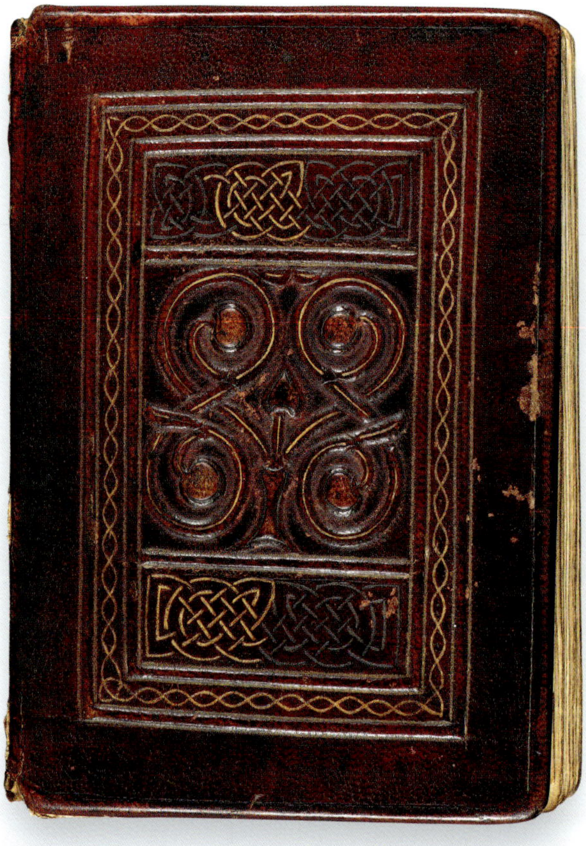

ABOVE This late seventh-century red goatskin binding over beech boards, decorated with coloured paint, is the earliest surviving Western binding in Europe, and possibly a unique example of decorated Insular (i.e. post-Roman, British-style) leatherwork. It covers a pocket-sized manuscript of the Gospel of St John, once owned by Saint Cuthbert of Lindisfarne (d.687), and was buried with him, protected by a satchel, which accounts for its remarkable condition. It was rediscovered in 1104, when the tomb was opened to move St Cuthbert's remains to a new shrine behind the altar in Durham Cathedral. The interlace and raised double-vine scroll design on the upper (front) cover differs from the pattern of the lower (back) cover, which is based on step motifs within a panel. Both designs draw inspiration from geometry. The sections of the parchment pages are linked by chain stitch (as with Coptic sewing) and the boards are also sewn on. As this may be a sole survival one cannot draw reliable conclusions about binding structure and decoration in this period, but Anglo-Saxon and Coptic influences are discernible.

England, late seventh century
137 x 95 x 35 mm (5.4 x 3.7 x 1.4 inches)
Loan 74

OPPOSITE 'The most beautiful ivory covers in the British Library', adorned with garnets and turquoise, enclose a sumptuous twelfth-century illuminated Latin Psalter. Ivory was a luxury material and particularly difficult to obtain during the Middle Ages. The skill of the workman and the rarity of the materials would have made it one of the most expensive possessions of its owner, possibly Melisende (1105–1161), Queen of Jerusalem. The binding serves as an indication of her wealth, status and piety, as well as depicting the sophistication of court taste. The design shows influences from Islamic, Byzantine and Western art.

Eastern Mediterranean (Jerusalem),
mid-twelfth century.
Lower cover 142 x 220 mm (5.6 x 8.7 inches)
Egerton 1139

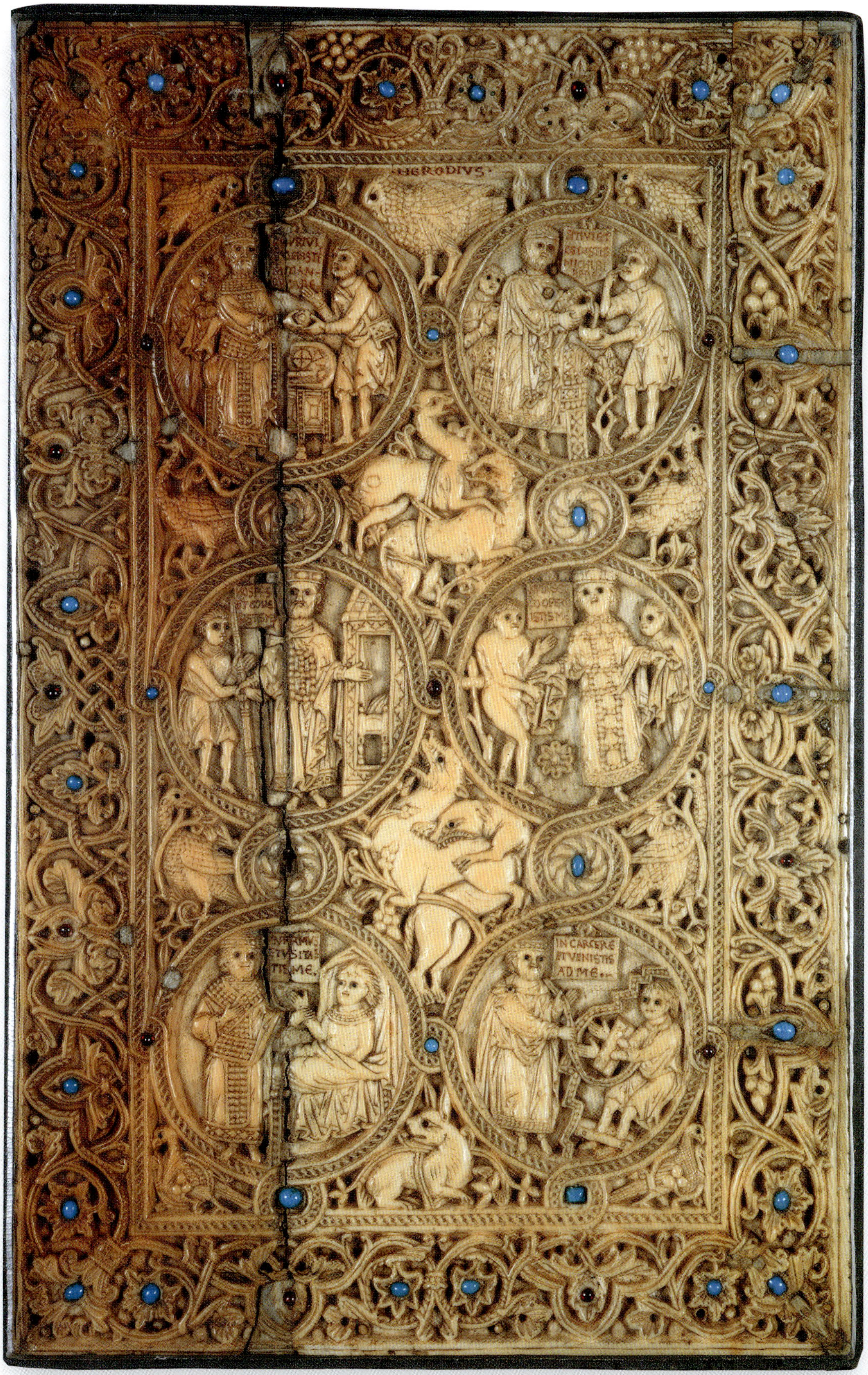
HERODIUS
IN CARCERE
ET VENISTIS
AD ME

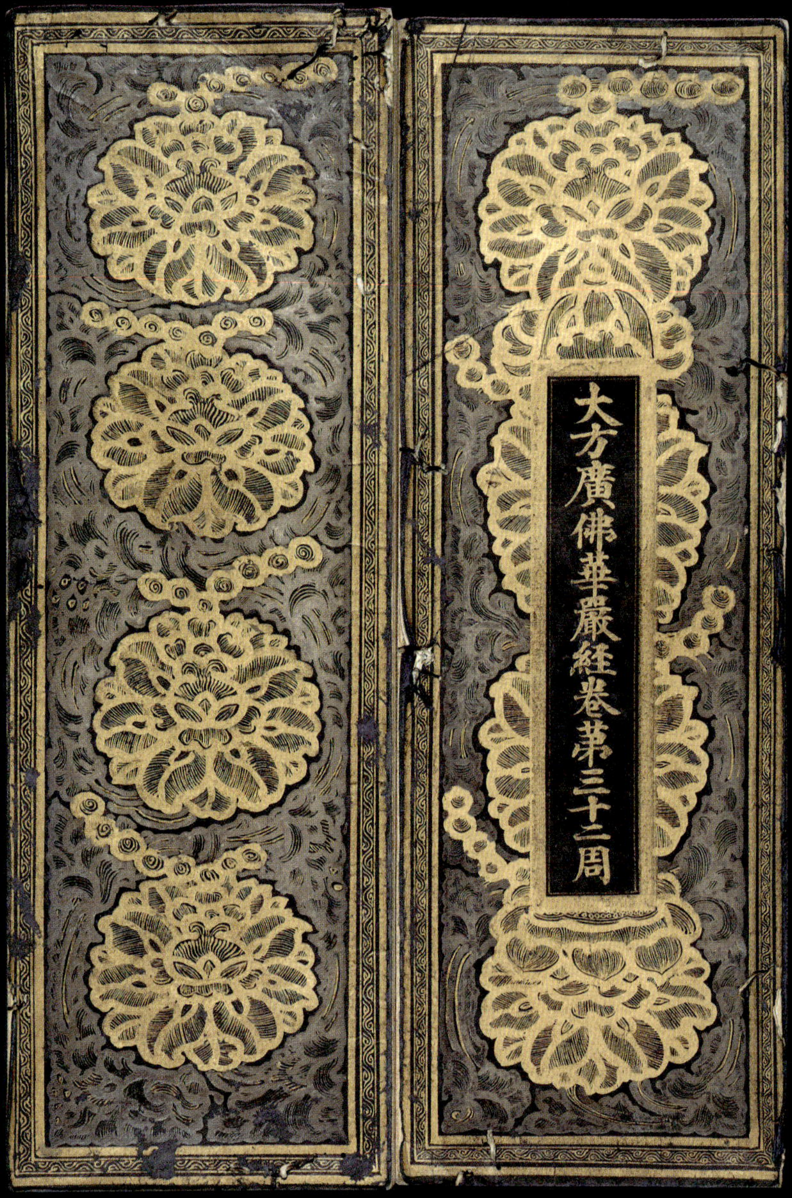

Paper scrolls which were folded into a concertina format are known as sutra bindings and are found exclusively on Buddhist scriptures. This manuscript, the *Garland Sutra*, was written in Korea *c.*1390–1400. Korean bindings were much influenced by Chinese and Japanese practices but characteristic differences emerged after side-stitched books began to predominate after the thirteenth century. The thick paper covers shown here are decorated in gold, silver and indigo with large floral medallions and a title panel with gold ink on black.

Korea, late fourteenth century
325 x 110 mm (12.8 x 4.3 inches)
Or.7377

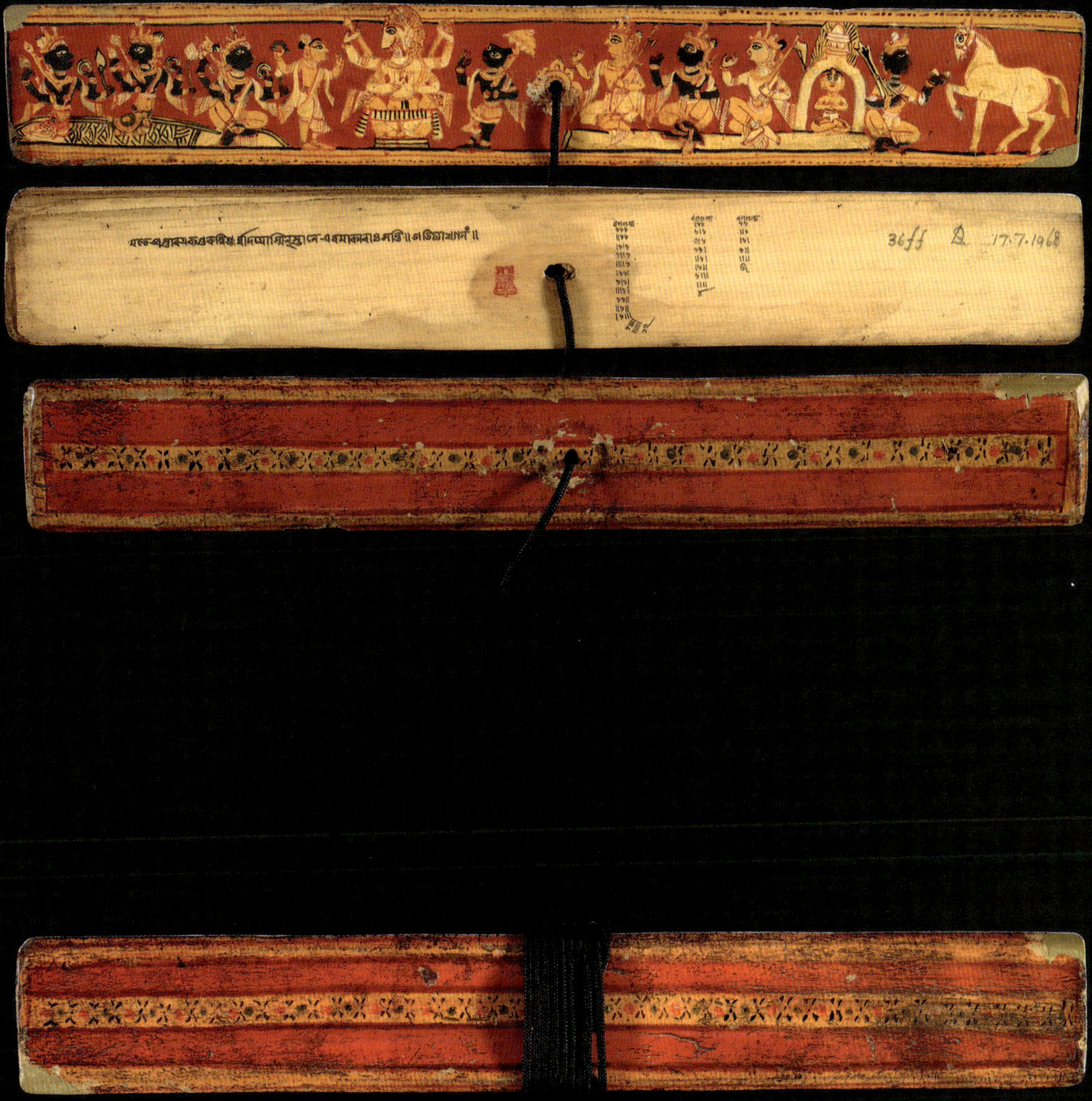

The Indian *pothi* was an early form of bookbinding. It consisted of religious texts written on split leaves that were stacked together, landscape-style, and secured by a thread (or threads) passing through each leaf; it was then sandwiched between two wooden boards, around which any excess thread was wrapped. The style spread, relayed by Buddhist monks, through Persia, Afghanistan and Iran, reaching China in the first century BC. Thenceforth, the format changed little. The structure of the binding, illustrated here, follows the same tradition but covers an anonymous Sanskrit commentary, which was probably produced in Bihar, eastern India, in 1491–92. The holes in the centre of the boards accommodated the threads. The upper board depicts the ten incarnations of the Hindu god Vishnu, and the lower board is painted with scenes of Krishna and his followers. J P Losty describes the boards as being 'securely anchored within the developing tradition of Indian miniature painting'.

India, late fifteenth century
37 x 53 x 18 mm (1.4 x 2.1 x 0.7 inches)
Or.13133

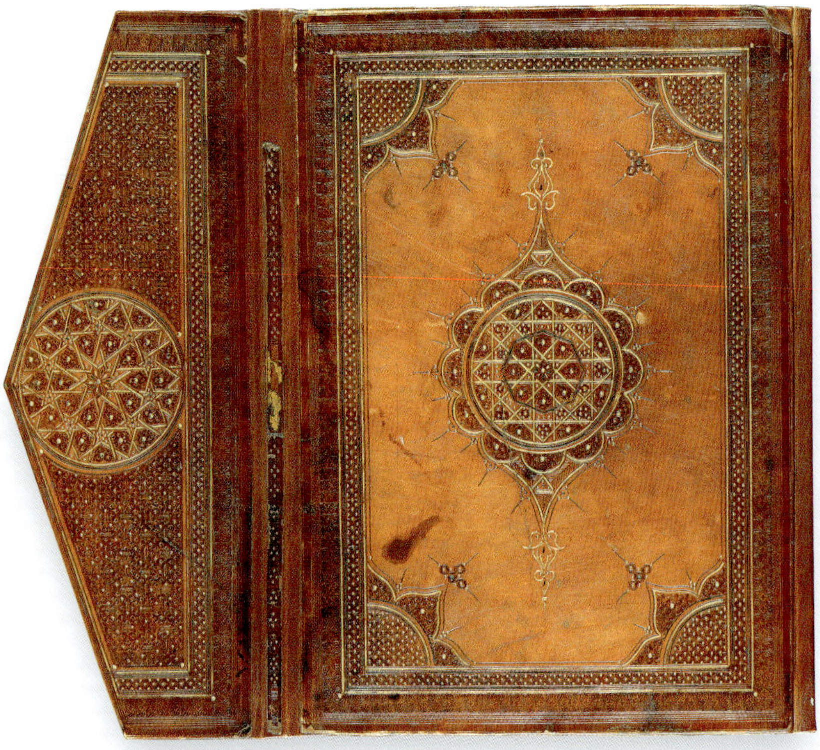

ABOVE Early North African bindings, of which this is a tooled goatskin example, were produced in the Islamic tradition. Our knowledge of them owes much to works including the *Book on the Staff of the Scribes and Implements of Discerning*, which was written by the Zirid King al-Mu'izz ibn Badis of Tunisia in the eleventh century. The binding of this Qur'an was probably made during the Marinid dynasty (which ruled the Berber tribe in the thirteenth century). The Marinids lived in present-day Morocco and Spain, and their considerable leather-working skills and traditions spread to mainland Europe, influencing the native craftsmen. The Mudéjar bindings in Spain are an example of this influence, and were characterized by the geometrical patterns with interlacing ribbons that are clearly evident here. Gold tooling was an Islamic invention and this thirteenth-century example is one of the earliest known.

Morocco (?), thirteenth century
280 x 220 (250 with flap extended) x 288 mm
(11 x 8.7 [9.8 with flap extended] x 11.3 inches)
Or.13192

OPPOSITE This late fourteenth-century Egyptian binding from the Mamluk period, with its characteristic pentagonal flap (not shown), displays one of several designs that were common in the Islamic world. It covers part seven of a Qur'an written for Amir-Aitmish al-Bajasi (executed in 1400), and is decorated in gold and blind 'in the elegant and restrained style which is typical of the best in Islamic art'. Its quality reflects the status of the holy book and the rank of its owner, who was a commander under Sultan Barquq. The other parts of the manuscript that survive are bound in a similar style and may originate from the same workshop, which continued to bind Qur'ans for the top echelons of Mamluk society. The elegant centre and corner-piece pattern used on the covers was found on many decorative items, including carpets, and became influential in Europe, probably travelling along the trade routes from the East to Italy, and thence to France and England.

Egypt, late fourteenth century
374 x 278 x 15 mm (14.7 x 10.9 x 0.6 inches)
Or.9671

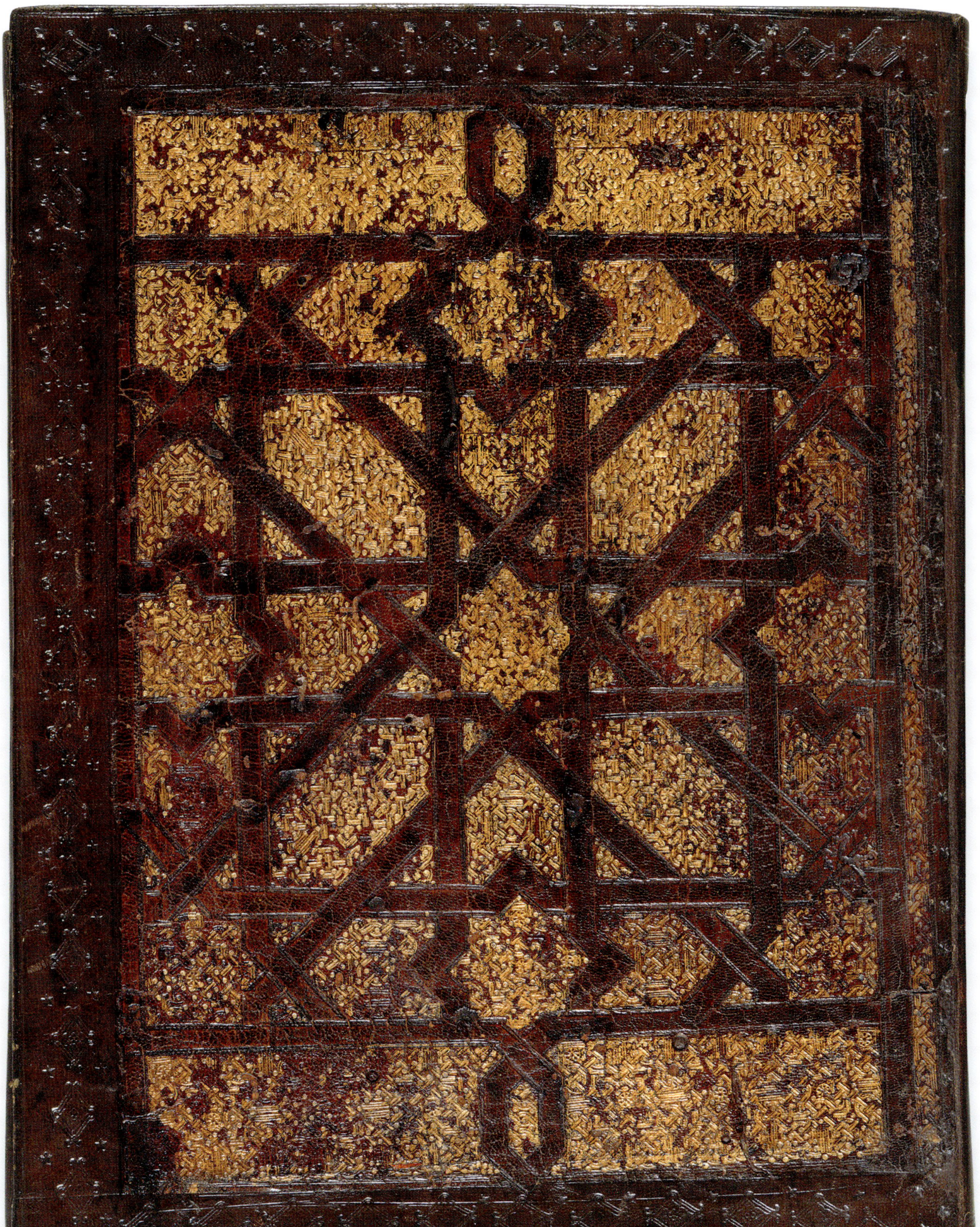

TREASURE BINDINGS

Devotional works have always merited costly and lavish bindings, for their owners would frequently demonstrate their piety by choosing as elaborate a binding as they could afford. In 384 St Jerome was moved to voice his displeasure about the jewel-covered books carried by rich Christian women, but exhibitionism of this sort prevailed at all levels of society, with monarchs and wealthy institutions such as cathedrals and monasteries commissioning metal 'treasure' bindings adorned with gold, silver, gemstones, enamelwork and carved ivory panels. The craftsmen involved were not binders but metalworkers, and the bindings were often more expensive than the manuscripts they contained. Despite St Jerome's view, there was some justification for this, however, as the text could be argued to have a liturgical use and the binding a ceremonial one. Certainly other religions venerated holy texts by giving them expensive bindings, though this particular format was more characteristic of the Christian West.

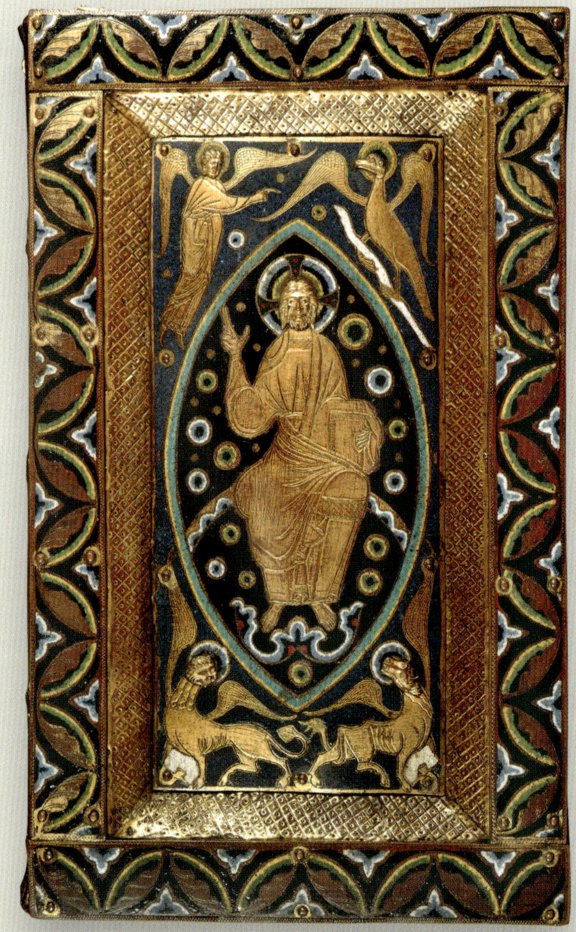

LEFT This Gospel book is bound in red sheepskin over wooden boards and decorated with small blind-tooled motifs and Limoges enamelled copper plates. Most surviving Limoges enamel book covers come from *c.*1180–1230. Enamelling was a new technique, inspired by the work of Byzantine craftsmen, and was adopted in centres that, like Limoges, produced such decorative items on an almost industrial scale. This particular binding may have been owned by the Heiningen Nunnery in Hildesheim. Note the figure of Christ in Majesty holding a bound book, while the lion, representing St Mark, and the ox of St Luke clasp bound copies of their gospels. The eagle of St John grips an old-fashioned scroll.

Limoges (?), late twelfth century/early thirteenth century
327 x 200 x 55 mm (12.9 x 7.9 x 2.2 inches)
Add Ms 27,926

OPPOSITE The Armenian plateau was rich in ores, and the craftsmen of the region were skilled metalworkers, as we can see from this seventeenth-century silver gilt repoussé treasure binding decorated with a scene of the crucifixion. The red leather-covered wooden boards and outer flap (not shown) offer a high degree of protection to the precious contents, an illuminated manuscript of the four Gospels. The spine structure comprises a link-and-rod mechanism (see p.00 for a similar but modern version). The colophon tells us that the binding was designed by Nahapet and made by Smawon (a doctor of the church).

Lake Seven region, Armenia, seventeenth century
180 x 132 x 54 mm (7.1 x 5.2 x 2 inches)
Or.14839

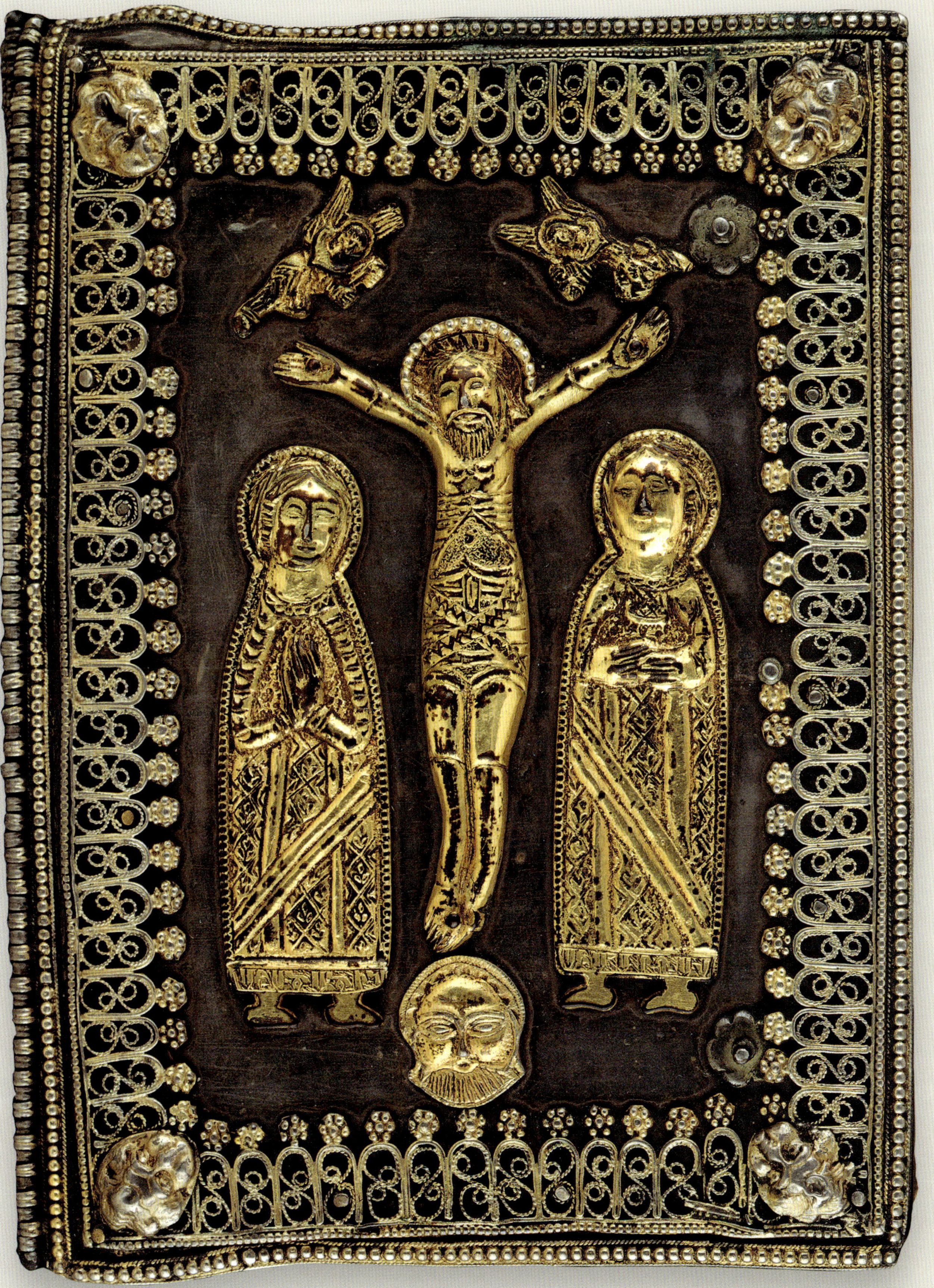

This seventeenth-century German book in its silver-gilt covers provides an unusual example of a treasure binding on a secular text, in this instance a chronology. Its provenance is ambiguous and the binder and researcher, S T Prideaux, has suggested that it is a 'remboitage', or a new text, inserted into an older binding. A metal worker would have made the case, which has filigree in the central panel and spine and is also ornamented with onlays of black niello (a metallic alloy often used in jewellery). At this time, silver bindings were rarely stamped with a maker's mark so it is difficult to source the work, but there were famous goldsmithing families in Augsburg, Nuremberg and Konigsberg who were known to create such pieces. They were also fashionable in the Netherlands and Sweden.

Germany (?), late seventeenth century (?)
142 x 80 x 36 mm (5.6 x 3.1 x 1.4 inches)
C.27.c.32

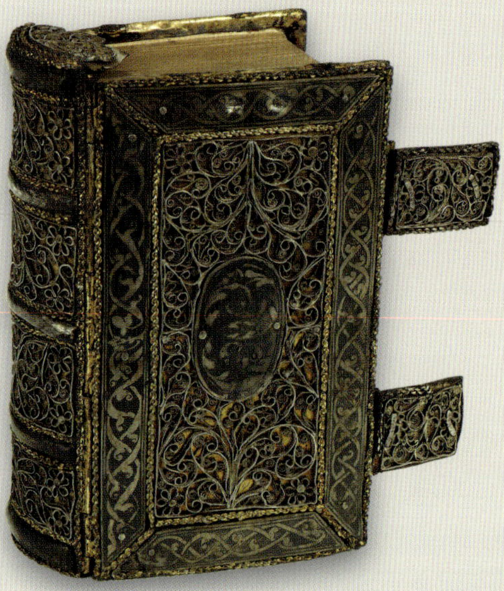

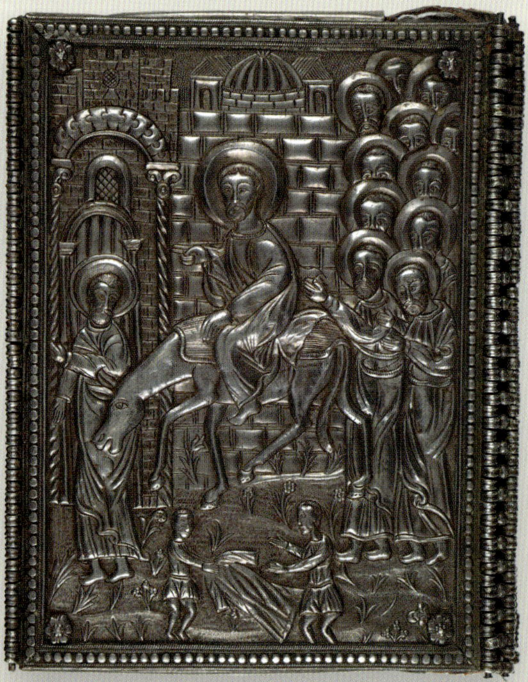

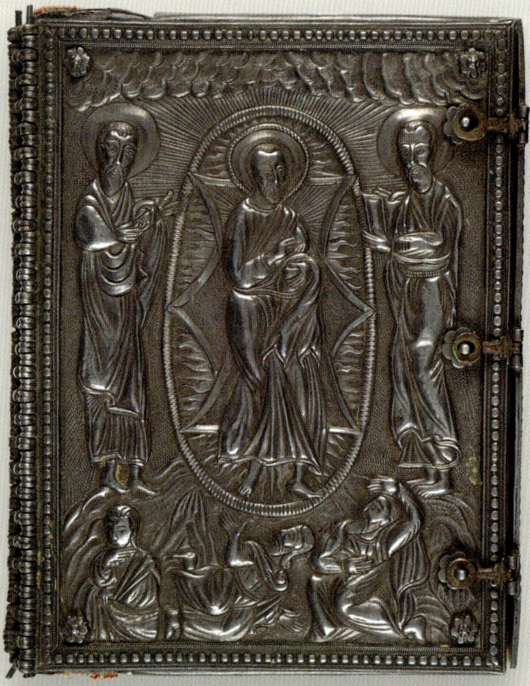

The tradition of treasure bindings is not restricted to the Middle Ages. This copy of the Gospels – according to an inscription inside it – was restored and encased in silver covers by a craftsman named Elia (or perhaps Eghiay) in 1755. It was made in Caesarea (eastern Turkey) and its upper cover depicts the Transfiguration of Christ; its lower, the entry into Jerusalem.

Caesarea, eastern Turkey, 1755
194 x 142 x 70 mm (7.6 x 5.6 x 2.8 inches)
Or.13895

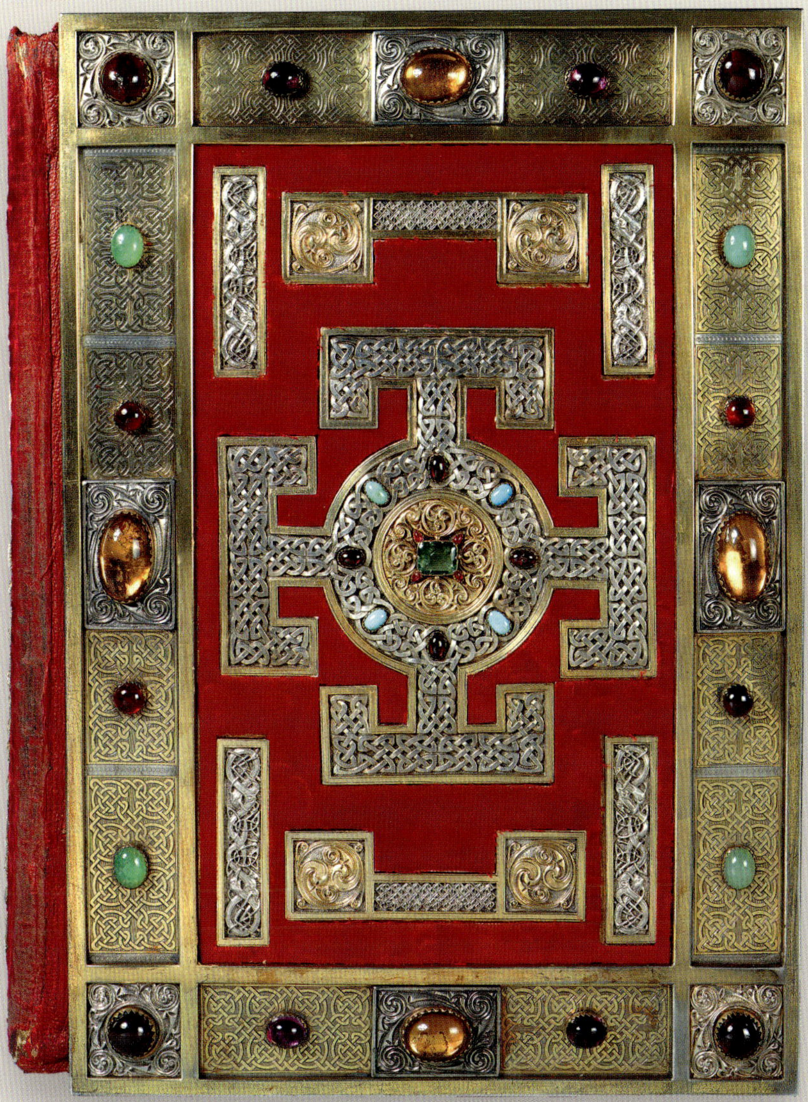

The Lindisfarne Gospels were written and decorated by the monk Eadfrith, Bishop of Lindisfarne, to celebrate the life of St Cuthbert (d.687), and such was the fame of the manuscript that it was venerated as a relic and housed in a treasure binding. We are indebted to the inscription it carries, which informs us that Eadfrith's successor as bishop, Æthelwald, was the binder and that the hermit, Billfrith, added jewels and precious metals; but – tantalisingly – the original binding does not survive and it fell to Edward Maltby, Bishop of Durham, to provide funds to replace it. This Victorian binding commissioned in 1853 from Smith, Nicholson and Co. of Lincoln's Inn is the result of Maltby's generosity. It attempts to capture the magnificence of the original with its frames, gold-plated alloy plaques, coloured stones and spine embroidered in gold thread. The design was inspired by decorative motifs in the manuscript itself. Unfortunately, scandal and controversy dogged Bishop Maltby's life. Queen Victoria famously described him as 'remarkably maladroit' when he passed her the orb during her coronation service in 1837, but this pales into insignificance beside his interference in elections, challenges to contemporary religious orthodoxy and the questions raised in Parliament about the propriety of his enormous wealth.

London, 1853
372 x 265 x 84 mm (14.7 x 10.4 x 3.3 inches)
Cotton Nero D. IV

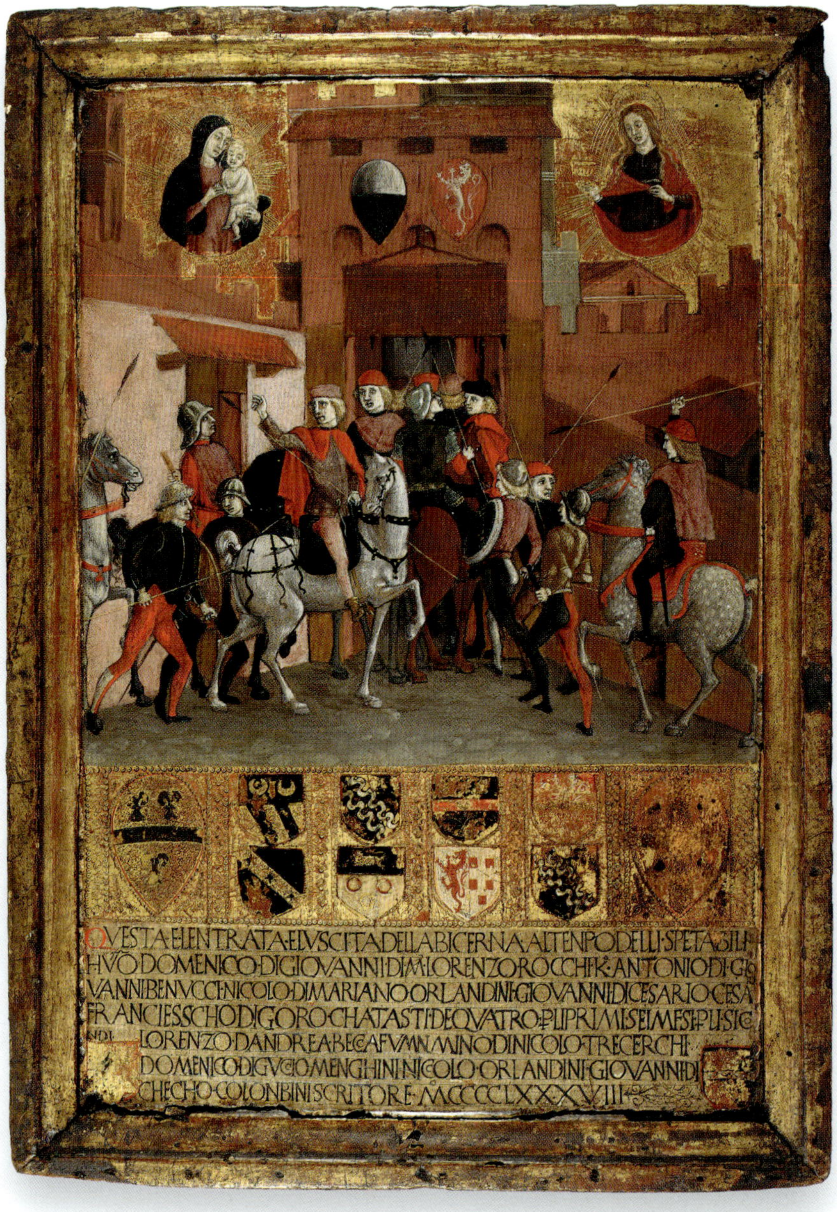

From the thirteenth century on, the accounts of the Sienese exchequer, written on parchment, were stored under painted wooden covers (*tavolette di Biccherna*) to keep the pages flat. In the late 1450s, paper replaced parchment and the wooden covers assumed a purely decorative function and were hung in the Treasury building. The subject of the paintings reflected the history of Siena, or celebrated the noble families who served as Treasury officials by incorporating their coats of arms. This panel illustrates a recent event, the triumphant return of the exiled Noveschi political faction to Siena in 1487. The leader of the group, Pandolfo Petrucci (later de facto lord of the city), is shown on a white horse. Cozzarelli (d.1516/17) was a Sienese painter known for his depiction of cityscapes, as can be seen here. His workshop also produced the majority of decorated wooden cupboards and chests in late fifteenth-century Siena.

Siena, 1488
500 x 335 mm (19.7 x 14 inches)
Davis 768

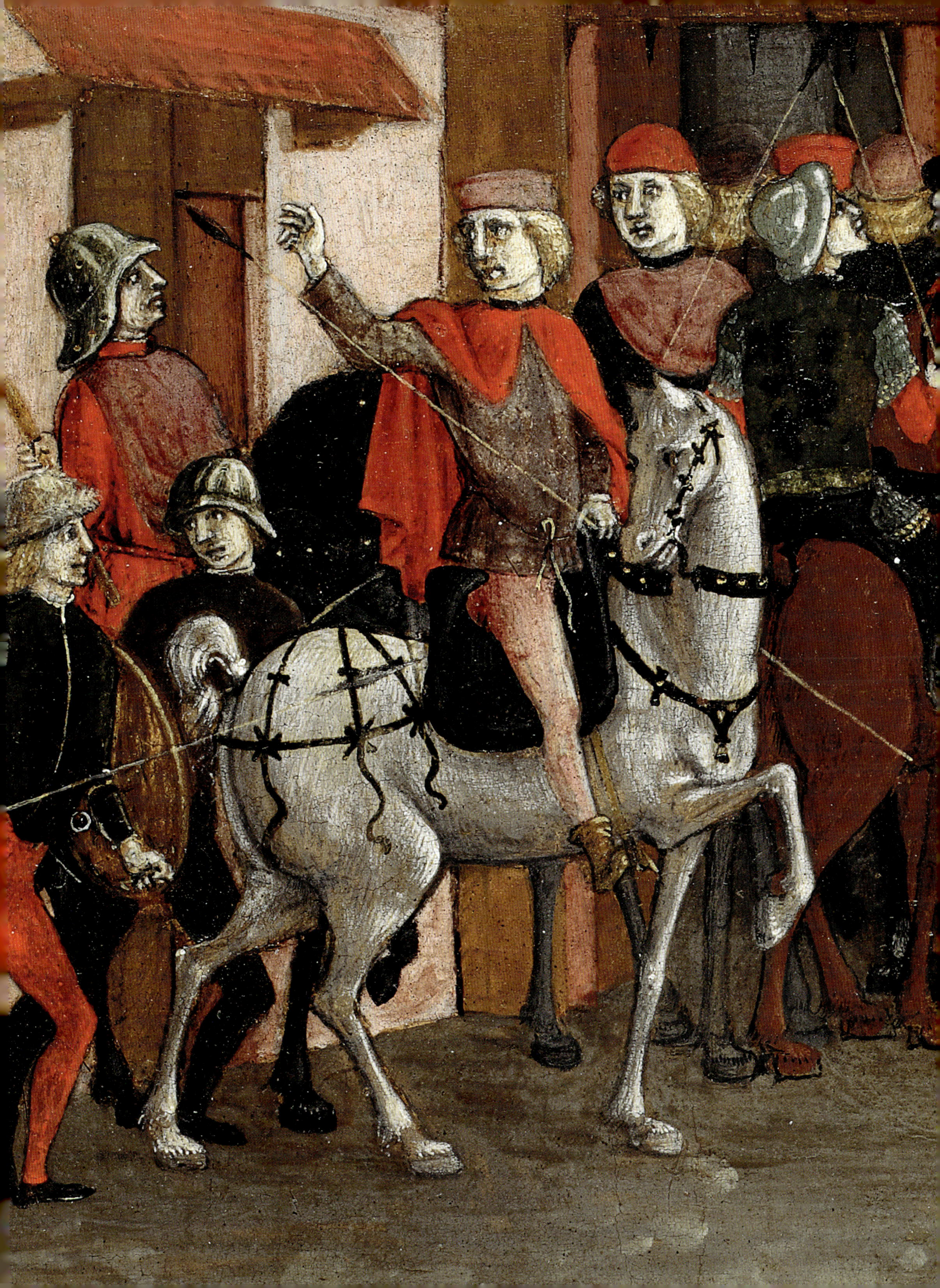

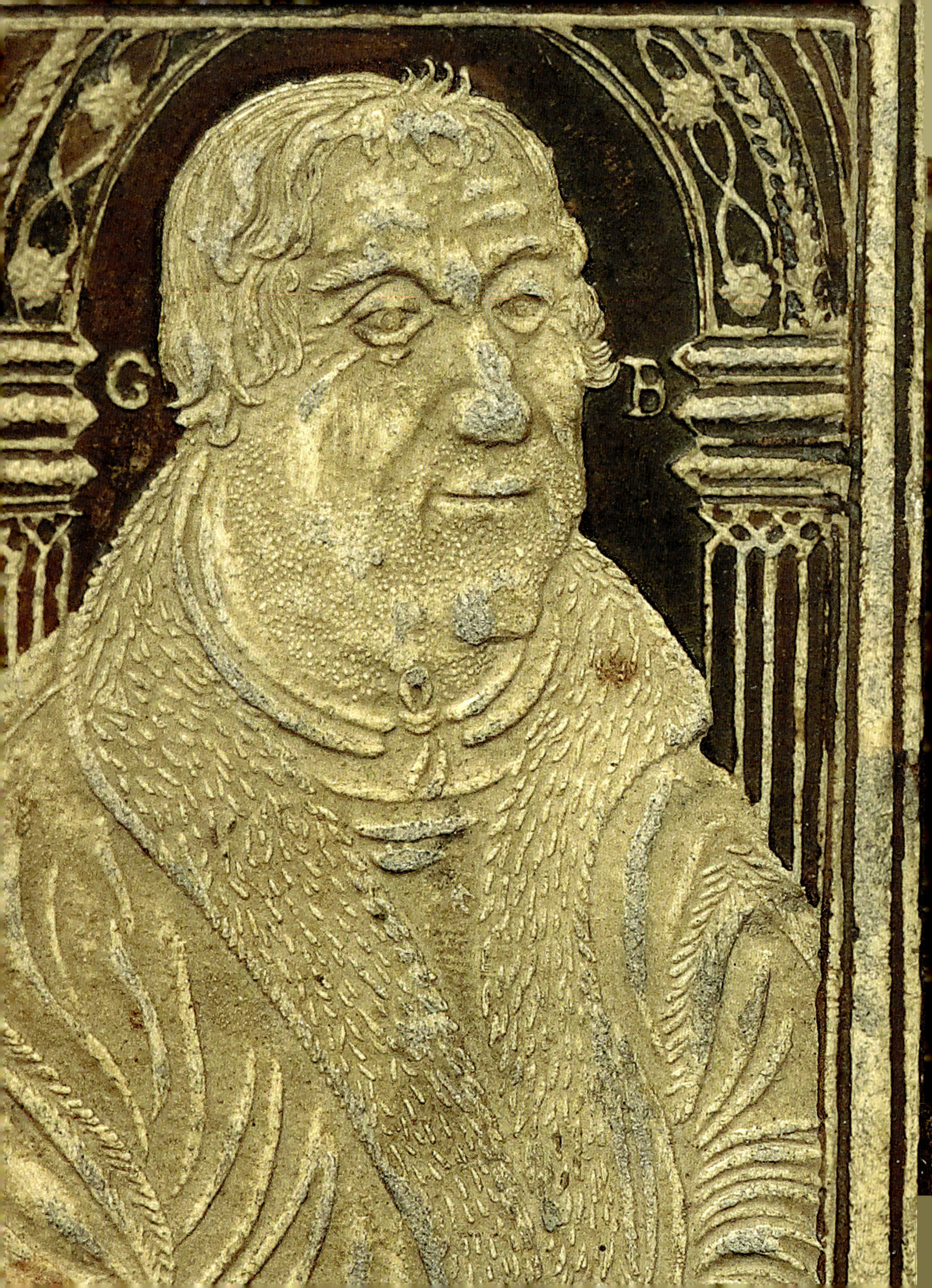
G
B

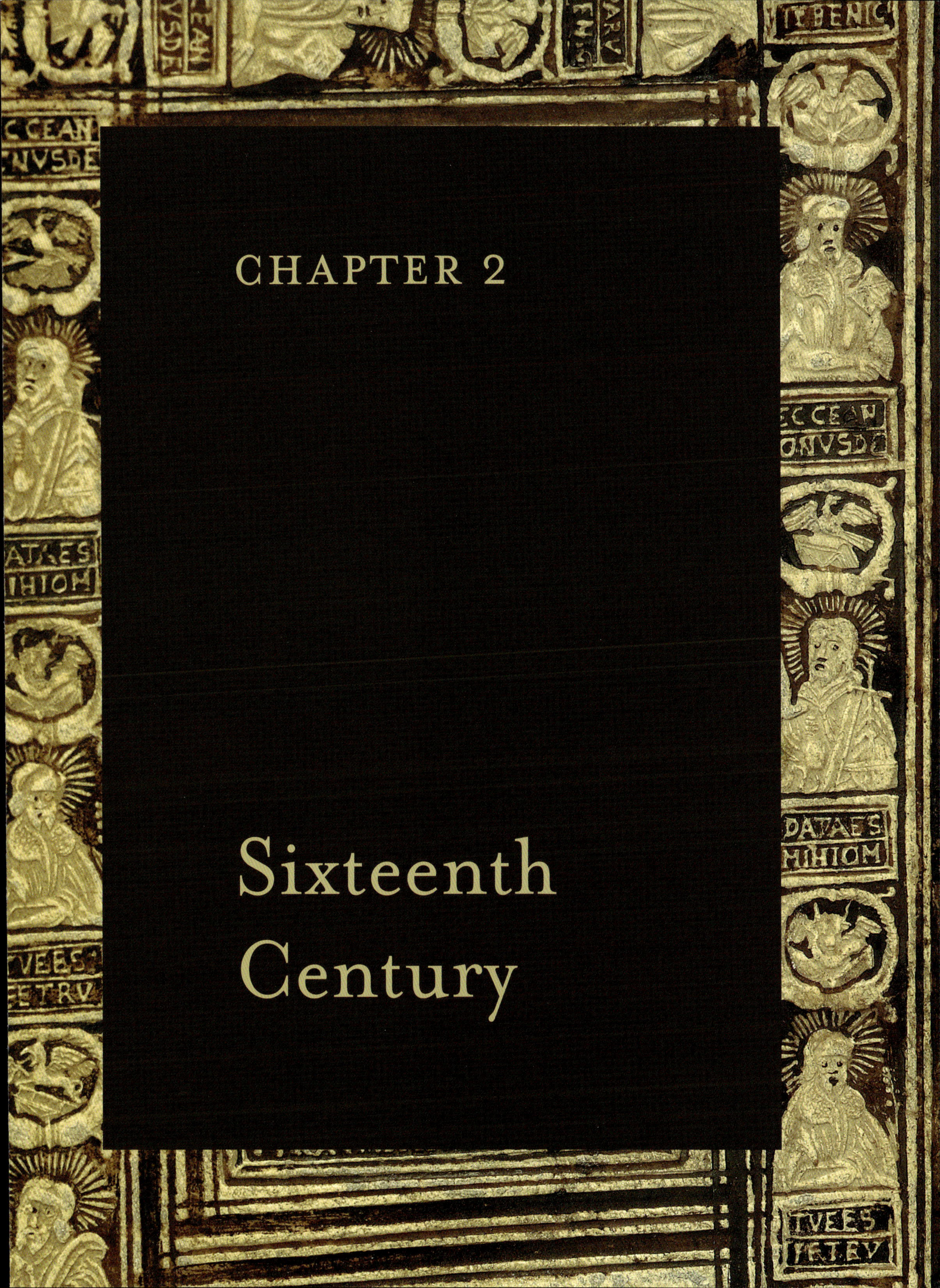

Sixteenth Century

RIGHT AND OPPOSITE The Westminster Charter, which was the foundation document of Henry VII's chapel in Westminster Abbey, *c.*1505, was bound in pink silk and given an extra burgundy-red velvet 'chemise' binding (a protective 'outer coat' where the covering was extended beyond the edges of the book). The tail edge has a generous allowance of fabric to enclose five silver and silver-gilt seal containers attached by silk cords (not shown). The two fore-edge clasps have gold buckles featuring a Tudor rose topped by an angel, and are attached with embroidered straps. There are five painted enamel badges. Folio 60 of the indenture (shown opposite) actually depicts the opened pages of this manuscript surrounded by monks. The protective fabric is clearly visible.

London, early sixteenth century
385 x 280 x 50 mm (15.5 x 11 x 2 inches)
Harley Ms 1498

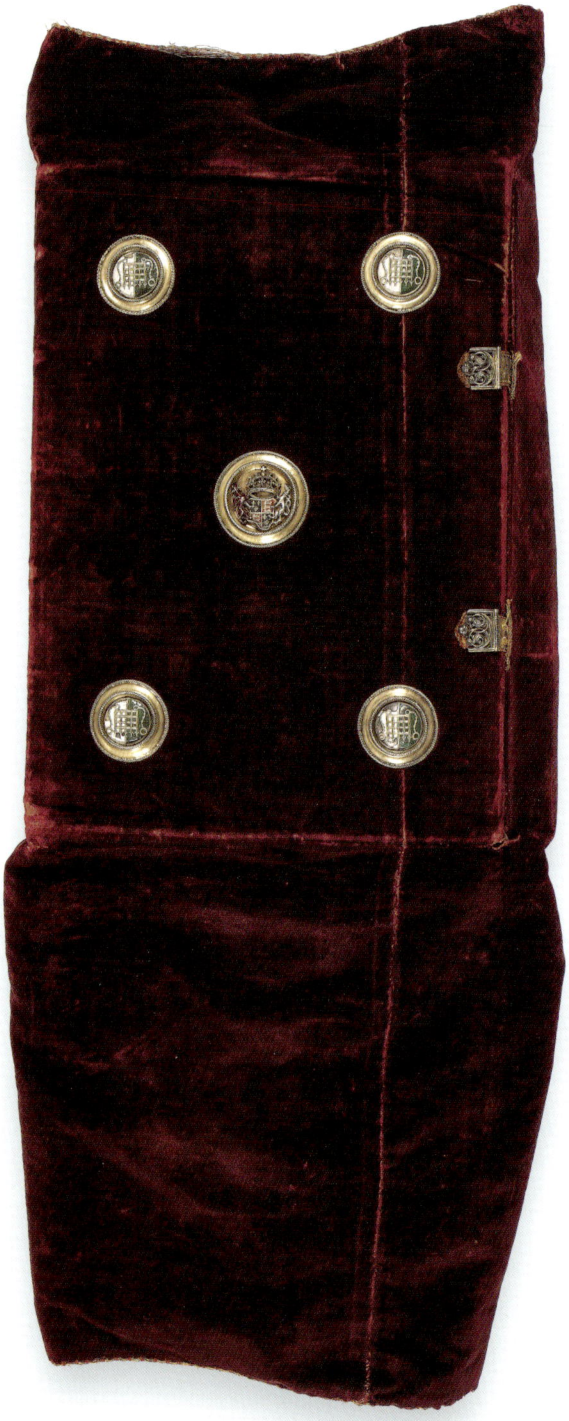

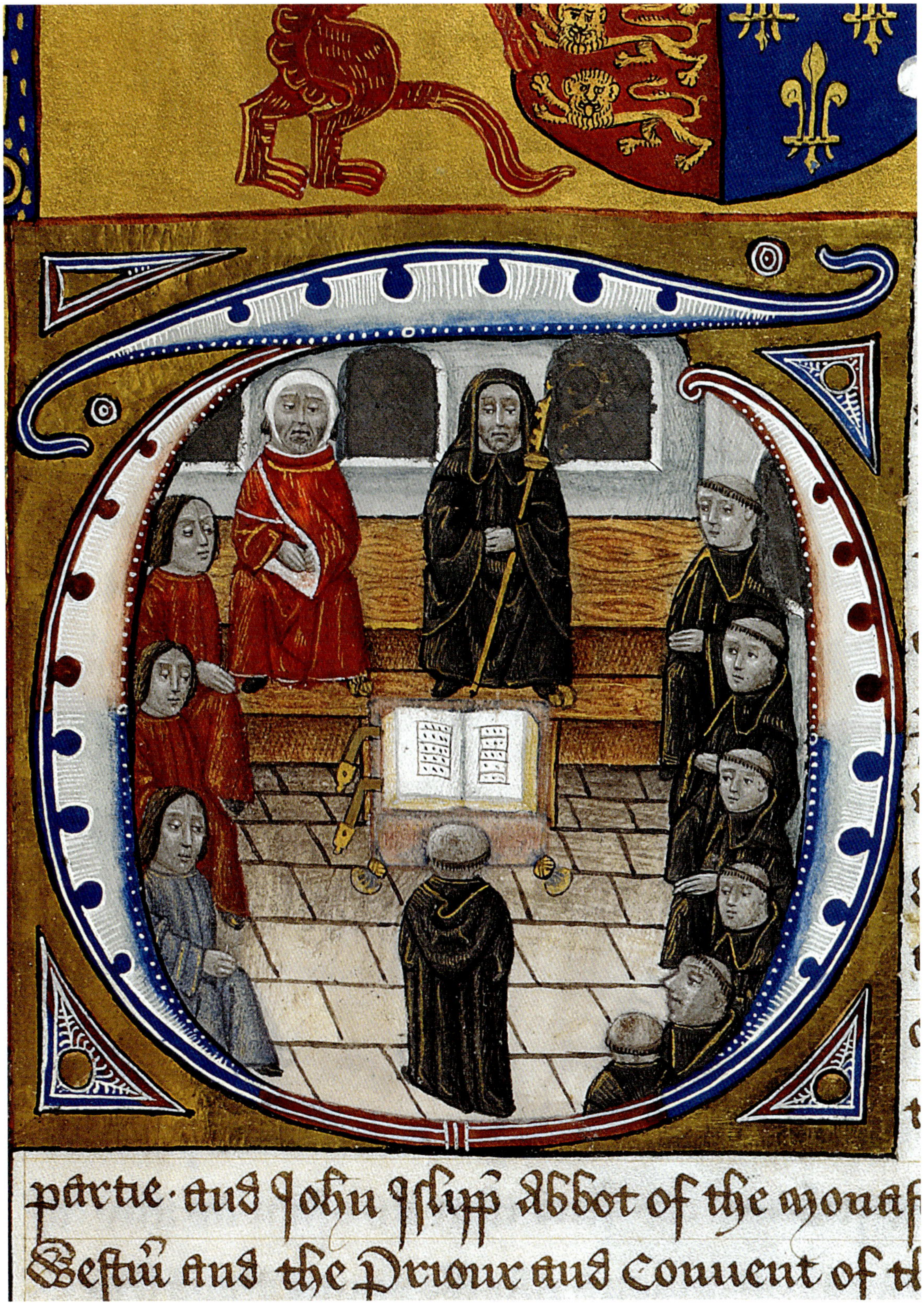
partie · and John Islipp Abbot of the monast
Westm̄ and the Priour and Couent of th

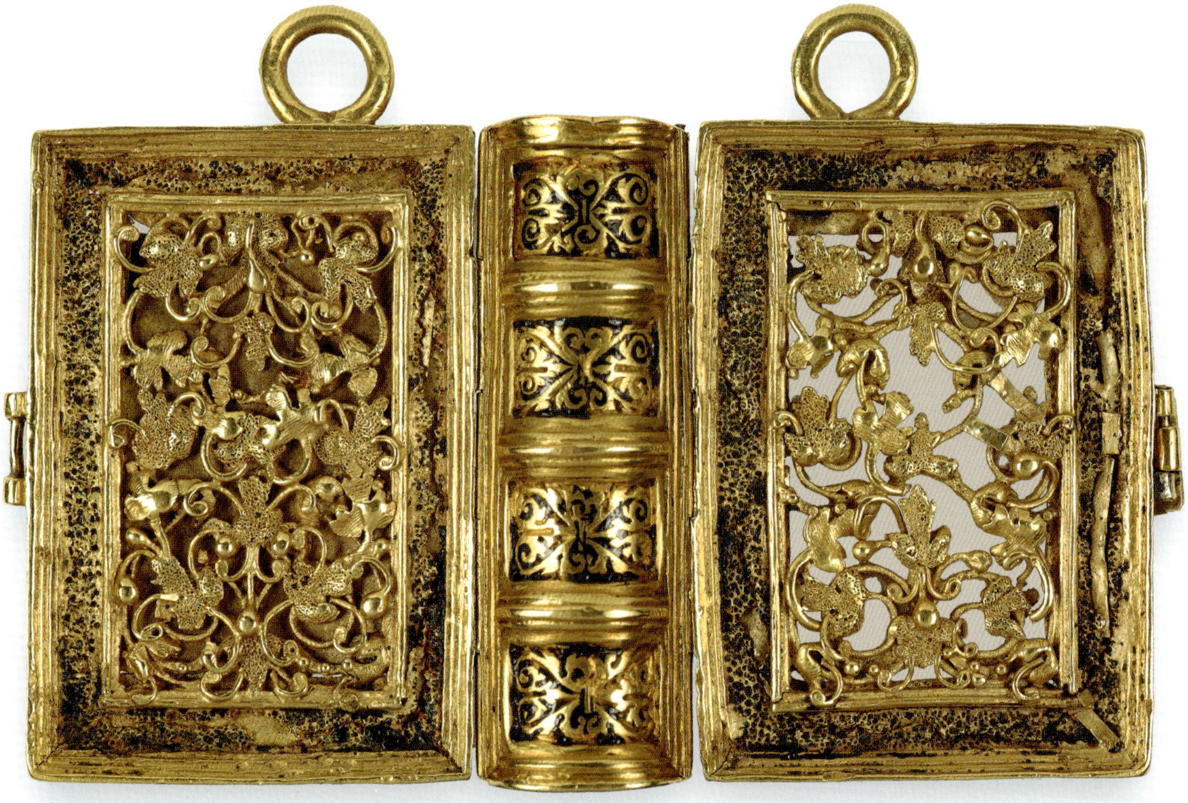

ABOVE This copy of Psalms in English verse was intended, as were many devotional works, to be portable in order to enable private prayer. A cord would have been threaded to the metal roundel on the top edge of the book, and this was then tied to a girdle or belt. Such 'girdle books' were particularly popular with women during the fifteenth and sixteenth centuries, and this example in its metalwork case is believed to have been owned by Anne Boleyn (*c.*1500–1536) who, when on the scaffold, gave it to one of her maids. Books of this kind were affordable only by the rich. This one is further distinguished by a painting of Henry VIII inside.

Probably England, sixteenth century
431.8 x 330.2 mm (17 x 13 inches)
Stowe 956

OPPOSITE Books of hours, in use from the thirteenth to sixteenth centuries, have been described as medieval bestsellers, and were popular because they enabled the laity to adopt a framework of daily prayers relating to the eight canonical hours observed by the clergy. This is a French sixteenth-century example bound in silver, partially gilt and enamelled, and engraved with the Nativity (and the Virgin and Child on the upper cover). Its quality follows the pattern for books of this type, which were invariably highly illustrated and sumptuously bound, reflecting the wealth and taste of the owner.

France, sixteenth century
70 x 50 x 10mm (2.8 x 2 x 0.4 inches)
Add Ms 22751

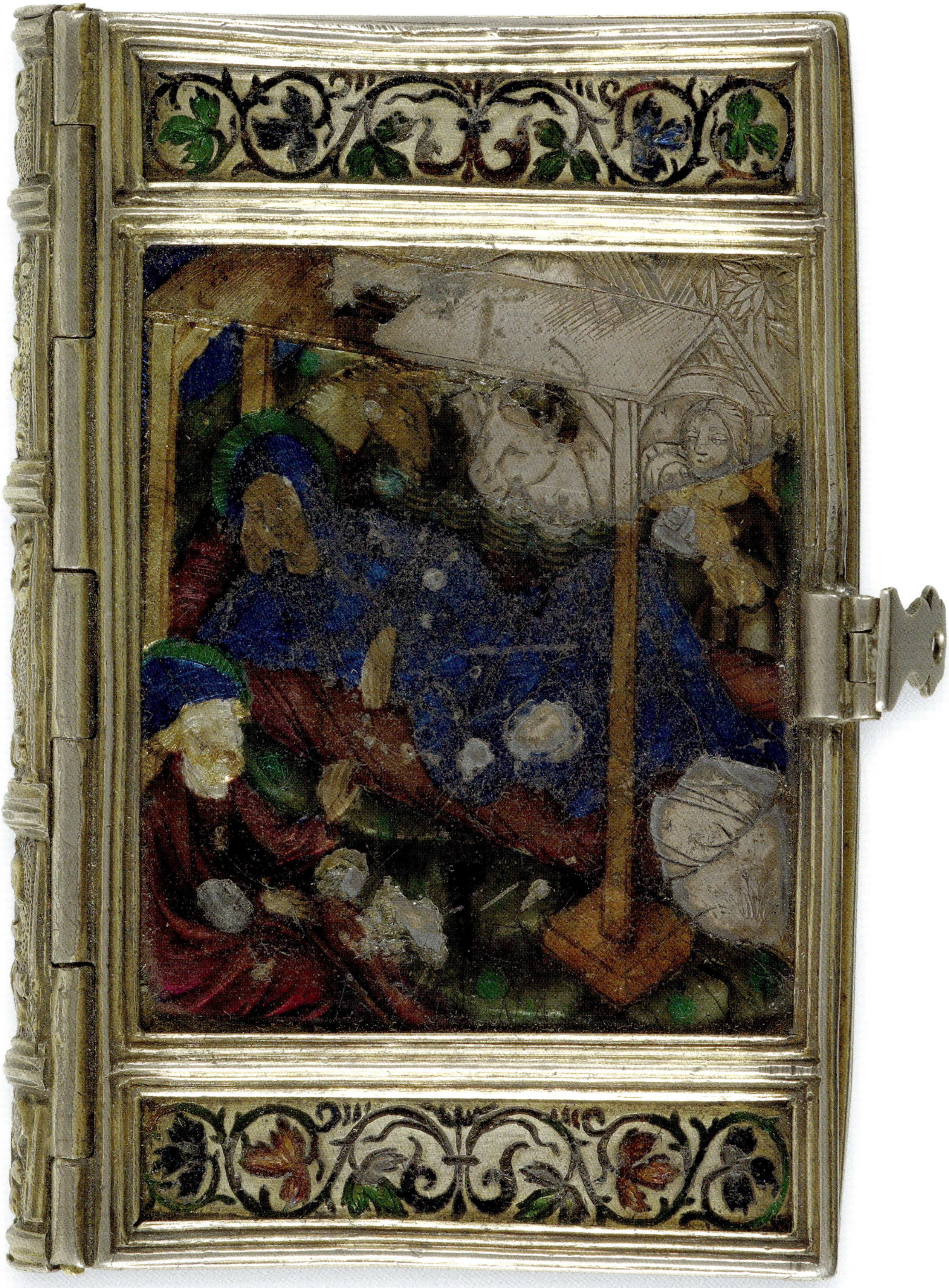

MEDALLIONS

The revival of interest in classical studies during the Italian Renaissance had its inevitable effect upon bookbinding design. During the sixteenth century, medallions (some inspired by Roman coins) were often used as the focus of a binding, and allegorical figures, classical heroes and legends became frequent sources of inspiration, although depictions of more recent historical (and indeed contemporary) figures are also to be found. The rarity and lavishness of these bindings, for which specially commissioned tools were made, indicates that their owners were people of consequence and the neo-classical style quickly spread to the rest of Europe's elite, notably in France, Germany, Switzerland and England. A selection of medallion details from French, Italian and Swiss bindings is shown opposite.

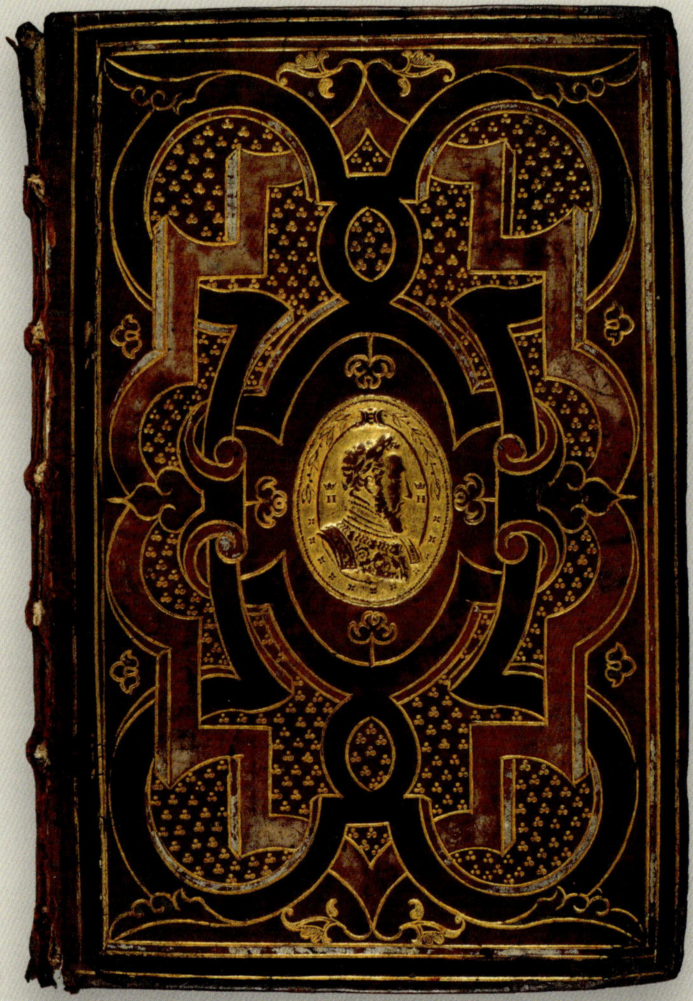

ABOVE
Paris, mid-sixteenth century
244 x 164 x 55 mm (9.6 x 6.5 x 2.2 inches)
C.29.k.8

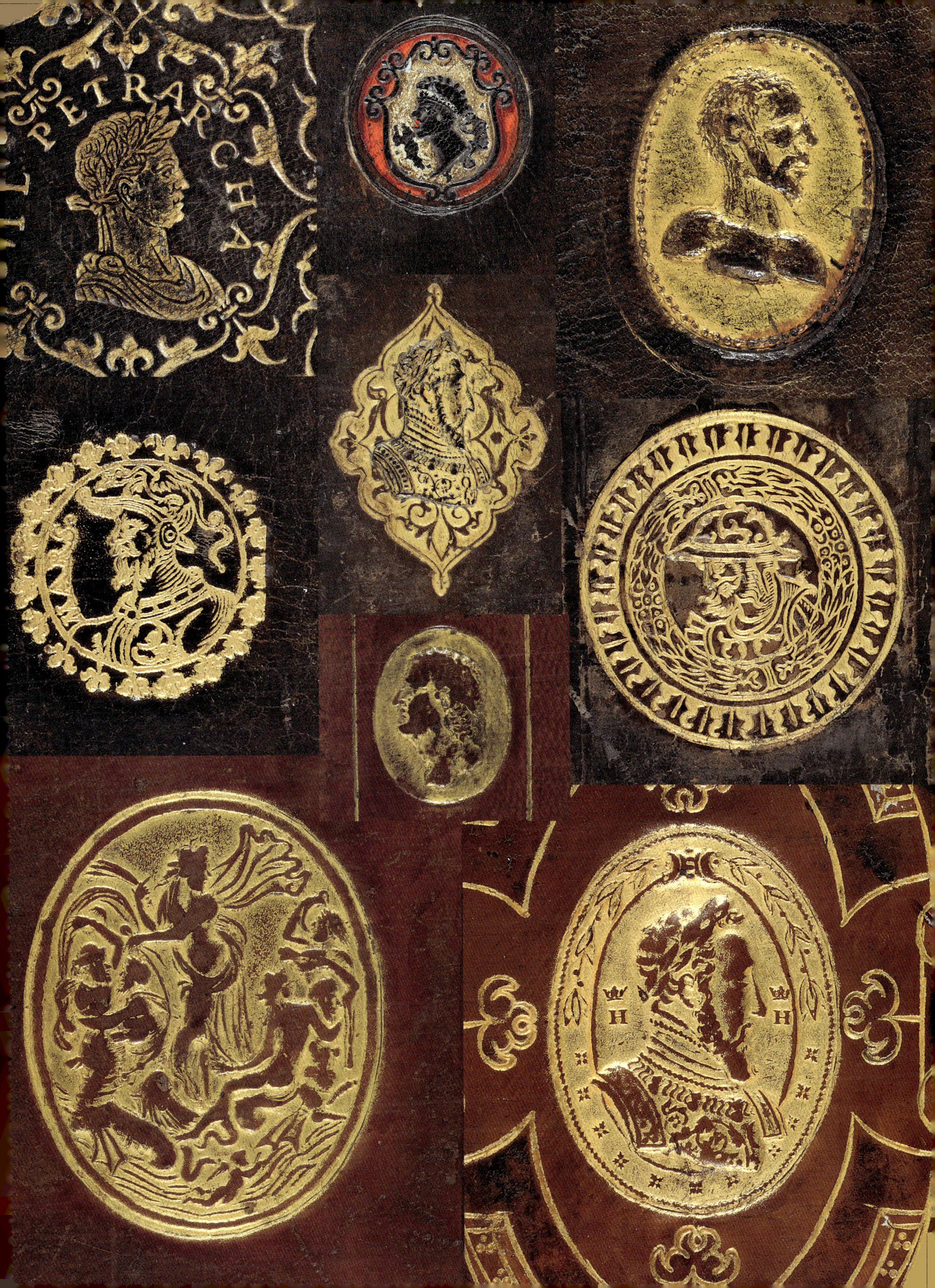
PETRARCHA

Jean Grolier (1479–1565) was arguably the most famous collector of bookbindings in history. He was secretary to the French king on campaign in Milan at a time when Italian publishing was flourishing. He must have encountered many of the newly discovered and published classical texts with their exciting, modern gold-tooled bindings. Italian workshops were quick to adopt the technique that had travelled via the trade routes from the Islamic East, and bindings featuring this innovation must have been very enticing to those who could afford them. Grolier's subsequent post as Treasurer of France ensured his financial security, and he took pains to employ the finest craftsmen to bind his extensive library – though not, presumably, using national funds, since he survived accusations of malpractice!

Grolier's collecting coincided with the golden age of French bookbinding, almost in a literal sense, for the Parisian workshops perfected the skills of gold tooling learned from their Italian counterparts. This mainly blind-tooled, brown goatskin binding features painted gesso plaquettes of classical scenes, and is an example of one of the earliest Italian bindings in Grolier's collection. His ownership inscription, 'Est mei Jo Grolier lugd. & amicorum', is visible on the pastedown of the lower cover (and is illustrated on the contents page). An abridged form of the inscription (indicating that the book was meant for Grolier and his friends), was frequently tooled onto the upper cover of later bindings, including a brown goatskin binding tooled in gold to an architectural design based on a 1539 woodcut (shown on p.45).

Italy, early sixteenth century
312 x 213 x 20 mm (12.3 x 8.4 x 0.8 inches)
G.9026

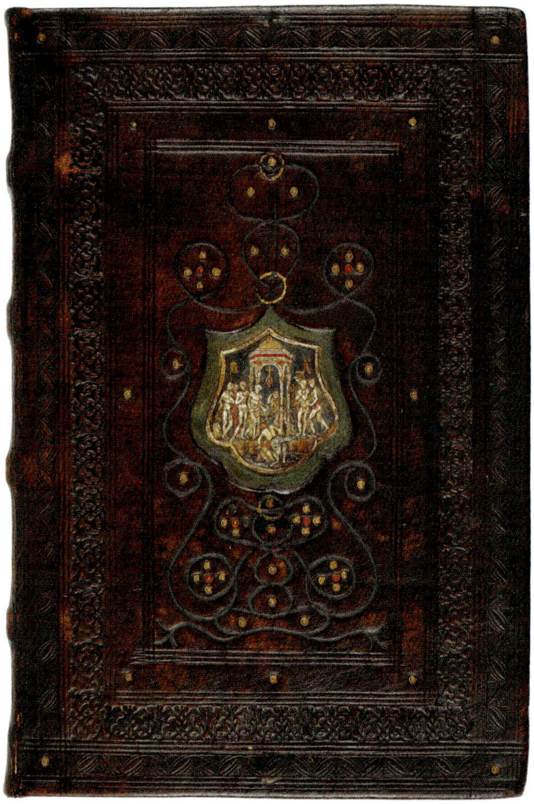

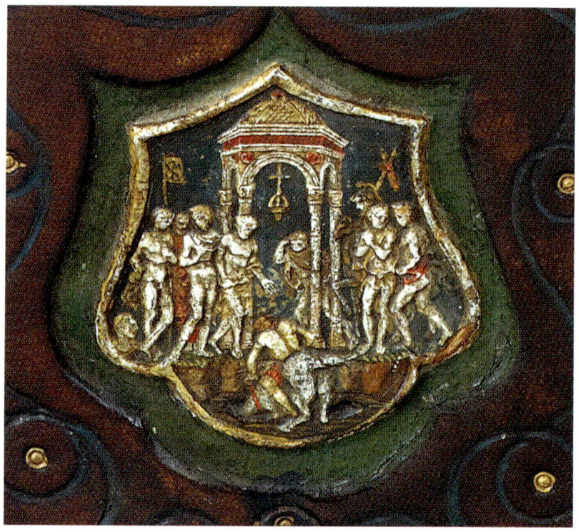

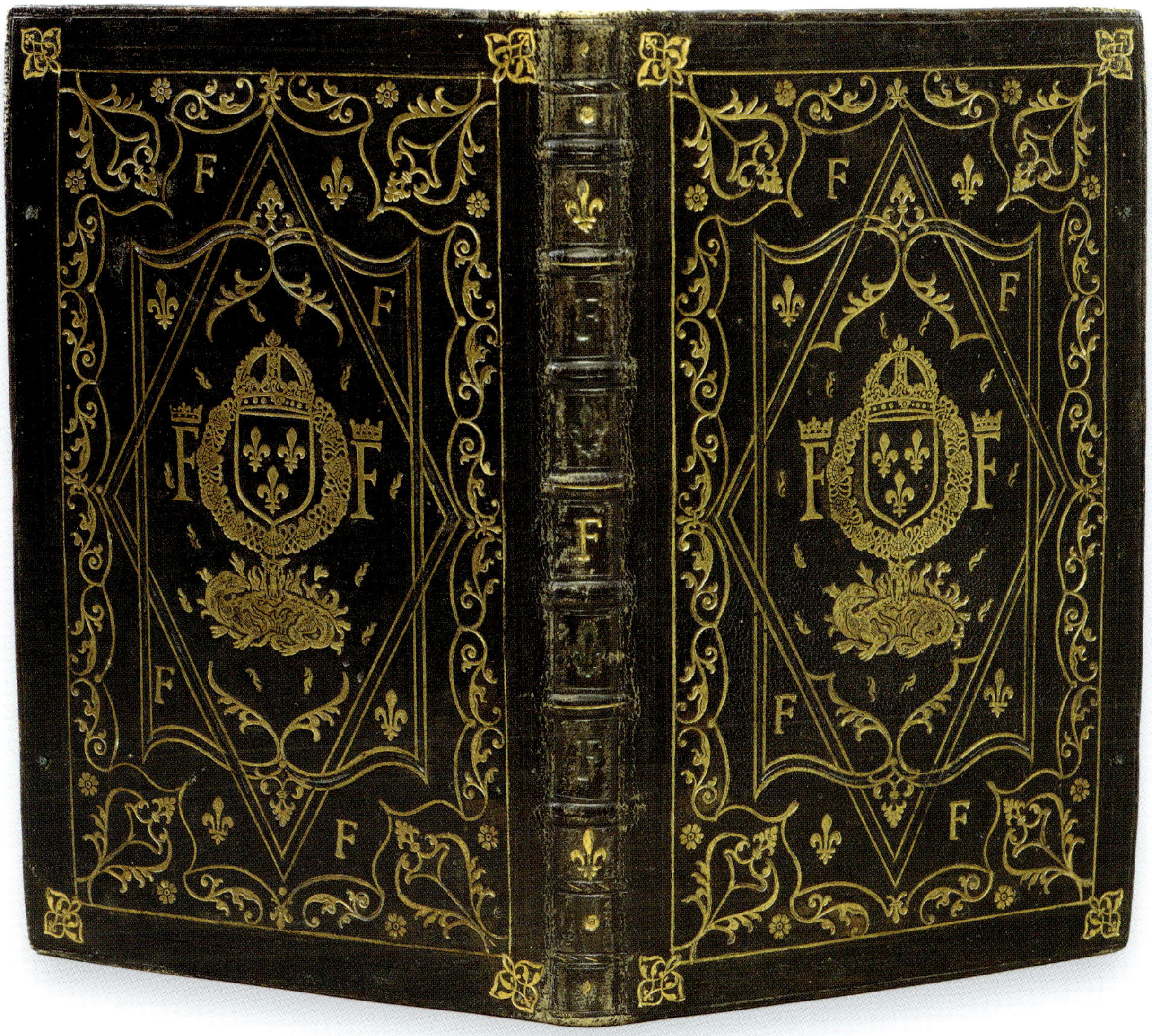

This elegant black goatskin binding, made by Etienne Roffet for Francis I (1494–1547) shows how quickly French binders mastered the new technique of tooling in gold, a skill originating in the East and picked up by Italian craftsmen in the fifteenth century. The corner motifs reflect the Eastern influence, whereas the splendid coat of arms, with Francis's personal salamander badge, represents a Western tradition. Francis gathered together all the royal manuscripts and printed books in the recently refurbished palace of Fontainebleau, thus forming the basis of a national collection that would become the Bibliothèque Nationale. This unprecedented programme of rebinding continued, and such royal patronage stimulated the Parisian trade and raised bookbinding 'au rang d'art décorative à part entière'. Roffet was the first to receive the title 'Royal Binder' in France.

Paris, c.1542
240 x 155 x 21 mm (9.4 x 6.1 x 0.8 inches)
Davis 367

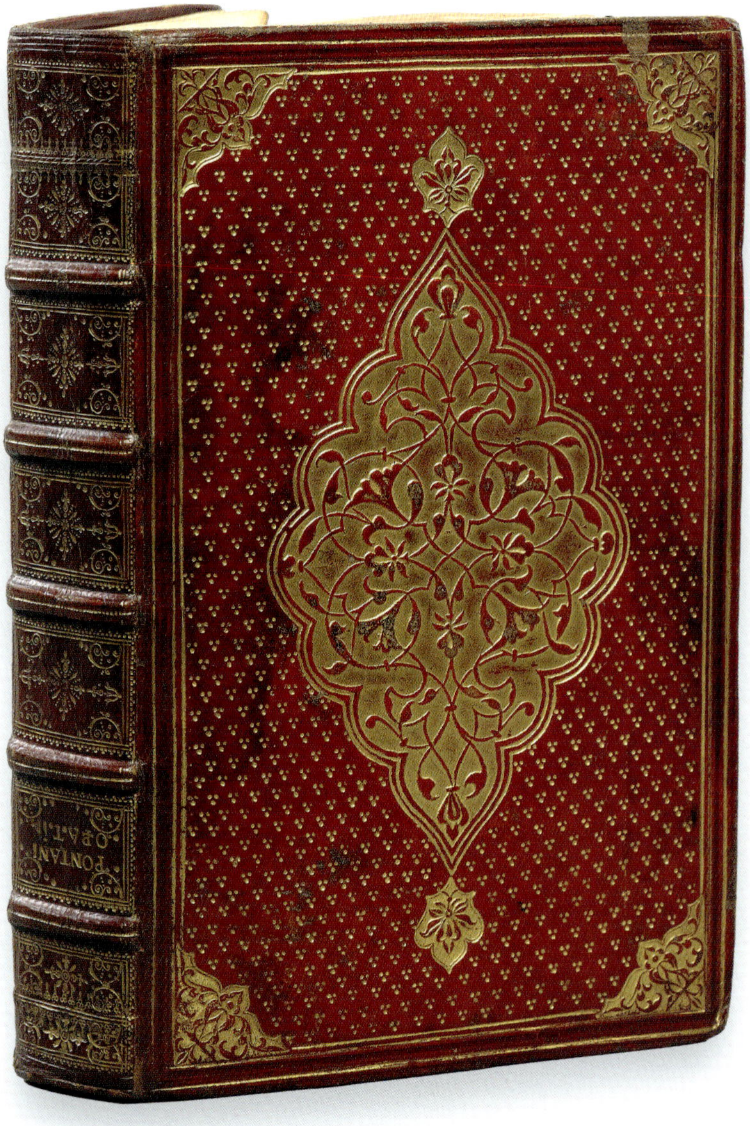

Attracted by the humanist study of classical civilization while on a military campaign in Milan, Francis I of France (1494–1547) acquired a number of humanist books bound in Italy. Some of these bindings exhibited the influence of Islamic artistic traditions (spread via Venice, the major point of trade between East and West). The new acquisitions had a demonstrable effect upon the French royal binders who were exposed to them. This gold-tooled, red goatskin binding clearly displays an Islamic influence, notably the '*şalbek*' placed above and below the centrepiece, a pattern that frequently appeared on Qur'ans. The *semis* of three dots comprising the background of the pattern is also characteristic of Western imitations of the Islamic style. It seems likely that the binder was either Gommar Estienne or Claude Picques, but little is known concerning contemporary ownership of binding tools or, indeed, about the practices of the trade (some binders, *doreurs*, specialised in gold tooling and may have worked for several workshops, making precise attribution difficult). Both were royal bookbinders, and Picques followed Estienne in the post in the 1550s.

Paris, *c.*1560–1565
217 x 140 x 40 mm (8.5 x 5.5 x 1.6 inches)
Davis 381

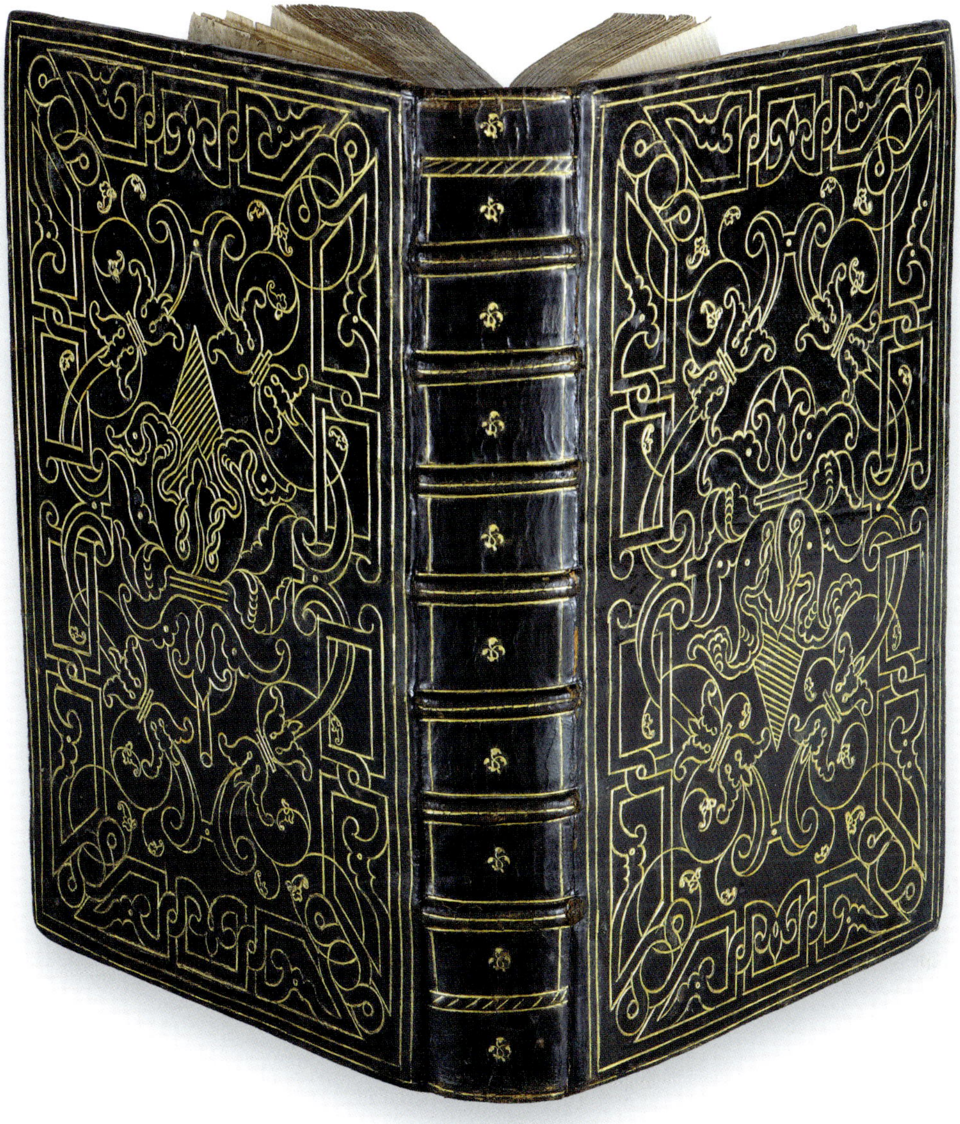

The *doreur* (a French craftsman specialising in gold tooling) who decorated this sixteenth-century Parisian goatskin binding was clearly at the height of his powers. Patterns that cover the entire space available are sometimes applied with large engraved panels in a single operation. This example, however, relies on fillets and gouges, which are more difficult to apply than small individual hand tools, and require confidence and a steady hand, particularly on an unforgiving black background. This technique lends fresh energy and movement to a traditional design featuring interlacing ribbons and compartments.

Paris, sixteenth century
380 x 250 x 62 mm (15 x 9.8 x 2.4 inches)
C.183.b.1

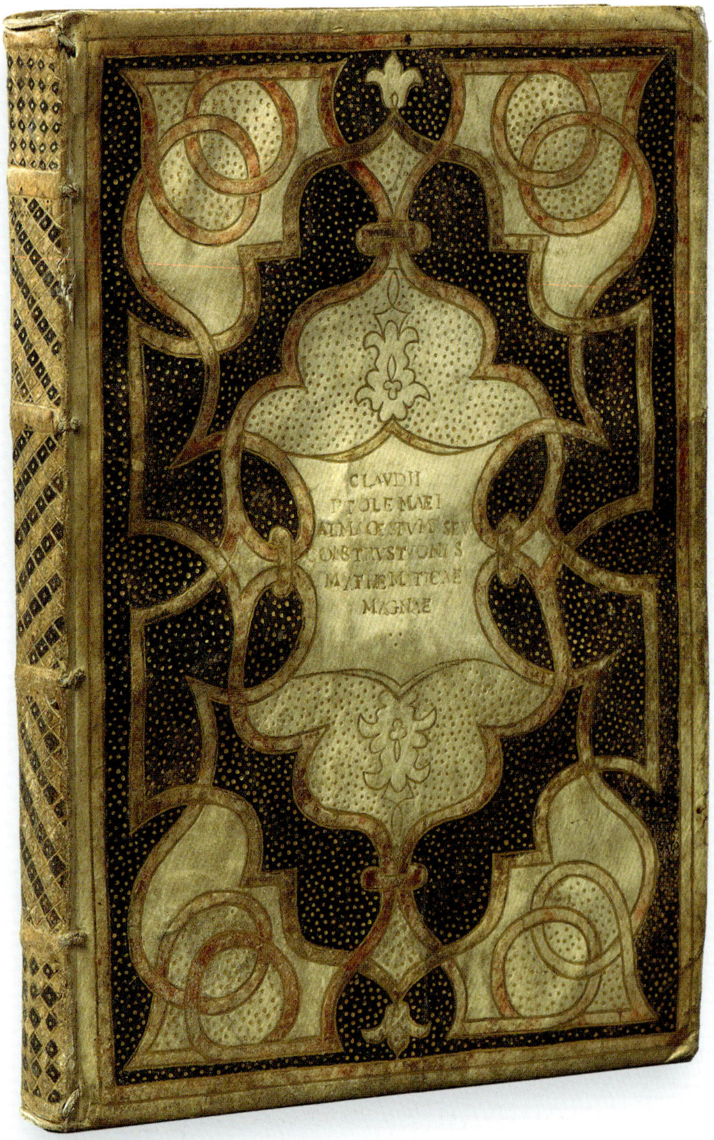

Documents have been written on parchment (thin calf, sheep or goatskin dried under tension) for centuries, but bookbinders often used it as a wrapper for texts. Its virtue is that it is lighter, cheaper and more flexible than leather and surprisingly robust, as this sixteenth-century French example demonstrates. These covers have been tooled in gold and painted to an all-over design incorporating interlacing ribbons. Its owner, Thomas Mahieu, secretary to Queen Catherine de Medicis and Treasurer of France, was a protégé of the famous book collector, Jean Grolier, and adopted Grolier's habit of incorporating Latin phrases into the binding design. The most common, shared by both, was a Latin statement of ownership that included the owner's friends 'et amicorum'. The bindings were produced in the best Paris workshops. Most were leather, and it has been suggested that Mahieu purchased this parchment text already bound.

ABOVE
Paris, *c*.1550–58
318 x 215 x 25 mm (12.5 x 8.5 x 1 inches)
Davis 406

OPPOSITE
Paris, mid-sixteenth century
312 x 207 x 37 mm (12.3 x 8.1 x 1.4 inches)
C.46.i.12

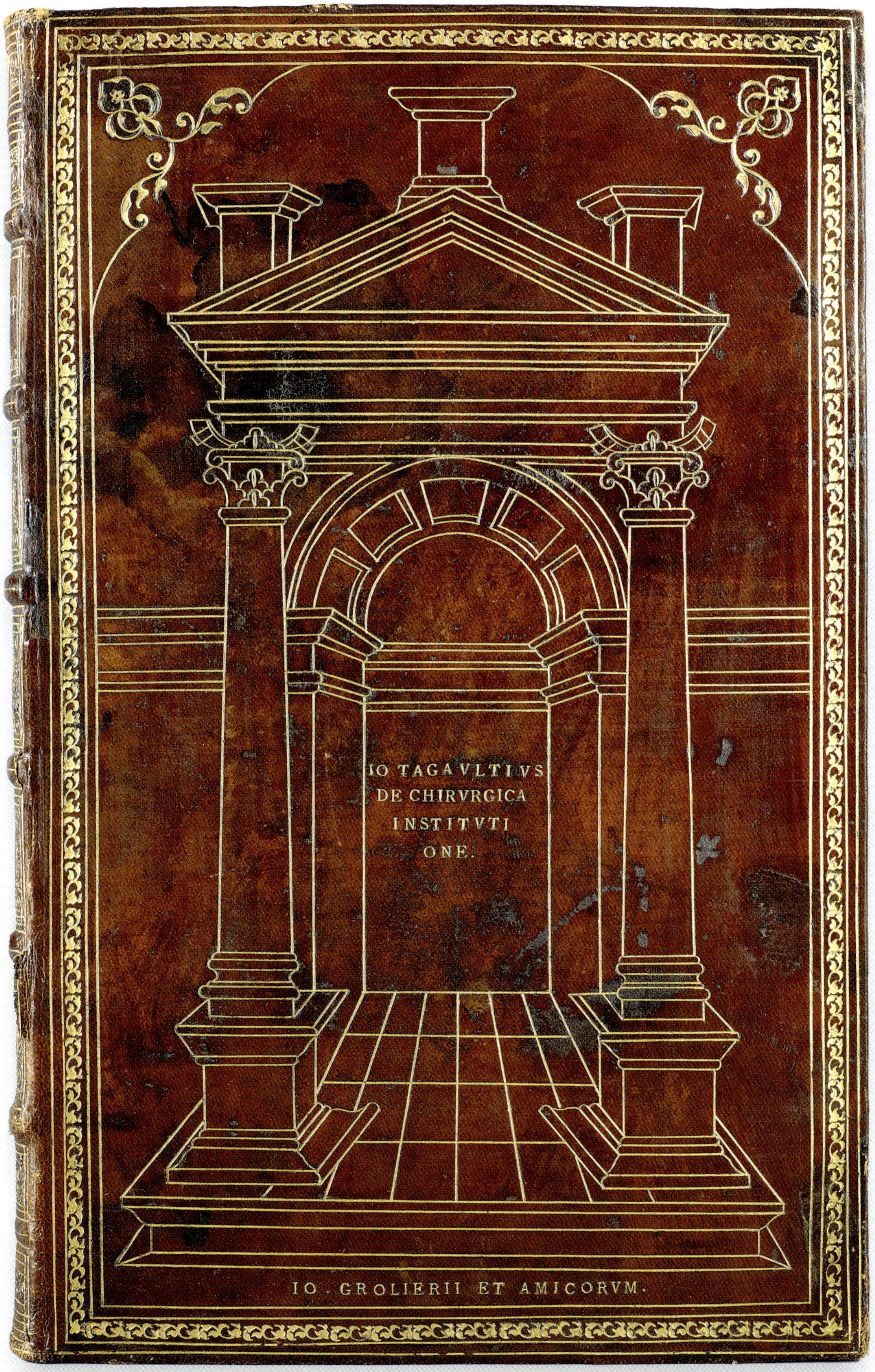
IO TAGAVLTIVS
DE CHIRVRGICA
INSTITVTI
ONE.
IO. GROLIERII ET AMICORVM.

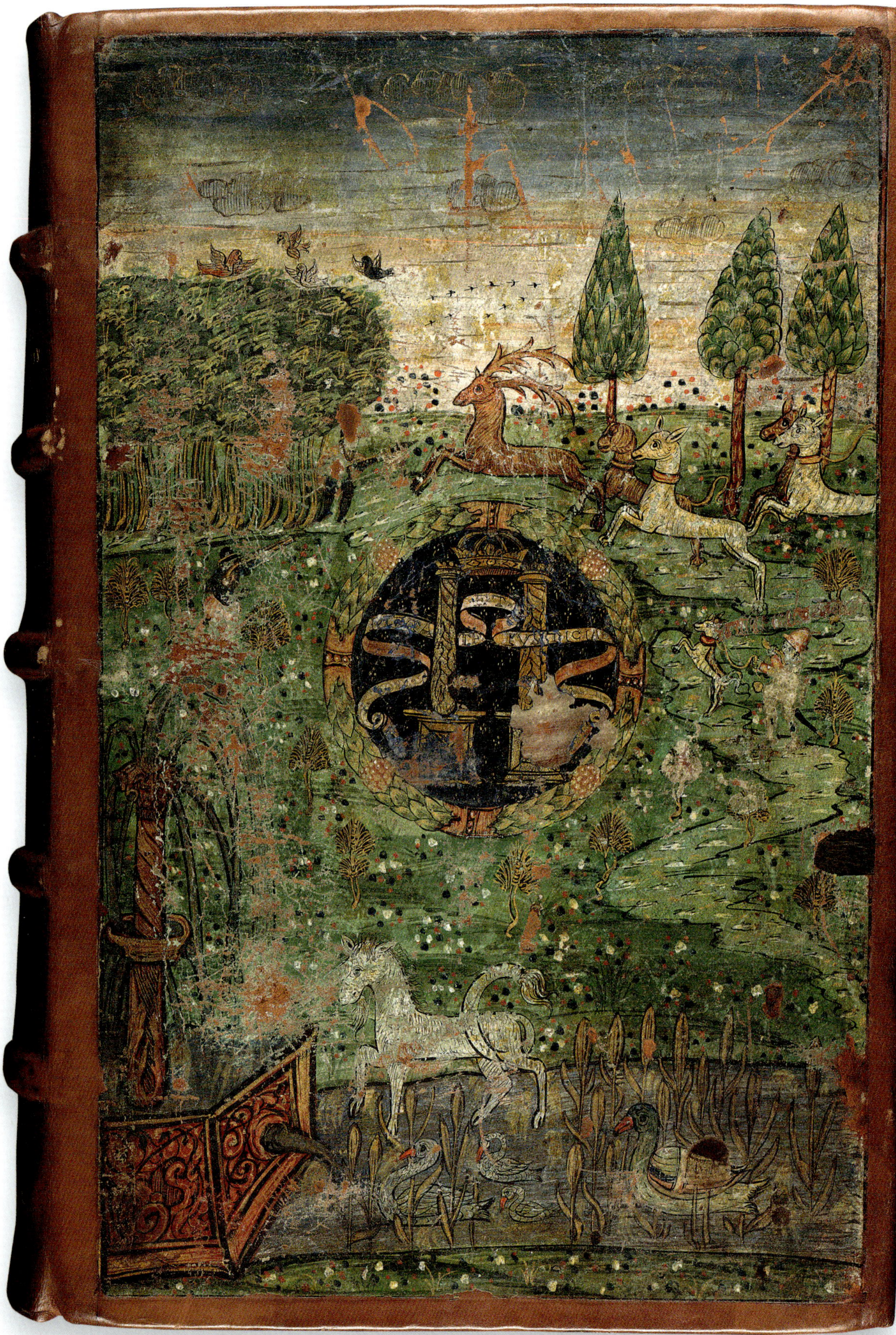

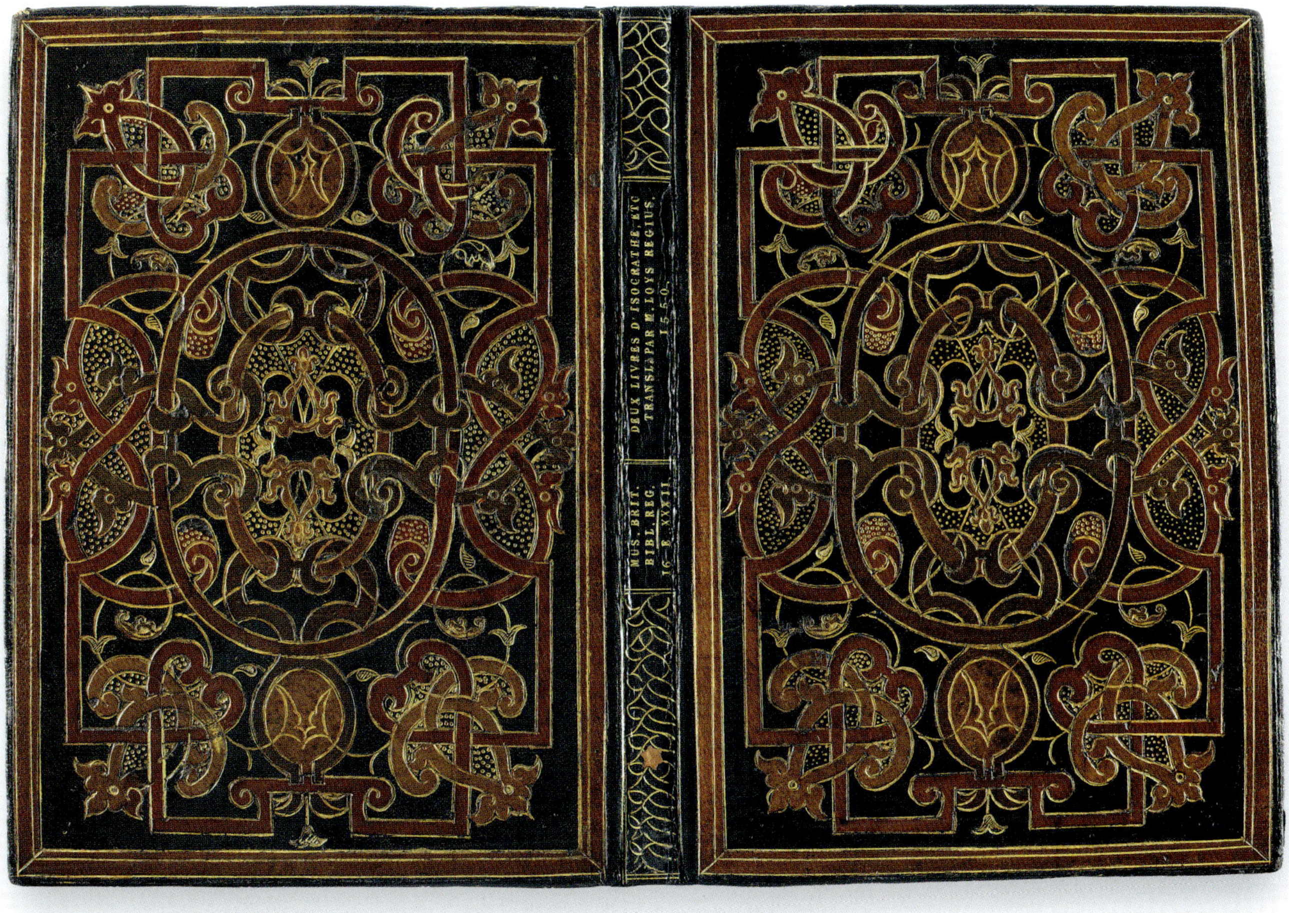

OPPOSITE This modern binding incorporates the original painted leather covers of a sixteenth-century French manuscript dedicated to King Charles IX of France (1560–1574). Charles's personal device, two columns linked by the motto 'Pietate et Justicia,' forms the centrepiece of the design on the upper cover, and surrounding this is a scene depicting the hunt. This subject, popular with the aristocracy who practised it, can also be seen in a sixteenth-century Mughal interpretation on pp.66–7. As we have seen, French binders were more than equal to the task of producing lavishly tooled bindings, but here the medium of paint has been chosen to create a much more subtle effect in the form of a harmonious pastoral illustration.

Paris, 1569
315 x 205 x 45 mm (12.4 x 8.1 x 1.8 inches)
Egerton 2388

ABOVE This design, a form of which can be found on eighth-century Coptic bindings, is particularly versatile. Each cover is divided up by interlacing ribbons, and the spaces between filled with single tools or left empty, as with this example. This elaborate, black goatskin-tooled and onlaid presentation was intended as a gift for Edward VI (1537–1553); he was the recipient of several unusual bindings, usually on academic texts, presumably to encourage him to pay attention to his school books. Edward's library also contained a novelty 'backless' binding which appeared to have four edges and no spine.

Paris (?), mid-sixteenth century
203.2 x 152.4 mm (8 x 6 inches)
Royal MS 16 E

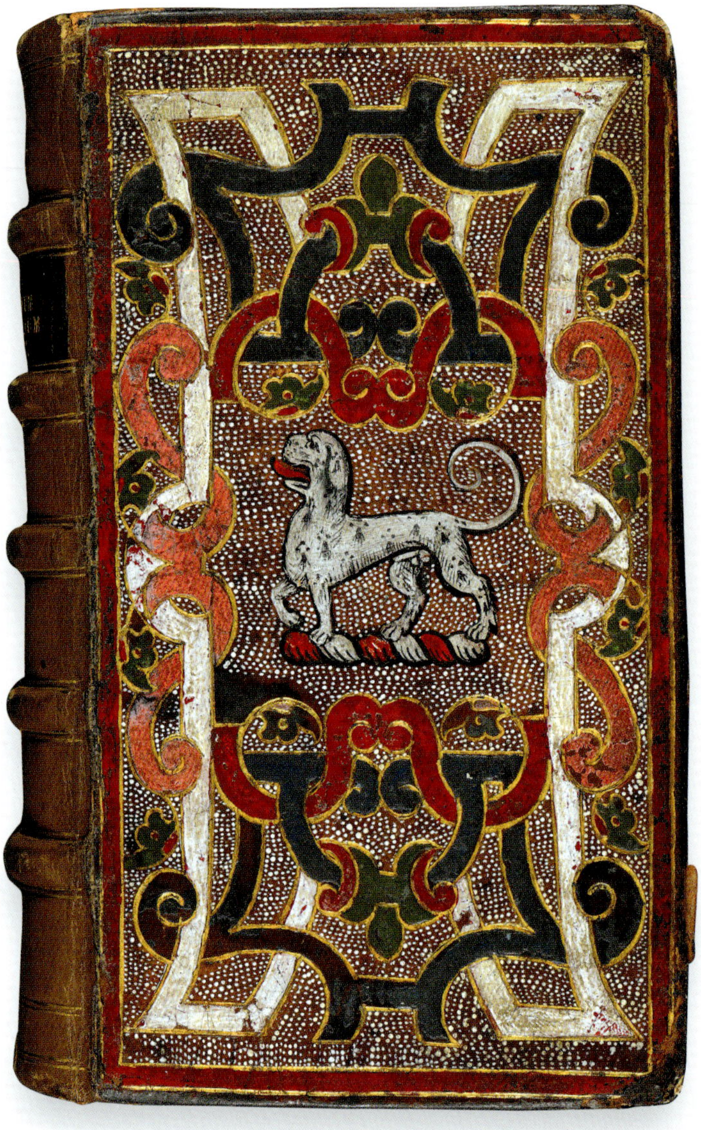

The dog depicted on this English, brown calf binding is described in heraldic terms as 'a talbot passant'. It is the badge of Elizabeth Grey (née Lady Elizabeth Talbot), Countess of Kent (1582–1651), the first lady of the bedchamber to Queen Elizabeth I and an influential noblewoman. Coats of arms, crests and other emblems signifying rank were commonly found on bookbindings. Frequently the design was simple, with a central coat of arms being framed with a gold- or blind-tooled panel. The example shown here is more sophisticated as it features the painted interlacing ribbons fashionable in contemporary France (see p.50).

Books were expensive and, like heirlooms, great care was taken of them. The text bears the signatures of Henry Fitzalan, twelfth Earl of Arundel (d.1580) and his scholarly daughter, Jane (1537–1578), who in 1552 married John, Lord Lumley (d.1609). Lumley inherited Fitzalan's library and became the owner of the largest private library of the period, eventually bought by King James I. It seems likely that Lady Elizabeth Grey had the book rebound when it came into her possession.

English or French, early sixteenth century
169 x 100 x 40 mm (6.65 x 3.94 x 1.57 inches)
C.20.a.6

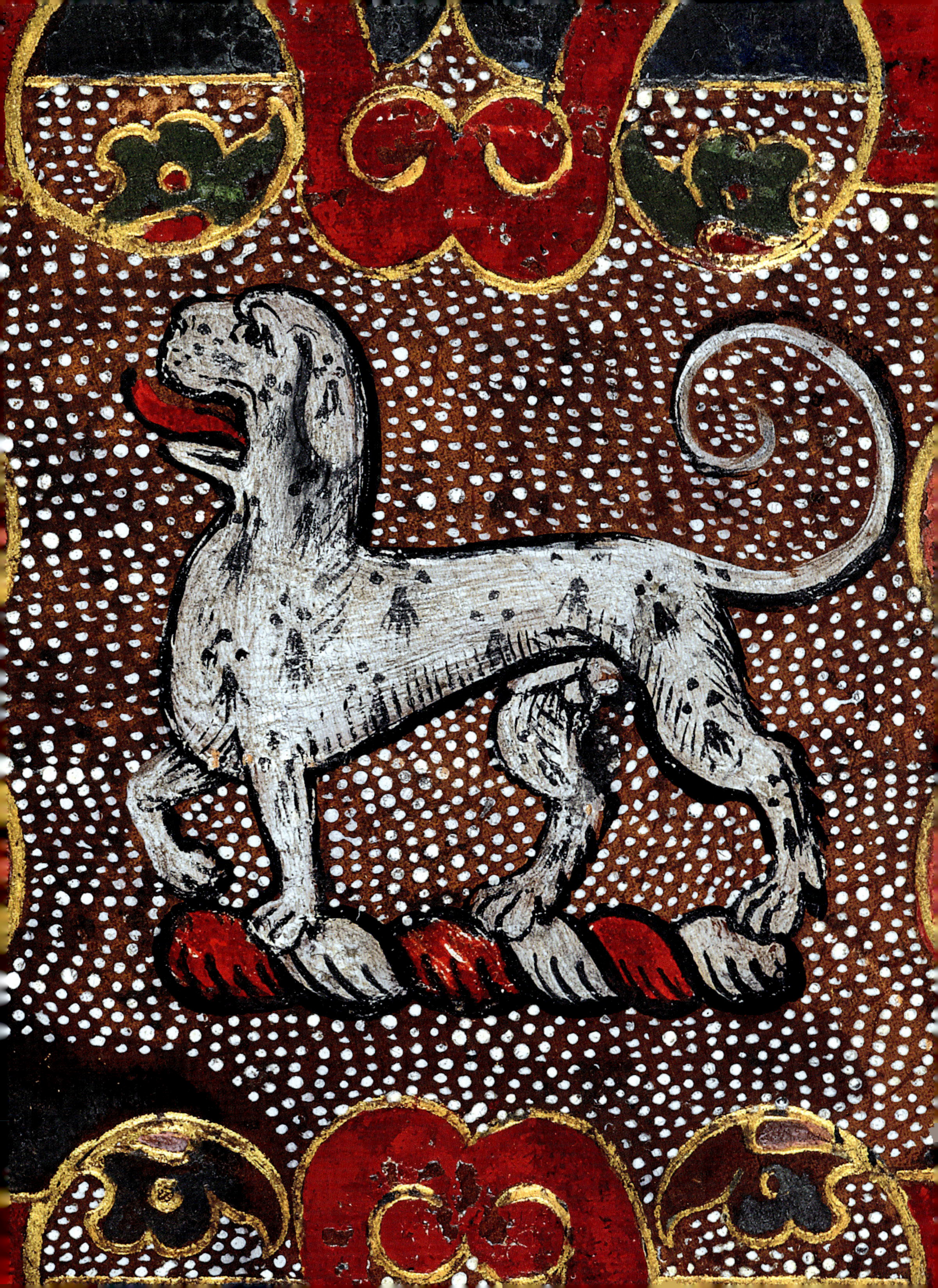

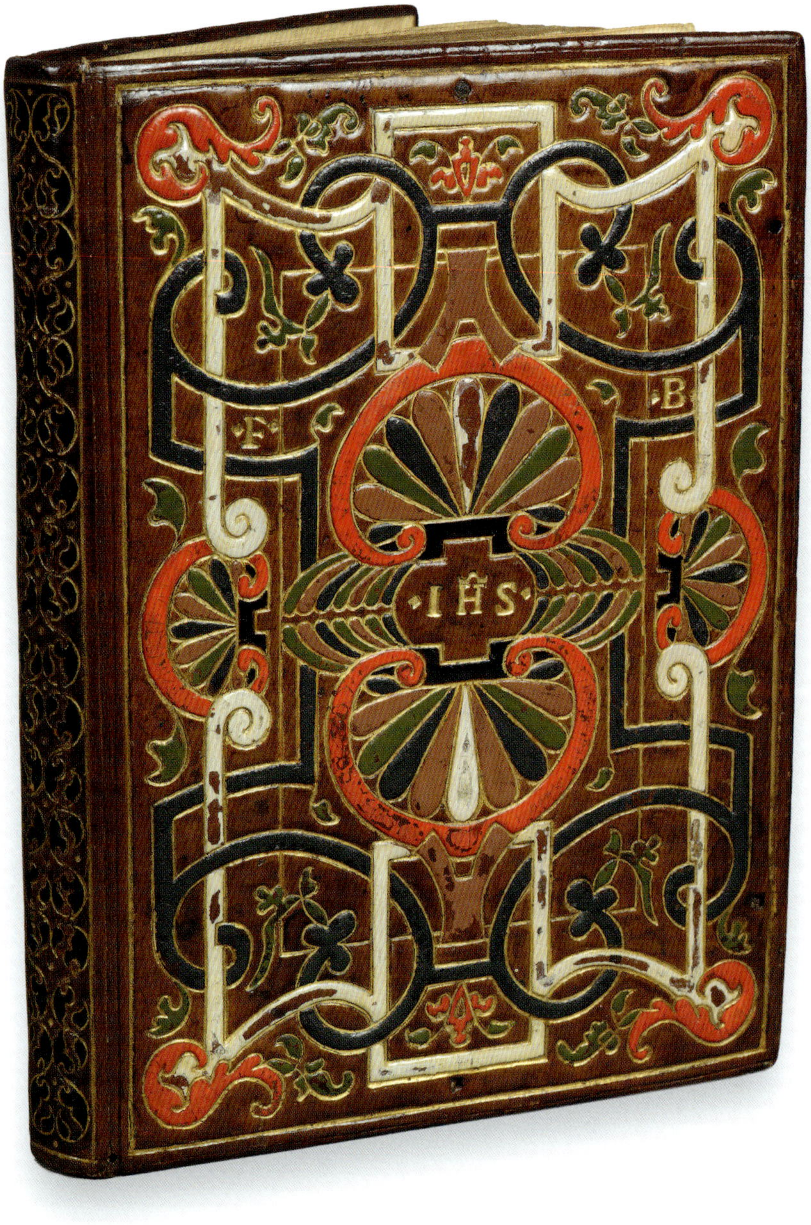

The interlacing design used on this sixteenth-century French brown calf binding has been economically applied using a single large decorative block. This block would probably also have been used on other bindings of the same size (covering both this text and others). To distinguish each binding, appropriate lettering and coloured paints could be applied. Here, the Sacred Monogram (IHS, denoting the first three letters of the Greek name of Jesus, *iota-eta-sigma*) has been gold-tooled on the upper cover and the initials M A for Maria on the lower, both appropriate for a devotional work.

The initials F B may represent the owner's name. The appearance of historic bindings can be misleading. Today, some examples can seem particularly subtle due to the fading of the leather and pigments. In fact, many bindings were vibrant, with colour being central to the scheme. The repainting on these covers helps us to visualise what the binding would have looked like to the sixteenth-century eye.

Paris or Lyons, *c.*1550
232 x 168 x 25 mm (9.1 x 6.6 x 1 inches)
Davis 500

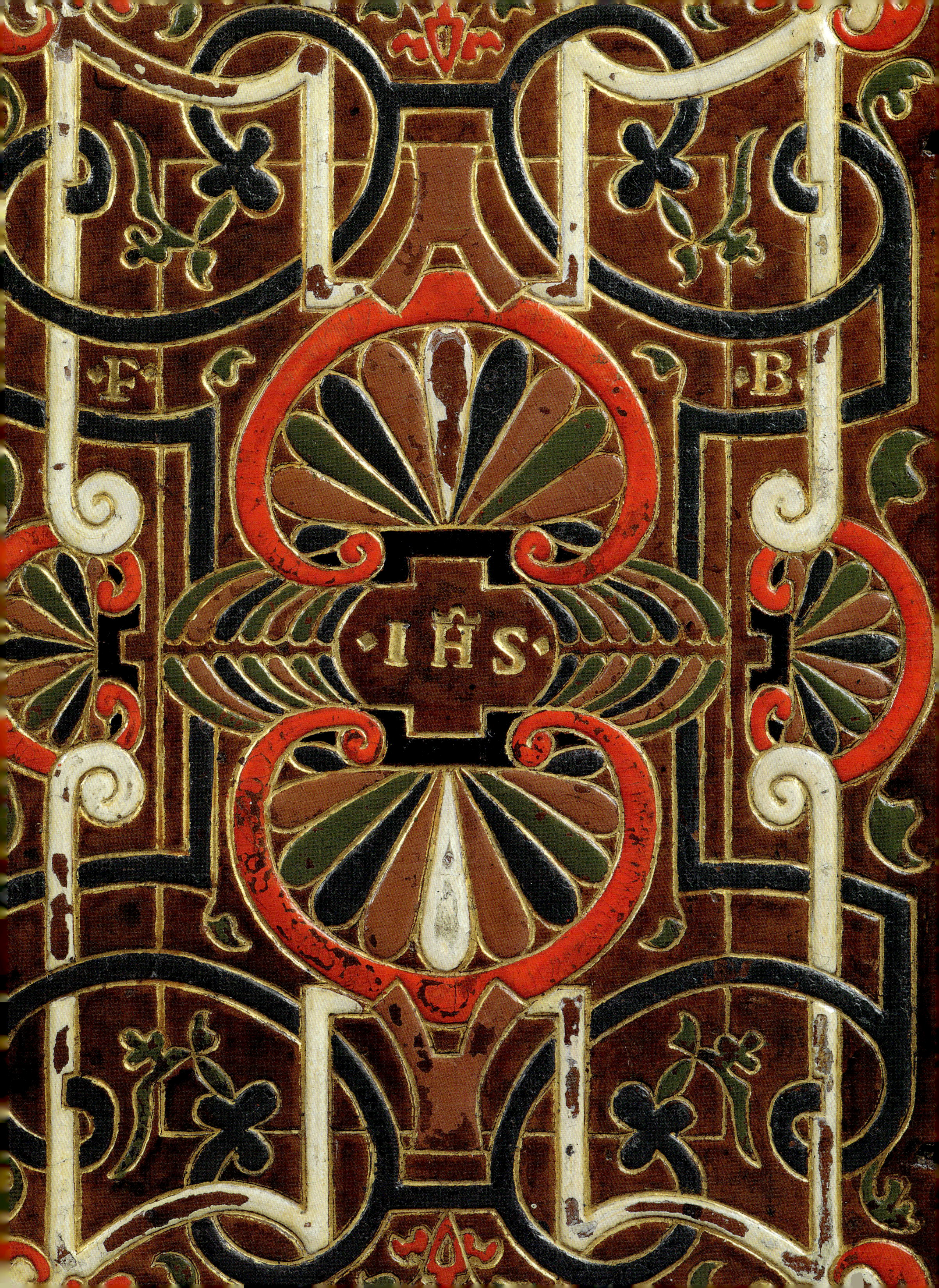
F
B
IHS

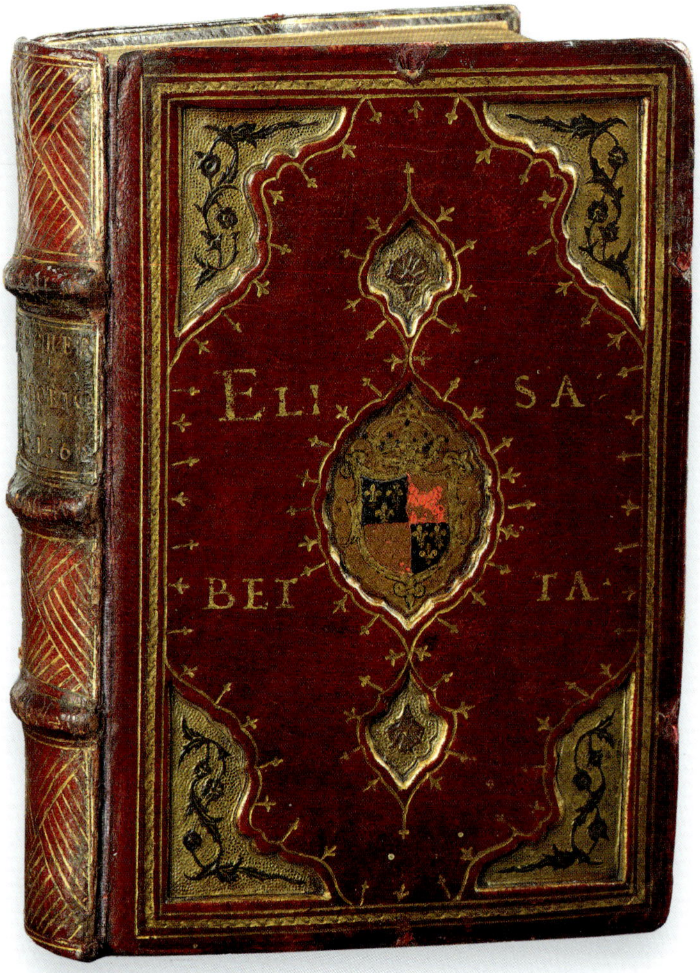

ABOVE This sixteenth-century Venetian binding, with its painted centre and corner-piece design and varnished surface, draws inspiration from Islamic sources. The text was dedicated to Queen Elizabeth I of England (1533–1603), and bears her name and arms on the upper cover. Nearly 200 printed books were dedicated to Elizabeth during her lifetime, and their authors invariably had them expensively bound in the hope of benefiting from royal favour. The Venetian red goatskin binding, with its eye-catching use of gold, would have provided an appealing alternative to the luxurious fabrics frequently chosen for such presentations. There would originally have been four pairs of red ties (a common Italian practice), one each on the top and tail edges and two on the fore-edge.

Venice, mid-sixteenth century
155 x 95 x 29 mm (6.1 x 3.7 x 1.1 inches)
C.20.a.21

OPPOSITE Elizabeth preferred her books to be 'bound in velvet of different colours ... with clasps of gold and silver', and this is an example of just such a binding. The glowing jewel-like colours of the metalwork give an impression of its original beauty (somewhat marred by the abraded surface of the velvet).

England (?), *c.*1570 (?)
127 x 80 x 20 mm (5 x 3.2 x 0.8 inches)
168.i.30

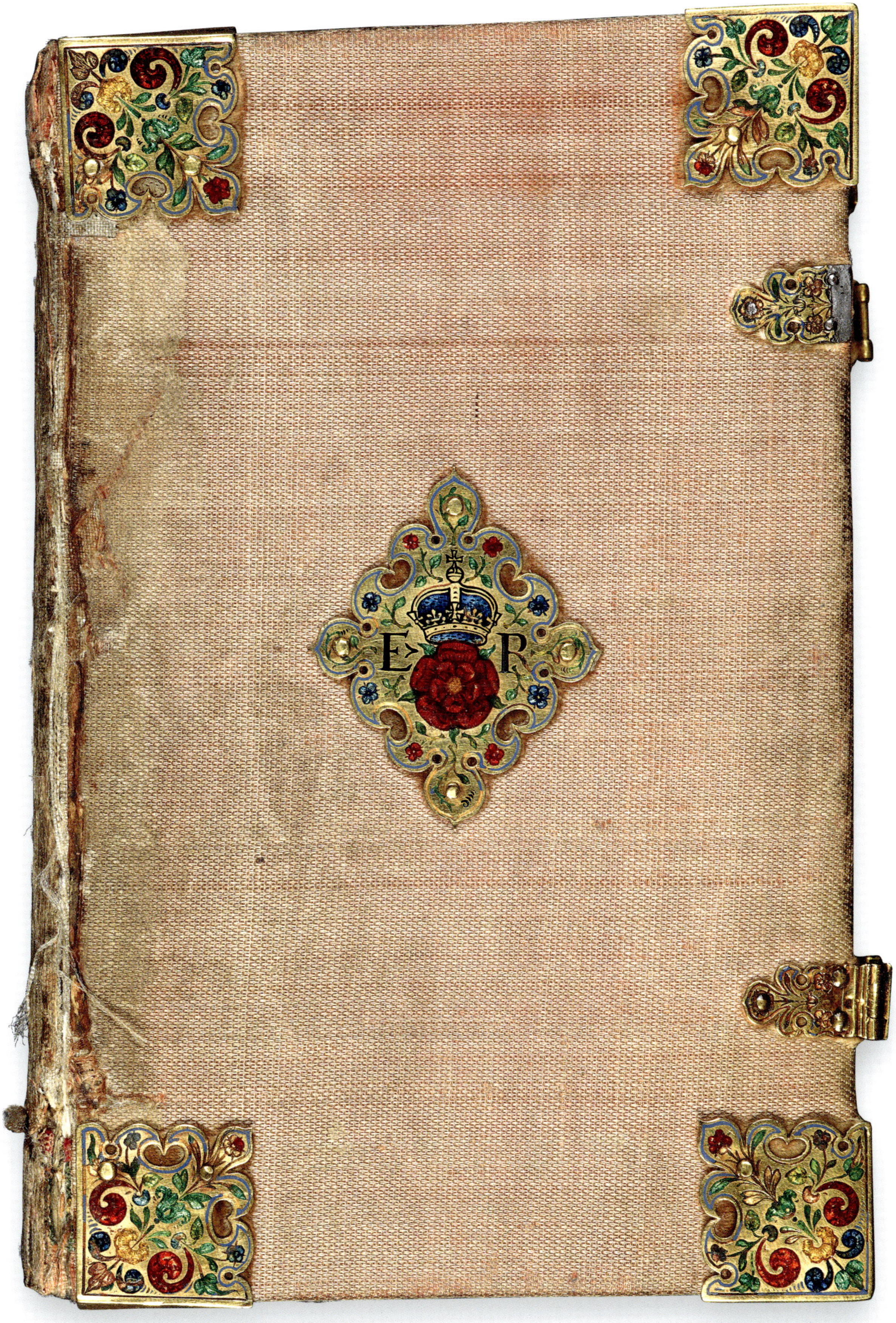
E R

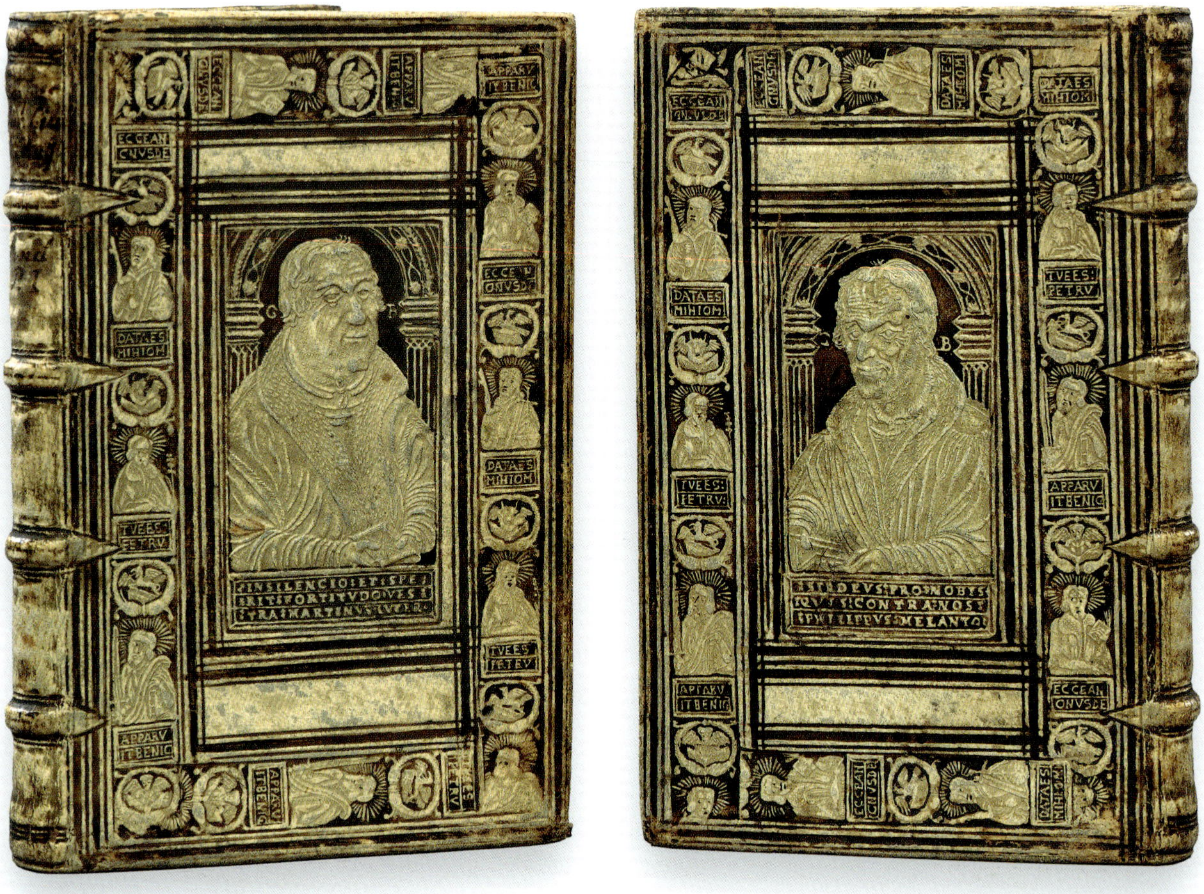

ABOVE Binders in the German-speaking world tended to be conservative in both style and technique, but the use of colour to emphasize the blind-tooled design here is unusual. The motifs on this alum-tawed pigskin binding from Wittenberg are traditional, with a border roll of the four evangelists and a central panel depicting a realistic likeness of Martin Luther (1483–1546) on the upper cover, and Philip Melanchthon (1497–1560) on the lower cover. Protestant reformers were often found on German bindings. In this instance the binder, Gregor Bernutz (working *c.*1560–74), has his own initials in the central panel. Luther's image was familiar, due to his depiction in the many prints and books that had become widespread since the development of printing. Controversies, including that provoked by Luther's *Ninety-Five Theses* which challenged the Catholic faith, energized all sectors of the book trade, including bookbinding.

Wittenberg, *c.*1570
177 x 114 x 25 mm (7 x 4.5 x 1 inches)
Davis 628

OPPOSITE Robert Dudley, created Earl of Leicester in 1564, was perhaps the most active non-royal patron of English bookbindings in the sixteenth century. His library contained books bound by most of the leading London workshops of the day. Although some may have been personal commissions, others were probably given to him as gifts by those of lesser status to gain his favour. The majority bore Dudley's badge, depicting a chained bear with a crescent on his shoulder (the mark of a second son) and holding a ragged staff in its paws. It seems likely that Leicester's household owned several versions of this badge, which were lent to binders to personalise the covers. The bear on this gold-tooled brown calf binding is in silver, now tarnished. The identity of the binder is not known, but as he bound at least nine books for Leicester, he was called the 'Dudley Binder'.

London, mid-sixteenth century
230 x 145 x 14 mm (9.1 x 5.7 x 0.6 inches)
C.19.c.23

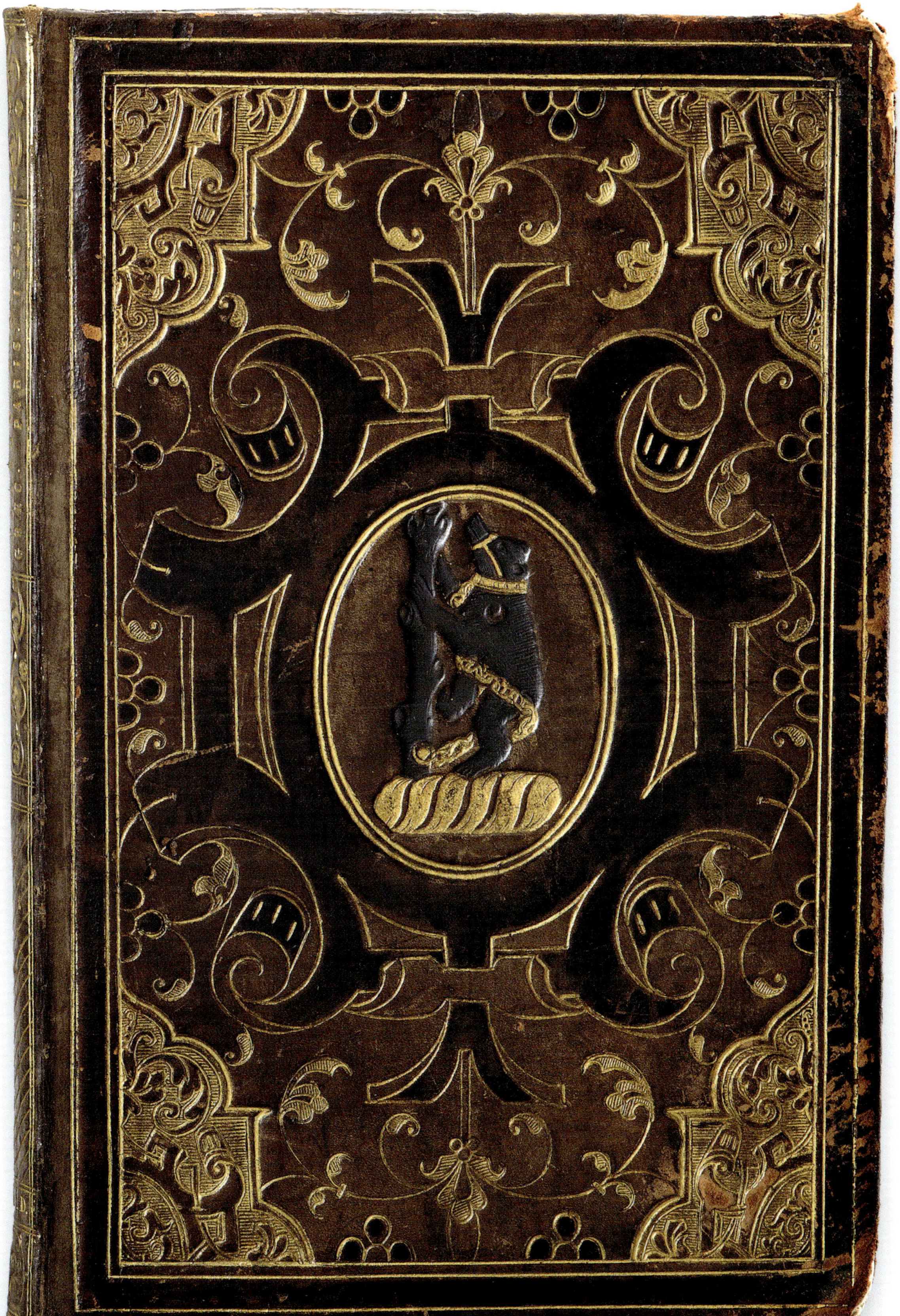

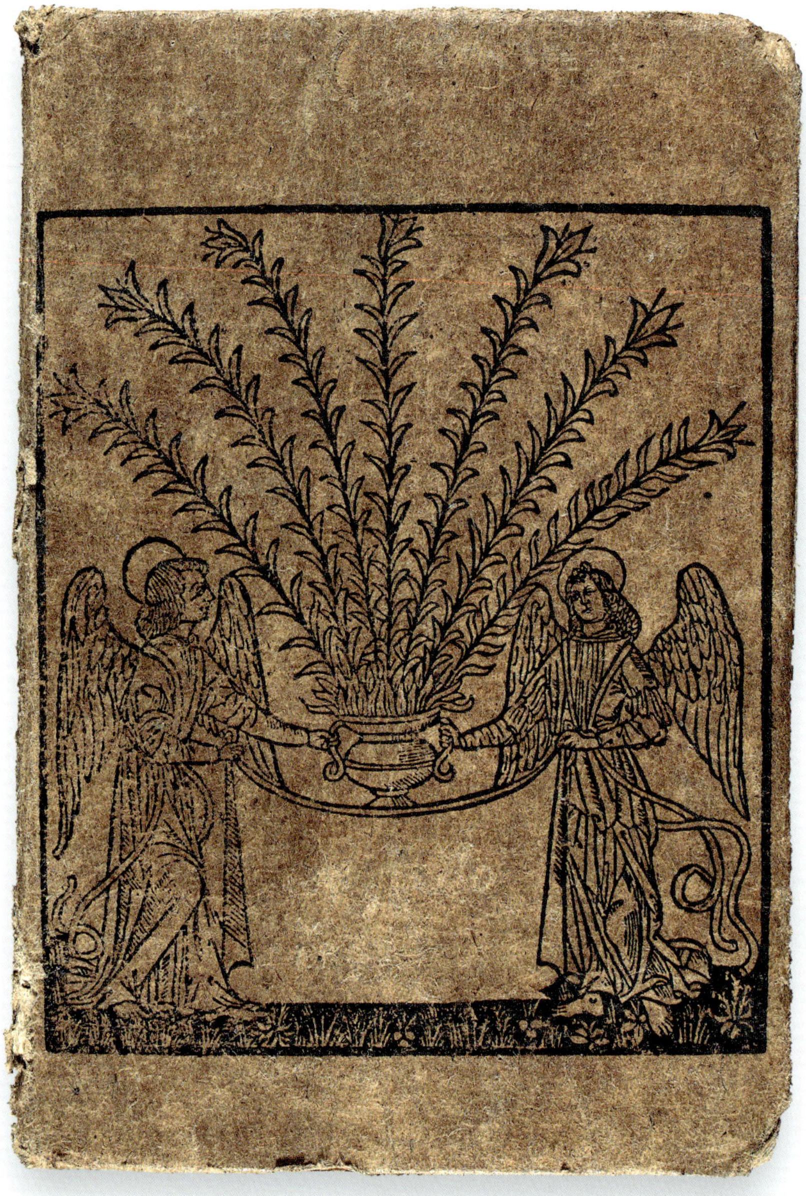

Bindings do not have to be expensive to be beautiful. This woodcut on paper depicting a vase of lilies flanked by two angels is a simple yet effective decorative addition to the inexpensive pasteboards that protect the text. The images on a binding were not expected to relate directly to the subject of the text itself, and binders were therefore at liberty to use any woodcut of an appropriate size. The Arabic technique of paper-making (adapted from first-century Chinese methods) reached Italy around the twelfth century. Local craftsmen modified it to meet their needs, becoming proficient in its decoration as well as its production. Ferrara in the late fifteenth and early sixteenth centuries was perhaps the most important centre for the production of woodcut paper bindings, but they were also made in sixteenth-century Venice, from where this example derives.

Venice, 1547
154 x 105 x 15 mm (6.1 x 4.1 x 0.6 inches)
Davis 802

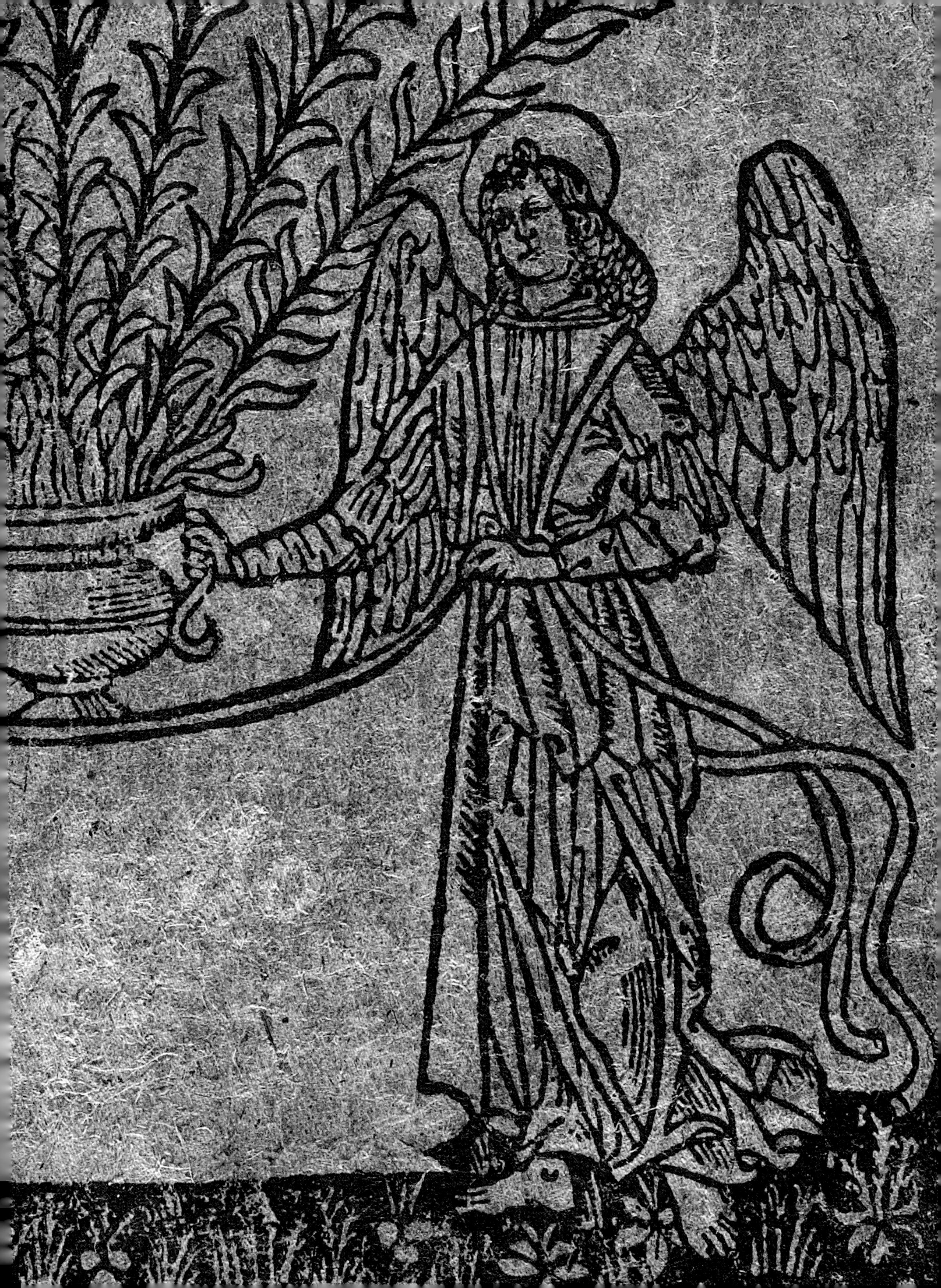

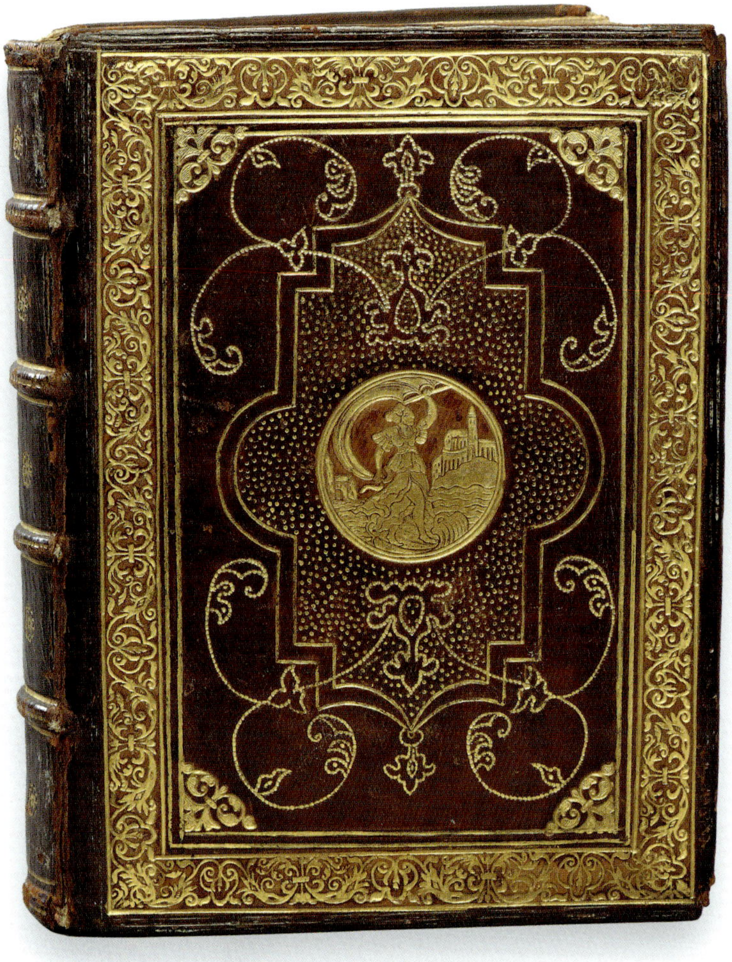

ABOVE This German binding clearly shows the influence of both Italian and French styles. The dotted background and open tools are reminiscent of Parisian bindings, while the medallion and the shape of the gold-tooled panel (with a semi-circular outline on each side) recall Venetian motifs. The book is inscribed by the author to Johann Fugger (1531–1598) of the Augsburg mercantile and banking family, many of whom were noted bibliophiles. Indeed, Antoine Louis of Flanders, the personal binder of Johan Jakob Fugger (1516–1575), was trained in Venice and brought his newly learnt skills to Augsburg, where the Italian style of binding had a great influence on the German binders. This binding has been attributed to Matthias Gärtner, also resident in Augsburg.

Augsburg, *c.*1580
213 x 158 x 41 mm (8.4 x 6.2 x 1.6 inches)
Davis 680

OPPOSITE This type of binding, which features pierced parchment with a coloured lining beneath (frequently silk), was produced during the sixteenth and early seventeenth centuries in the Low Countries, Germany, France and Italy (but rarely in England). The pierced leather technique was not new; examples are known from sixth-century Northern Italy, eighth- and tenth-century Egypt, and fifteenth-century Persia (on doublures). Binders still experiment with it today (see p.182). Hans Bapest von Erfurt, master bookbinder at Schmalkalden (central Germany), was a famous practitioner of this type of binding, but the work shown here has not been attributed and is plainer than some of his work.

Antwerp (?), *c.*1570
260 x 142 x 40 mm (10.2 x 5.6 x 1.6 inches)
C.46.f.5

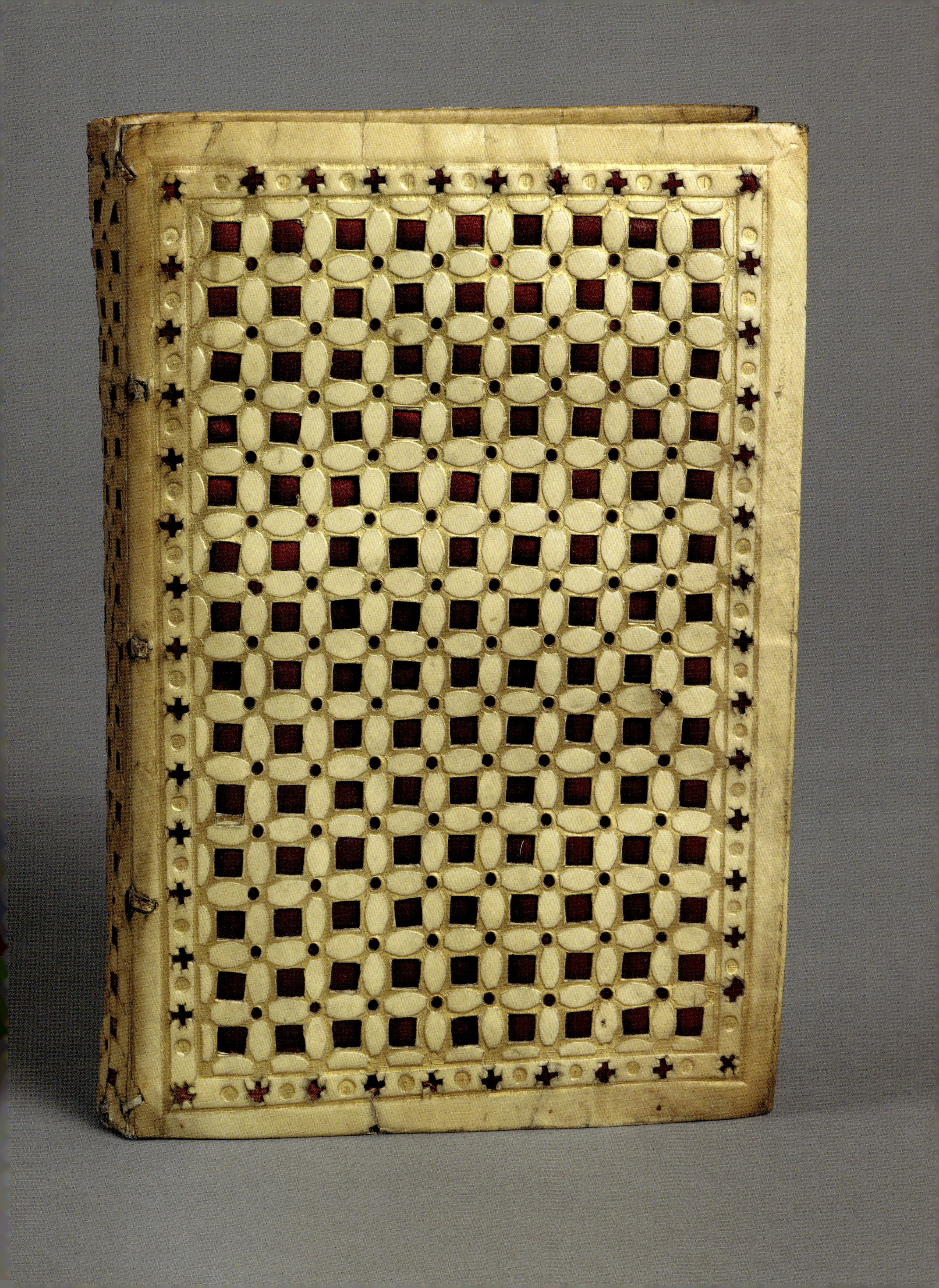

PAINTED EDGES

'A gilt edge is as necessary to a well-bound book as the gold chain is to an alderman's robes' pronounced the journal *Bookbinder* in 1888, and its approbation is well earned, for a gilt edge is not only decorative, but functions as a buffer, protecting the contents from dust. It is not surprising, then, that decorated edges have been recorded on manuscripts from the tenth century onwards and have been produced in Greece, Italy, France, Germany, Switzerland, the Netherlands and England (although it can be difficult to tell if they are contemporary).

The type of decoration ranges widely, from simple abstract patterns, to coats of arms and pictorial images. Bibliographical details have also been lettered onto some edges, indicating that these books were stored with the edges rather than the spine outwards.

The quality of the work undoubtedly varied. Some examples appear to be by amateurs, but we know that professional artists were involved, such as Cesare Vecellio, a cousin of the Renaissance artist Titian, in sixteenth-century Italy. John Edwards (1758-1791) of the Edwards of Halifax bindery, himself an accomplished painter on vellum, may also have contributed to the famous examples, which were signed with the Edwards name and much imitated.

There were fashions in edge decoration, as with other aspects of the craft. Religious motifs were always popular, and in seventeenth-century England verses from the scriptures decorated with flowers and insects were much admired. During the eighteenth century, with its more secular tastes, buildings and landscapes made an appearance. They were painted, then covered with gold, so the hidden image could only be seen as the text block was angled. Marbled edges were a common feature, but marbling under the gilt was less so.

Edge designs were eclectic. They could be stained one or more colours, marbled, coloured with paste paper, and sprinkled. Today, their decoration is considered integral to the look of the whole binding.

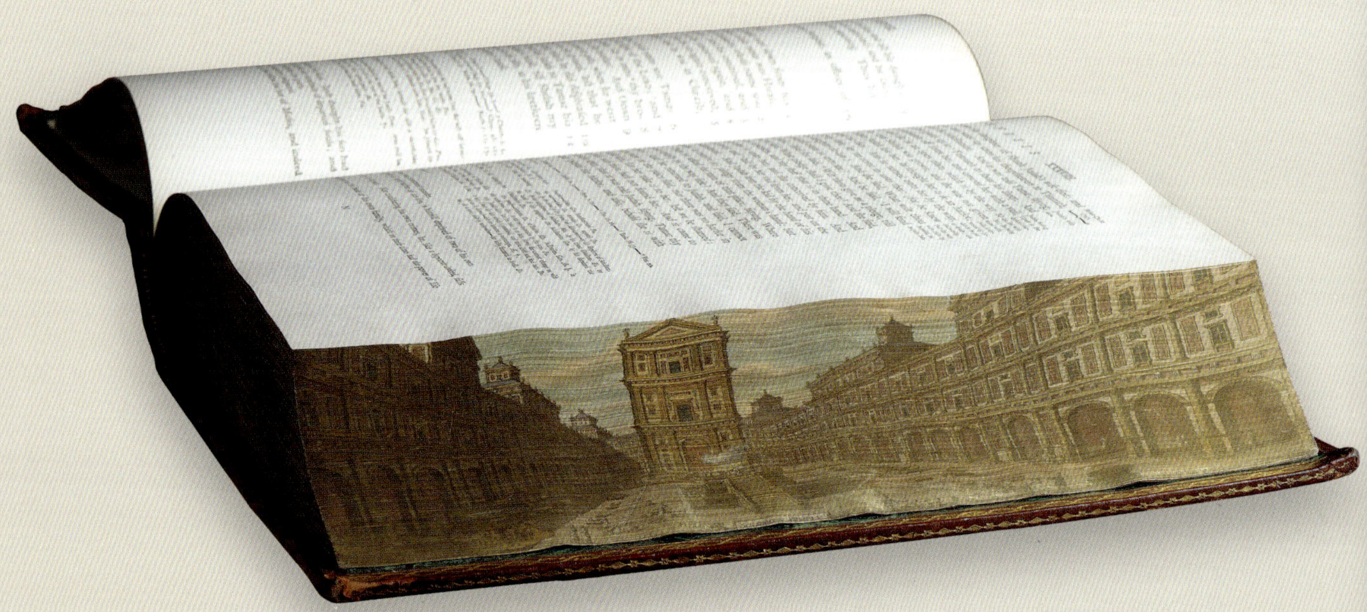

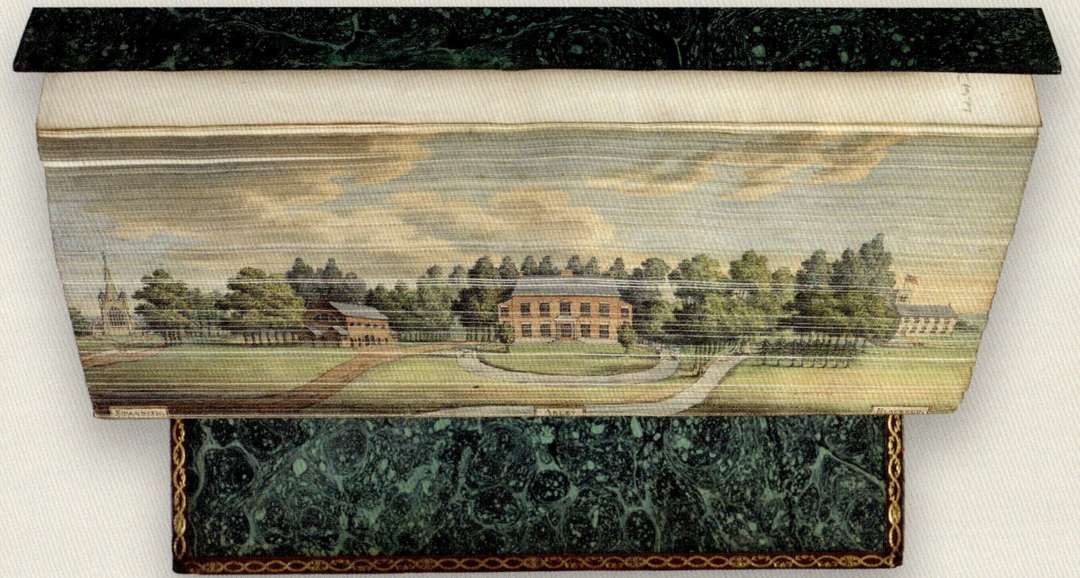

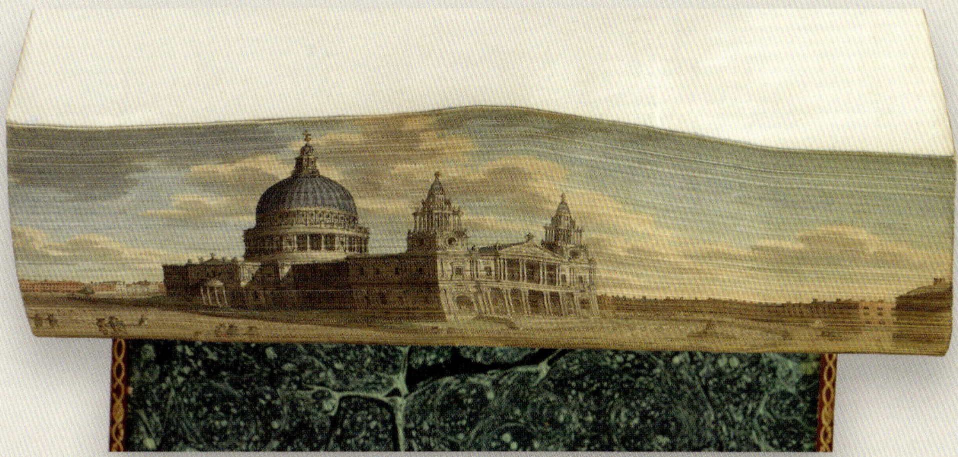

ABOVE AND OPPOSITE This simple gold-tooled, diced brown calf set of three bindings conceals a secret. Hidden beneath the gold on the fore-edges are painted scenes of Solomon's Temple, St Paul's Cathedral and Arley Hall, the country seat of John Johnson, who commissioned the bindings. Although the practice of decorating the edges of text blocks was long established, concealed paintings were particularly admired in eighteenth-century England. Accompanying documents confirm that these fore-edges were contemporary with the binding (during the nineteenth century, many fore-edge paintings were added to books to increase the price). A surviving fragment of a bill for the work includes a small sketch of buildings, which appear in the Arley Hall painting (top). All three of these volumes bear the binding ticket of German-born Benjamin Frye of Halifax and Manchester (at work from *c.*1793–1820). Pictorial images often appeared on his bindings (sometimes as drawings on parchment inlaid into the covers, sometimes on fore-edges), perhaps influenced by the fashionable Edwards of Halifax bindings.

England, early nineteenth century
Each volume 325 x 235 x 65 mm (12.8 x 9.3 x 2.6 inches)

This blind-tooled, sixteenth-century German brown calf binding is one of 172 books from the distinguished Pillone Library with decoration by Cesare Vecellio (1530–1600), a cousin of Titian. The Pillone family lived in Belluno, northern Italy, and were actively collecting from 1490–1590. Vecellio, who came from the same region, drew pen-and-ink images on texts with parchment covers and painted the edges of the leather-bound books, as is the case with this example. The painting depicts Alexander the Great and also includes the title.

Southern Germany, *c.*1547–50
349 x 220 x 90 mm (13.7 x 8.7 x 3.5 inches)
Davis 690

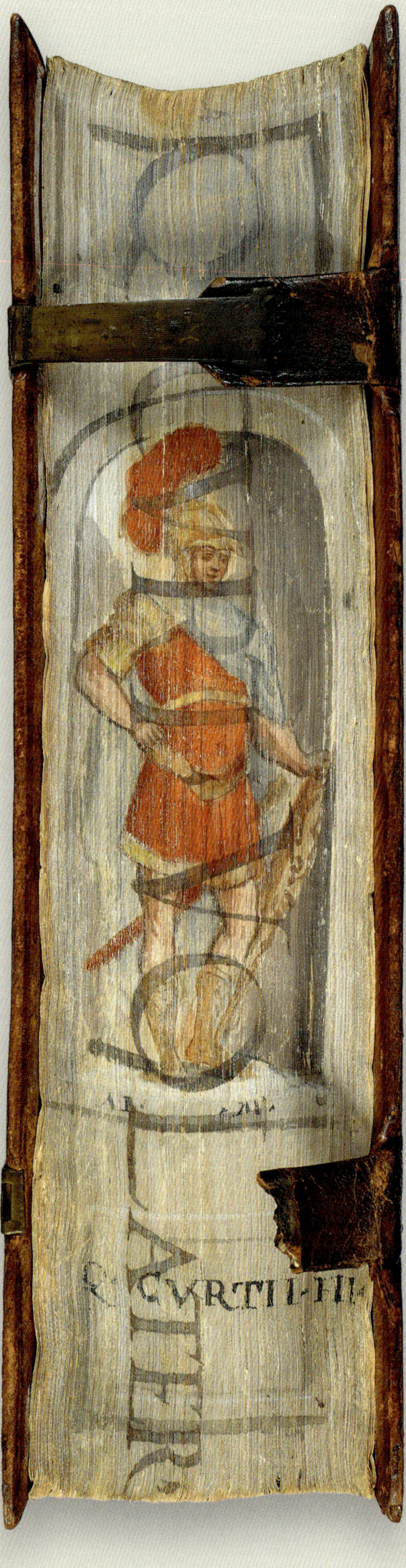

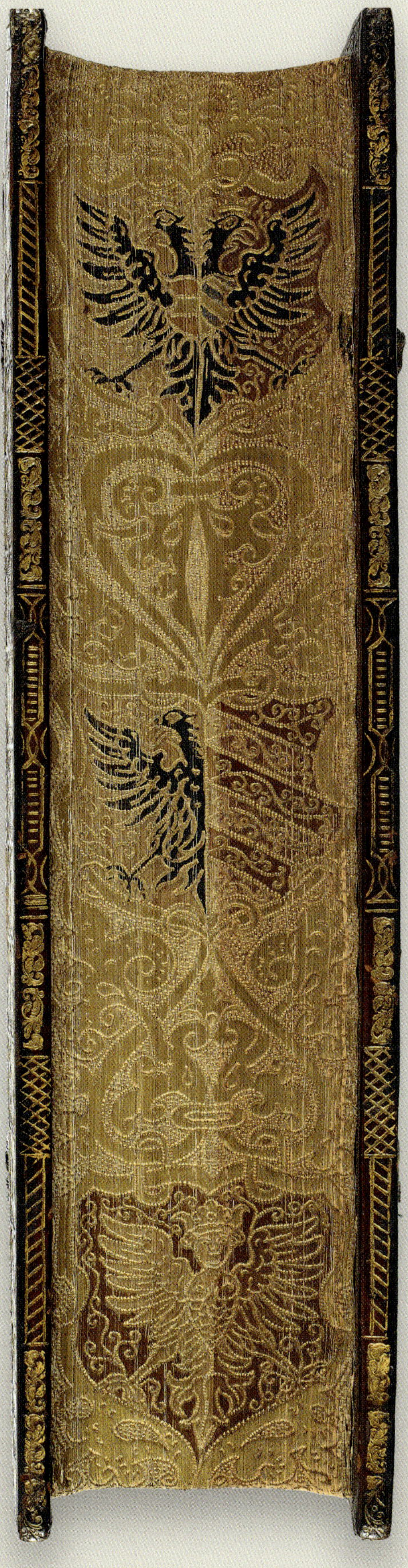

The edges of this elaborate brown calf binding have been gilt and gauffered (i.e. tooled) and the fore-edge has also been painted with the arms of the Holy Roman Emperor, Maximilian II (the top emblem). This binding has been attributed to the workshop of Hans Hermann of Nuremberg (a wealthy Imperial Free city and important centre of printing and bookbinding) and the book relates to the city's statutes.

Nuremberg, 1560s
325 x 200 x 89 mm (12.8 x 7.9 x 3.5 inches)
C.48.h.5

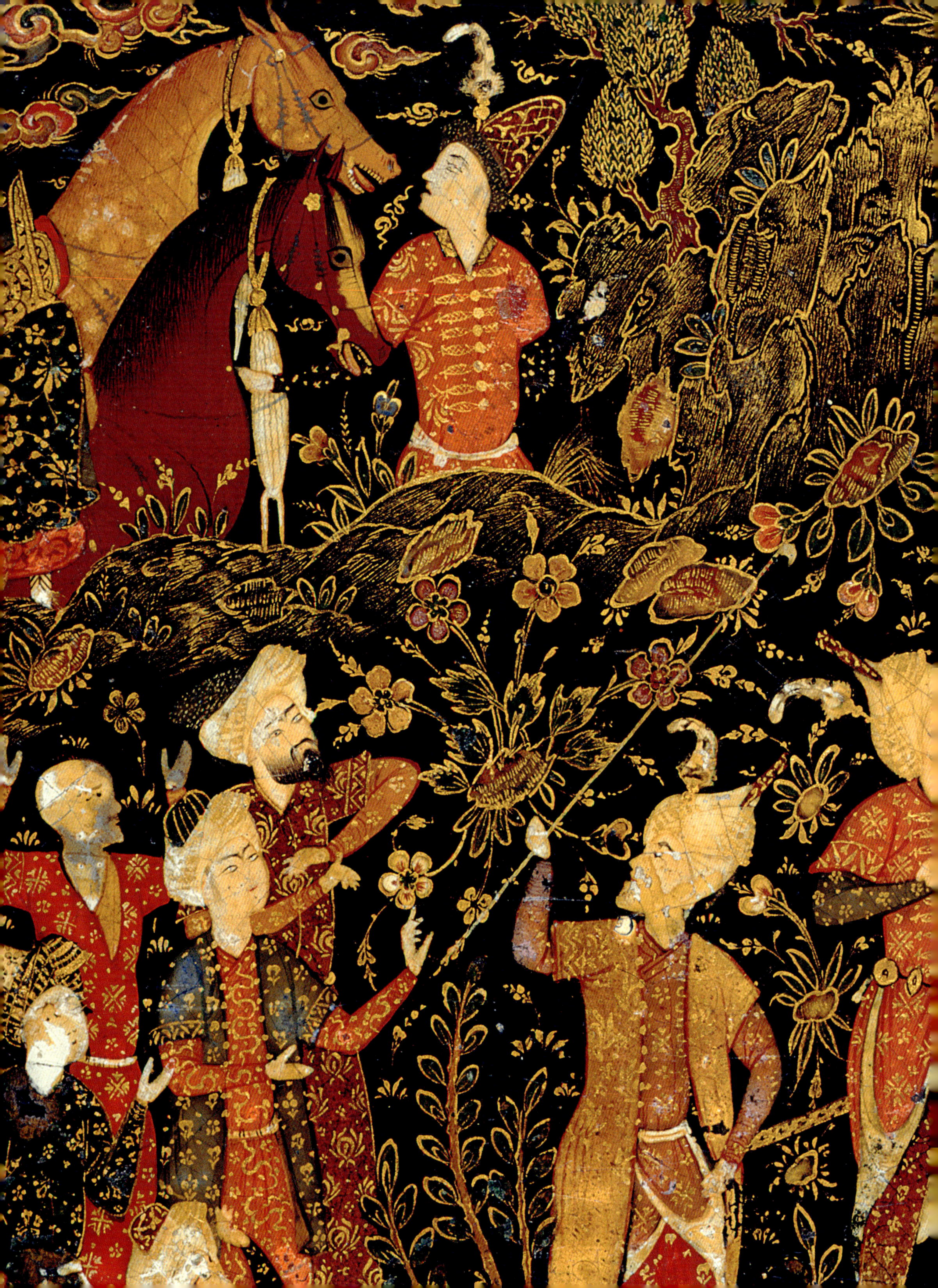

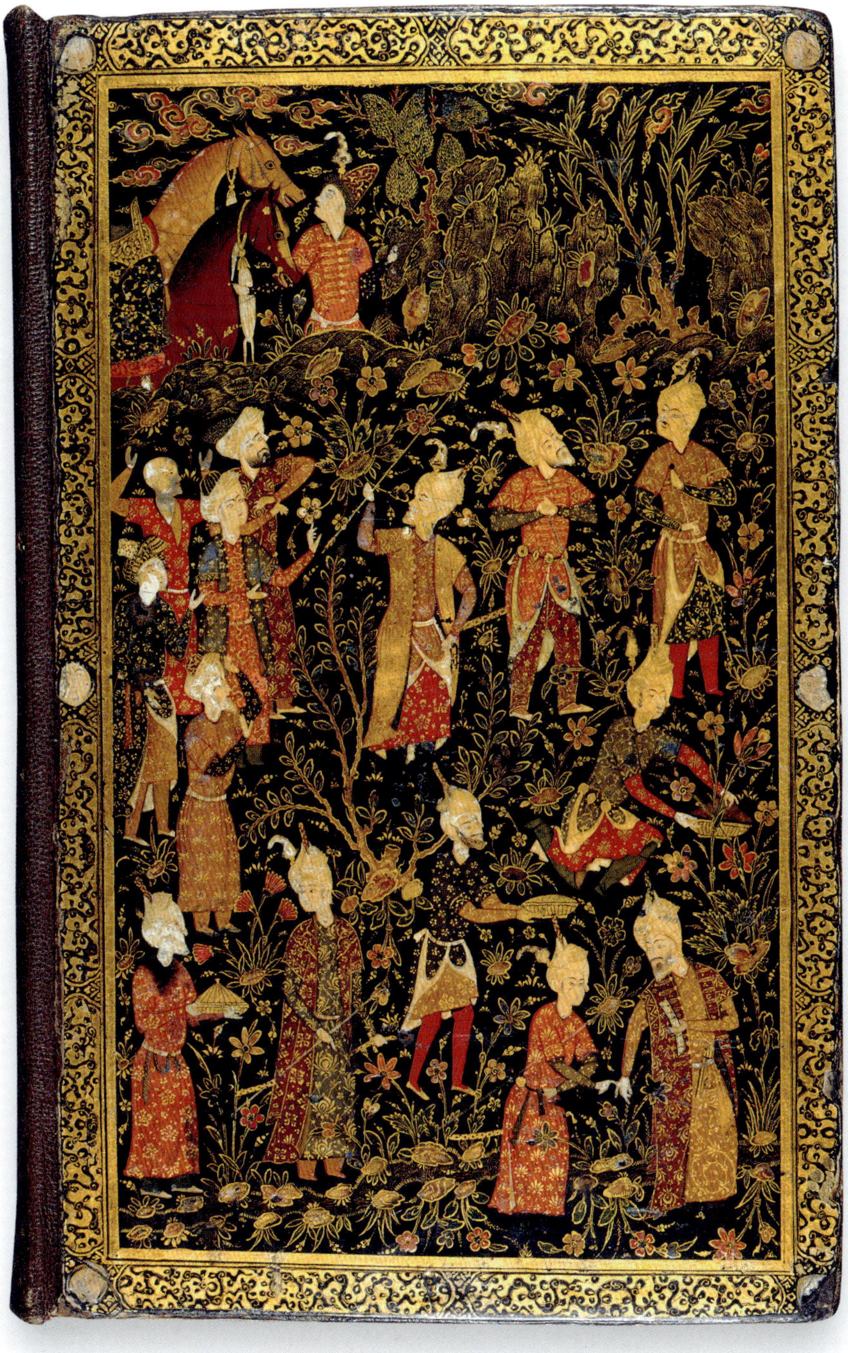

Lacquered bindings were a characteristic product of the Safavid period in Persia, and this cover is arguably one of the best examples. It depicts a busy scene of royal attendants in a garden and shows the attention to detail typical of this time. We are fortunate enough to know the names of several great contemporary painters who worked in the royal workshop. This particular work was signed by Mir Sayyid 'Ali (*c.*1540), an extremely influential artist who travelled to India and helped found the Mughal school of painting.

Persia, sixteenth century
243 x 147 x 27 mm (9.6 x 5.8 x 1.1 inches)
Or.1374

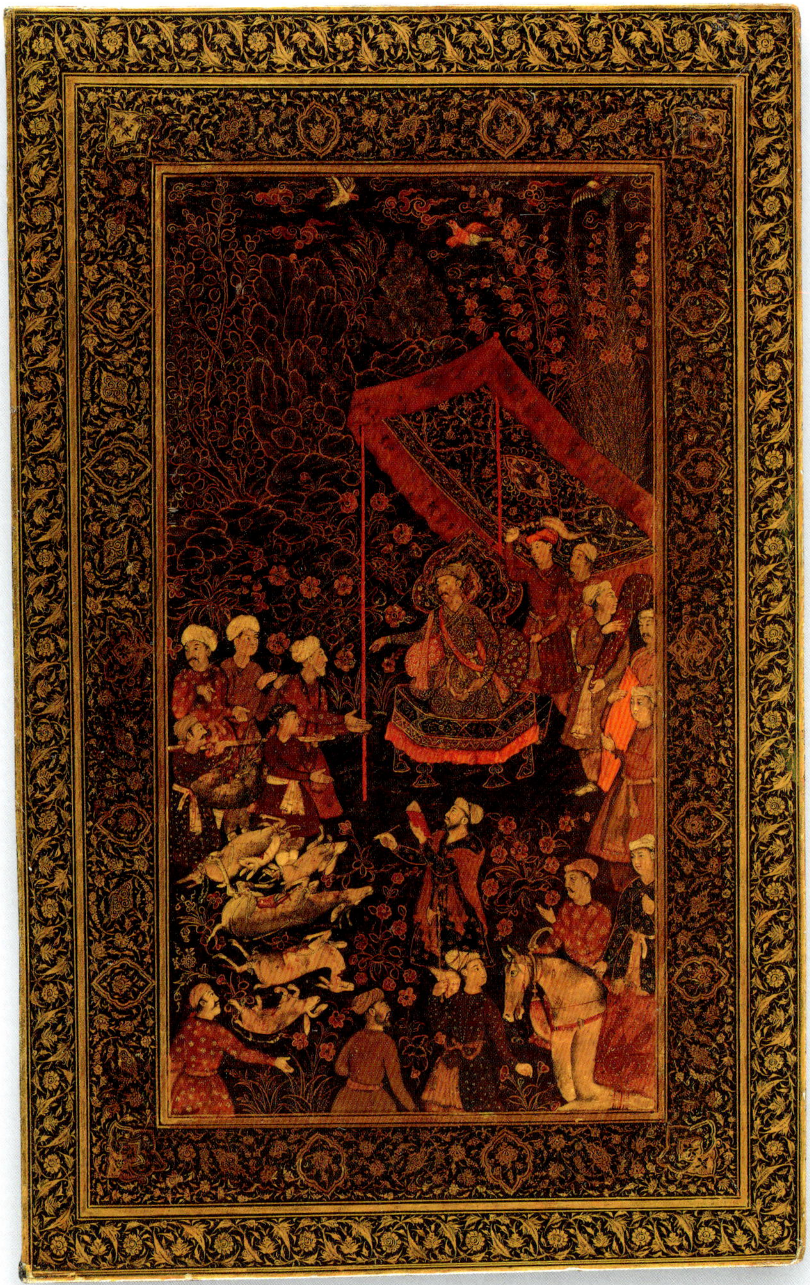

This varnished and gold-painted binding covers a manuscript copy of five narrative poems, copied in 1595 for Akbar, the third Mughal Emperor of India (1542–1605). Islamic binding historian Duncan Haldane suggests that 'in style and technique, Indian bookbindings are very close to their Persian precursors'. This example is thronged with animals, birds, foliage and natural features, reflecting the naturalism that is characteristic in Mughal art.

The lower cover depicts a princely hunt, while the upper cover shows a ruler (maybe Akbar himself) being presented with a bag of game. The design, workmanship and time taken would have made this a luxury item fit for an Emperor.

India, late sixteenth century
310 x 191 x 80 mm (12.20 x 7.51 x 3.14 inches)
Or.12208

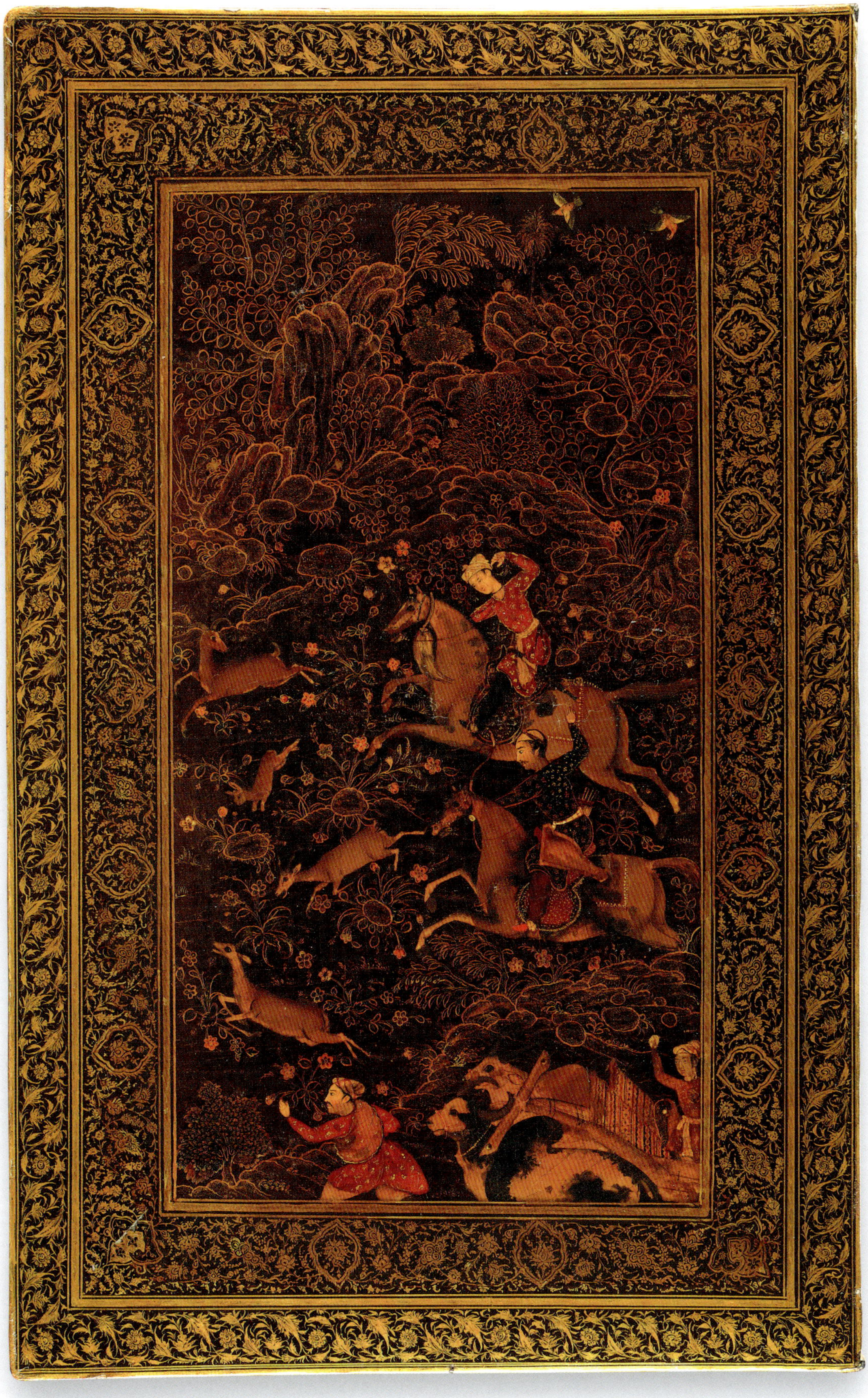

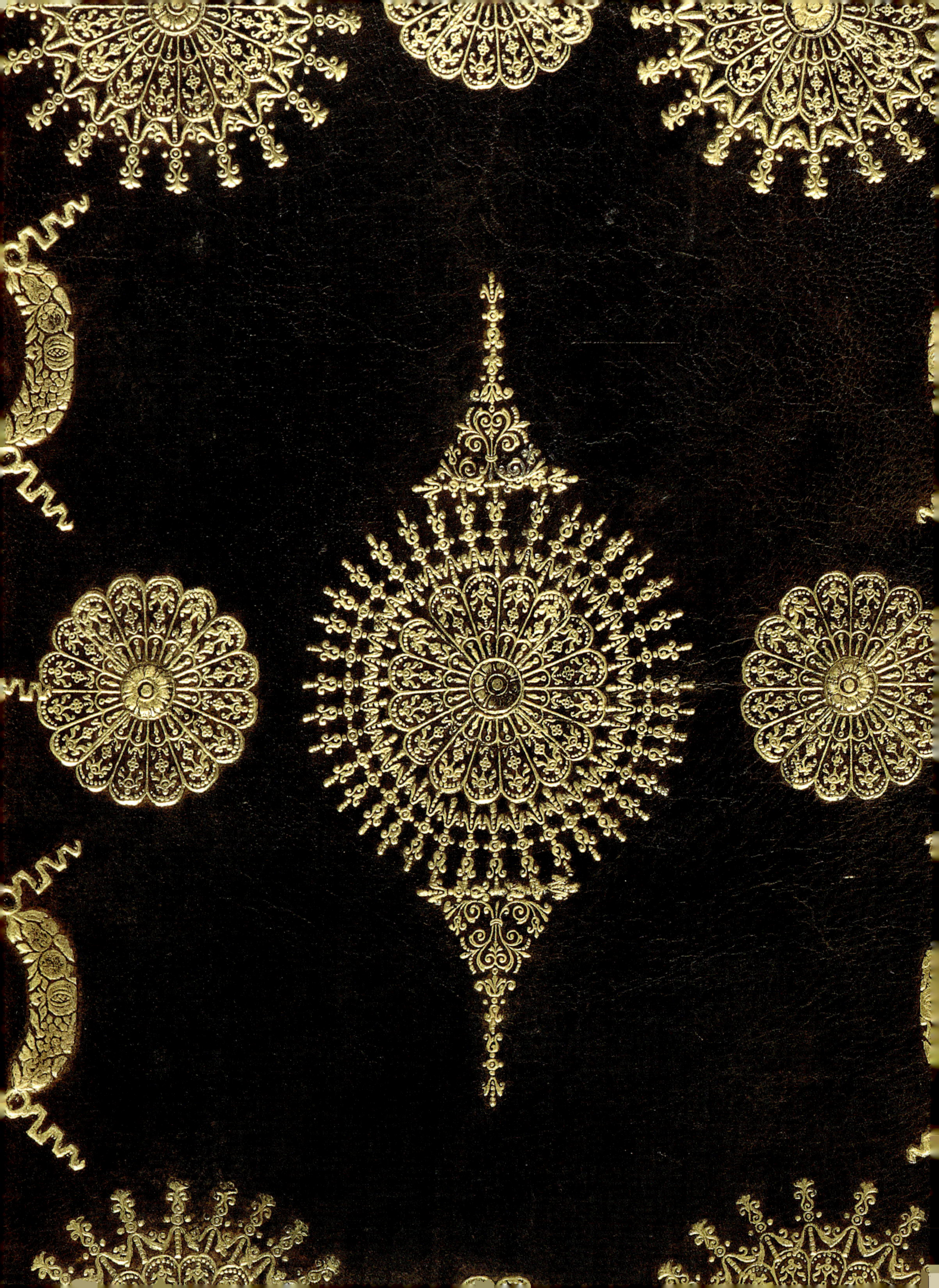

CHAPTER 3

Seventeenth Century

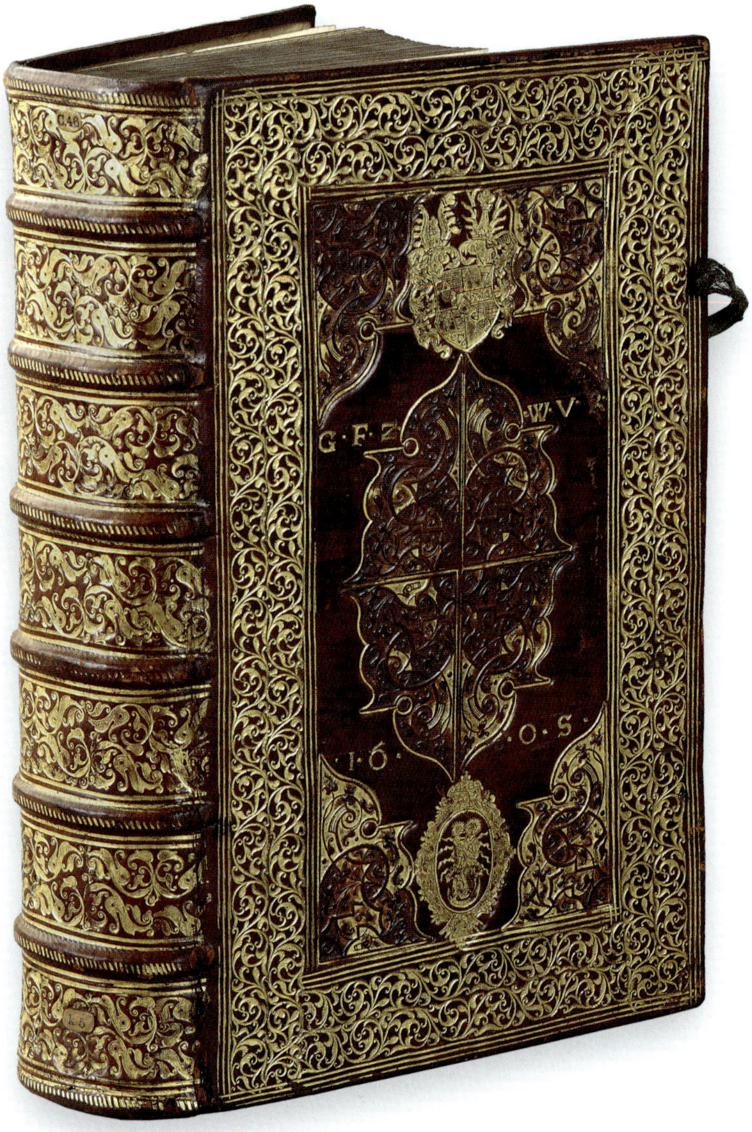

The coats of arms and initials gold-tooled on the upper cover indicate that this binding could be regarded as a status symbol. Its owner was the Austrian nobleman, Georg Frieherr von Wolkenstein Rodenegg (1559–1614). The lavish gold used to adorn the large, brown calf binding indicated his wealth, and the fact that such expenditure was for a seven-volume work on religion attested to his devotion and piety. The decoration has been influenced by the East – note the Islamic-inspired corner-pieces (also combined to form a centre-piece) and the two coats of arms acting as *şalbeks* (or pendants) – and by the West, in the form of the Italian-style border roll comprising curling branches (although few Italian borders were as wide). Western binders interpreted designs seen on Eastern bindings and often re-worked them to appeal to their own clients. The heavily rounded back is a characteristically German trait of this period. If the book was placed in a shelf with the spine visible, the extensive gold tooling would contribute to the opulent appearance of the library.

Germany, 1605
317 x 190 x 71 mm (12.5 x 7.5 x 2.8 inches)
C.46.k.5

The illustration shows a sophisticated example of an 'all-over' design, in which the entire surface of the book is decorated with a mosaic of coloured leather onlays, featuring *pointillé* motifs contained within a gold-tooled fanfare framework. This style is associated with Macé Ruette (1584–1638), a significant figure in the Parisian bindings trade, being master of the Guild of St Jean for five years before achieving the rank of royal binder in 1634. This exalted position subsequently passed to his son, Antoine. The Ruette workshops produced some of the finest French bindings of the seventeenth century.

Paris, mid-seventeenth century
340 x 250 x 60 mm (13.4 x 9.8 x 2.4 inches)
C.14.c.12

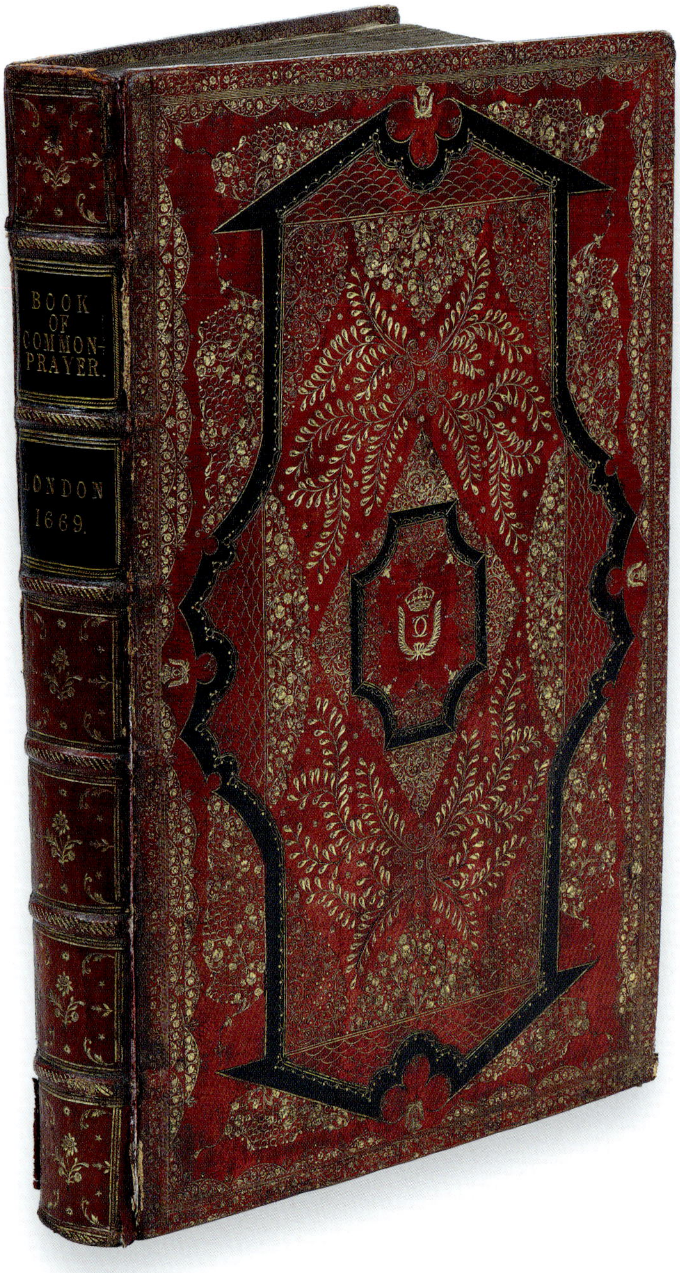

One of the duties of the English royal bookbinder, Samuel Mearne (d.1683), was to bind service books for the chapels in all of the king's palaces, the most important being the Chapel and the Closet at Whitehall, where the furnishings (including the bindings) had to be replaced at intervals of three to five years. These books were richly bound, as befitted the royal status, and this sumptuously gold-tooled and painted 'cottage roof' design with the cipher of King Charles II on red goatskin (and with the fore-edge painted under the gold) is a typical example.

Fortunately for Mearne, his publishing, bookselling and stationery supply activities provided an income, for the king rarely paid his bindings bills on time, or remitted the official fee of £6 a year for the position of King's Binder. The title was also granted to Mearne's sons, Charles (d.1686) and Samuel (until the revolution of 1688).

London, *c.*1669
370 x 245 x 50 mm (14.6 x 9.6 x 2 inches)

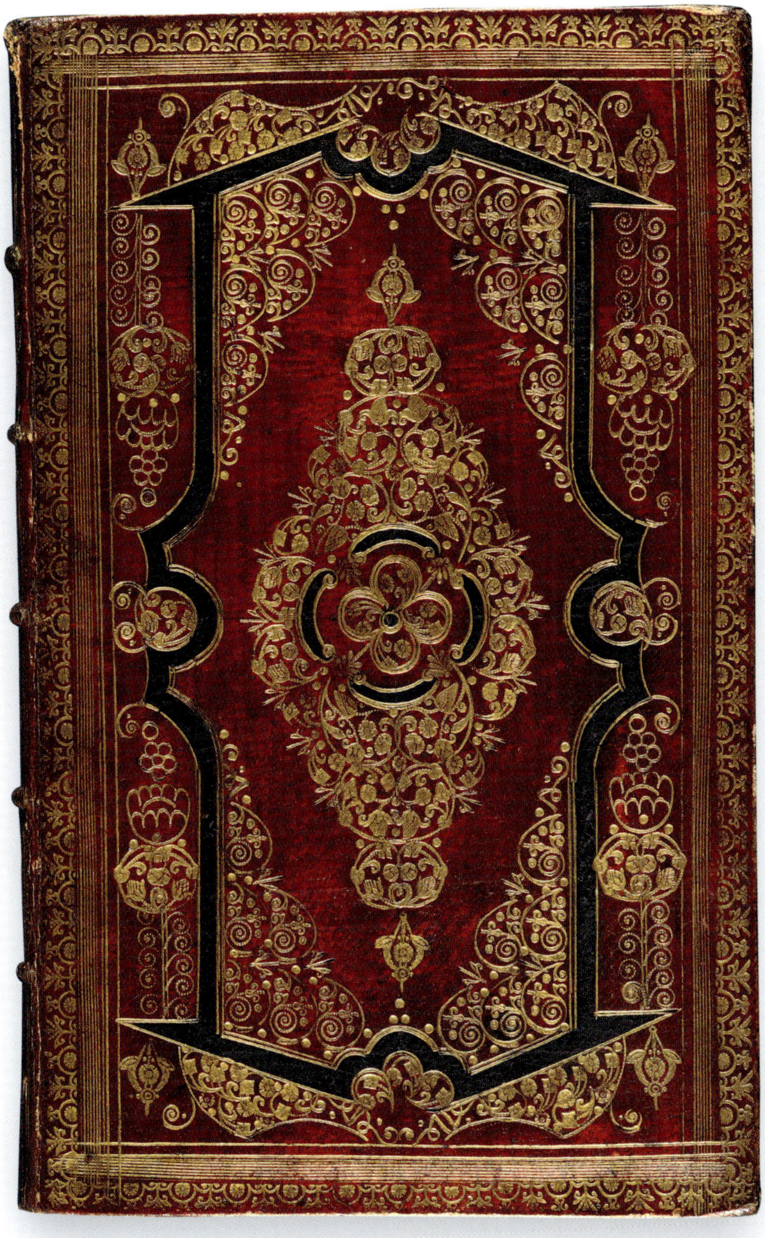

The style of binding remained remarkably consistent, as is demonstrated by the gold-tooled and painted red goatskin example shown here which was produced by Charles Mearne. The title page of the book, tracts by Sir Thomas Browne, indicates that it was 'printed for Charles Mearne, Bookseller to his most Sacred Majesty'. It seems likely that this binding and several others (covering the same text), which were decorated with identical tools, were specially bound for Browne to give as presentation copies to his friends and patrons.

London, *c.*1683
183 x 114 x 20 mm (7.2 x 4.5 x 0.8 inches)
Davis 112

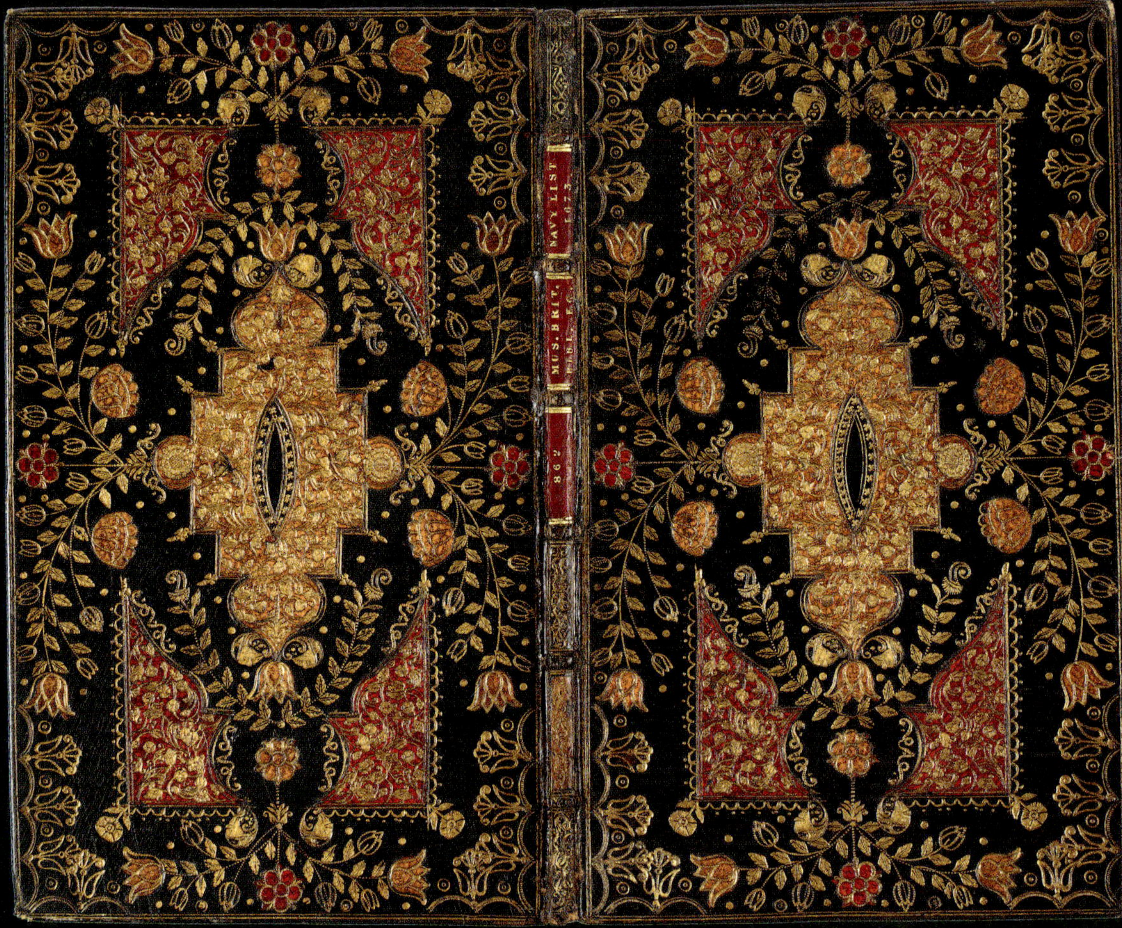

The binding historian Howard M Nixon considered the seventeenth century to be 'the greatest period in the history of English decorative bookbinding'. Certainly there was much demand for binding skills at this time, not only from individuals but also from institutions, including government departments. The Navy Office was a particularly good client and instructed a craftsman – later given the name the 'Naval Binder' (fl.1670s–80s) – to bind its manuscript records. It may well be that Samuel Pepys, a noted binding collector and the Treasurer of the Navy's Accounts, was responsible for commissioning this colourful, gold-tooled and onlaid black goatskin binding, which derives its pattern from those used on oriental carpets. In his diary entry of Monday 18 February 1666/67, Pepys noted: 'Up, and to my bookbinder's, and there mightily pleased to see some papers of the account we did give the Parliament of the expense of the Navy sewed together, which I could not have conceived before how prettily it was done.'

London, 1670s
170 x 105 x 12 mm (6.7 x 4.1 x 0.5 inches)
Egerton MS 862

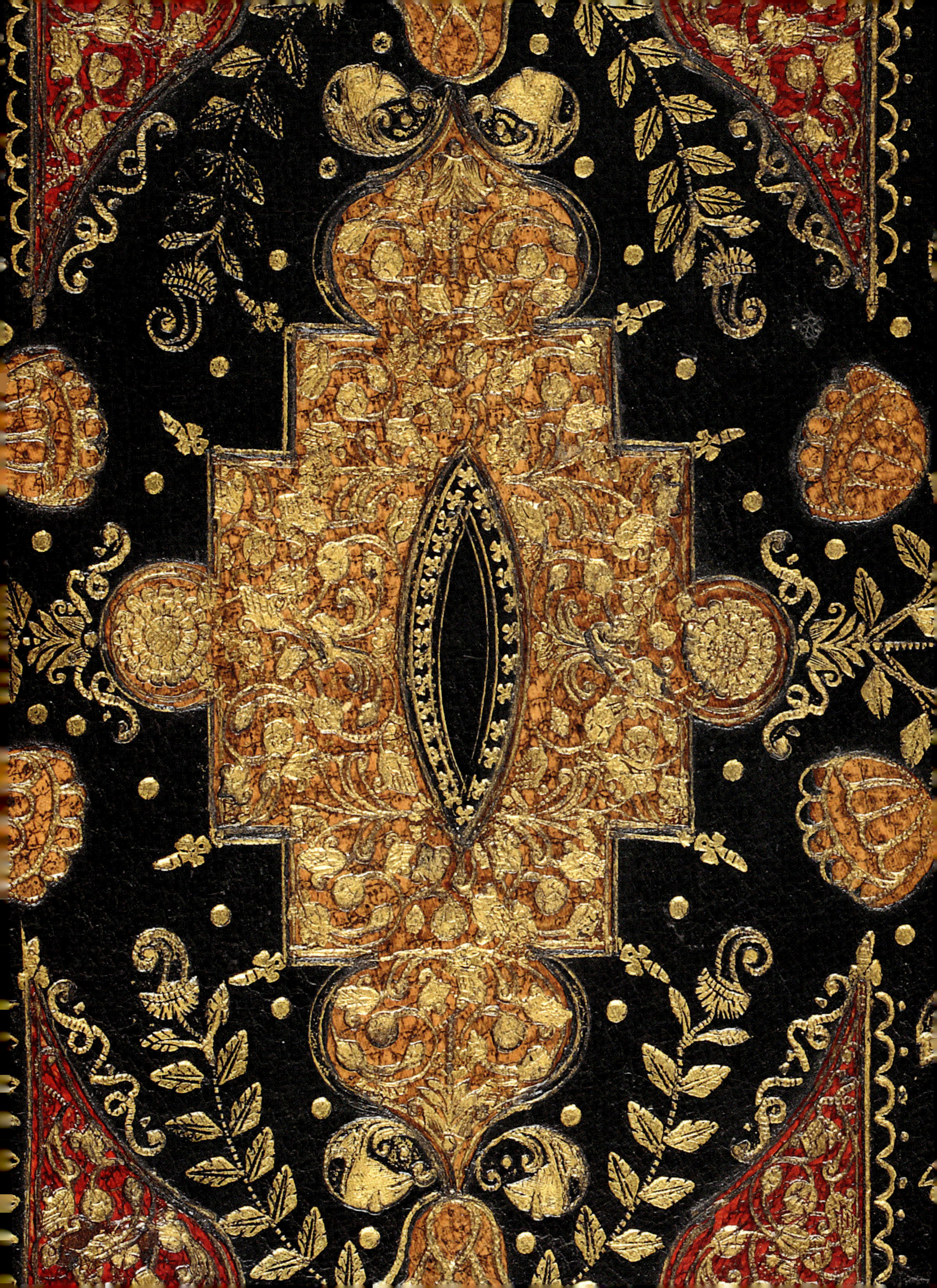

CLASPS

By the seventeenth century, many book clasps were used mainly for decoration. In western Europe particularly, pasteboard had supplanted wooden boards and paper had replaced parchment, so it was no longer necessary to fasten the wooden boards tightly together to keep the parchment pages flat. Ties made of fabric could serve to keep the covers together. In the East, boards were always made of lightweight materials and Islamic bindings had flaps, making clasps redundant. Convention dictated, however, that certain categories of Western book (devotional works for example) should have a fastening, and clasps therefore continued to be manufactured in a variety of shapes and sizes. These could be plain or highly decorated with engravings, stamps or embossing. Inventories of equipment in binders' workshops indicate that a number of them made their own clasps with metal-working tools, but there is also evidence of specialized craftsmen at work. Some bindings still required wooden boards, notably the 'Greek style' bindings which commonly featured four catches mounted on plaited leather thongs. Clasps were frequently made from brass, but by the seventeenth century silver had become popular on devotional works. Sometimes the placement of clasps can inform us as to where the binding was made. During the hand-press era, the hooks of the clasps usually caught on to the upper cover of German and Dutch bindings, a practice which was reversed in English and French bindings.

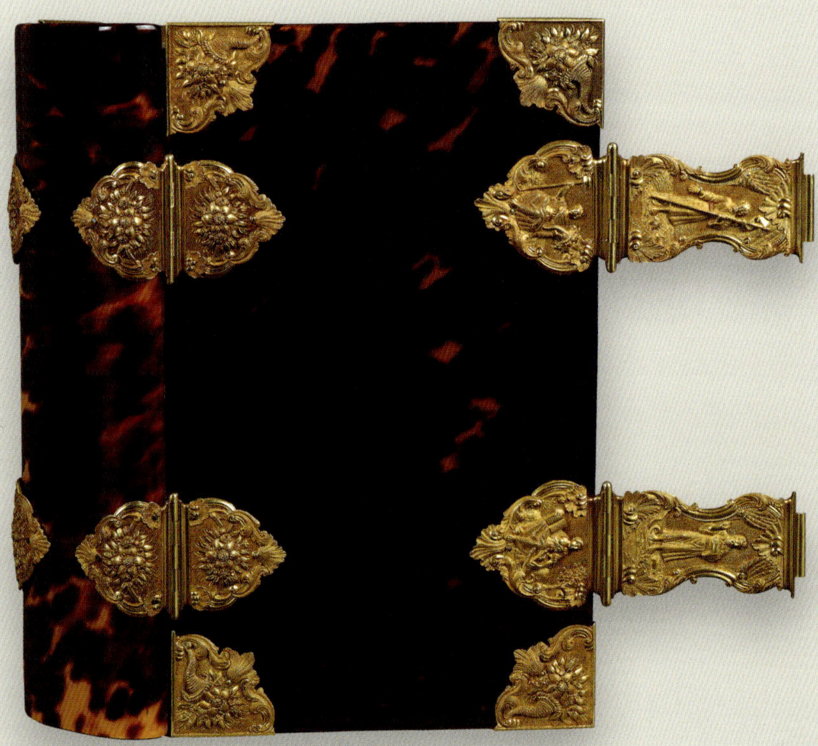

Amsterdam (?), *c.*1756
191 x 120 x 55 mm (7.5 x 4.7 x 2.2 inches)
Davis 672

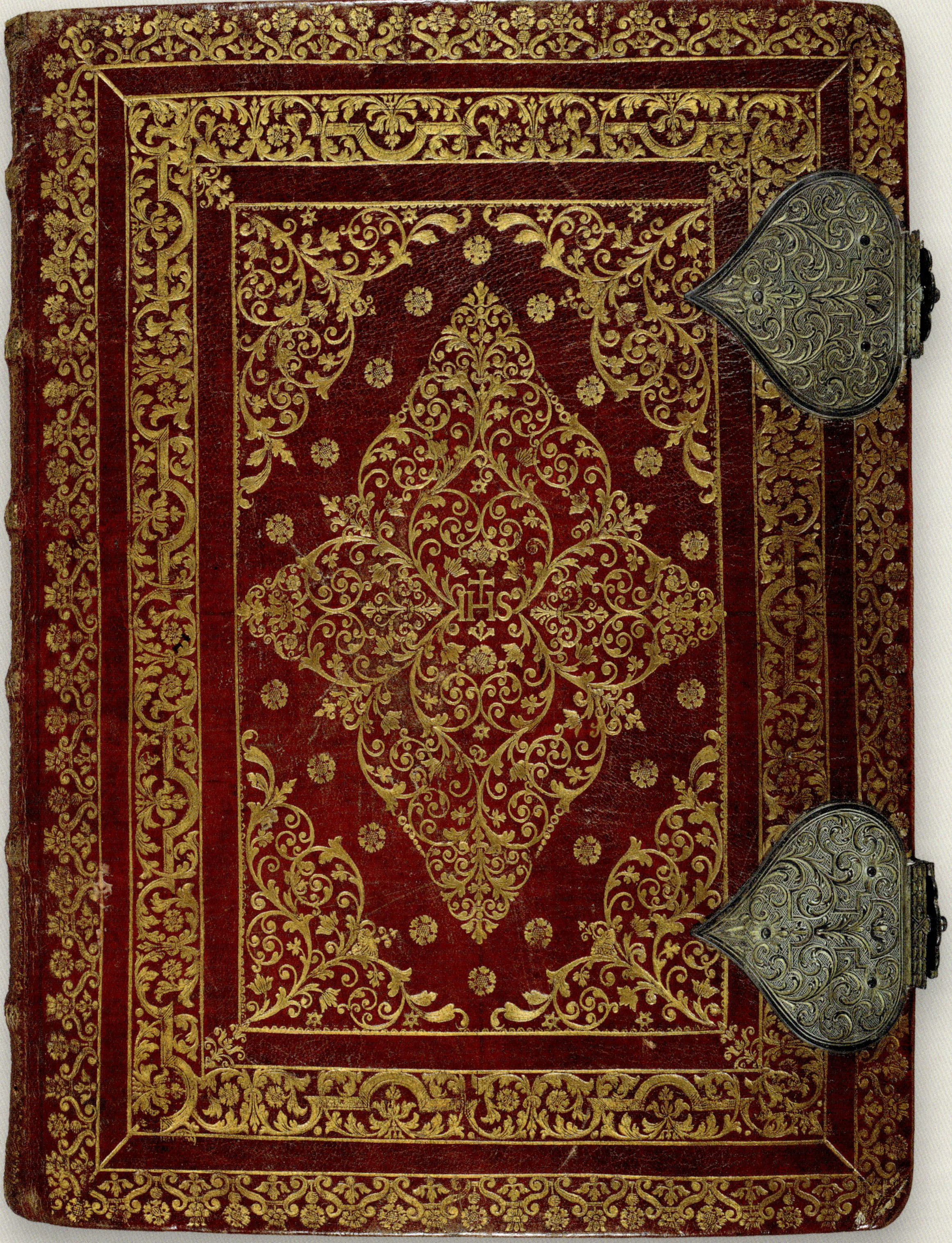

Flanders, *c.*1730
291 x 216 x 62 mm (11.4 x 8.5 x 2.4 inches)
Davis 686

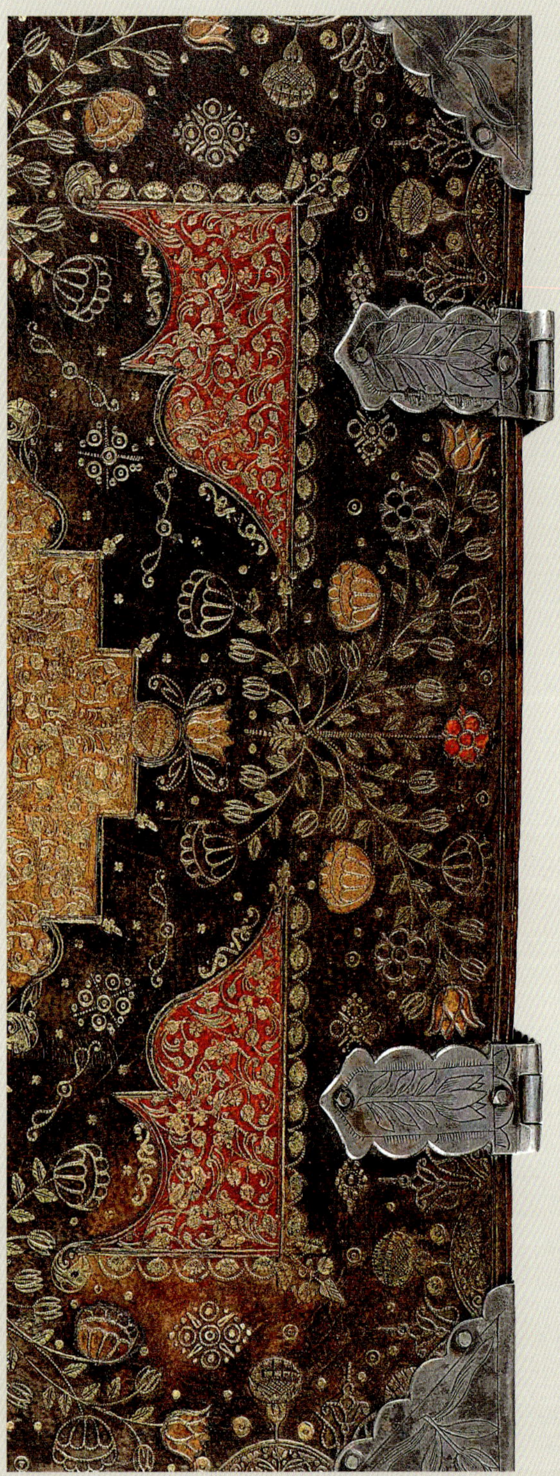

England, 1670s
238 x 175 x 63 mm (9.4 x 6.9 x 2.5 inches)
Davis 70

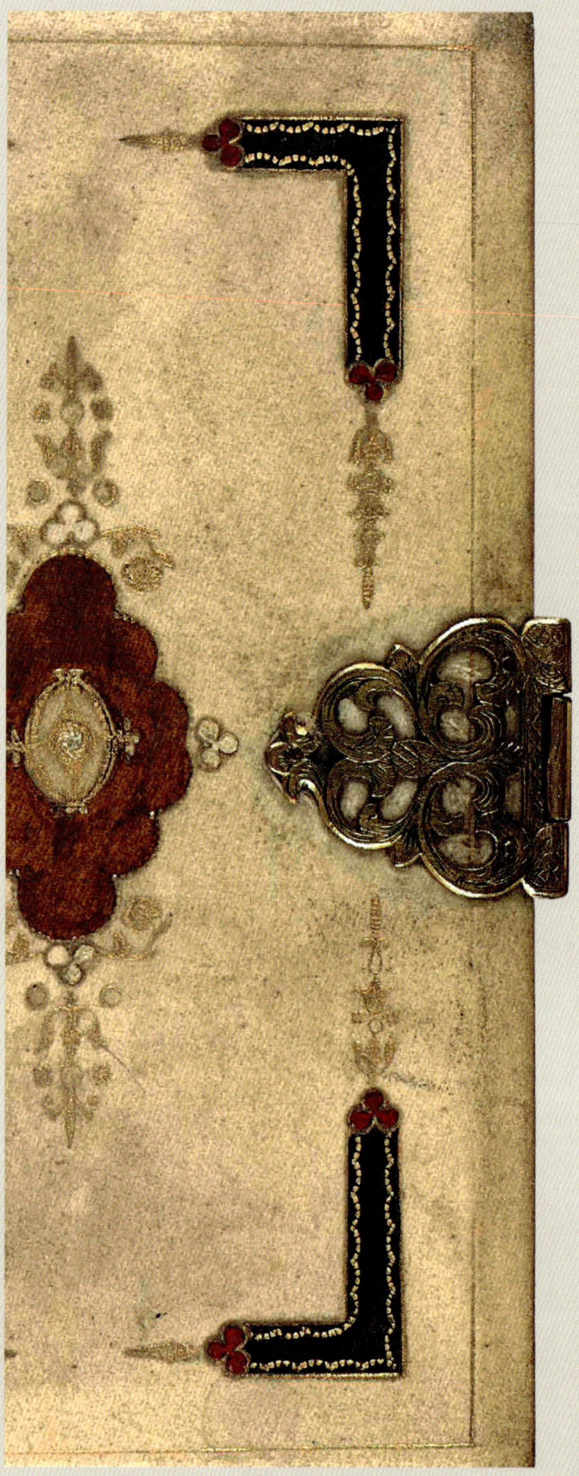

England, 1840s
151 x 95 x 30 mm (5.9 x 3.7 x 1.2 inches)
C.150.e.12(1)

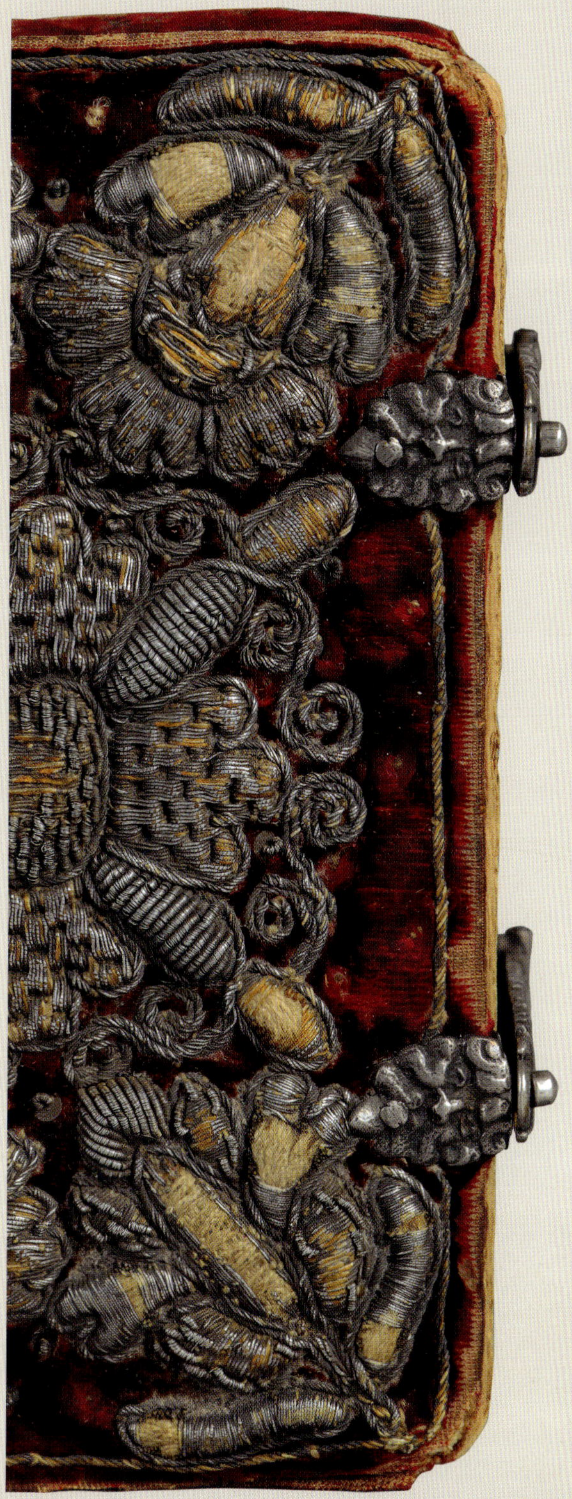
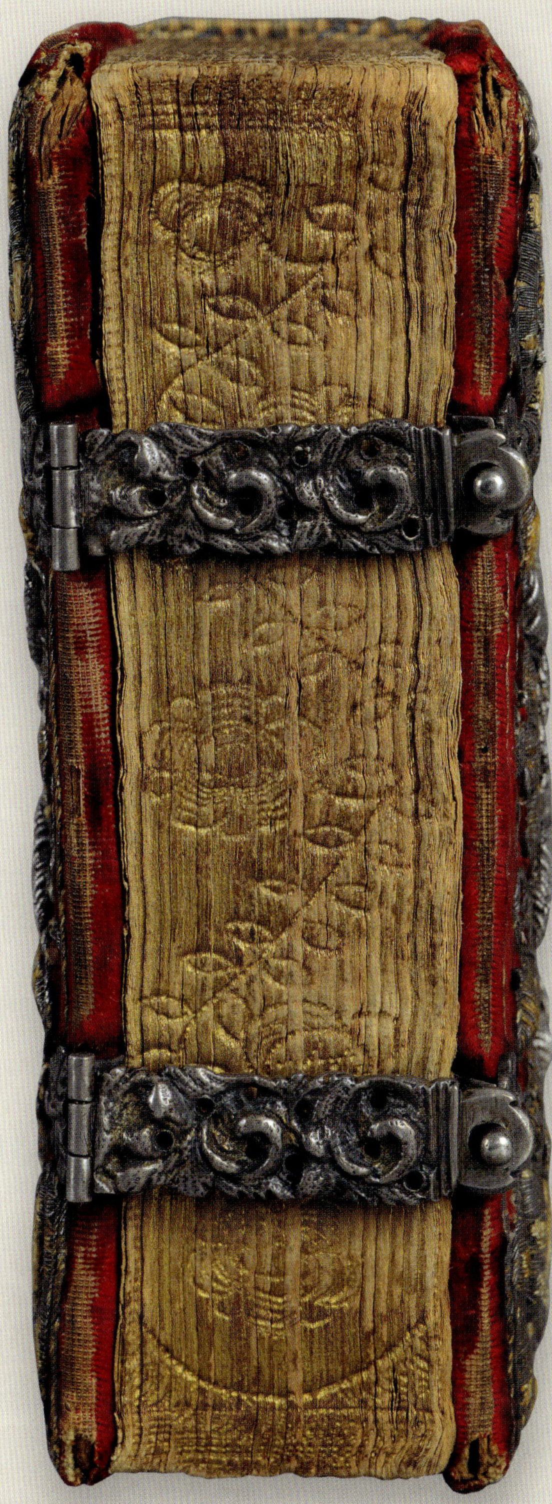

ABOVE AND RIGHT Denmark, 1670s
130 x 80 x 40 mm (5.1 x 3.1 x 1.6 inches)
C.188.a.130

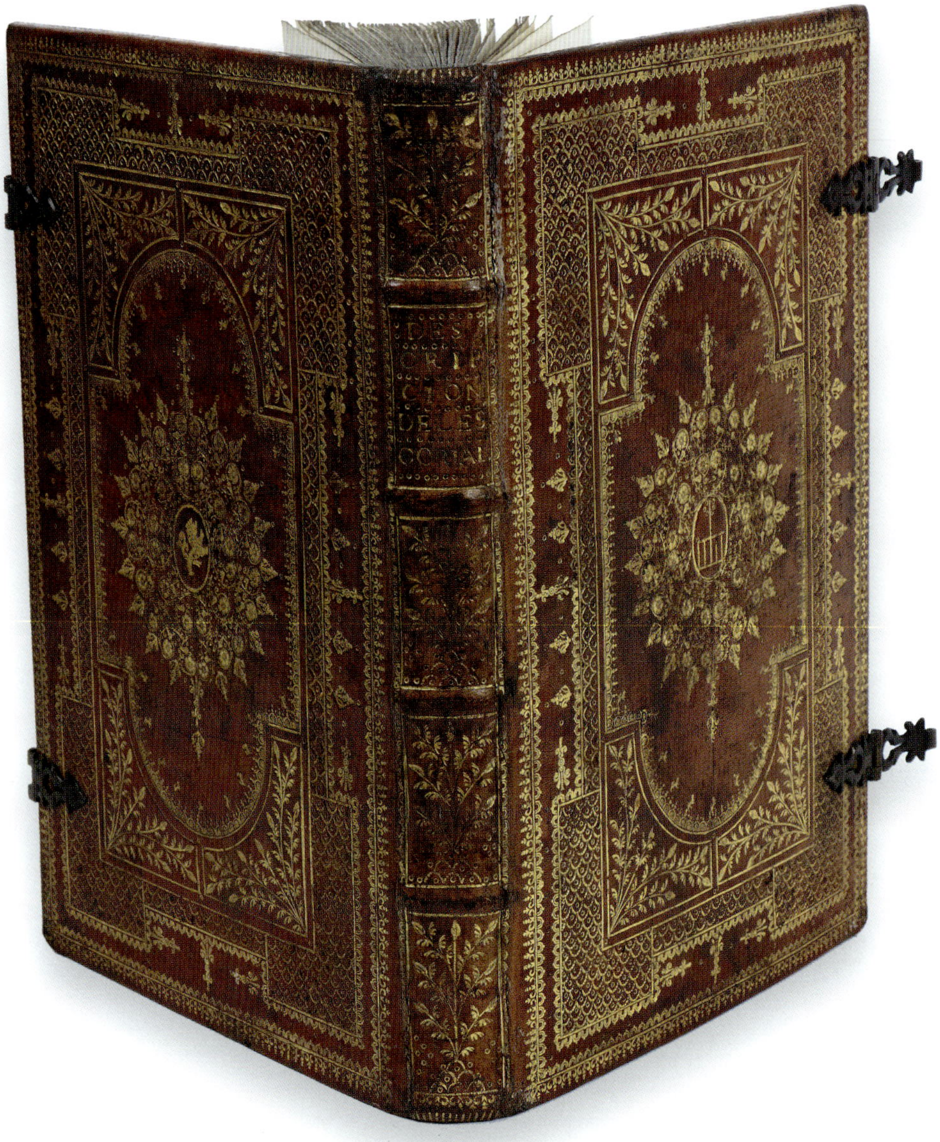

ABOVE Styles of decoration were influenced by a variety of sources, as the gold tooling on this seventeenth-century Spanish brown goatskin binding demonstrates. The compartments and leafy sprays owe much to the French fanfare style, while the repeated 'fish scale' motif is frequently found on Italian bindings. Even the small lions are relics of the earlier plateresque style. In the centre of the upper cover is the emblem of the Royal Monastery of San Lorenzo de El Escorial in Spain, which provides the subject for the text. Two elaborately shaped silver clasps catch onto the lower cover.

Madrid (?), late seventeenth century
290 x 190 x 30 mm (11.4 x 7.5 x 1.2 inches)
C.108.f.12

OPPOSITE The name of the London craftsman responsible for this gold-tooled blue turkey (a type of goatskin) binding is unknown, but he was active in the 1680s and 1690s. The workshop is now referred to as Barlow's Aesop Binder, due to the fact that it bound three presentation copies of the *Fables*, illustrated by Francis Barlow. It produced work of the highest quality, and supplied the Duke of Devonshire and noted binding collector Samuel Pepys, as well as King William and Queen Mary.

London, 1680s
370 x 250 x 40 mm (14.6 x 9.8 x 1.6 inches)
671.l.6

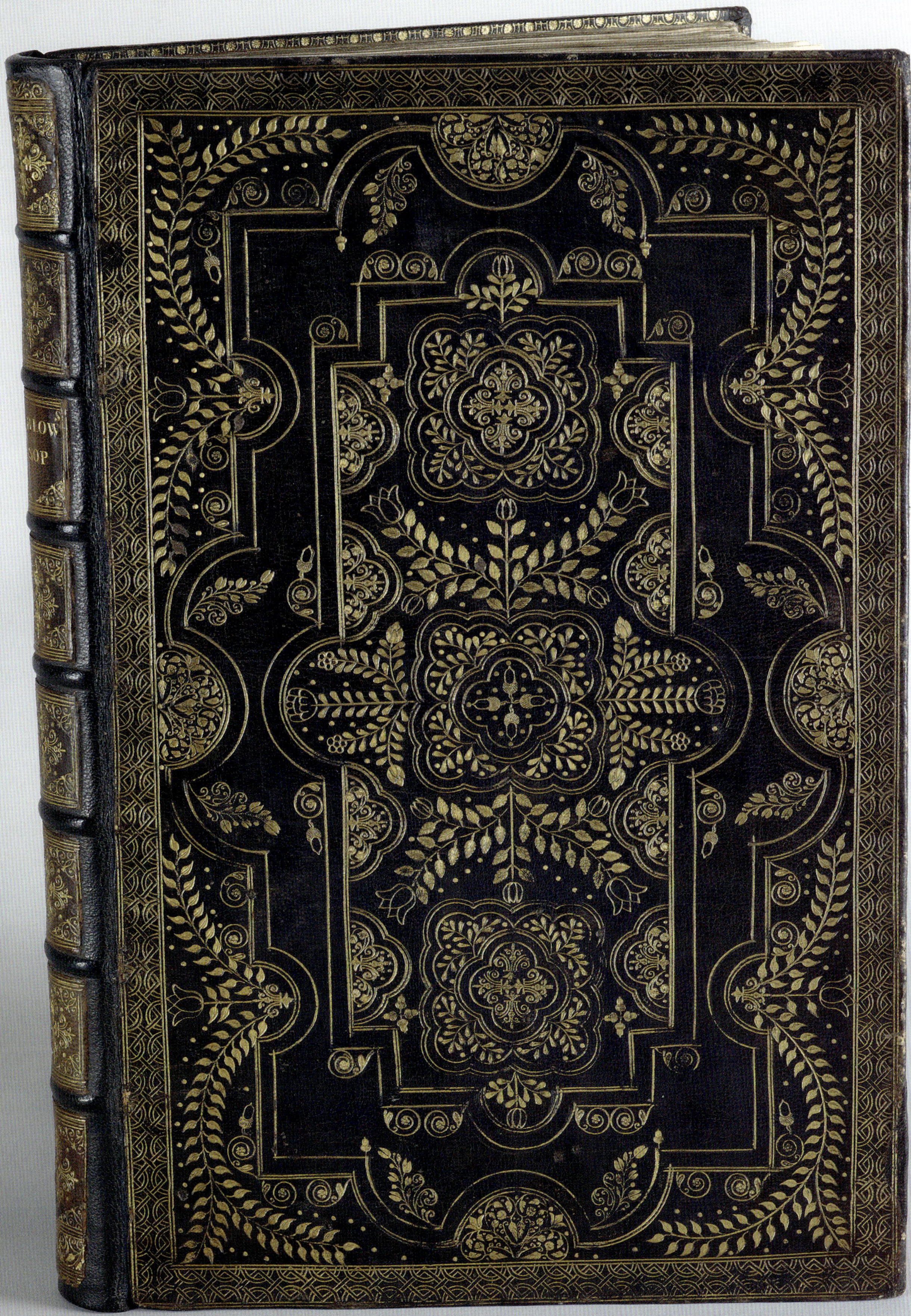

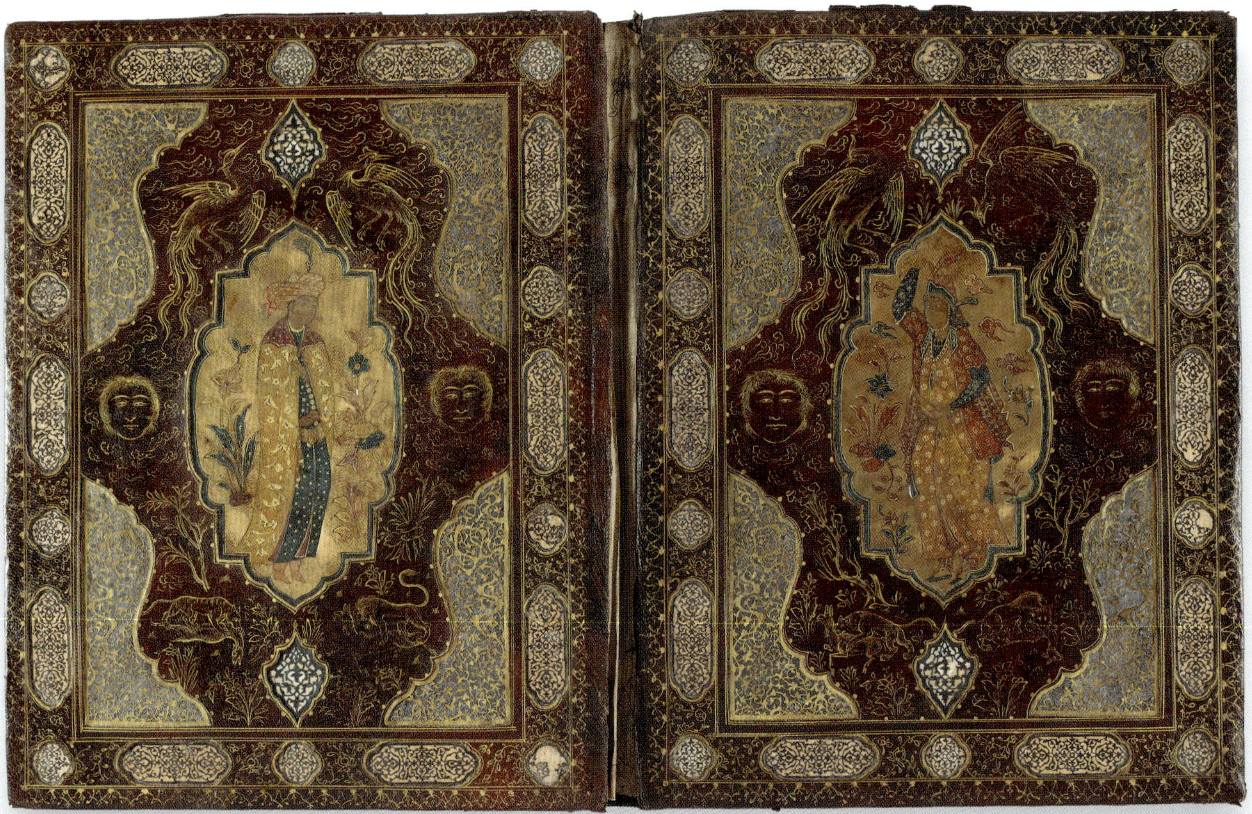

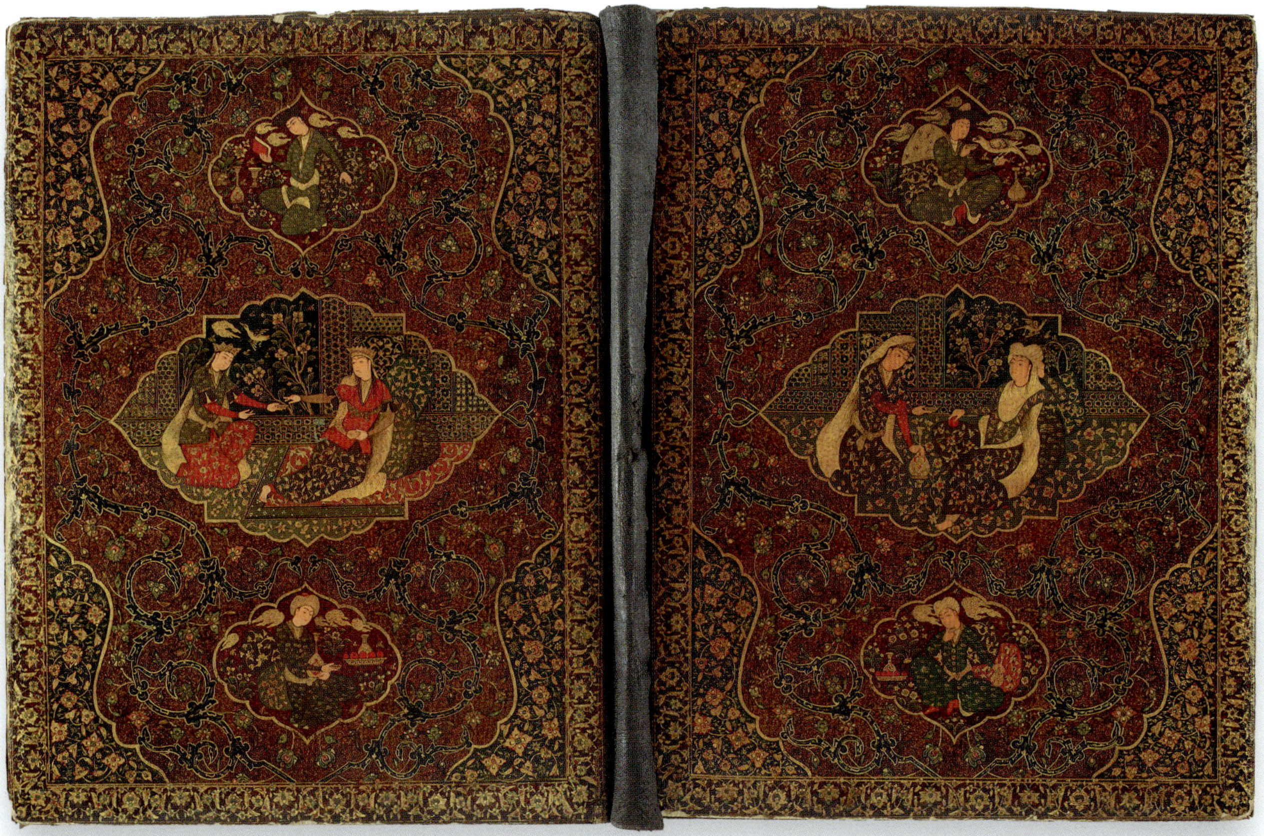

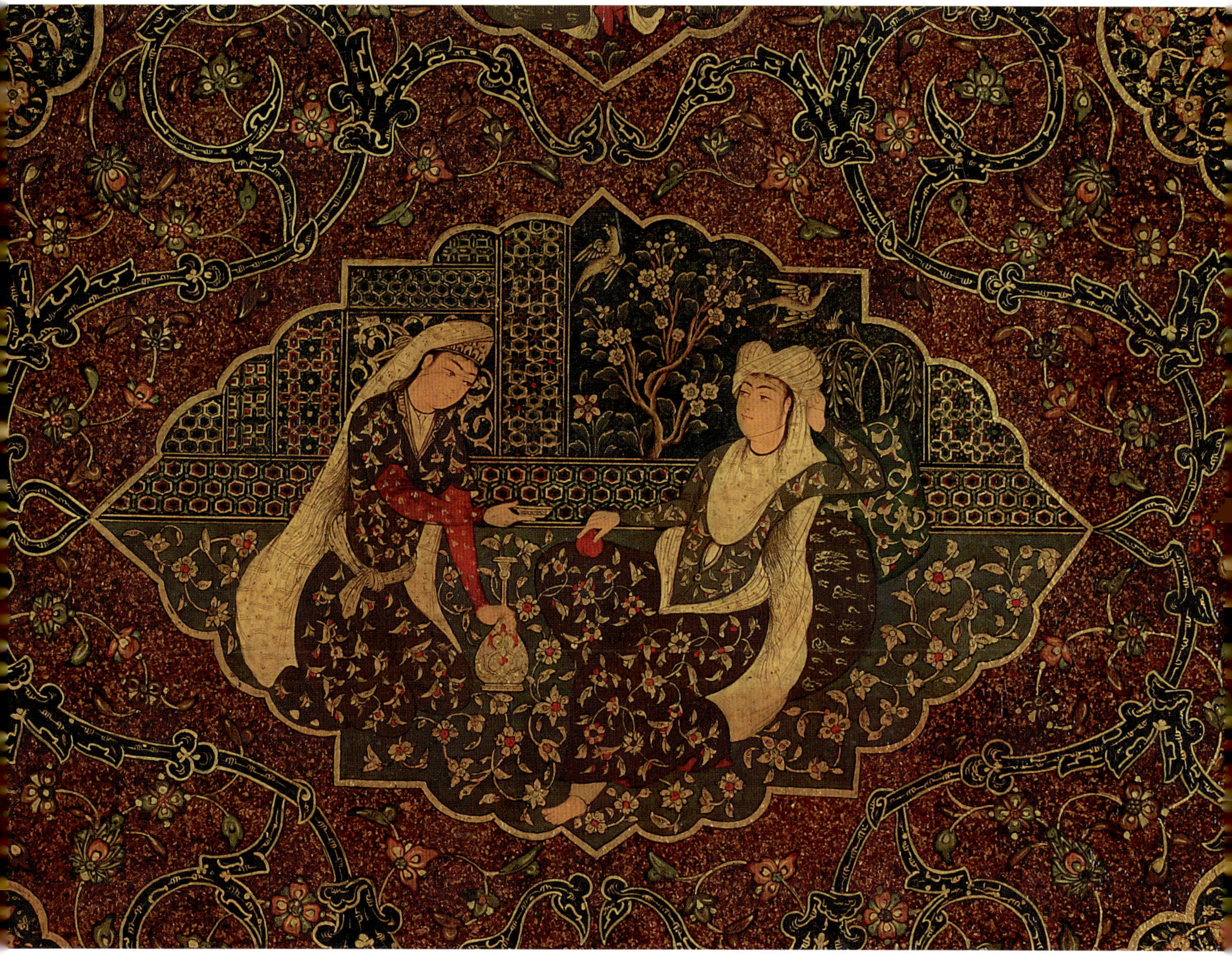

OPPOSITE AND DETAIL ABOVE This type of painted and lacquered book cover appeared in Persia in the fifteenth century, although the advent of the Savafid dynasty in the sixteenth century saw the spread of tooled bookbindings. Figurative illustration was disapproved of in many Muslim circles, but it did feature in a sizeable number of Persian, Turkish and Indian manuscripts with miniature paintings, and these book covers are decorated in the same tradition. Flowers and foliage surround human figures, birds and animals on a powdered-gold background. As was common, the brown goatskin doublures were also adorned, and this example features gold paint, blue paper filigree inlays and cut-out compartments. The 'spine', also of brown goatskin, is plain. It seems likely that such accomplished work would have been made for a high status recipient, possibly the Shah himself. Some have attributed the figures to Reza Abbasi, the most renowned miniaturist and calligrapher of the Isfahan School.

Persia, *c.*1650
418 x 323 x 12 mm (16.5 x 12.7 x 0.5 inches)
Davis 719

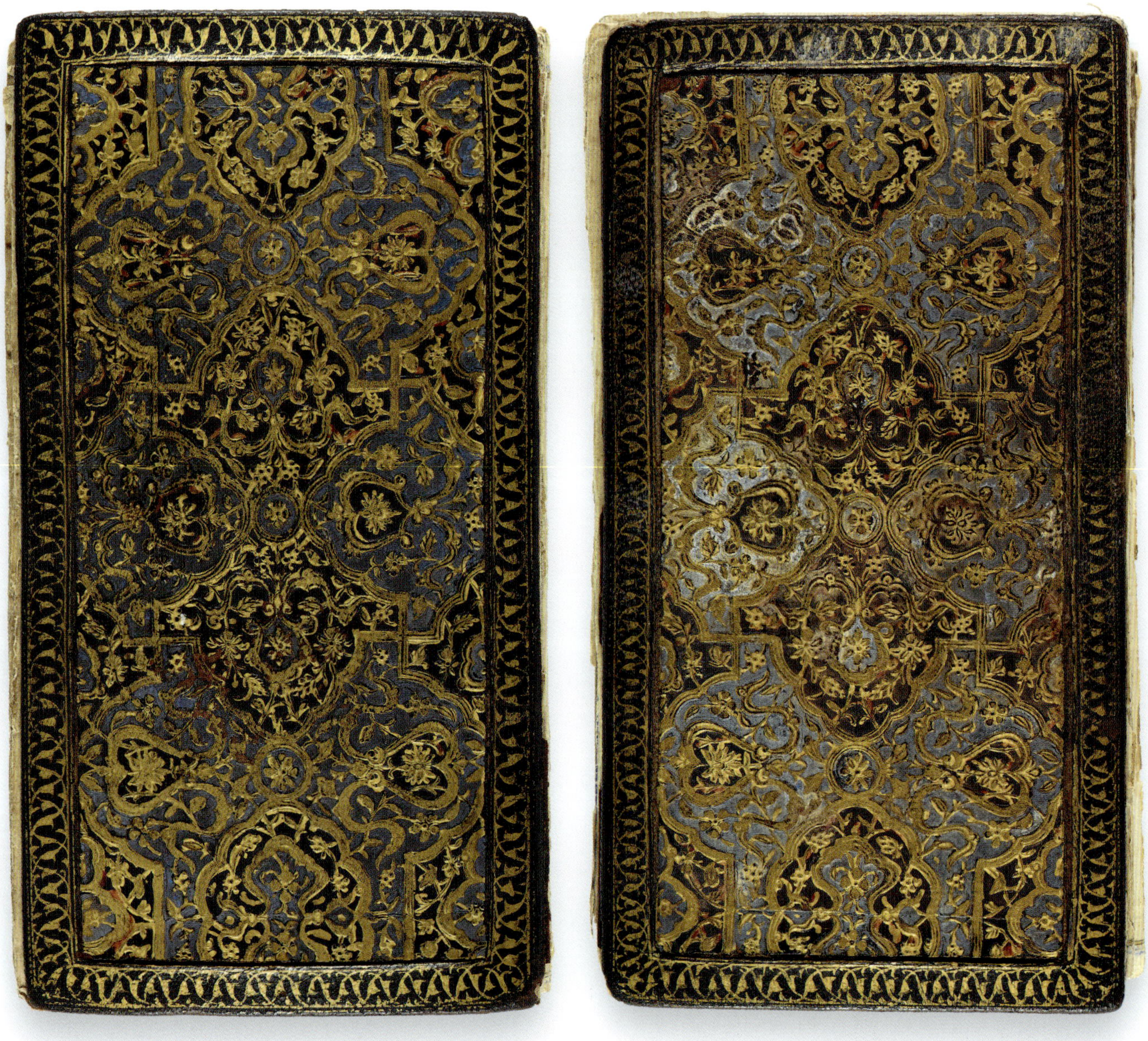

This brown goatskin binding may have belonged to the Mughal Princess Jahanara, who was the daughter of Shah Jahan who ruled India 1628–58. Its decoration recalls the filigree (or cut-pattern technique) doublures on sixteenth-century Persian bindings, which featured gilded designs against a blue background. Duncan Haldane laments such derivative styles, suggesting that 'the seventeenth-century witnessed a decline in the art of binding in Persia'.

Persia or India, *c.*1630–50
45 x 80 x 25 mm (1.8 x 3.1 x 1 inches)
Davis 652

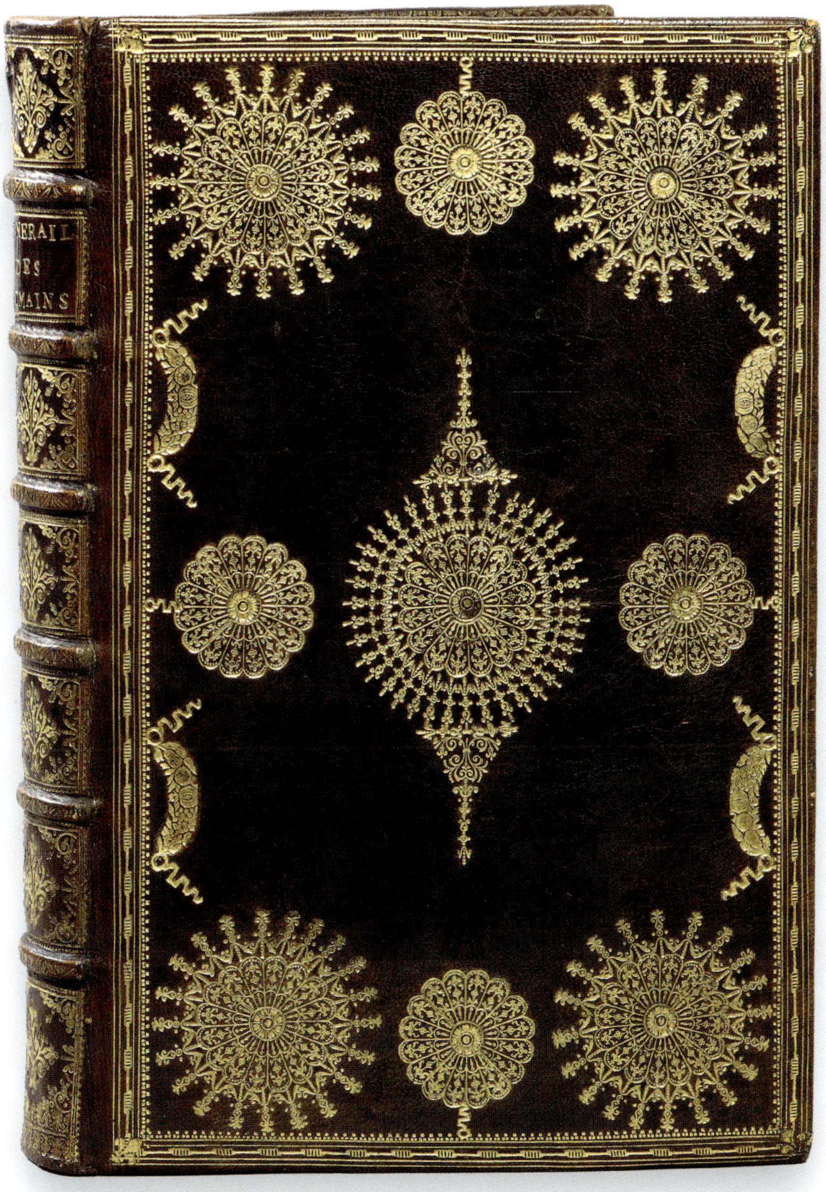

This late seventeenth-century French goatskin binding is tooled in gold *à l'évantail* (with a fan motif). It was once was owned by Antoine Leriche (1643–1715), who was Secretary to Louis XIV and a noted bibliophile and collector. He was famous for his paintings, objets d'art and 'cabinet of select books, among which there are a number of very beautiful and very unusual tooled bindings'. Fan motifs were popular in Italy, Spain and to a lesser extent in Germany, but, as with most fashions in binding, it was in France that the style reached its apogée.

Paris, 1690–1700
418 x 323 x 12 mm (16.5 x 12.7 x 0.5 inches)
Davis 512

EMBROIDERED BINDINGS

Embroidered fabric (usually canvas, satin or silk) was the costliest and most highly regarded of book coverings. The work is frequently ascribed to amateurs, usually noblewomen, since such an activity was seen as suited to their status, but the sophistication of many existing examples implies the involvement of professional needleworkers (many of whom were men). Regulatory guilds, which grew up in the major cities of Europe, including London and Paris, maintained a high standard of workmanship and their craftsmen were in great demand, both from the aristocracy and from the Church.

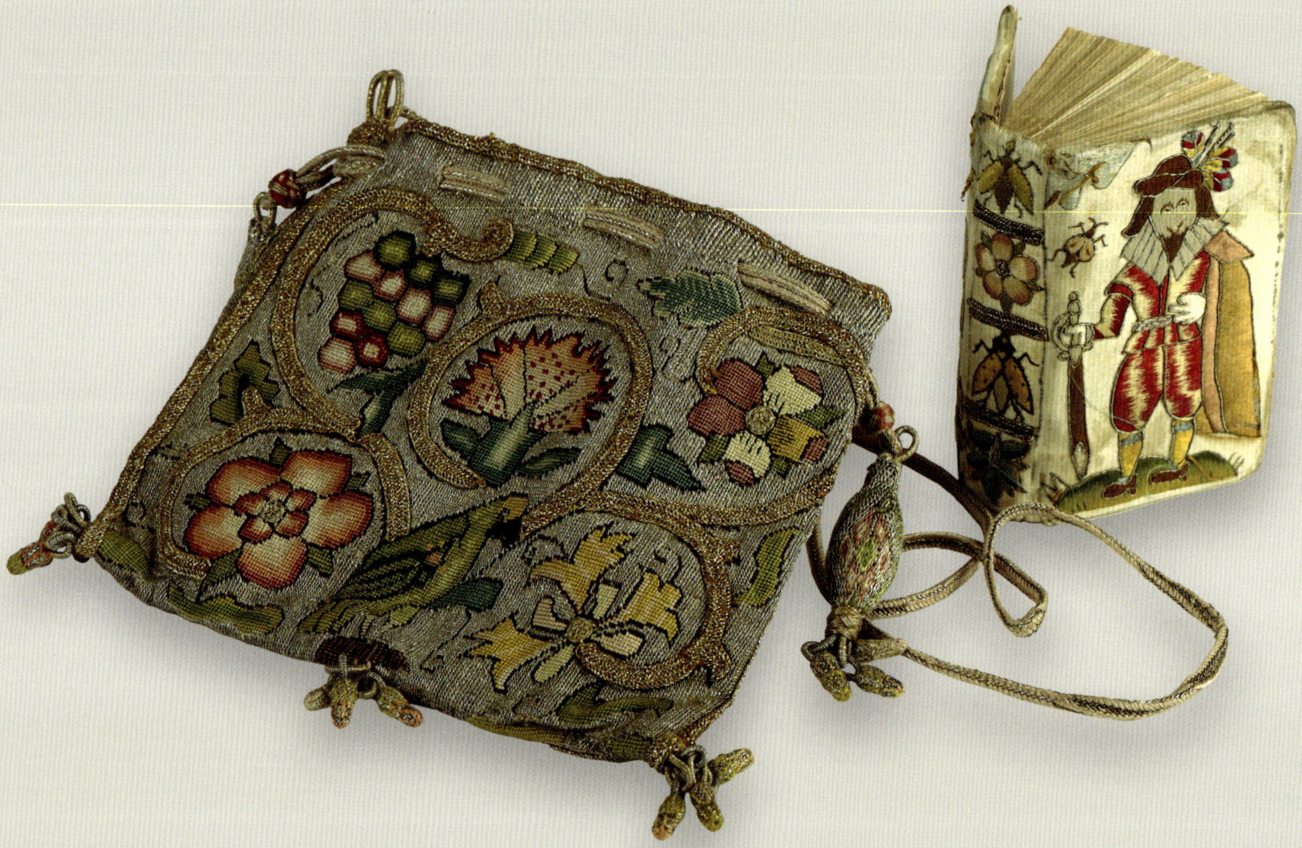

This tiny satin-covered book is embroidered with the figures of a seventeenth-century English nobleman with his sword (a status symbol) and his lady dressed in their Sunday best. Its size is a particular novelty. Prayer books were sometimes carried in fabric bags. These were decorated with fashionable motifs including parrots, flowers, leaves and grapes.

England, mid-seventeeth century
80 x 53 x 25 mm (3.2 x 2.1 x 1 inches)
C.194.c.27

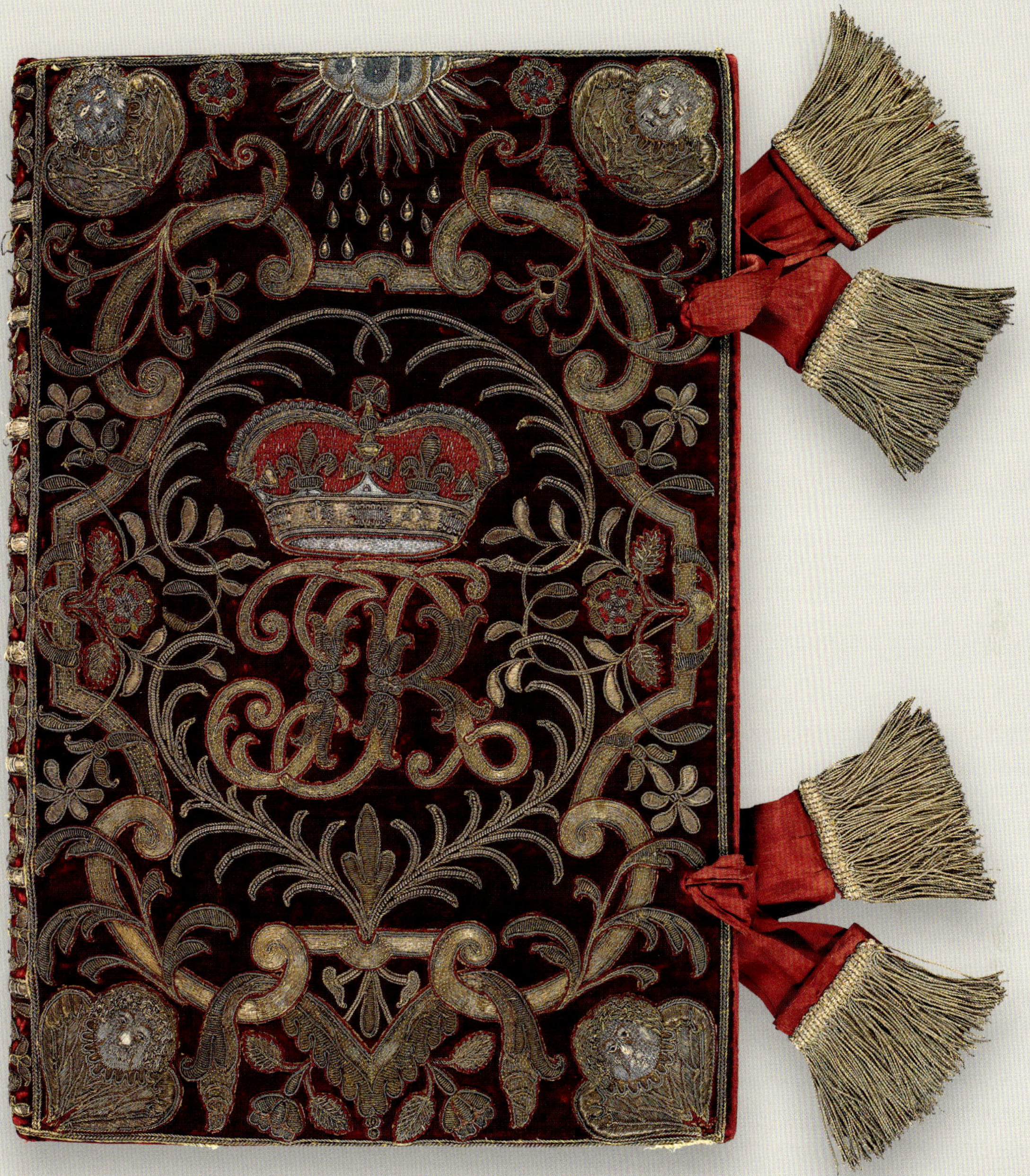

The crowned initials J R (standing for Jacobus Rex) embroidered onto this sumptuous seventeenth-century English, red velvet binding show that it was made for King James II of England (1633–1701). The professional needleworkers responsible used a variety of techniques and materials, including costly silver threads (which have tarnished with age). Cherubs' heads (comprising raised work), a small blue cloud and a floral and laurel wreath complete the design. According to Victorian researcher Cyril Davenport, the golden age of English embroidered bindings had passed. He declared the binding to be good and strong but 'utterly wanting in any of the artistic qualities either of design or execution which characterised so many of the earlier examples'.

England, 1670s
473 x 315 x 65 mm (18.6 x 12.4 x 2.6 inches)
C.18.e.11

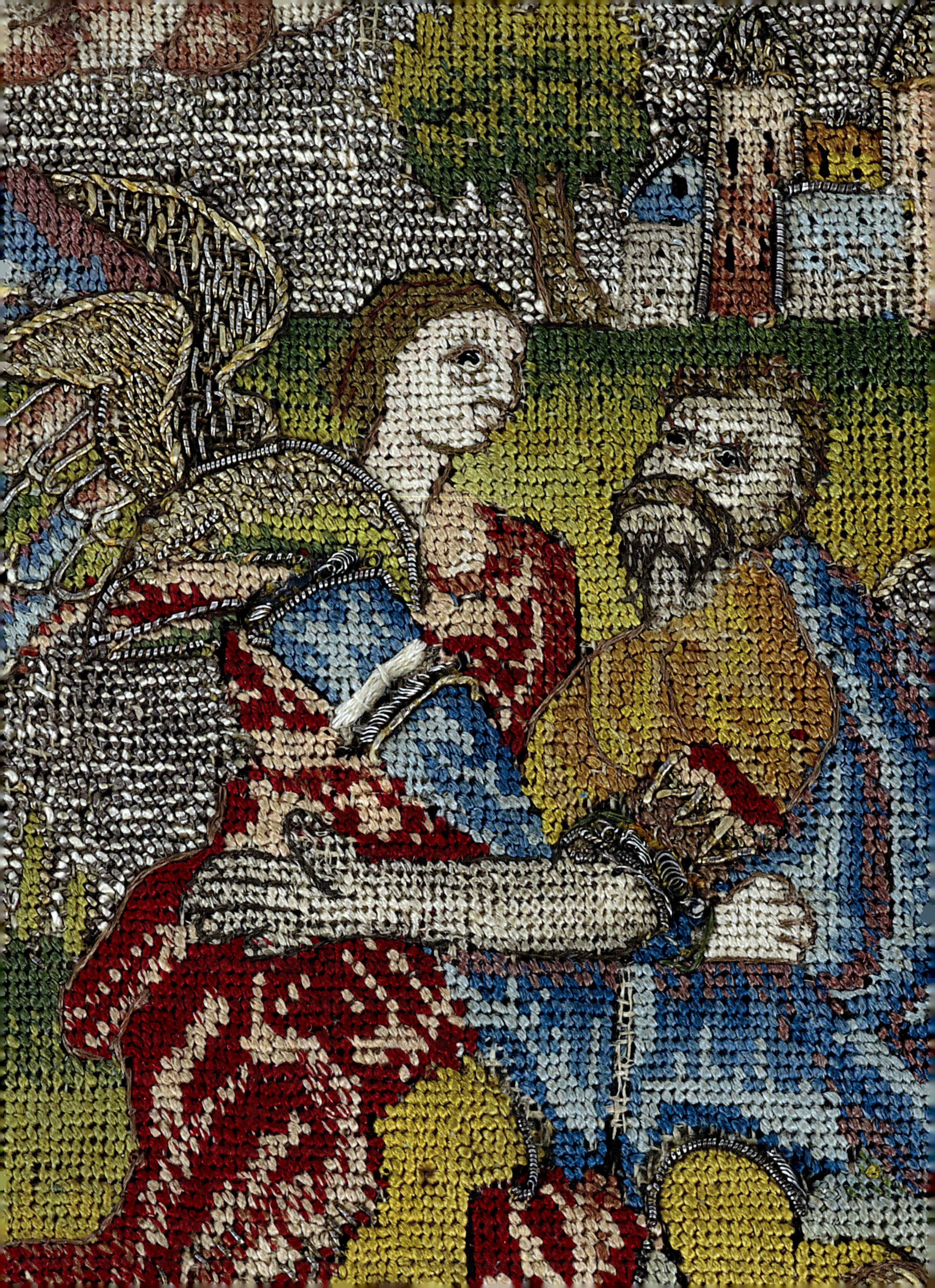

Going to church was a social act as well as an act of obedience, and members of the congregation were sensitive to signs of status. Possession of a Bible or prayer book finely bound in the latest style indicated not only the owner's literacy, but also their piety, wealth and taste; hence the popularity of embroidered bindings in England from the mid-sixteenth to mid-seventeenth centuries. The texts, usually devotional, were bound in the normal way, but passed to professional needleworkers to decorate the textile covers (which were of canvas, velvet, silk or satin). Subjects depicted could be scriptural, such as this example of Jacob wrestling with the Angel, worked in coloured and silver threads over canvas; symbolic (for example figures of Hope and Faith); armorial, or portraits (usually of royal or noble personages).

England, early seventeenth century
176 x 110 x 46 mm (6.9 x 4.3 x 1.8 inches)
C.65.l.6(1-2)

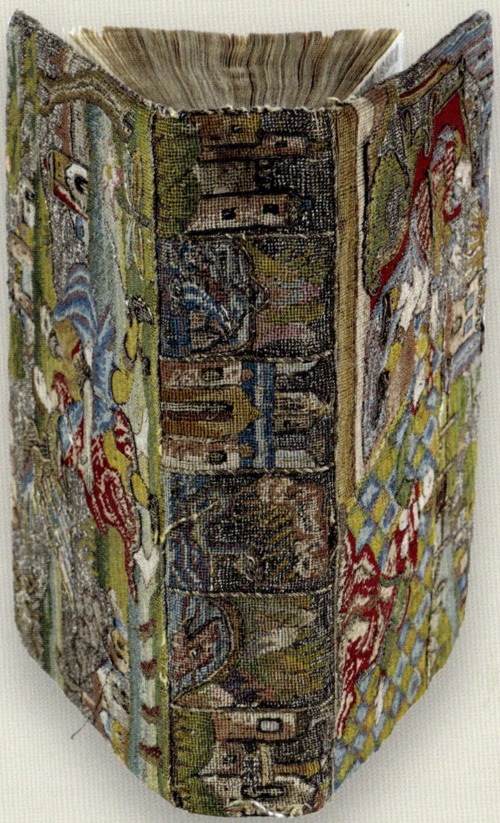

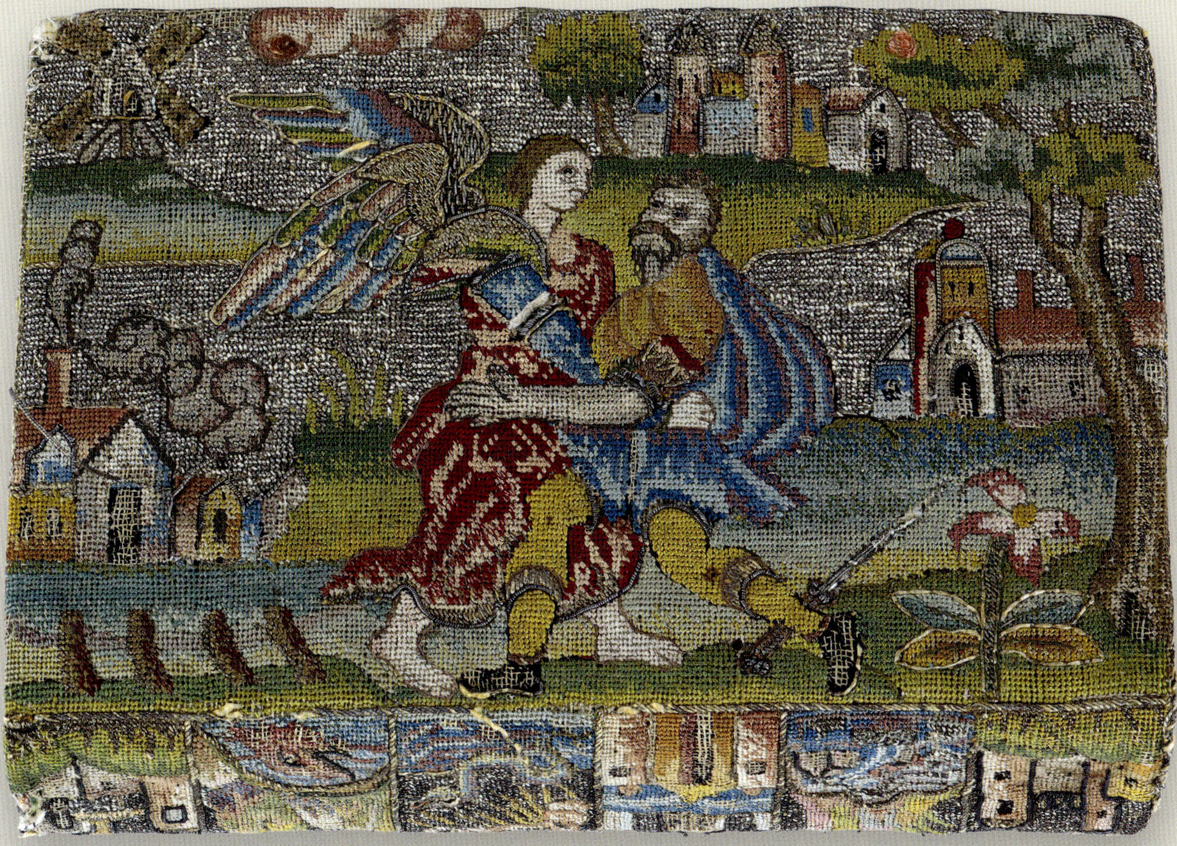

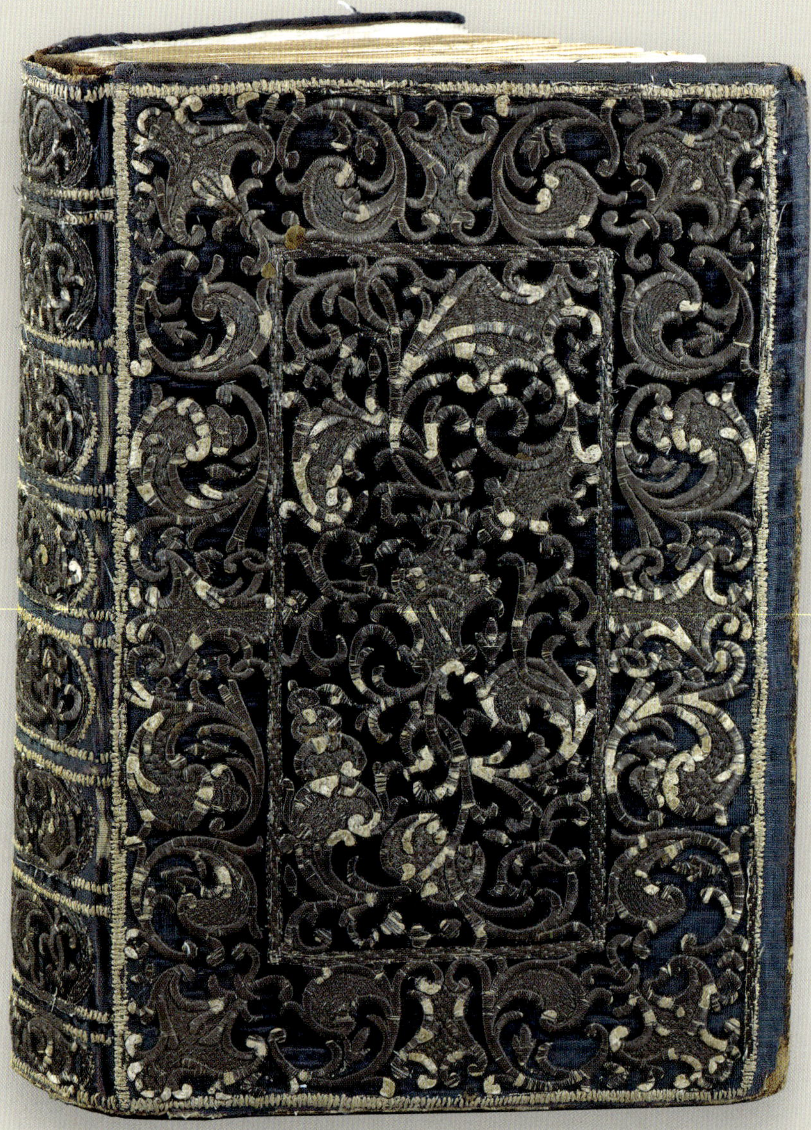

ABOVE Not all embroidered bindings were small, as is shown by this folio-sized Italian, eighteenth-century blue velvet example, embroidered with silver threads. The centre of the design features a coat of arms, now sadly indistinguishable. The text warranted such an expensive binding because it contained all the prayers and instructions necessary for the celebration of Mass throughout the year. The binding has several ribbon markers attached to allow the celebrant to keep his place during the service.

Italy, early eighteenth century
380 x 250 x 80 mm (15.0 x 9.8 x 3.1 inches)
C.188.c.5

OPPOSITE This nineteenth-century Portuguese pink satin binding has been embroidered with the royal arms. As with many fabric bindings, it has deteriorated and the silver threads and sequins have tarnished, but the amount of embroidery and the skill required would have made this a particularly attractive item at the time of production.

Portugal, *c.*1828
101 x 54 x 14 mm (4.0 x 2.1 x 0.6 inches)
C.108.u.2

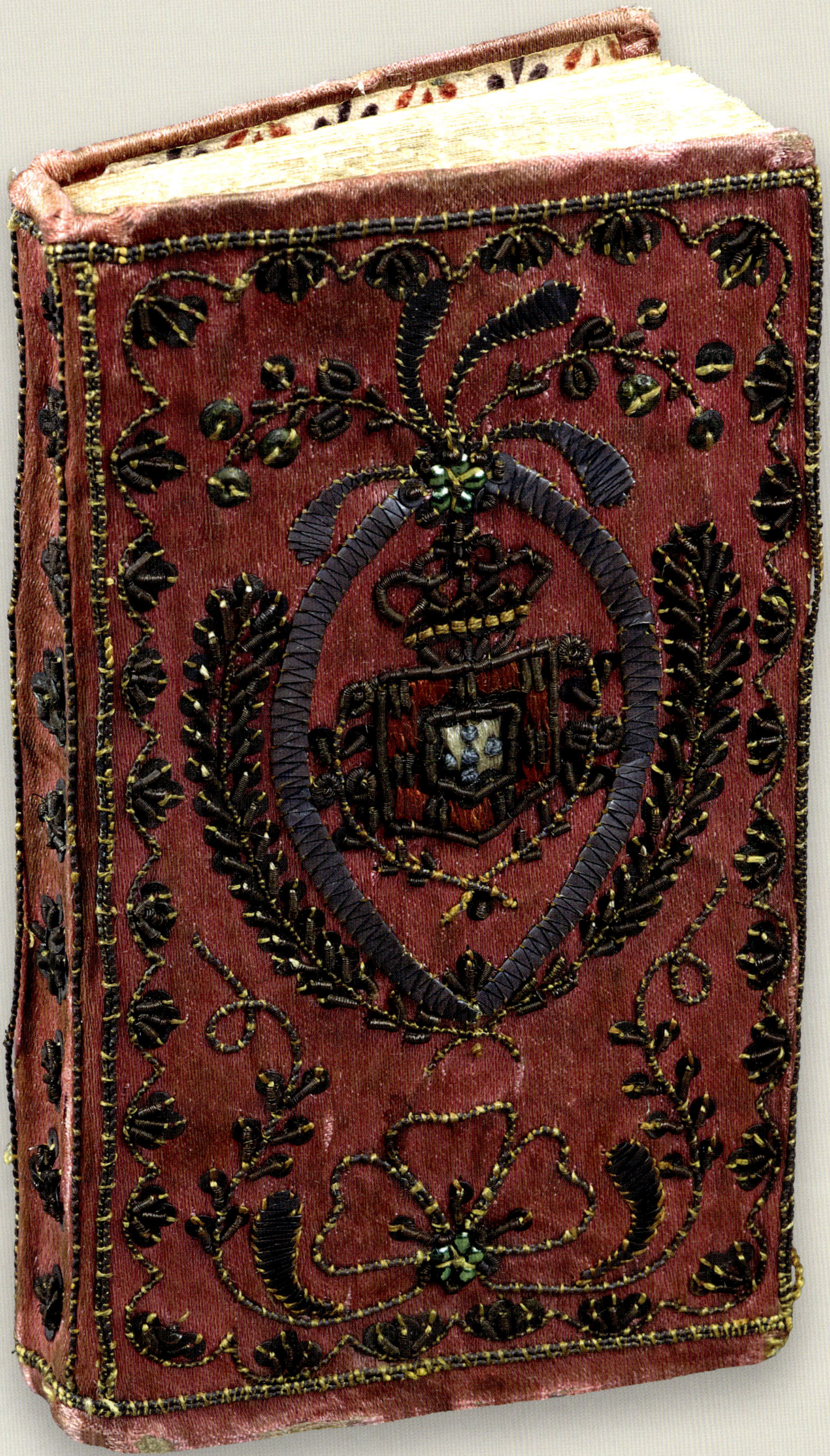

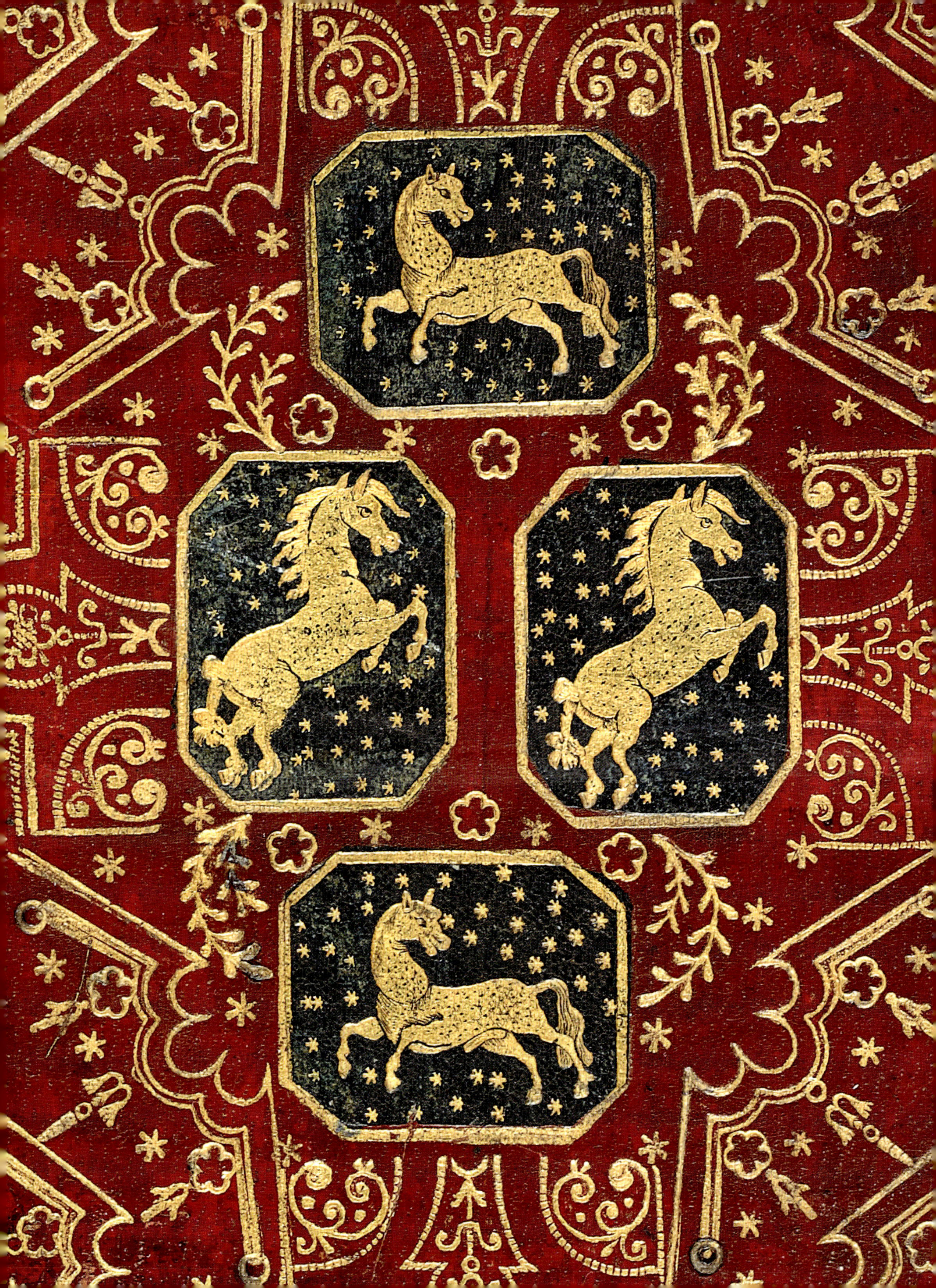

CHAPTER 4

Eighteenth Century

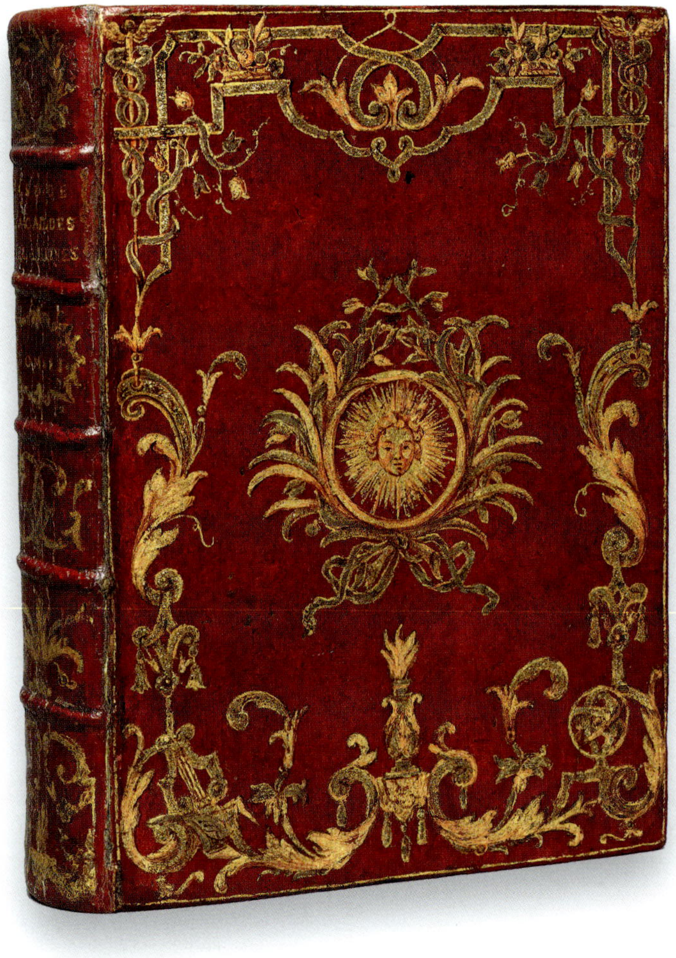

ABOVE The use of varnish or lacquer is common in the Eastern bookbinding tradition, less so in that of the West. However, in the eighteenth century, there was something of a trend for reproducing the high gloss seen on Chinese furniture. This was achieved by using a new French technique called 'vernis Martin' (although the application of this description to bindings, while prevalent, is incorrect). The gleaming surface of this painted, contemporary French red leather binding shows elements of this style.

Paris (?), *c.*1717–20
264 x 193 x 53 mm (10.4 x 7.6 x 2.1 inches)
Davis 536-537

OPPOSITE Bookbinding workshops grew up near to the markets they supplied. Rome had a flourishing bindings trade, due to its proximity to the Vatican, the headquarters of the Roman Catholic religion. The pope and his administrators required bound books related to their calling, as did the musicians who took part in the ceremonies. The author of this book, a history of the papal choir, was an Italian musician and castrato, who ran the choir and was also a popular figure in aristocratic circles. Noble families based in Rome, as well as wealthy visitors, were another source of income for binders. Such demand helped maintain the vibrancy of binding decoration, as demonstrated here by this red goatskin binding: the foliage and hatched flower-head design is tooled in gold and fills the entire cover. The gilt, gauffered and painted fore-edge and the gold-blocked paper endleaves attest that this was a luxury item.

Rome, early eighteenth century
240 x 170 x 30 mm (9.4 x 6.7 x 1.2 inches)
C.20.c.4

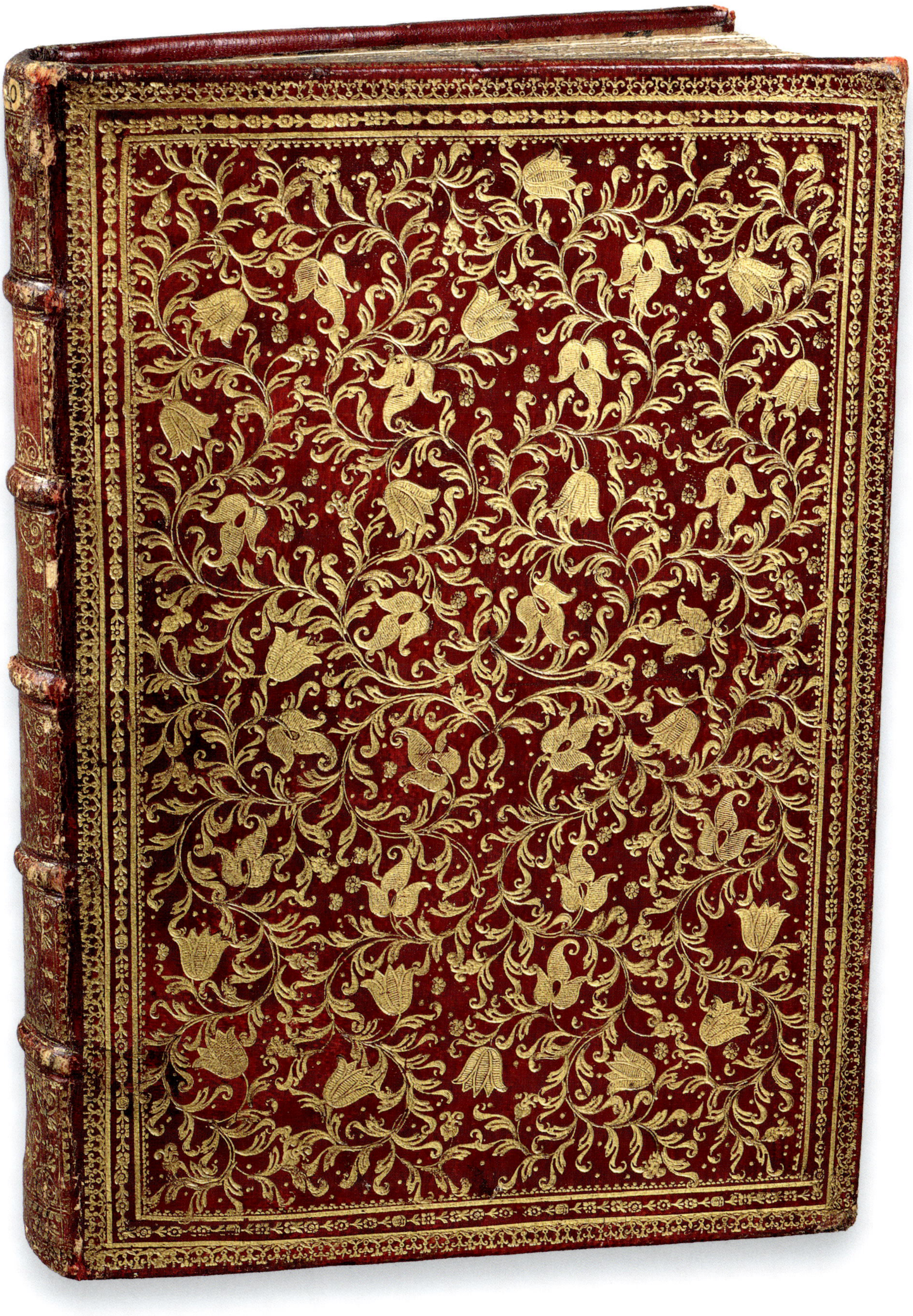

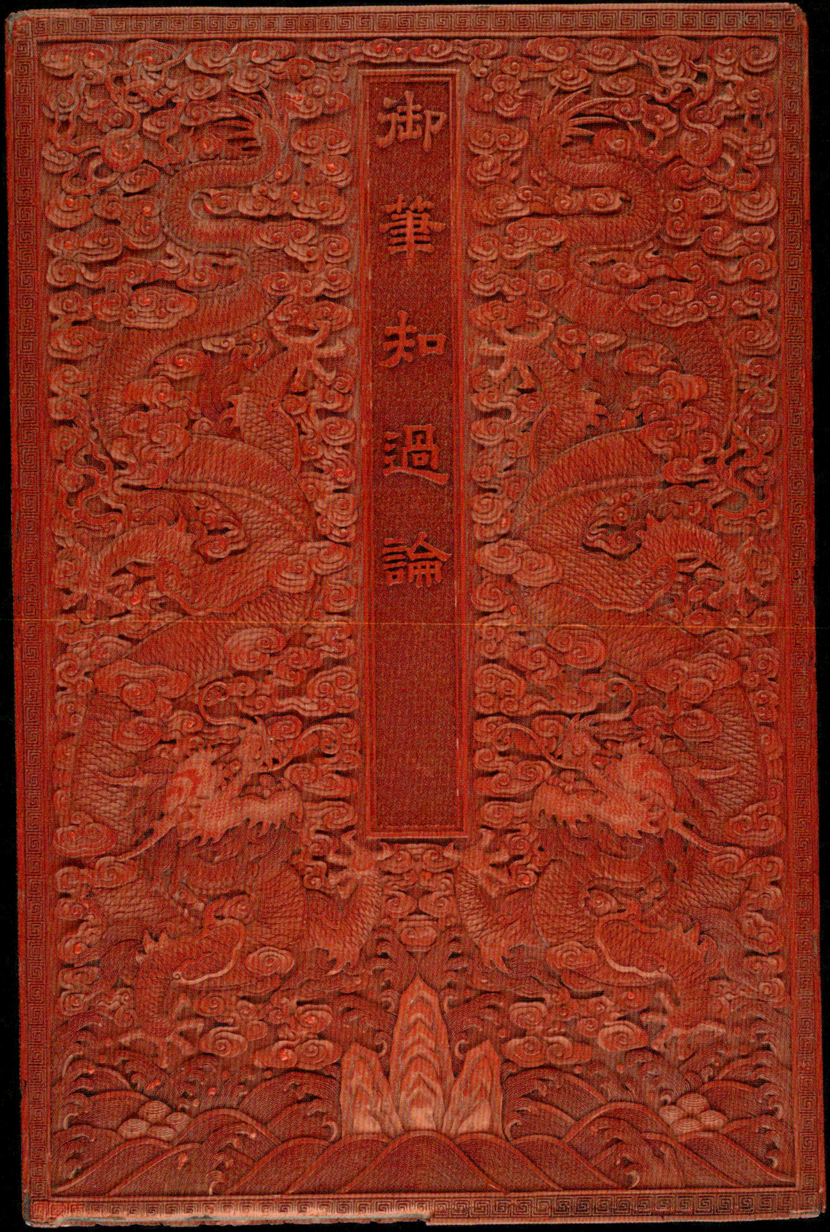

The dragons carved on this eighteenth-century red lacquer book cover are popular Chinese motifs, often associated with the emperor. They are particularly appropriate here as the book contains the calligraphic exercises of the Emperor Ch'ien-lung (1711–99), a patron of the arts who was interested in painting and literature. Lacquer is derived from the resin of a tree native to east Asia. It has a long history in the arts of China, with archaeological evidence of its use dating back to Neolithic times (10,000–2,000 BC). Raw lacquer was toxic and difficult to work, and a book such as this would have been available only to the highest echelons of society (red lacquer-ware was reserved for the royal family). Many thin layers were applied before carving could begin, and each coat took a considerable time to harden and dry. The result was an extremely expensive binding.

China, eighteenth century
452 x 305 x 50 mm (17.8 x 12 x 3.2 inches)
Or. 6682

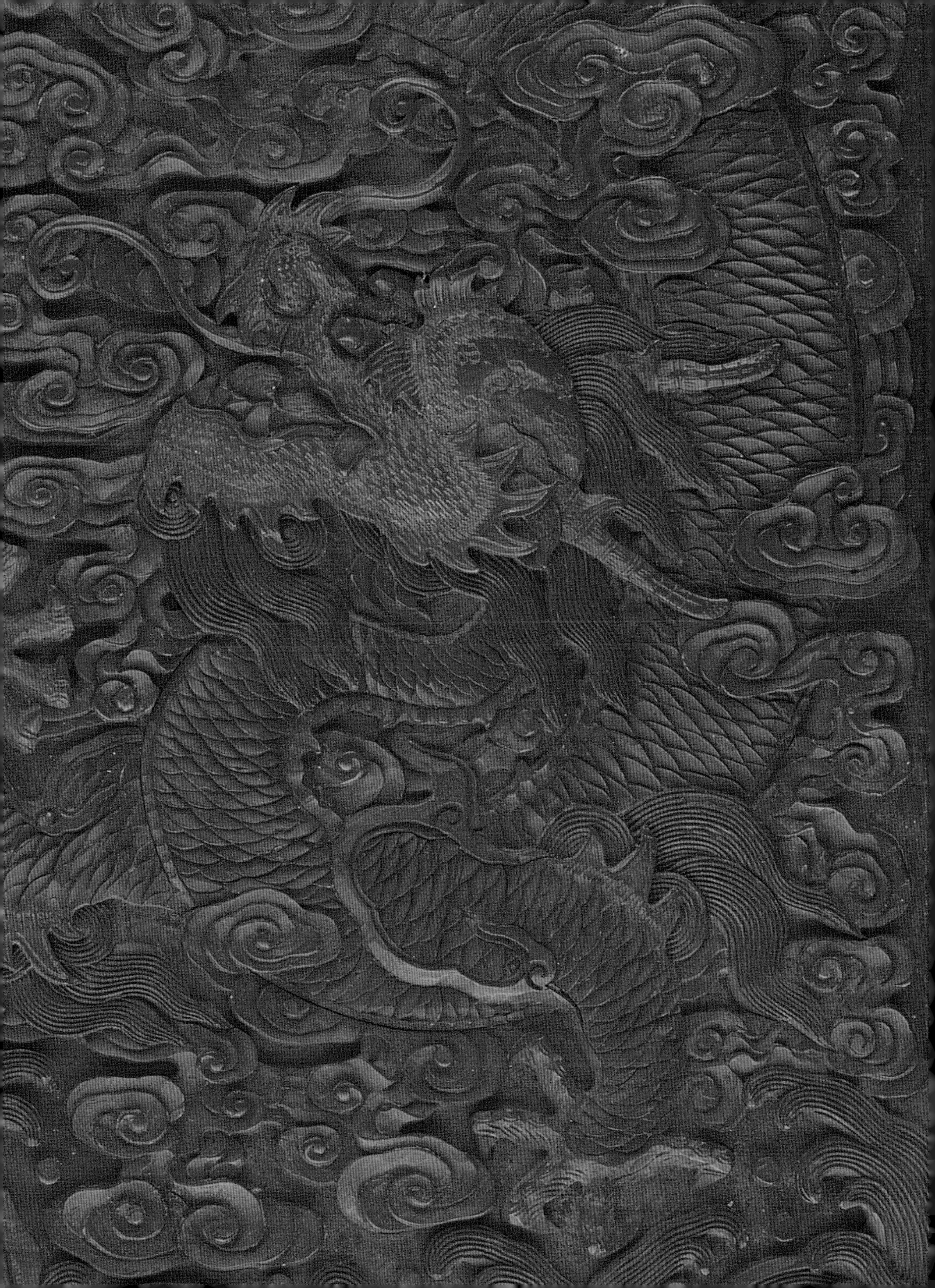

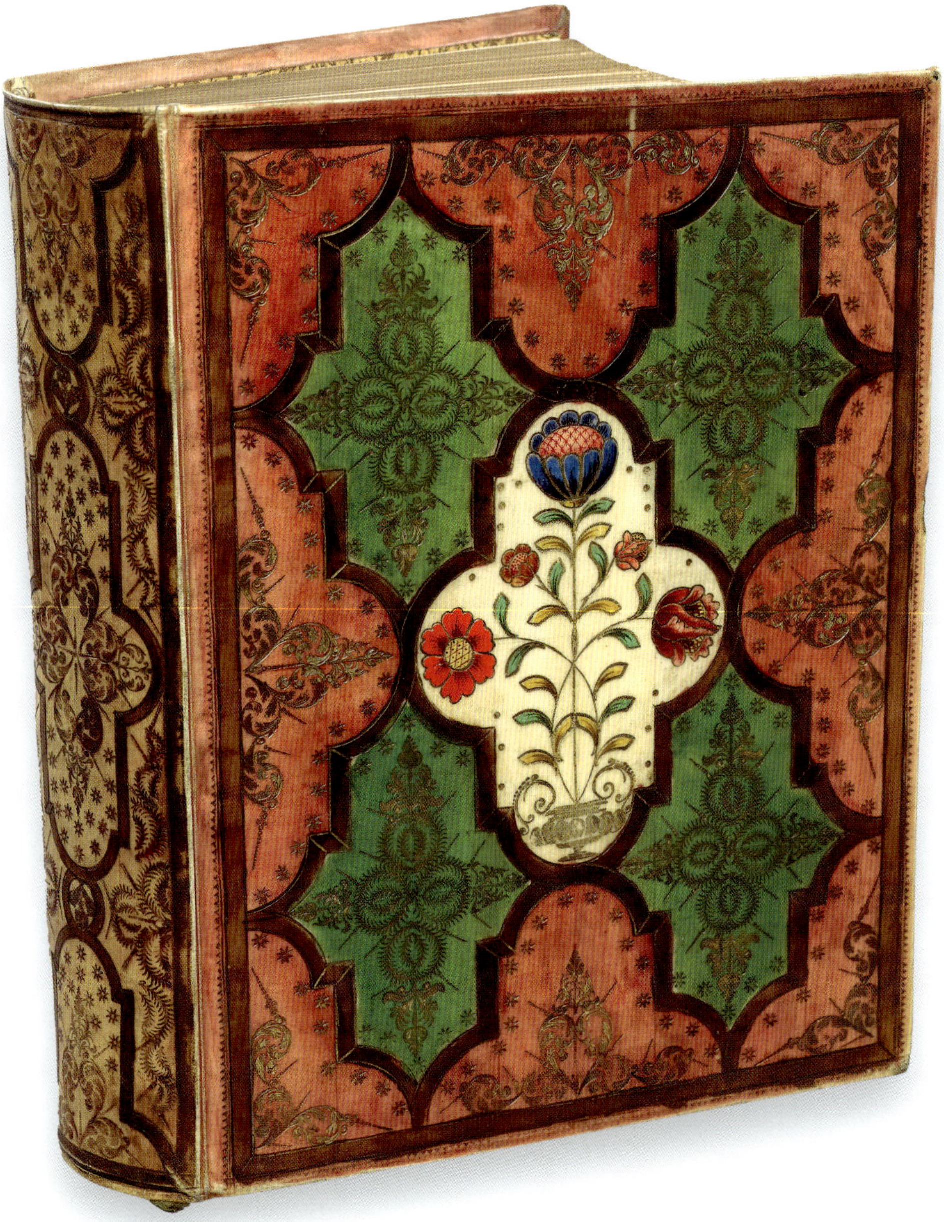

The appearance of this Swiss stained parchment binding is reminiscent of the colourful, floral peasant style known as 'Bauern Einbände', which was popular in the German-speaking areas of Europe, and also Scandinavia and Eastern Europe. This sort of design, featuring compartments and the use of gouges, was quite complicated to apply. Craftsmen could have looked to a binding manual for help, such as that written by a German binder Christophe Ernst Prediger, which included several tooling patterns for this type of work. The highly decorative nature of the binding is augmented by the gilt and gauffered edges, as well as the yellow decorated endleaves and green silk bookmarkers.

Bern (?), *c.*1731
260 x 198 x 63 mm (10.2 x 7.8 x 2.5 inches)
Davis 558

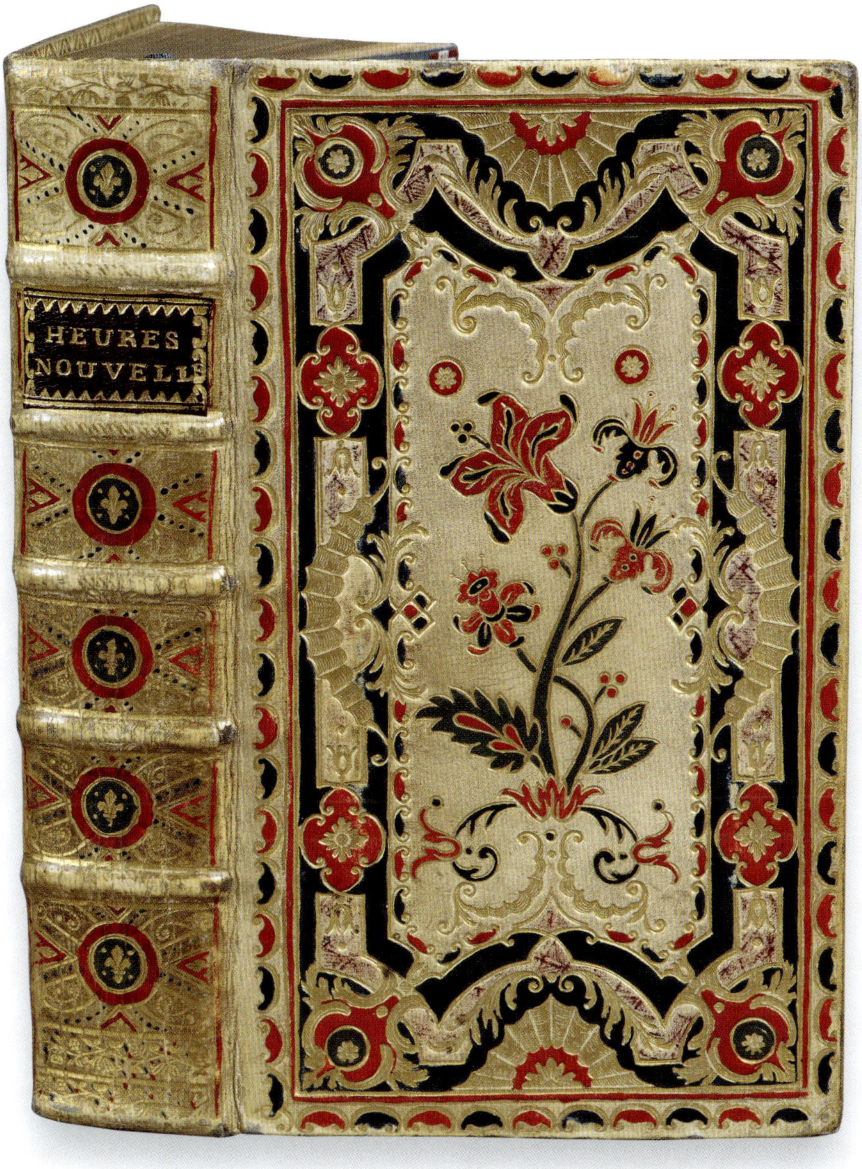

Pierre-Paul Dubuisson was made royal binder to the French king in 1758, and the output of his workshop was prolific. Unlike some Parisian binders, Dubuisson was both a binder and *doreur*; even so, it seems likely that other craftsmen were employed by his workshop to satisfy the demand, not only for commissioned work but also for 'more standard octavo-type bindings in a fancy style ... to meet the New Year market for almanacs or the like'. In these circumstances, timesaving techniques, notably the plaque for decoration, became particularly valuable, and Dubuisson became especially associated with it, although other binders also adopted the method. The plaques often produced an ornamental frame in gold, as seen here on this white calf binding. This particular style was called *à la plaque rocaille*. Coloured paints and a central flower motif have been applied to complete the design. The endleaves are lined with watered silk, and the edges have been gilt and marbled beneath the gold.

Paris, *c.*1750
171 x 112 x 38 mm (6.7 x 4.4 x 1.5 inches)
Davis 560

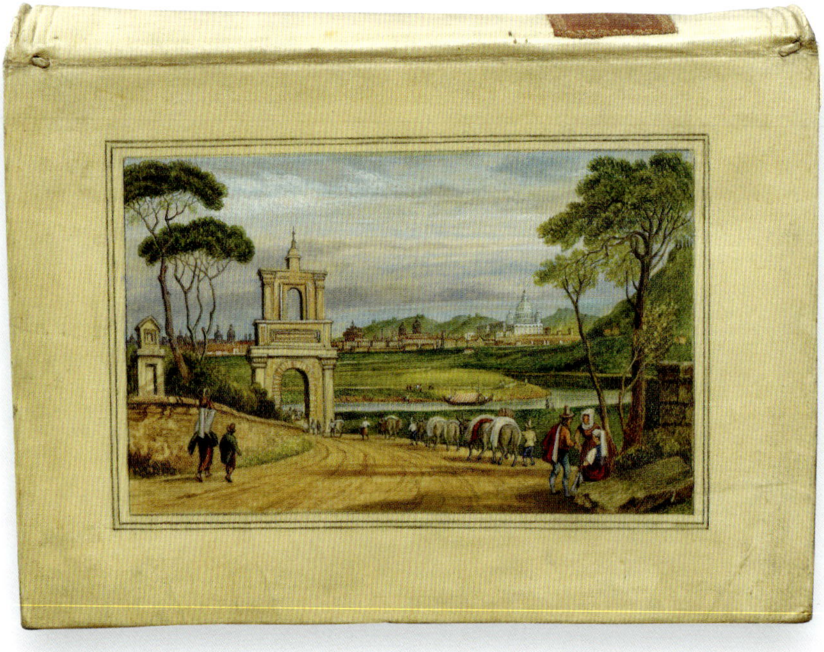

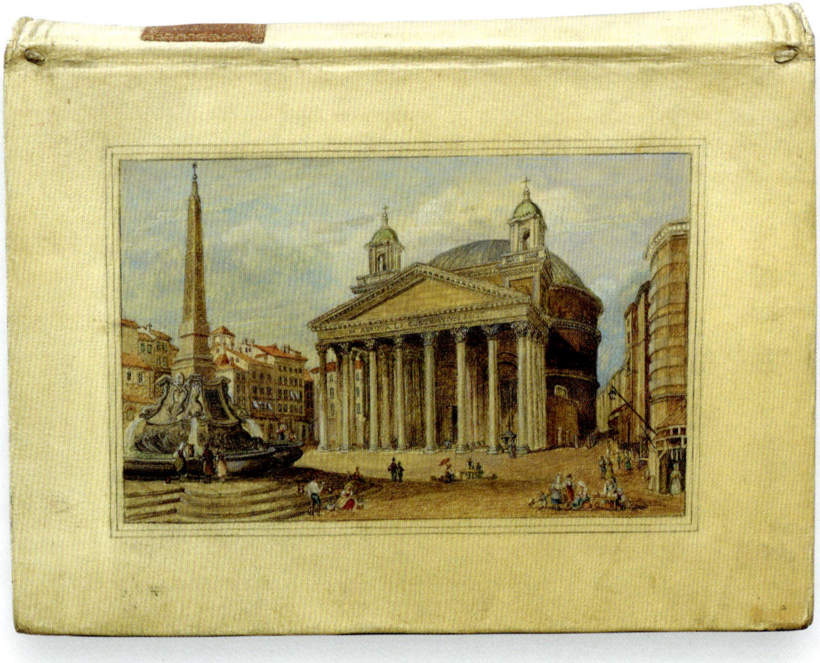

These eighteenth-century Italian parchment bindings over pasteboard feature watercolour paintings of the sights of Rome, and would, perhaps, have served as an attractive souvenir to a gentleman on the Grand Tour. Inexpensive plain parchment was frequently used to wrap around academic texts and dissertations, particularly in Italy and Spain, but parchment applied over pasteboard made the structure robust. Here, its smooth pale surface provides a perfect background for the colourful images of the landscape with St Peter's (in the distance) and the Pantheon.

Italy (?), late eighteenth century
250 x 182 x 38 mm (9.8 x 7.2 x 1.5 inches)
Davis 884-885

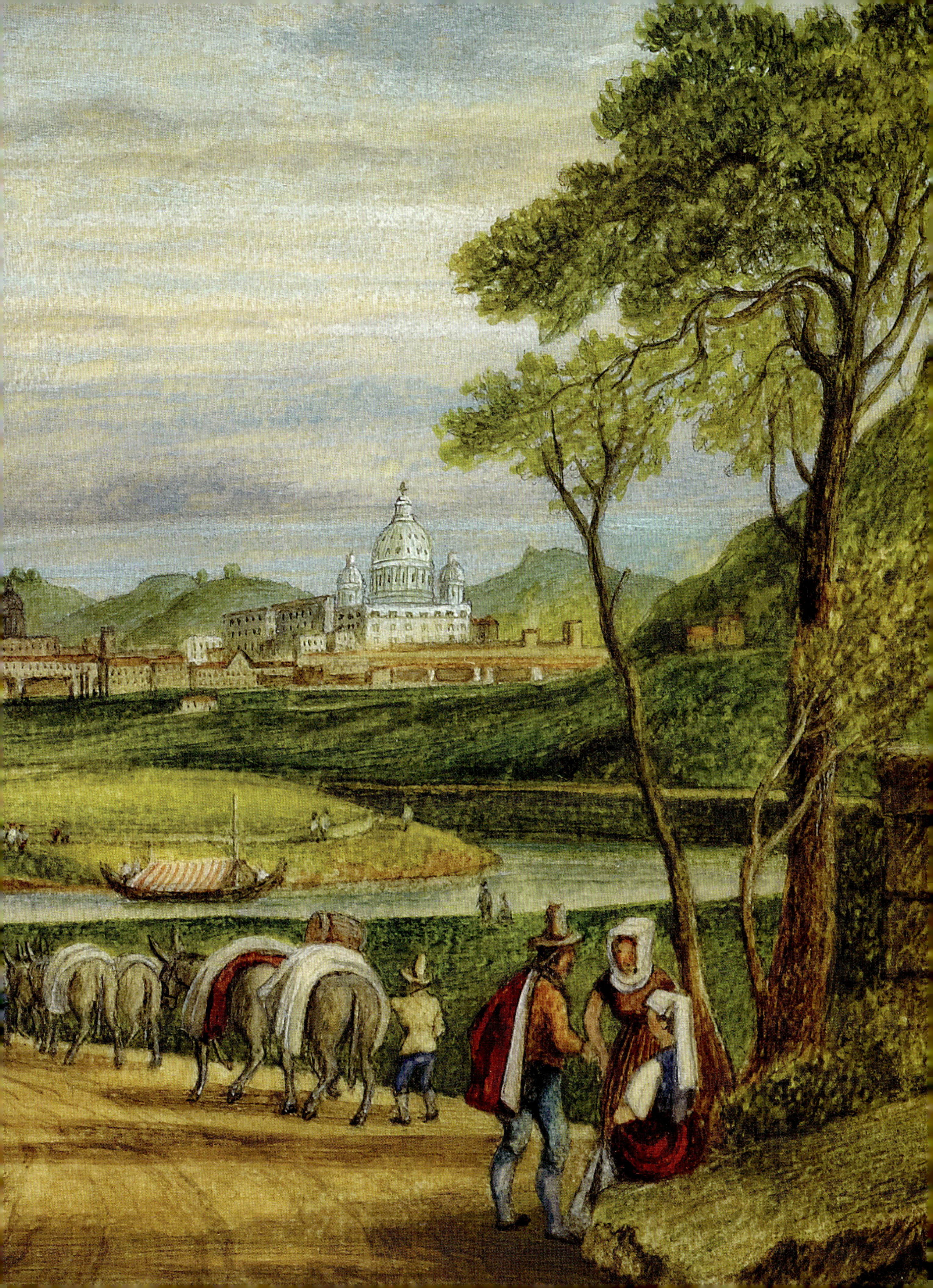

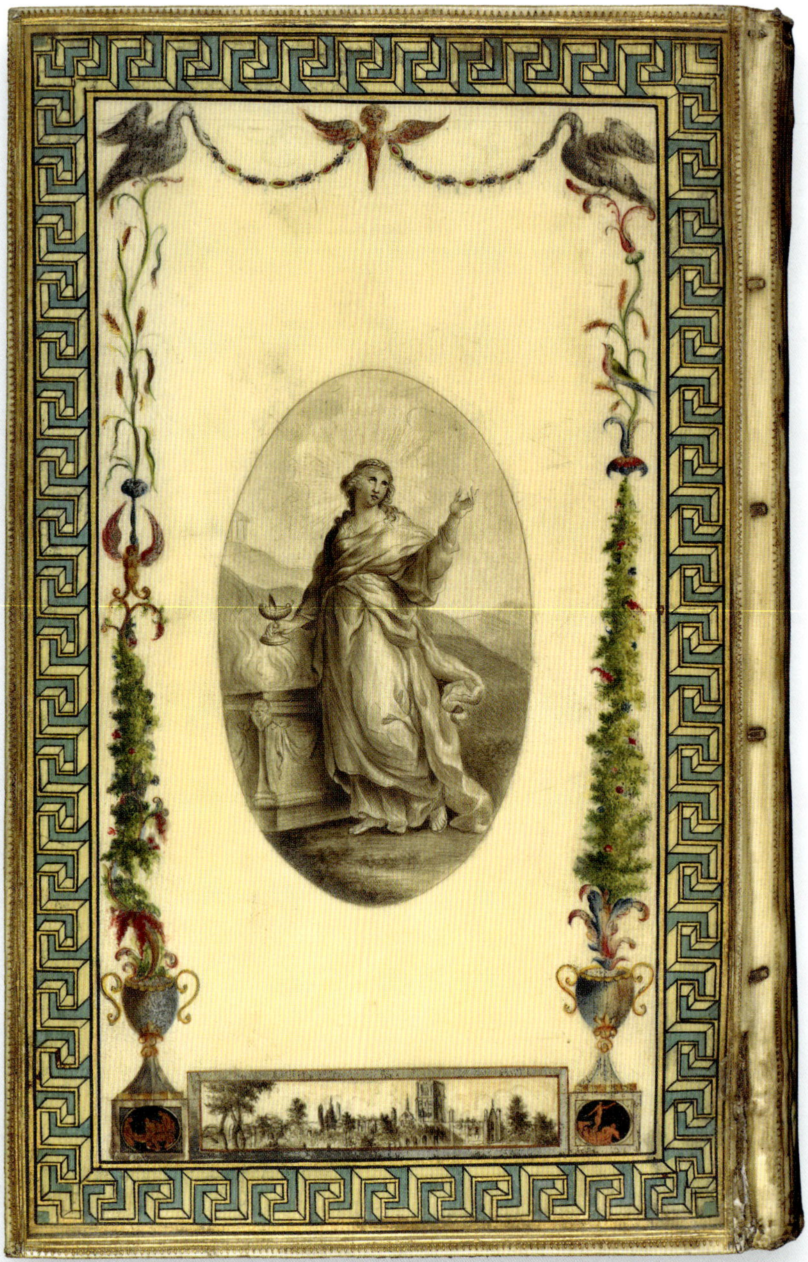

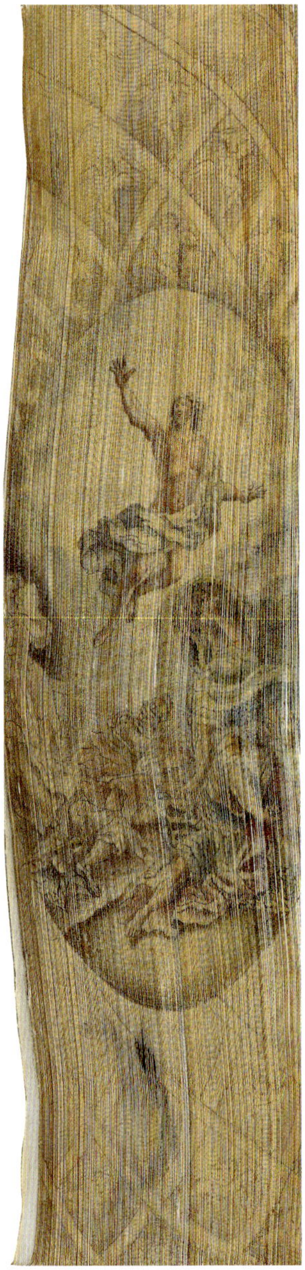

This prayer book was bound by the Edwards Bindery for Queen Charlotte (1744–1818), the wife of George III. The decoration has been applied on the underside of the translucent vellum covering, a technique patented by James Edwards in 1785, and the fore-edge conceals a painting of the Resurrection under the gold leaf. These new elements became very fashionable, and many aristocrats commissioned bindings incorporating paintings of their own coats of arms or country houses. An eighteenth-century commentator Thomas Hearne considered that 'people are in love with good binding more than good reading', and the Edwards Bindery profited from this by introducing a number of popular styles

England, late eighteenth century
256 x 163 x 45 mm (10.1 x 6.4 x 1.8 inches)
2.a.17

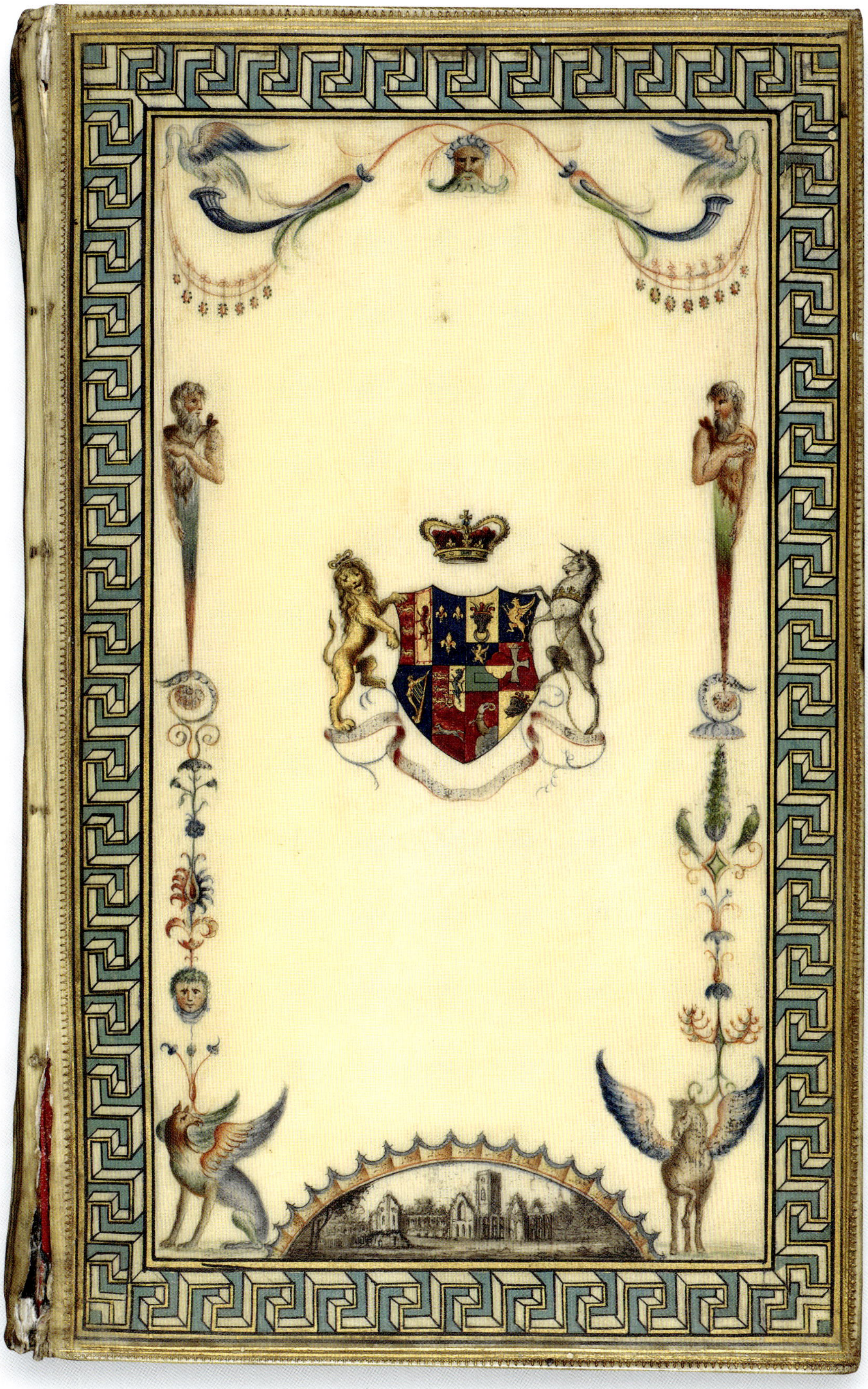

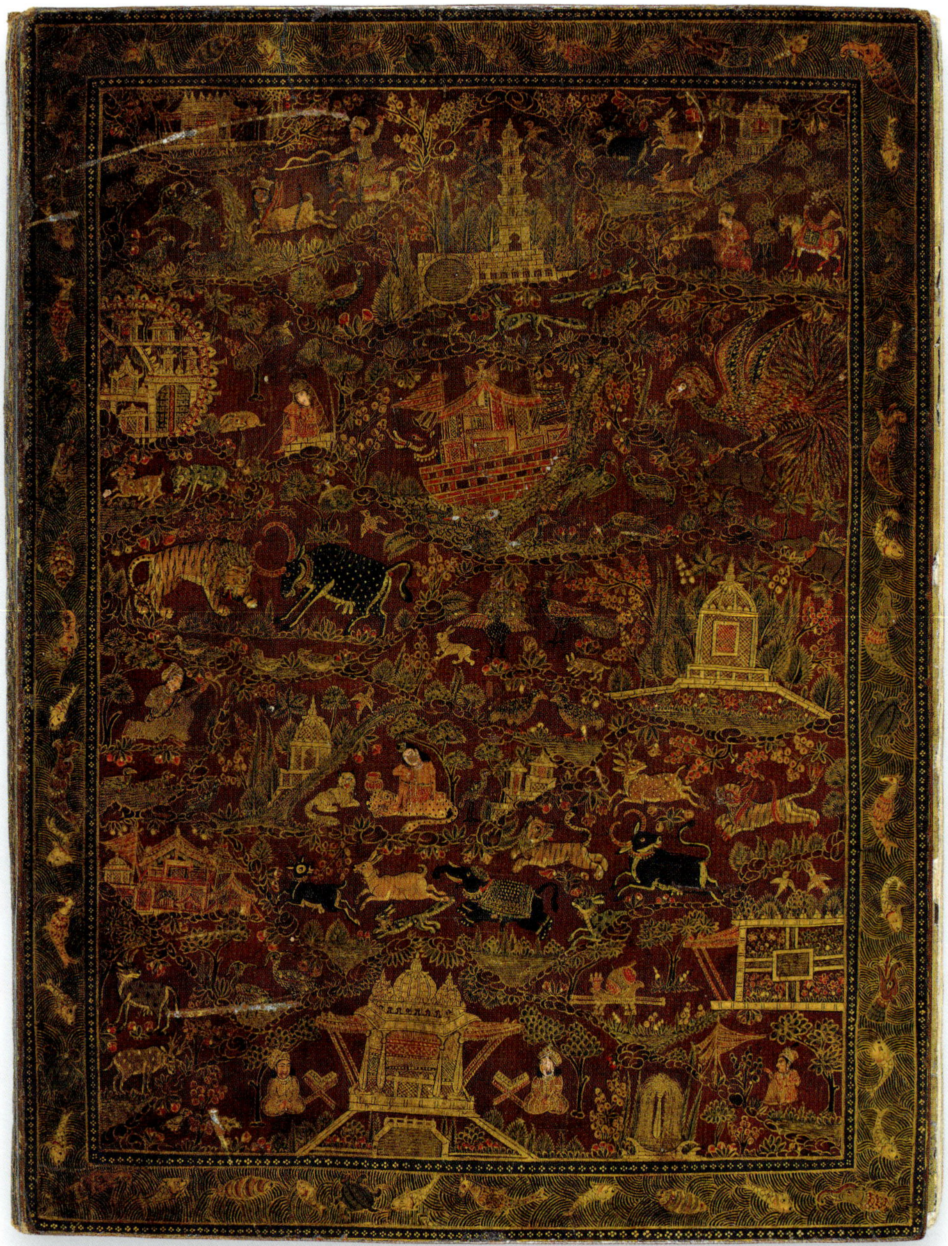

This early eighteenth-century lacquered binding, probably made in the Deccan Plateau, Southern India, is full of vitality and has captivated a number of binding scholars with its 'colourful composition' and its 'delightful animal figures'. The scene on the cover certainly reflects the spirit of the manuscript: a fanciful poem which related the adventures of Ali and his companions with 157 miniatures by the artist, Abd al-Hakim Multani. The manuscript itself was written in the 1680s, but it seems likely that the covers were added later, probably around 1760. Painting thrived in the Deccan under the patronage of its sultans, but when these rulers were superseded by the Emperor Aurangzeb, the old traditions were replaced by the Mughal styles that dominated during the eighteenth century.

Probably Southern India, *c.*1760
356 x 265 x 60 mm (14 x 10.4 x 2.4 inches)
Add. Ms 19766

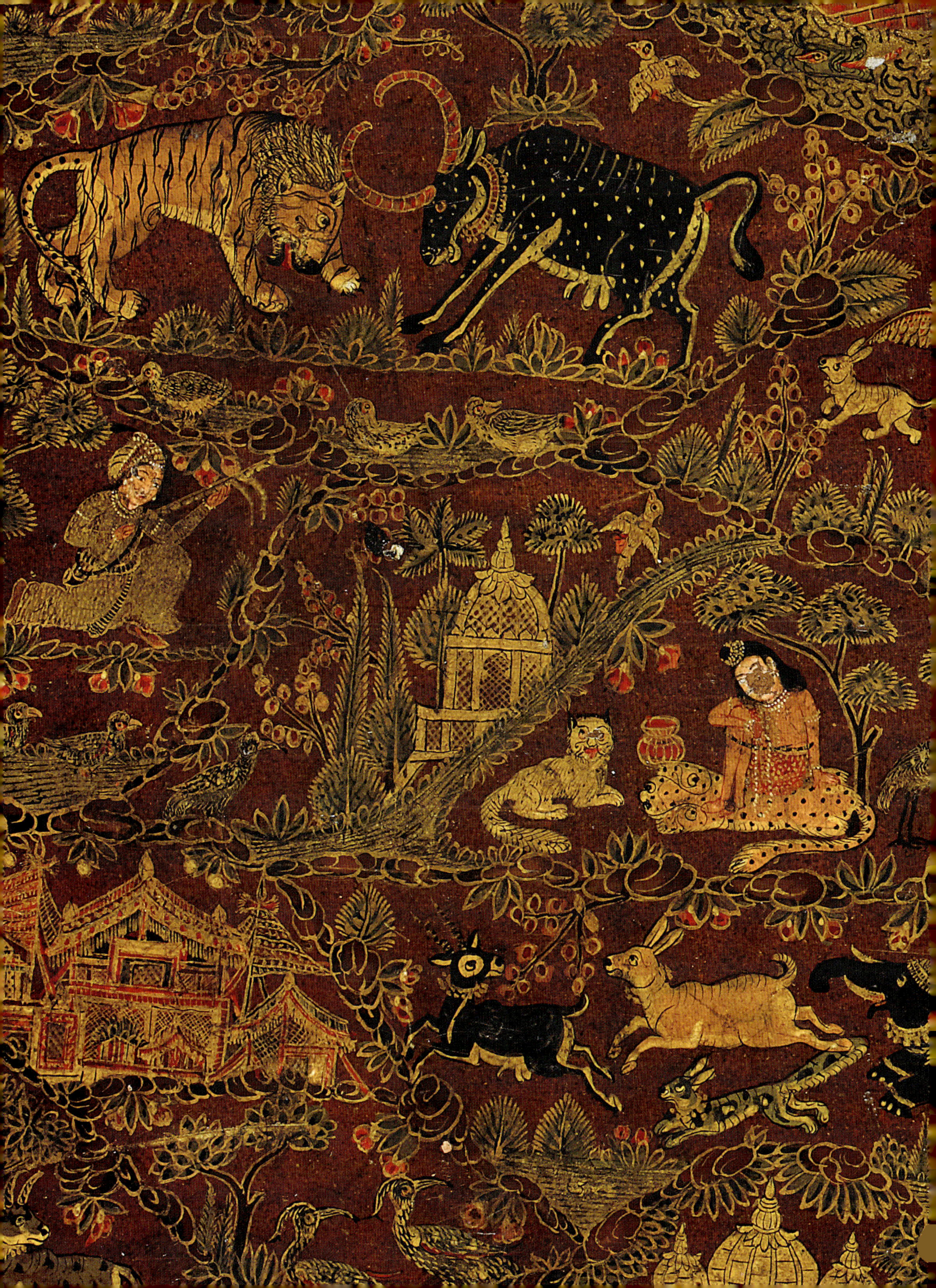

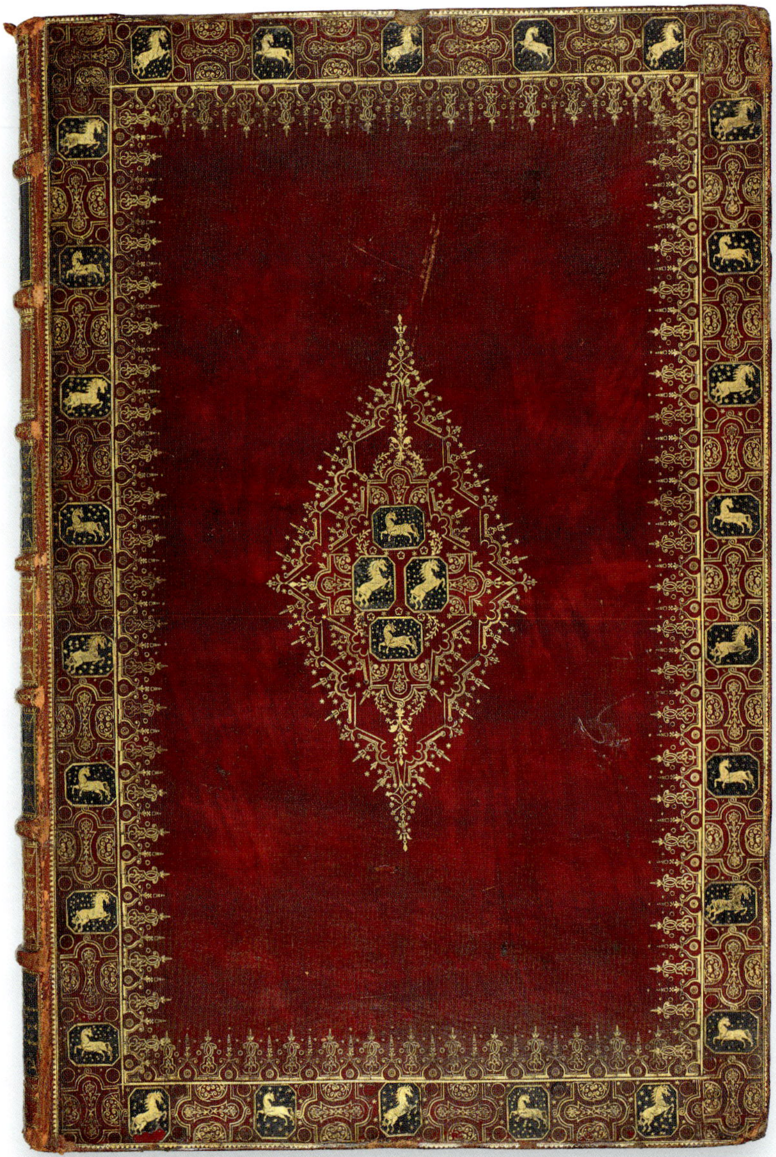

The bookseller and publisher, John Brindley, who bound this gold-tooled and onlaid red goatskin binding, held the appointment of bookbinder to Queen Caroline and Frederick, Prince of Wales. Brindley's specially commissioned bindings are particularly striking, and several found their way into the library of George III. The styles favoured by Brindley sometimes incorporated colourful and unusual elements (for example the horse motif shown here), and were often distinguished by decorative edges in the form of gilding, marbling and painting. The design comprizing a lozenge or diamond-shaped centrepiece made up with individual tools is similar to that found on bindings made for the Harleian Library (owned by the Earls of Oxford). The characteristic Harleian style arose when Thomas Elliott and Christopher Chapman bound at the library in the 1720s; Brindley was employed there in the 1730s.

England, *c.*1730s
542 x 370 x 60 mm (21.3 x 14.6 x 2.4 inches)

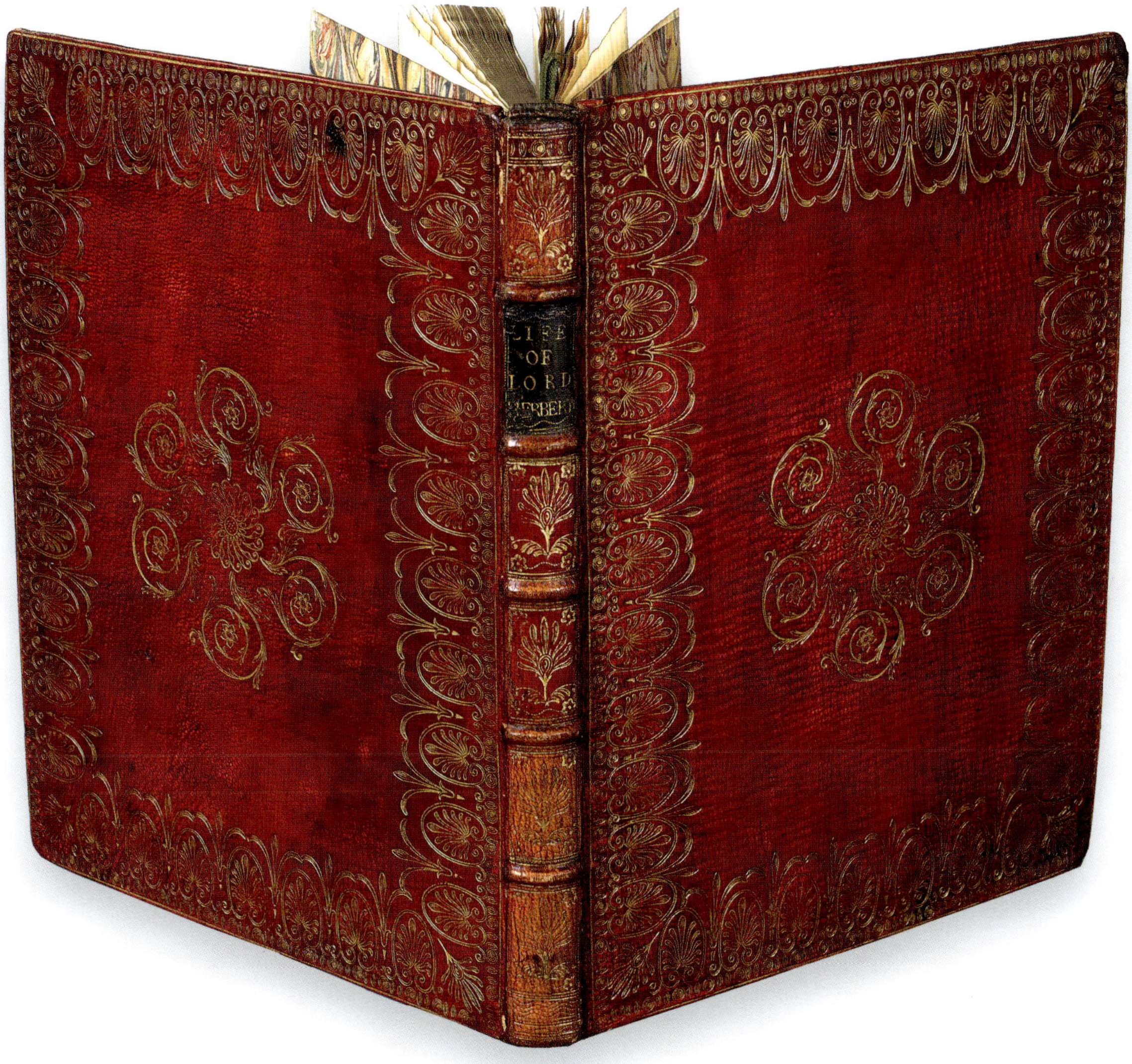

Bookbinders were not often in the forefront of artistic movements since it was expensive to have new-style decorative tools cut. Such a purchase was delayed until the binder could be sure the fashion was here to stay, and not just a passing fad. A notable English exception to this was neo-classicism. The binding historian, Howard M Nixon, explains that new motifs were used by Stuart and Adam as 'advertisements for the new style they were introducing into England' and they can be seen on this binding, for example in the decoration of the frame. This mid-eighteenth-century, lavishly gold-tooled red goatskin binding is likely to have been a gift from Lord Powis to George III: it covers a specially printed edition (produced by Horace Walpole's Strawberry Hill Press) of a manuscript owned by Powis relating to his ancestor, Lord Herbert. George III appreciated bookbinding as an art, even to the extent of establishing his own workshop in Buckingham House, so he would have been intrigued to see how this new style could be applied to a bookbinding.

London (?), mid-eighteenth century
235 x 190 x 20 mm (9.3 x 7.5 x 0.8 inches)
132.c.2

ALMANACS

Bookbinders sold certain categories of book ready bound because there was a constant market for them. Almanacs were particularly popular throughout Europe since they were bestsellers second only to the Bible, and contained interesting facts, medical advice, statistics of all sorts, as well as significant dates and religious festivals. Their attractive decoration made them excellent gifts, and ornamenting a pocket-sized volume was a relatively inexpensive process as a large motif could fill the entire cover. Some binders purchased engraved plaques that would ornament the cover in a single operation, but not all almanac bindings were produced along these 'industrial' lines. Some were rendered more individual by the addition of a family coat of arms, while others were bound in satin and embroidered with floral or pictorial scenes. A nineteenth-century Portuguese binding on an almanac is reproduced on p.91.

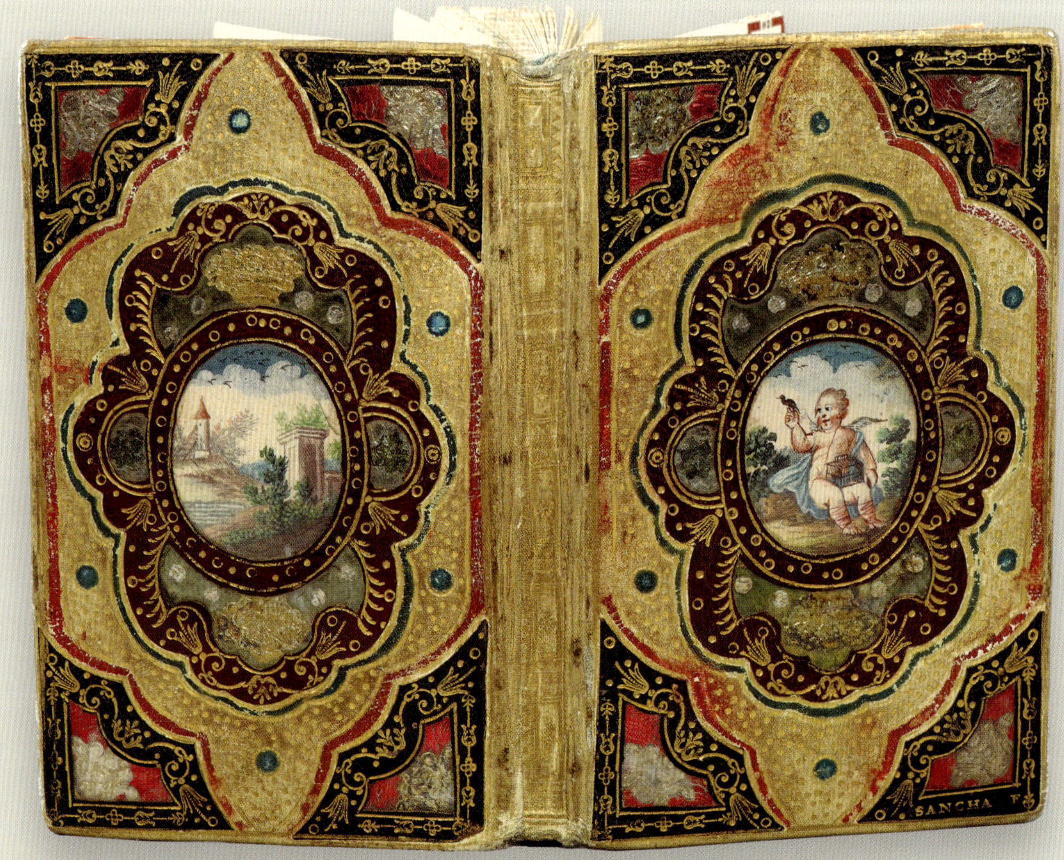

Spain, late eighteenth century
114 x 70 x 10 mm (4.5 x 2.8 x 0.4 inches)
Davis 660

LEFT Paris, 1792; 90 x 55 x 12 mm (3.5 x 2.2 x 0.5 inches); C.97.f.6/19

RIGHT Paris, 1787; 100 x 60 x 11 mm (3.9 x 2.4 x 0.4 inches); C.97.f.6/27

LYING FLAT Paris, 1786; 90 x 55 x 12 mm (3.5 x 2.2 x 0.5 inches); C.97.f.6/26

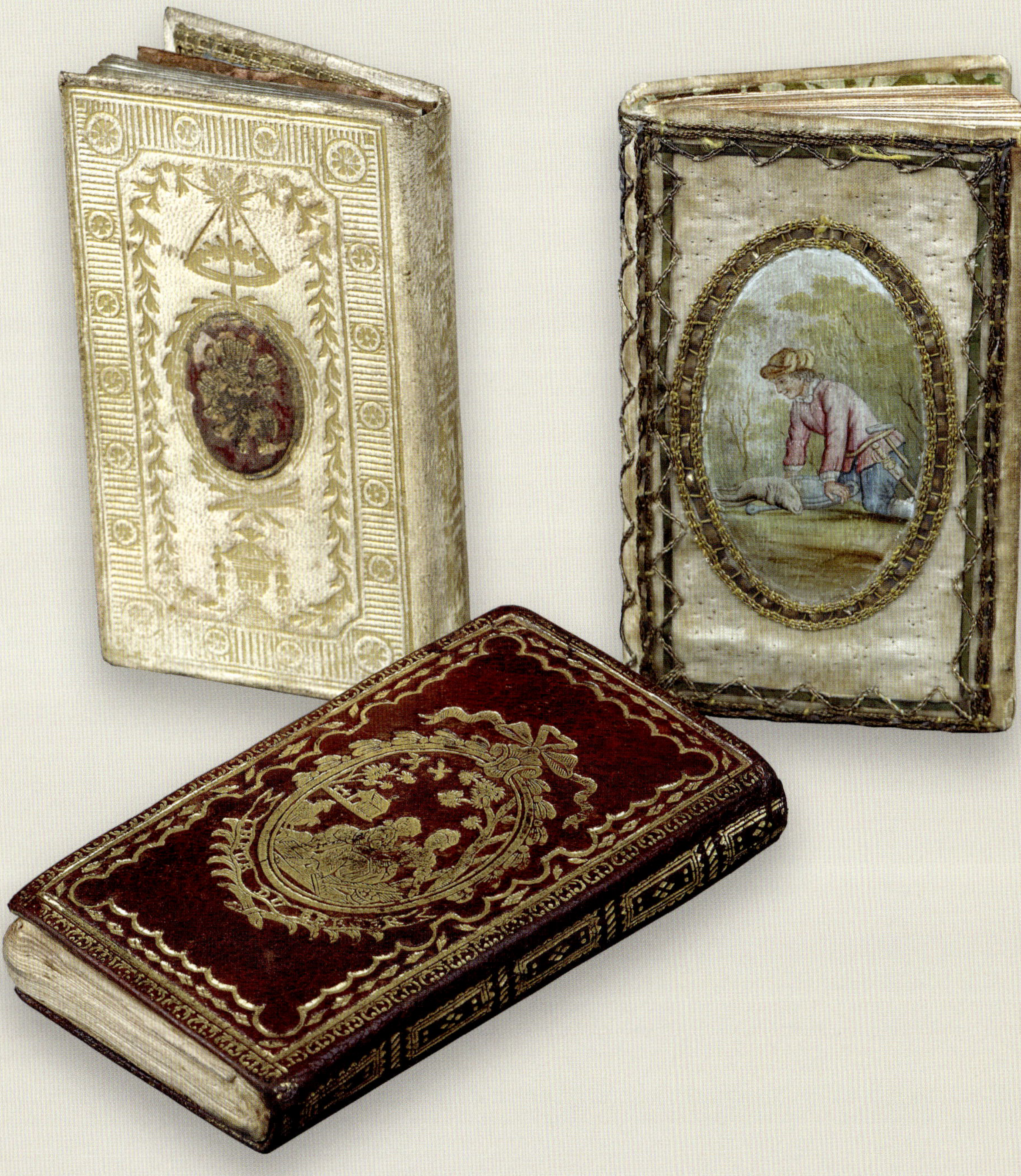

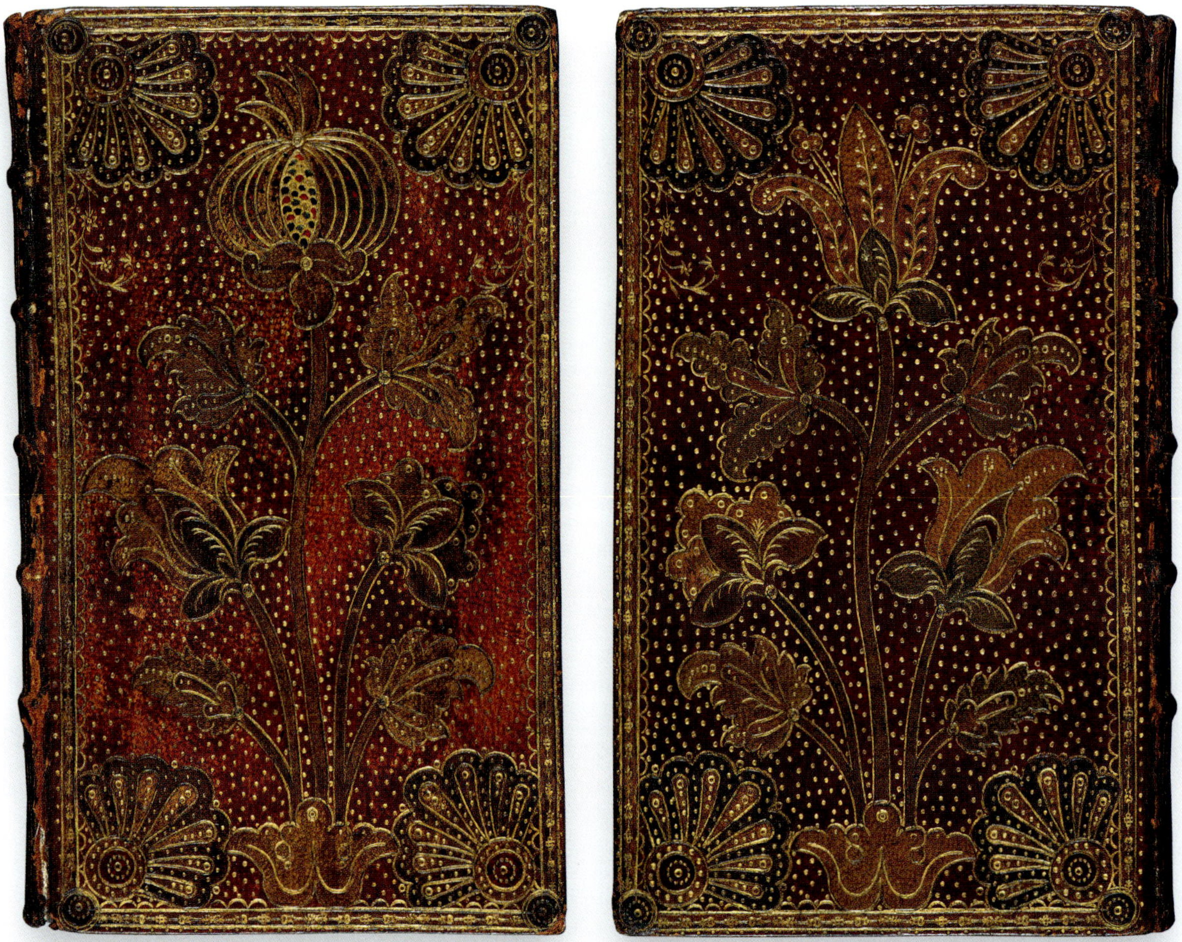

An inventory made after royal binder Antoine-Michel Padeloup's death in 1758 lists many finishing tools and equipment. The absence of forwarding tools suggests that Padeloup was predominantly a *doreur*, specializing in the decoration of book covers. The Padeloups were a famous Parisian bookbinding family, apparently comprising fifteen binders in five generations. Antoine-Michel (known as *le jeune*), who was responsible for this gold-tooled and onlaid red goatskin binding, was the most distinguished. His workshop not only bound books for King Louis XV, but also the aristocracy and important bibliophiles. The many illustrations included in *Beautiful Bookbindings* indicate that the eighteenth century was a golden age for the craft in France. Mirjam Foot describes the 'wonderful and fanciful mosaic effects', of which this is a characteristic example. The designs on the covers differ: the upper cover (now rather faded) displays an extraordinary plant, probably a pomegranate with seeds; the lower, a floral design. The pomegranate was a motif commonly found on bookbindings, and represented plenitude and hope. The bookmark and endleaves are of blue silk, and a small mirror has been affixed to the upper pastedown.

Paris, mid-eighteenth century
168 x 100 x 40 mm (6.6 x 3.9 x 1.6 inches)
C.48.b.8

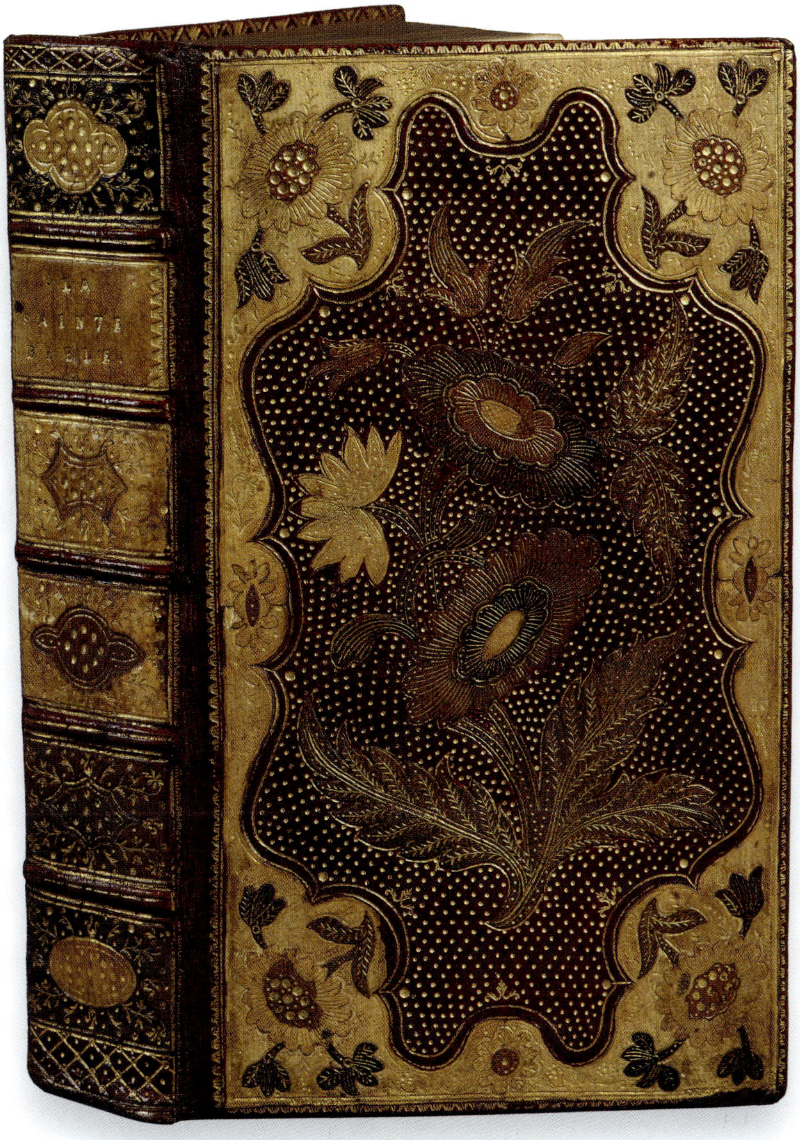

The flourishing market for bindings in France in the eighteenth century prompted the development of a variety of eye-catching designs, among them *dentelle* (a lace-like frame comprising small tools), *à la plaque rocaille* (see p.99) and mosaic, featuring colourful onlays. These were styles that all Parisian binders would be expected to master. This red goatskin binding is signed by Jean-Charles-Henri Lemonnier (sometimes known as Monnier), who has added his name in minute gold letters along the tail-edge of the border. The cover's bold floral and leaf onlays are characteristic of this striking mosaic style, with gold tooling restricted to simple motifs such as dots and curves. Lemonnier (d.1782) came from a distinguished binding family who worked extensively for the nobility, most notably Louis-Philippe, the Duc D'Orléans, who was not alone in holding him in high regard: the writer René-Martin Dudin consulted Lemonnier when compiling his *L'art du relieur doreur des livres* in 1772.

Paris, mid-eighteenth century
165 x 95 x 35 mm (6.5 x 3.7 x 1.4 inches)
C.72.a.9

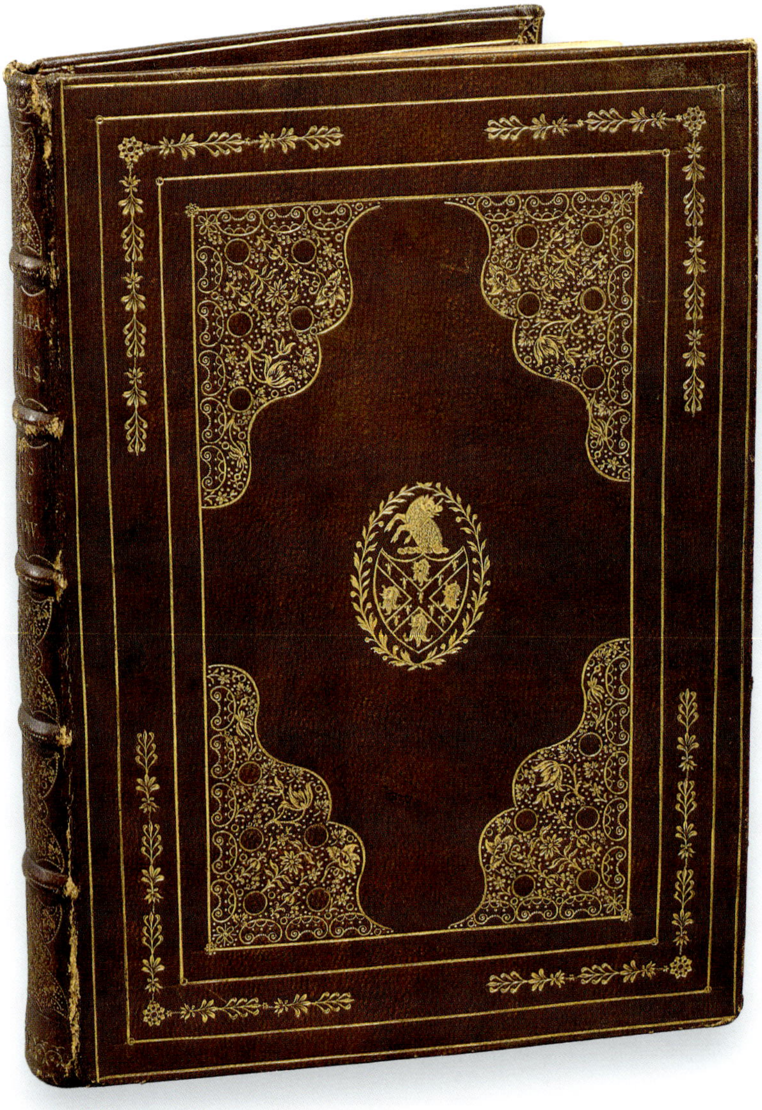

Descriptions of Roger Payne (d.1797), who was arguably the most famous of English bookbinders, often dwell on two of his particular traits: his skilful tooling and his fondness for barley beer. We have little actual proof of the latter beyond his accounts – which include sums for alcohol – and hearsay. This is reinforced by an etching made after Payne's death depicting him as an unkempt, gaunt figure in a dilapidated workshop, and a humorous poem praising alcohol written by Payne himself. We do know that he was not robust, for binding historian Mirjam Foot has described bills and letters that refer to his ill health, but the cause of this is not known. The bindings do not betray signs of infirmity and Payne was employed by the leading bibliophiles of the day, whose standards were exacting. One such was the Reverend Clayton Mordaunt Cracherode, whose coat of arms can be seen here on this gold-tooled, olive green (faded to brown) goatskin binding. Payne clearly took pride in his work, selecting the most suitable leathers and devising innovative designs. The small, delicate motifs he favoured were much imitated. His contemporaries, and later collectors, considered him the best of the English bookbinders.

London, late eighteenth century
210 x 150 x 25 mm (8.3 x 6 x 1 inches)
I.A.24382

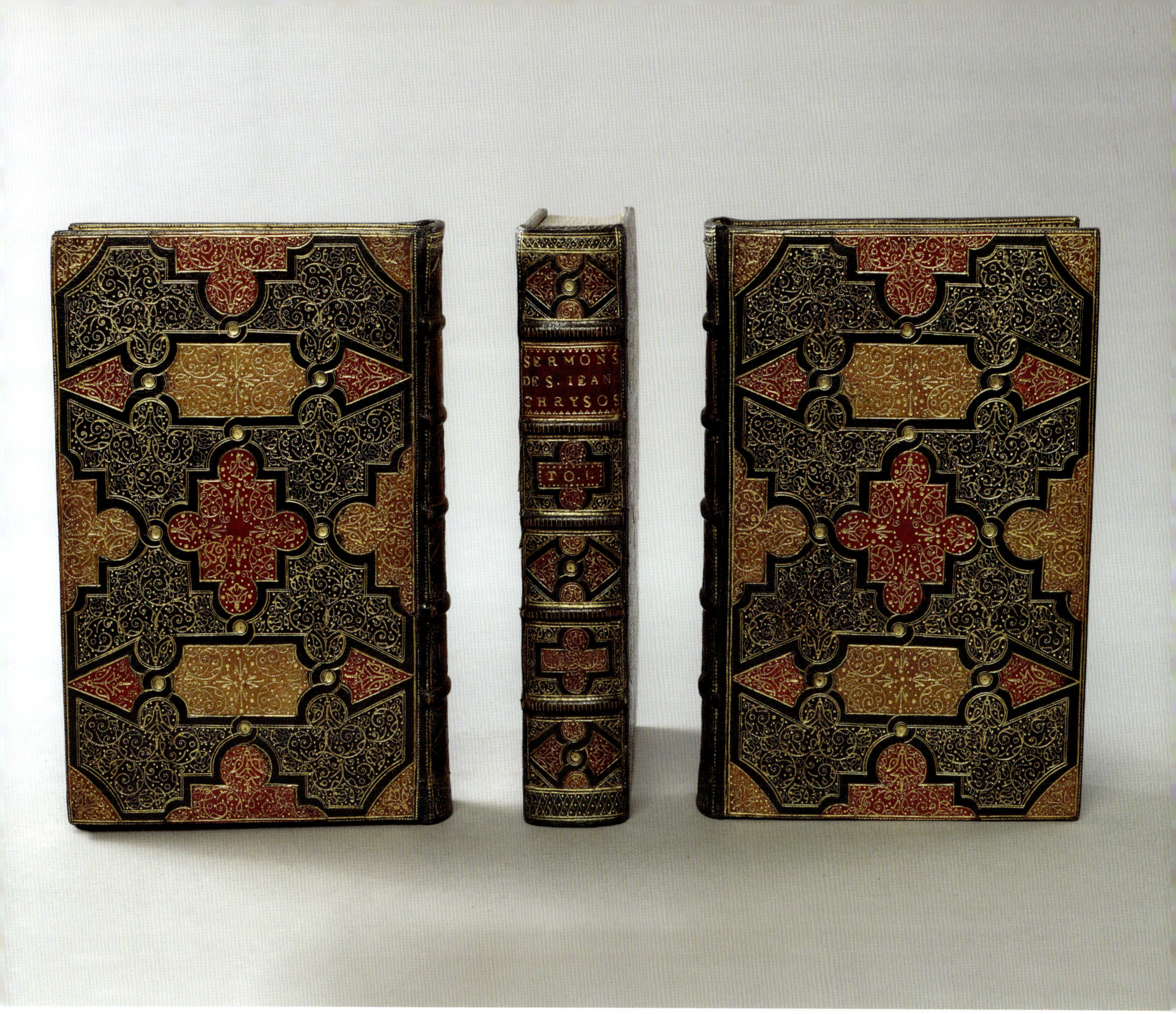

The set of gold-tooled black goatskin bindings above demonstrates the sophisticated nature of the craft in Paris. Antoine-Michel Padeloup (1685–1758), appointed royal binder to Louis XV in 1733, may have worked on this three-volume devotional work. It features several fashionable styles, including mosaic (the application of coloured onlays in a regular pattern), fanfare (compartments formed by a ribbon comprising a single outline on one side and a double outline on the other) and *pointillé* (motifs with dotted outlines). These types of decoration, combined with coloured and elaborately worked endbands, pink silk bookmarkers, floral paper pastedowns and gilt and marbled edges, involved an extremely labour-intensive process, and the binding would have been very costly.

Paris, mid-eighteenth century
195 x 125 x 36 mm (7.7 x 4.9 x 1.4 inches)
Davis 533

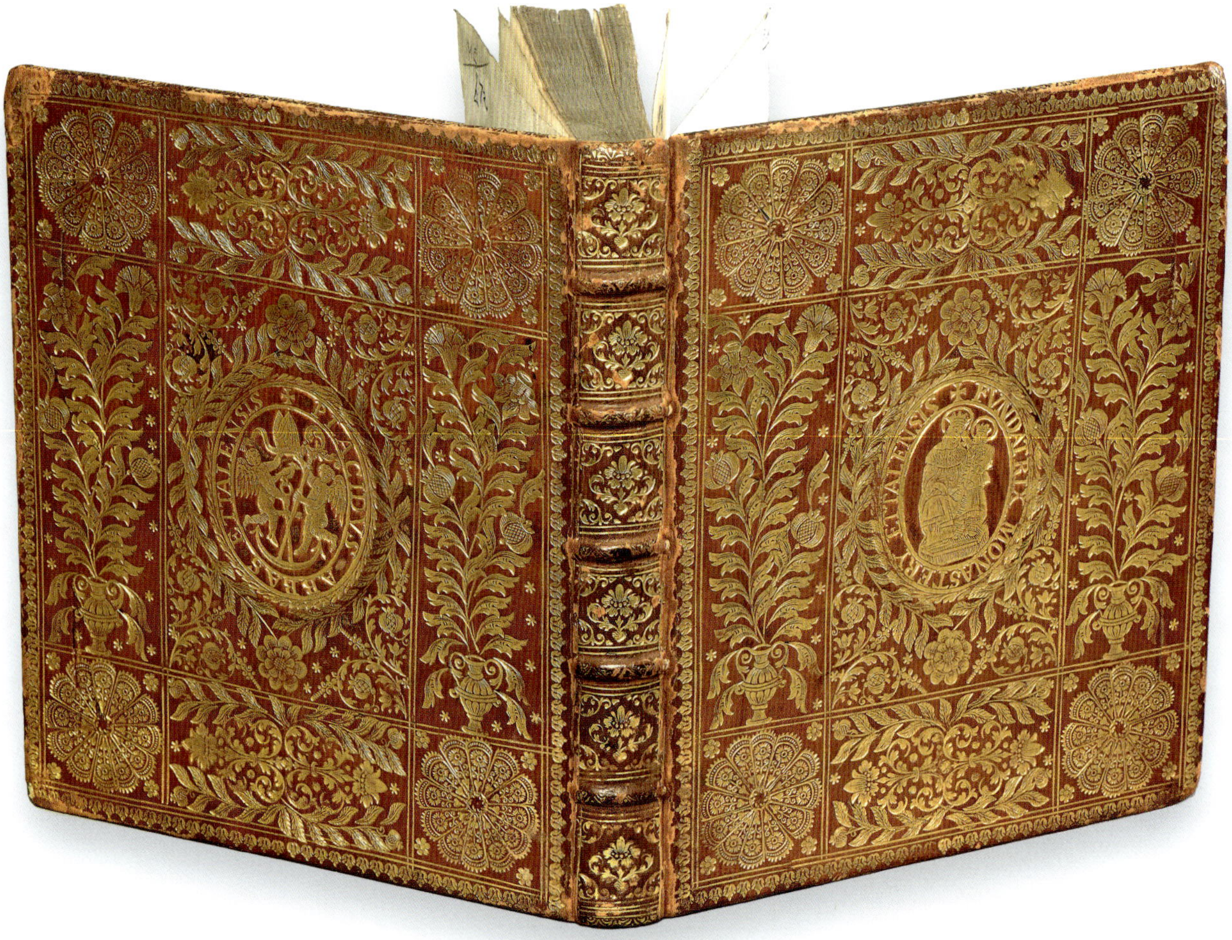

The emblems and arms on the covers of this German, brown calf binding reveal it to have been commissioned by Placidus Seitz II, who was abbot of the Benedictine monastery at Ettal, Bavaria, from 1709 to 1736. Seitz inaugurated a golden age in the monastery's history, and this extravagantly gold-tooled binding almost literally reflects his achievement. The corner fan motifs recall Italian and Spanish bindings, while the leaf and floral motifs evoke the so-called German peasant style ('Bauern Einbände') often found on painted parchment (see p.98). The monastery's binder at this time was Brother Gregory, formerly known as Ignaz Michael Kuen (1690–1737), a trained bookbinder from Tyrnau (now in Slovenia, then in Hungary).

Ettal, Germany, *c.*1710–30
202 x 170 x 28 mm (8 x 6.7 x 1.1 inches)
Davis 643

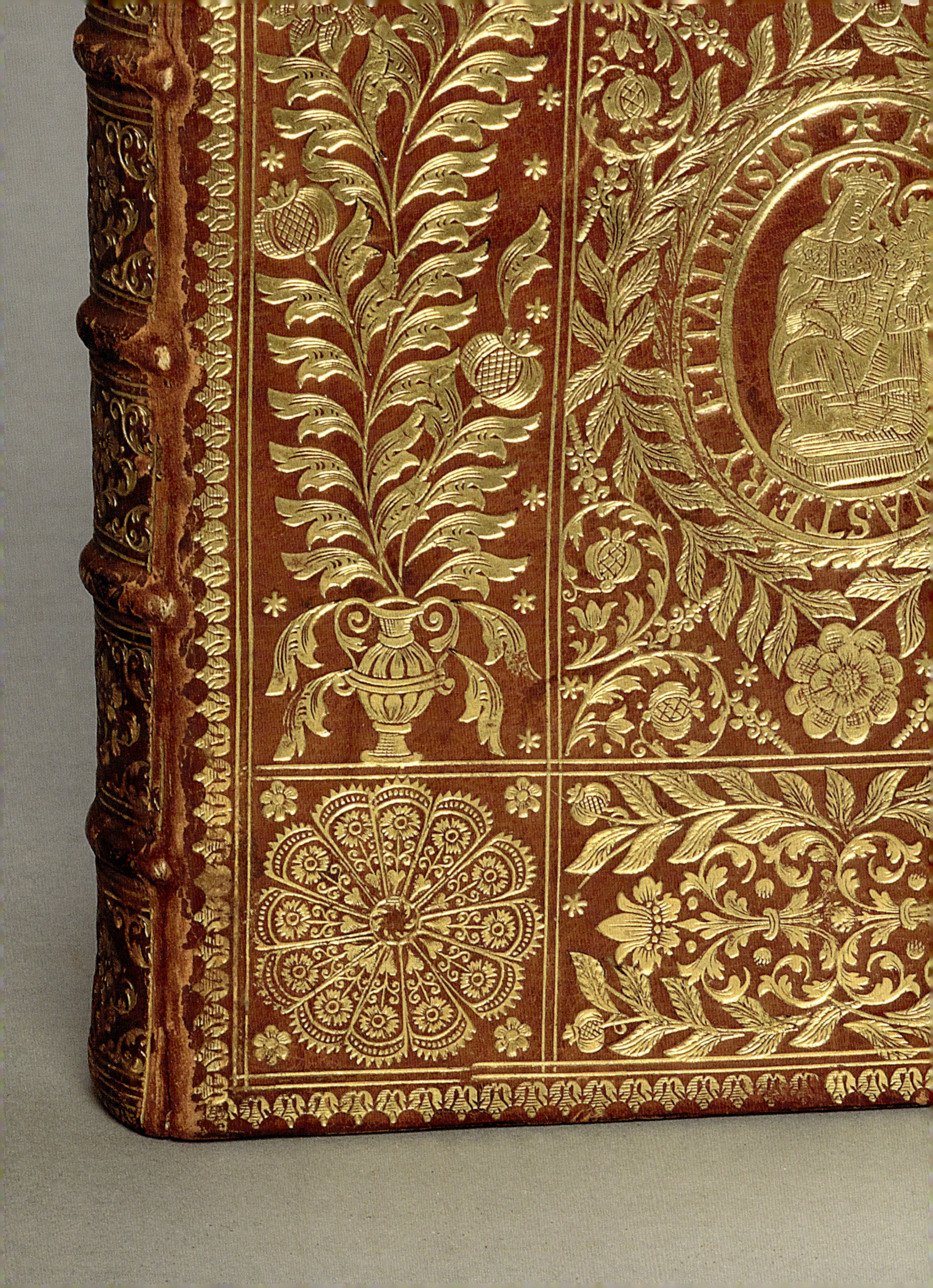

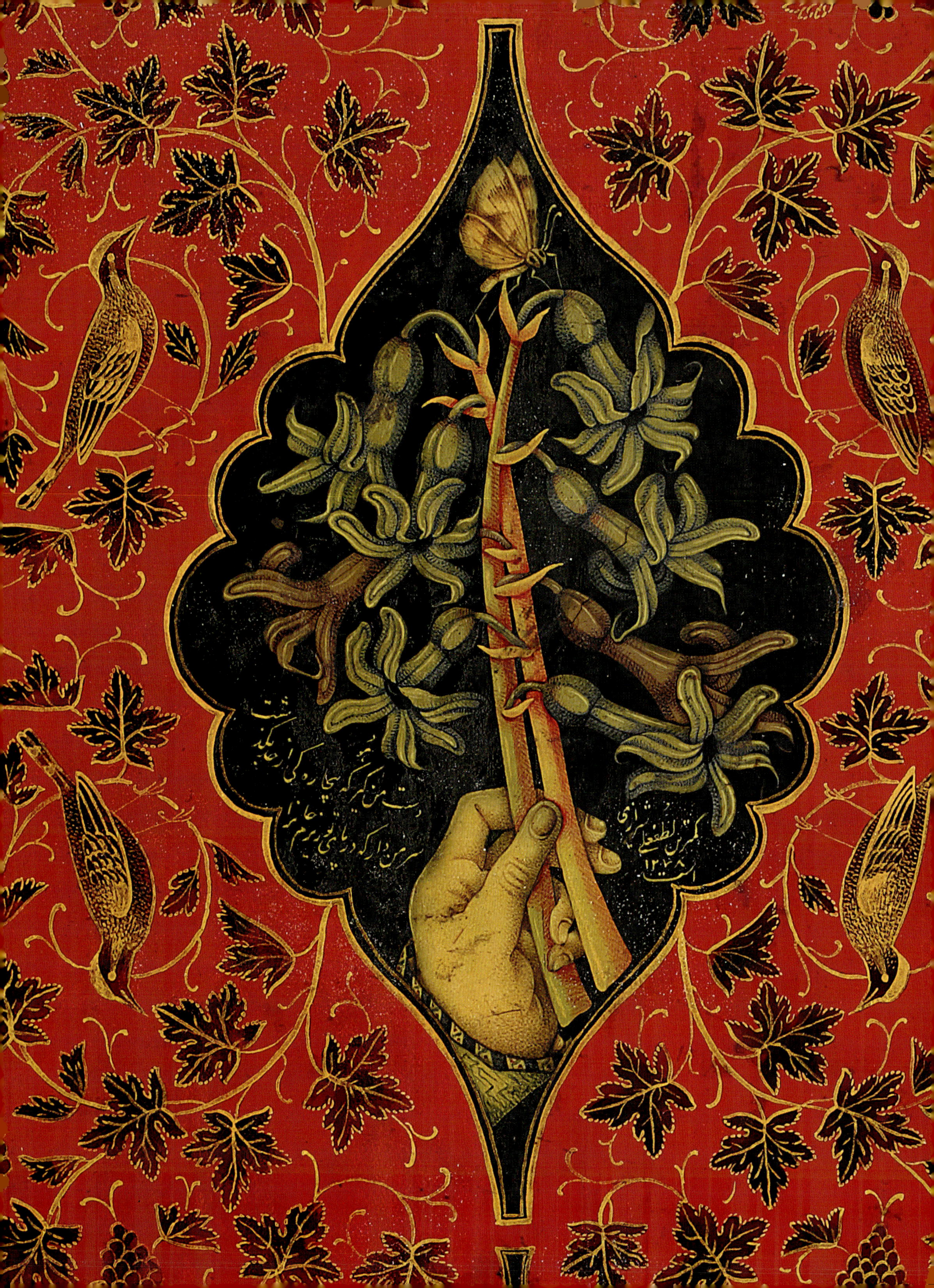
دست من گیر که بیچارگی از حد بگذشت
سر من دار که در پای تو ریزم جان را
کمترین لطفعلی شیرازی
۱۲۷۸

CHAPTER 5

Nineteenth Century

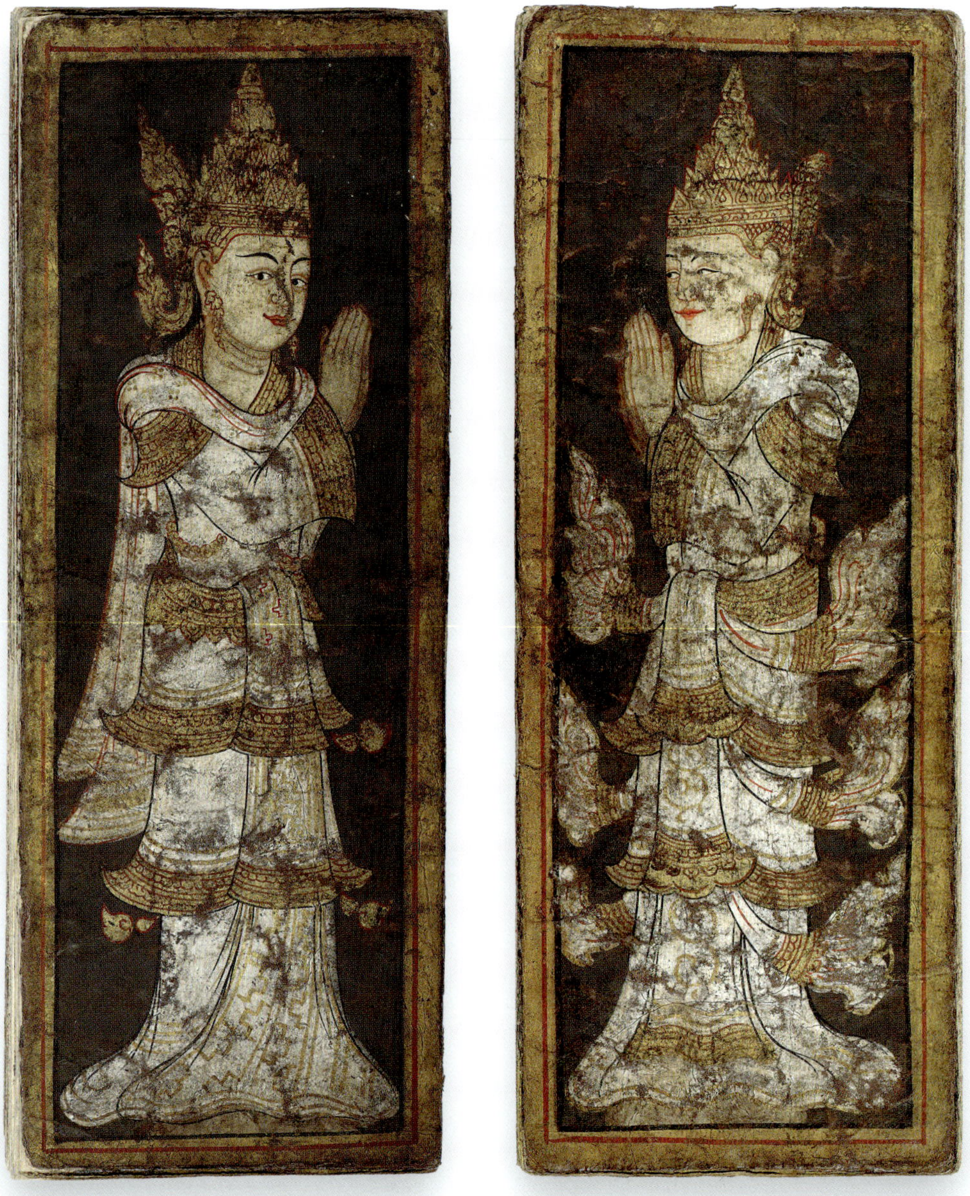

These painted covers protect one of the earliest surviving illustrated manuscripts from Burma, probably produced in the early 1800s. Folded manuscripts called 'Parabaik' were common to Burma, Cambodia, Laos and Thailand, and required strong paper made of bamboo, bark, straw or palm-leaf fibre. The covers were decorated by professional manuscript painters, and featured brilliant colours with gold embellishments frequently depicting a god, a king or the wealthy court official who commissioned the work. The status of the figure in white shown here would be clear to the Burmese reader, since the strict sumptuary laws of the region were rigidly enforced, and the three-tiered costume would have been reserved for those of the highest status.

Burma, early nineteenth century
502 x 199 x 48 mm (19.8 x 7.8 x 1.9 inches)
Or.14297

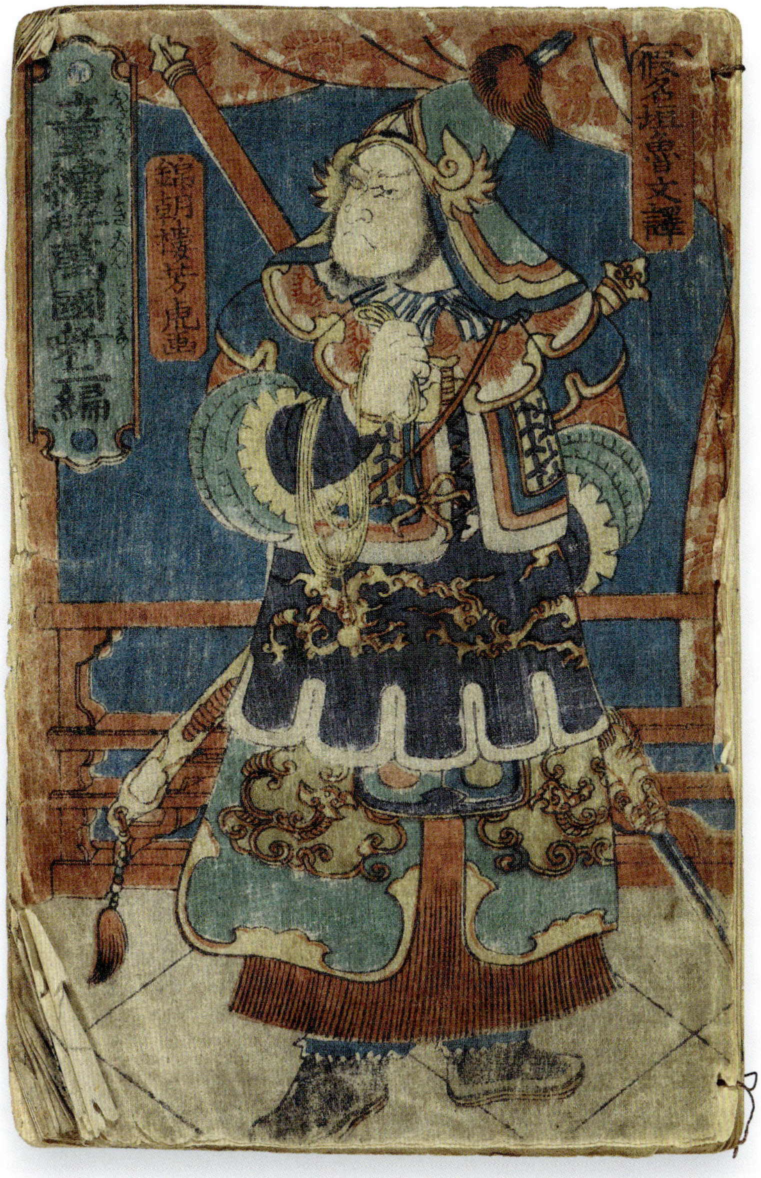

Japanese popular fiction of the nineteenth century is often distinguished by the lively and attractive wood-blocked paper covers which adorned the text. Famous artists were responsible for some of the designs, as with this example by Utagawa Yoshitora (fl.1850–1880) a proponent of *ukiyo-e*, which was the principal artistic genre for woodblock printing. Most Japanese people would have struggled to afford a print by this master, but they were able to purchase a book featuring his designs on the mass-produced covers. The author of this particular children's book, Kanagaki Robun (1829–94), was known for his humorous writings and he has even been credited with the creation of the first 'manga'-style magazine in 1874. Paper is an inexpensive bindings medium and is therefore common in both the East and West, though the method of attaching the pages differs. The sewing shown here is visible (as opposed to the more concealed Western style), passing along the outside of the right edge, threading through pierced holes and passing across the spine.

Japan, *c.*1860
177 x 117 x17 mm (7 x 4.6 x 0.7 inches)
ORB .30/3393

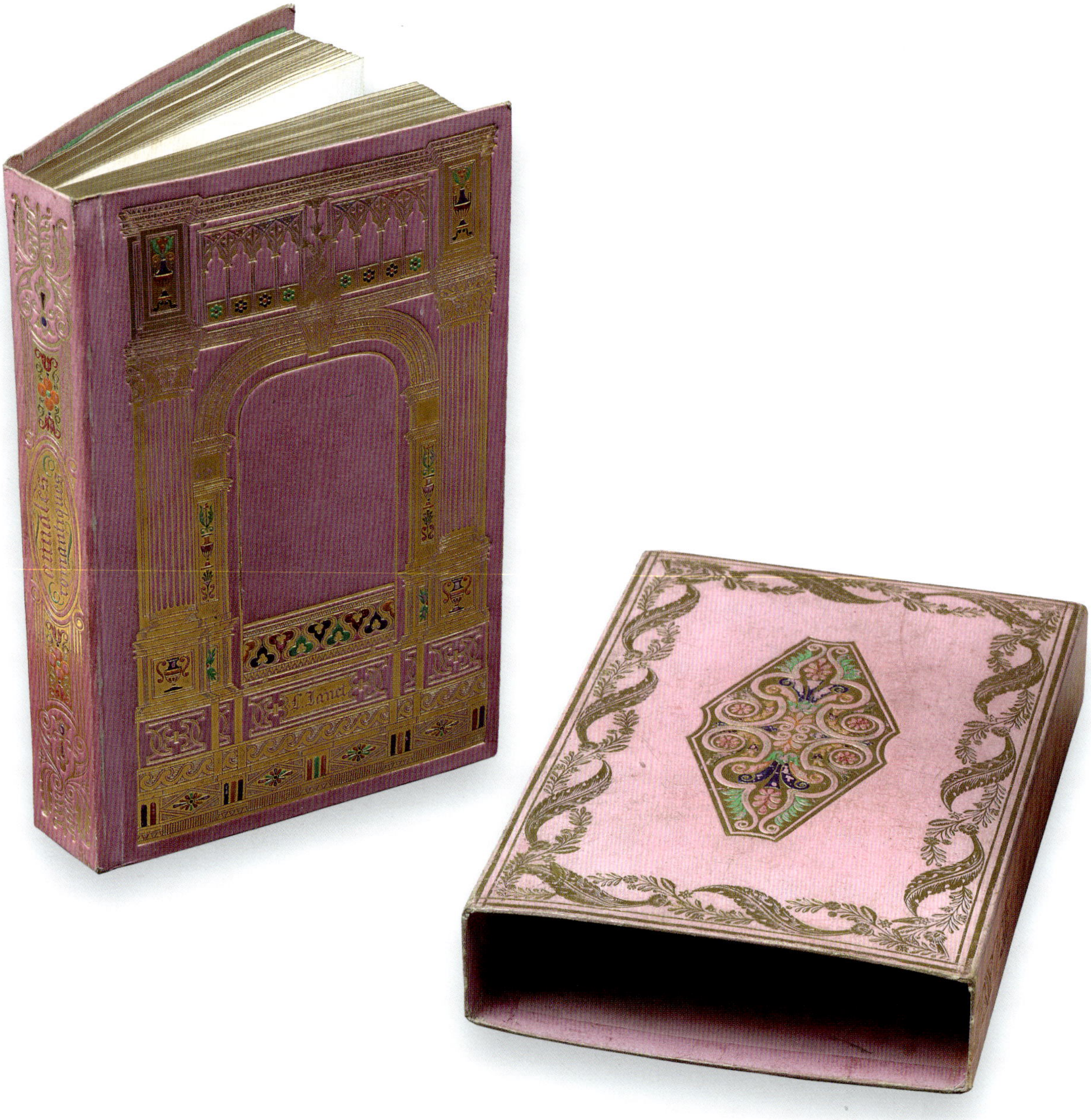

This small, pink paper gold-blocked binding by Louis Janet reflects the contemporary taste for the Gothic. The inclusion of colour lightens the tone and would have made the text, complete with its decorative slipcase, a charming present. The Janet establishment in Paris was a family concern that existed from 1776 to the 1850s. Louis Janet (1788–1840) specialized in the production of 'keepsakes', ready bound texts that could be given as gifts. Many decorative techniques were employed, including painting on glass and blocking on velvet. The Janet firm thrived under Louis, as confirmed in *Le Bazar Parisien*, a journal of 1822. It relates how the establishment was distinguished by its involvement in the book trade, the beautiful bindings produced by its workshops and the multitude of almanacs and Christmas gift books with which it constantly supplied not only France but other countries.

Paris, early nineteenth century
Book 145 x 86 x 24 mm (5.7 x 3.4 x 0.9 inches)
Case 148 x 95 x 25 mm (5.8 x 3.7 x 1 inches)
C.150.h.10

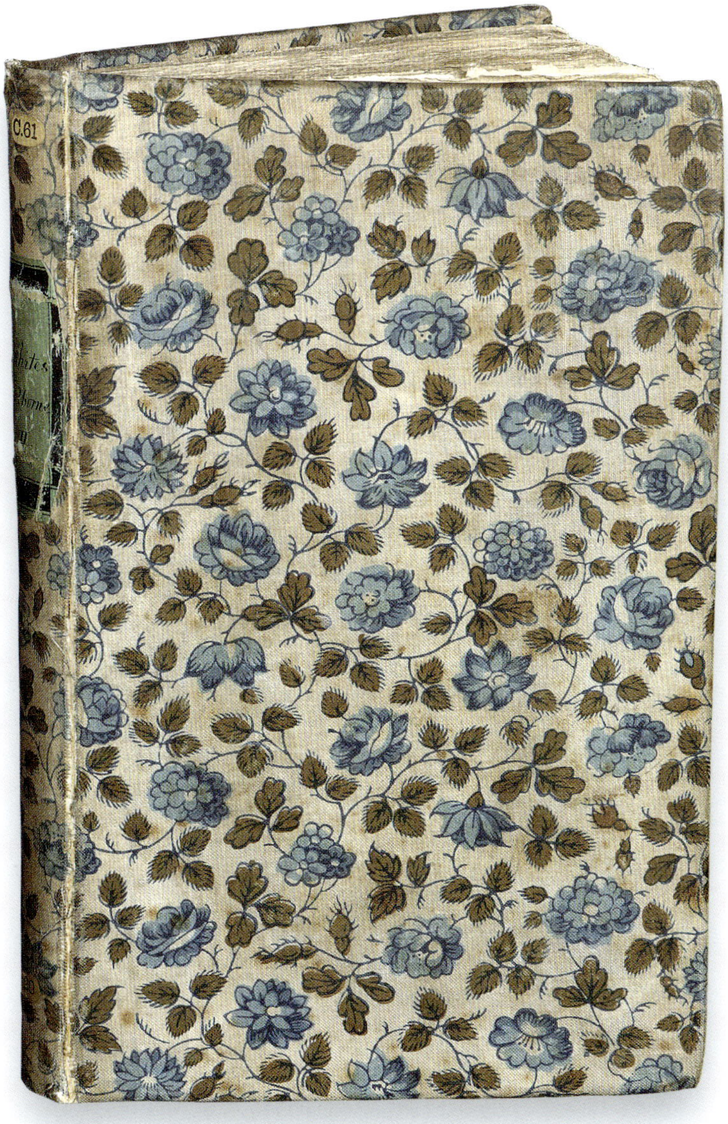

Some collectors cared for their books in idiosyncratic ways, notably the poet Robert Southey (1774–1843). His son described his collection of 'all those books of lesser value, which had become ragged and dirty … bound in coloured cotton prints … it being impossible to afford the cost of having so many [an estimated 1200 to 1400] put into better bindings'. The floral fabric and green paper label seen here would have been applied by one of Southey's five daughters or their friends. Southey's older parchment-bound books were spruced up with a layer of coloured paint and gold lettering. Don't try this at home!

England, early nineteenth century
222 x 141 x 25 mm (8.7 x 5.5 x 1 inches)
C.61.b.20

MAME BINDINGS

As with many craft-based processes, the nineteenth century saw the mechanization of bookbinding in western Europe. Some firms came to resemble factories, and this was particularly true of the family business of Mame in Tours, France, which was also known for its publishing and printing activities. Traditional craft bindings continued to be produced, but most workers (including women) were employed in the mass production of case bindings, in which the text block was made separately from the cloth or cardboard covers and attached by means of endleaves and lining material. This was an inexpensive but colourful format, with gilt, coloured or glazed paper used in combination with lithographic prints to make an immediate visual impact. Such bindings have been likened to chocolate boxes and sweet wrappers, but they were popular enough, often being used for such items as Sunday school prize books. Unusually for the time, Alfred Mame (1811–1893) instituted pensions and profit-sharing schemes for his workers.

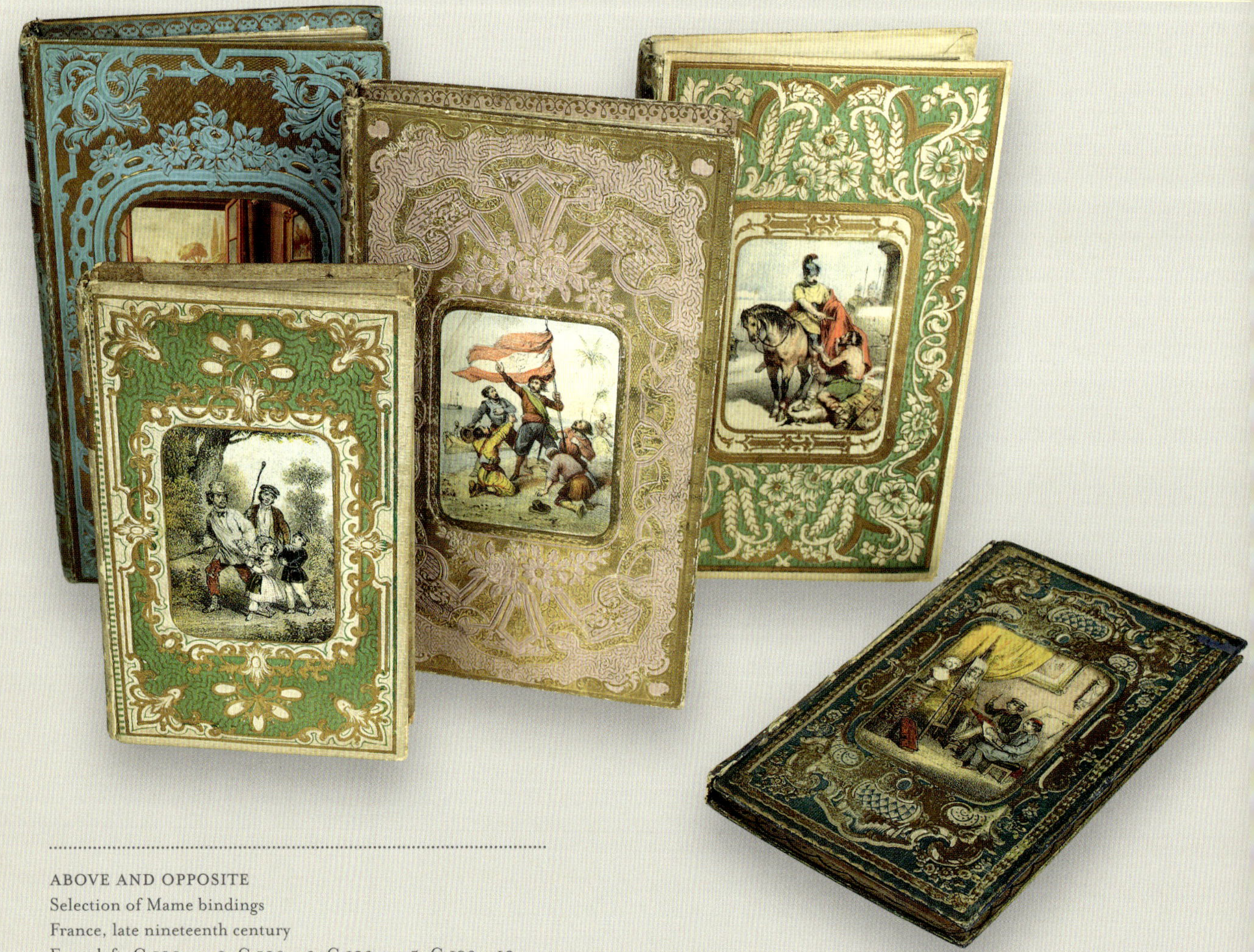

ABOVE AND OPPOSITE
Selection of Mame bindings
France, late nineteenth century
From left: C.109.aaa.3; C.109.a.9; C.109.aaa.5; C.129.c.10; C.109.e.4

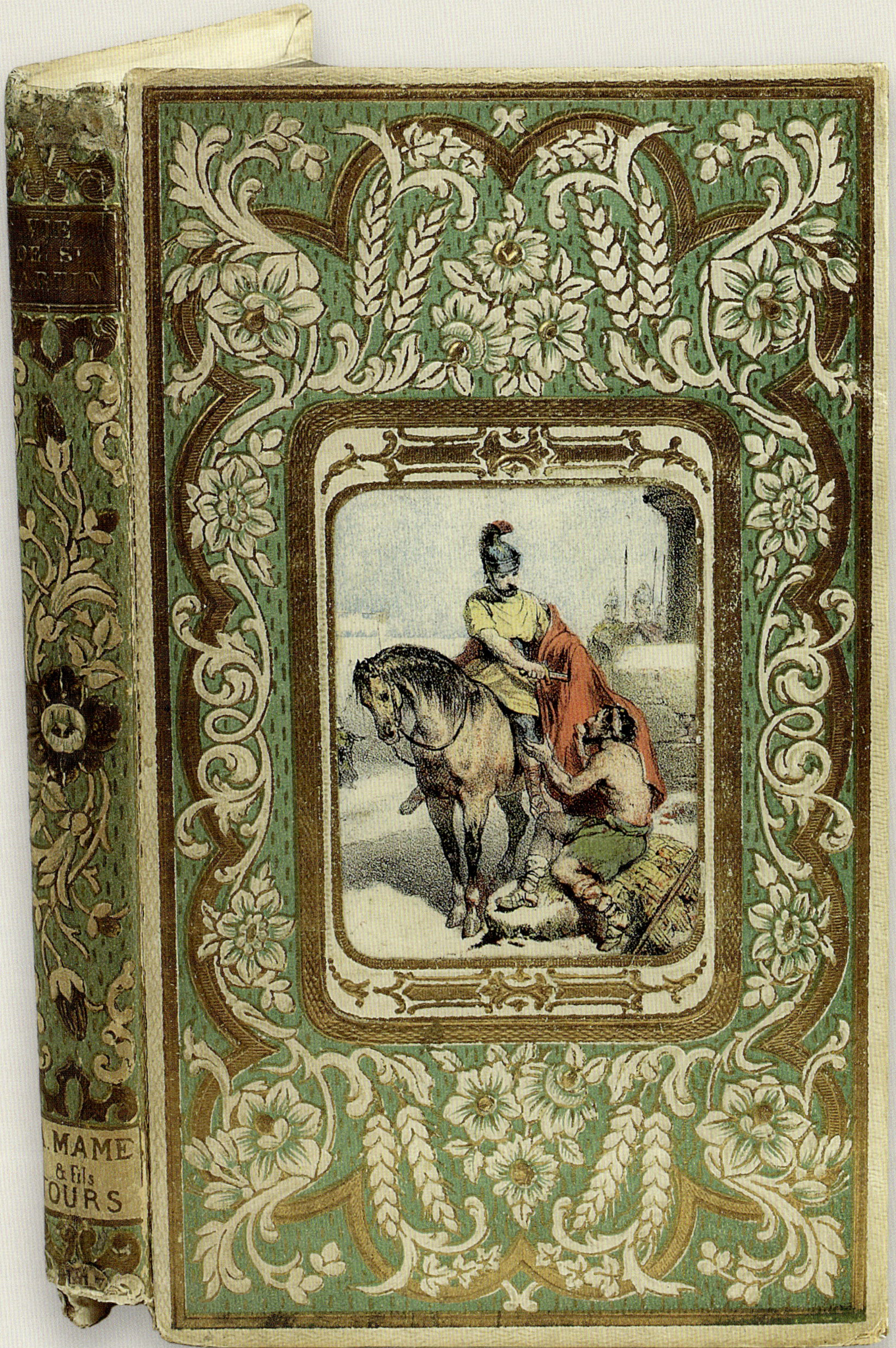
MAME
& fils

The nineteenth century gradually saw the emergence of binding designs that reflected the contents of the book, although traditional abstract or retrospective styles remained popular. An example is this gold-blocked, brown calf binding of *Don Quijote* by Alphonse Simier, which shows the bust of a knight surrounded by cathedral-style motifs. The decoration, although elaborate, was achieved relatively quickly and cheaply, due to the use of engraved plaques (which can be employed to cover the whole space available when applied skilfully). The Simier workshop was famous throughout Europe, partly because its founder, René Simier (1772–1843), could turn his hand to different styles. He established his business in Paris in 1798, where his subsequent work found favour with the Emperor Napoleon and the Bourbon Kings, and he received the title 'Relieur du roi', which was passed on to his son, Alphonse. Both binders publicized the royal connection in the form of their trade signature, seen here at the foot of the spine (a French custom of the period). In the unlikely event that the viewer overlooked this, a printed trade ticket was pasted to the endleaf inside.

Paris, *c.*1827
126 x 82 x 33 mm (5 x 3.2 x 1.3 inches)
Davis 575

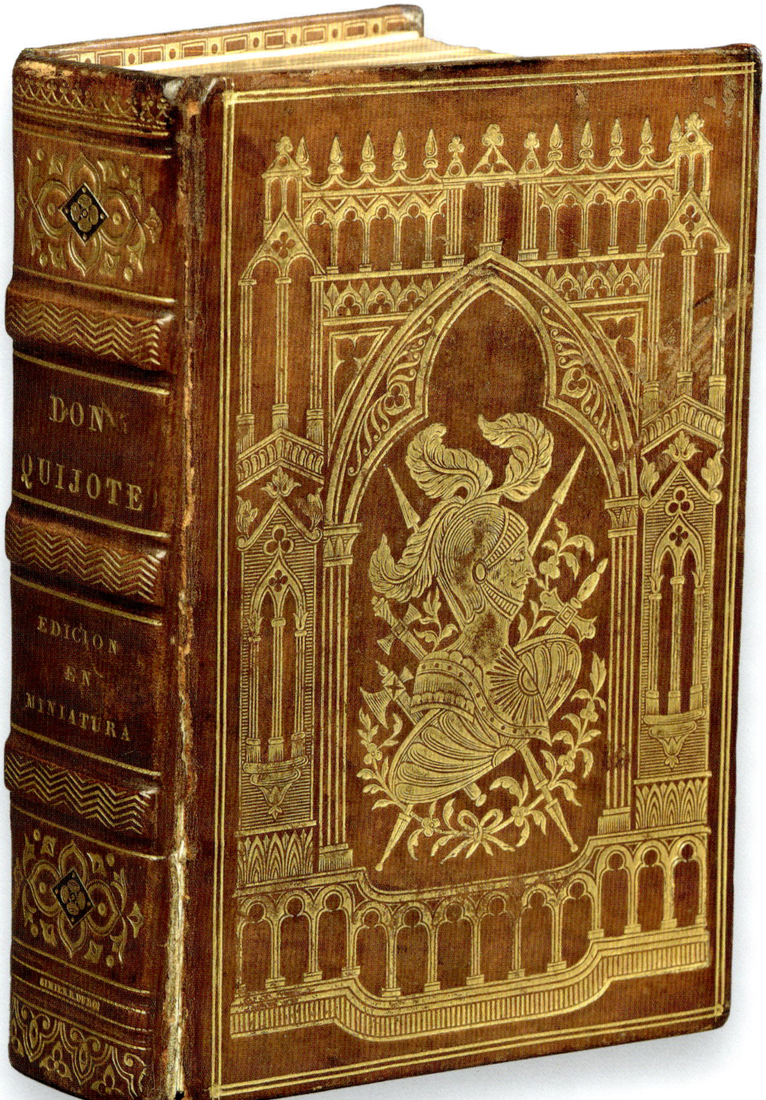

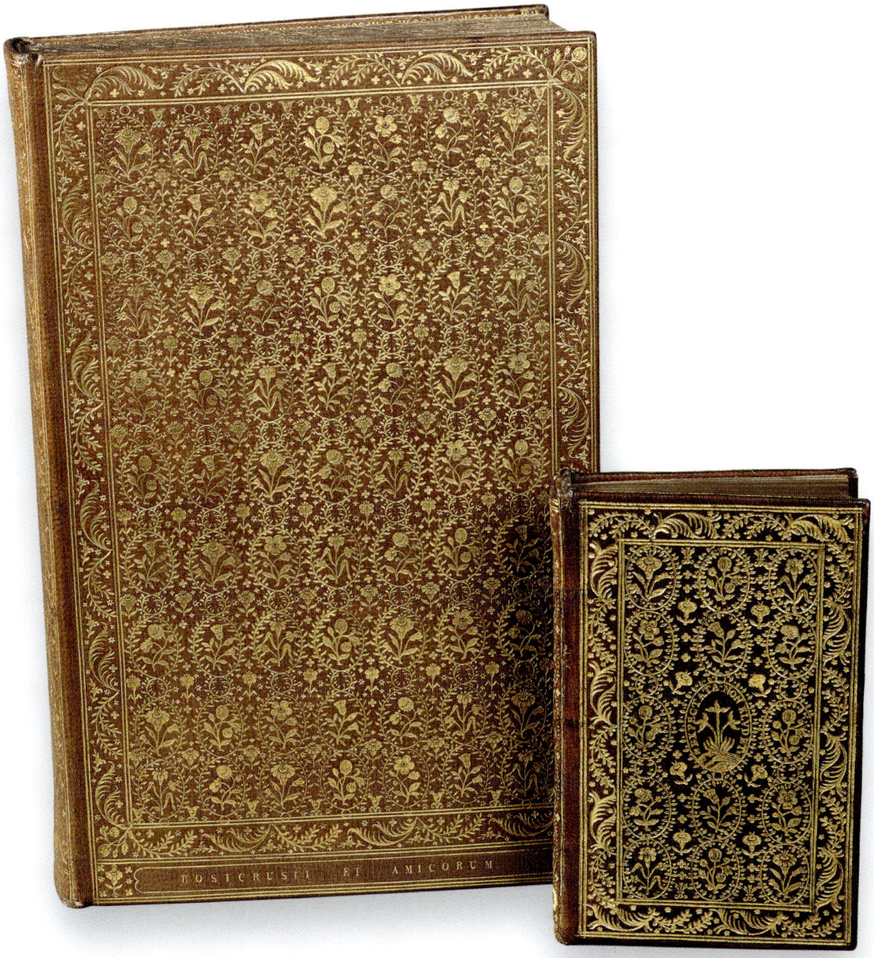

Throughout the nineteenth century, wealthy French and British bibliophiles were attracted to imitations of historic binding styles, particularly those of sixteenth-century France. Such bindings were certainly technically accomplished but – inevitably – they lacked the vitality of the original designs. The smaller binding depicted here was probably made in France as part of a travelling library for Pietro Duodo (1555–1611), Venetian ambassador to Henri IV. All the books were gold-tooled in the same way with Duodo's emblem and motto, 'Expectata non eludet' ('She whom I await with longing will not elude me'), but in different coloured goatskin according to the subject of the text. Theology, philosophy, law and history were in red goatskin, medicine and botany in citron and literature in olive (as seen here).

The bland appearance of the larger, nineteenth-century English work is not due to poor craftsmanship, for the binder, Charles Lewis (1786–1836), was acknowledged as the best London binder of his day. His natural skill responded to two stimuli: the vibrancy of the London trade fuelled by the many knowledgeable book collectors; and the influence of two figures, his bookbinder father, Johann Ludwig, and his apprentice master, Henry Walter. Both were Germans who emigrated to England to take advantage of the flourishing market. Lewis's large workshop was patronized by the most demanding collectors, including the second Earl Spencer. The author, Brunet, had this copy of his book specially bound for Spencer's librarian, Thomas Frognall Dibdin. The motto towards the tail edge of the front cover ('Rosicrucius et amicorum') alludes to Dibdin's *Bibliomania*, in which Dibdin himself appears under the soubriquet Rosicruscius, 'an ardent and indefatigable book-forager'.

ABOVE RIGHT France, late sixteenth century
127 x 78 x 35 mm (5 x 3.1 x 1.4 inches)
C.19.a.18

ABOVE LEFT London, early nineteenth century
232 x 149 x 29 mm (9.1 x 5.9 x 1.1 inches)
C.151.f.3

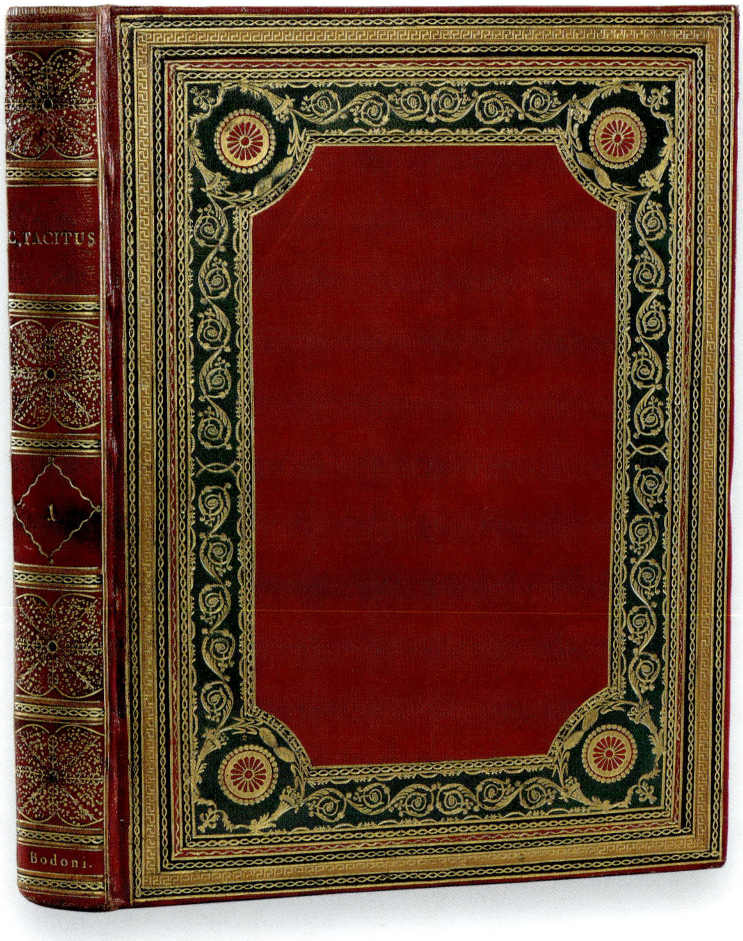

ABOVE There was no early tradition of secular books in Russian territories, although Treasure bindings often adorned the Bibles used in churches. New styles of bindings, influenced by those of western Europe, finally began to appear in the eighteenth century, further encouraged by the monarchy, notably Tsar Peter I (d.1725) and Catherine the Great (d.1796). This onlaid and gold-tooled red goatskin binding demonstrates that the western European taste for neo-classical bindings was firmly established in Russia by the early nineteenth century. Decorative binding styles were not confined by national borders. The work is unsigned, but Zaidler of St Petersburg produced bindings in a similar style, as did Staggemeier and Welcher in London, Georg Friedrich Krauss of Vienna and F W Standlander in Stockholm.

St Petersburg (?), early nineteenth century
331 x 253 x 40 mm (13 x 10 x 1.6 inches)
Davis 678–700

OPPOSITE George Mullen (d.1821) owned one of the most prestigious and successful binding workshops in Ireland. He fulfilled commissions from many notable institutions and individuals, including Trinity College, Dublin, and the Lord Lieutenant of Ireland. This large, red goatskin binding has been tooled in gold and blind to a Cathedral design (a retrospective style inspired by church Gothic), which was popular in Britain and France from 1810 to 1840. Unusually, the binder's signature has been tooled in gold on the fore-edge of the upper board.

Dublin, early nineteenth century
460 x 275 x 45 mm (18.1 x 10.8 x 1.8 inches)
C.156.i.2

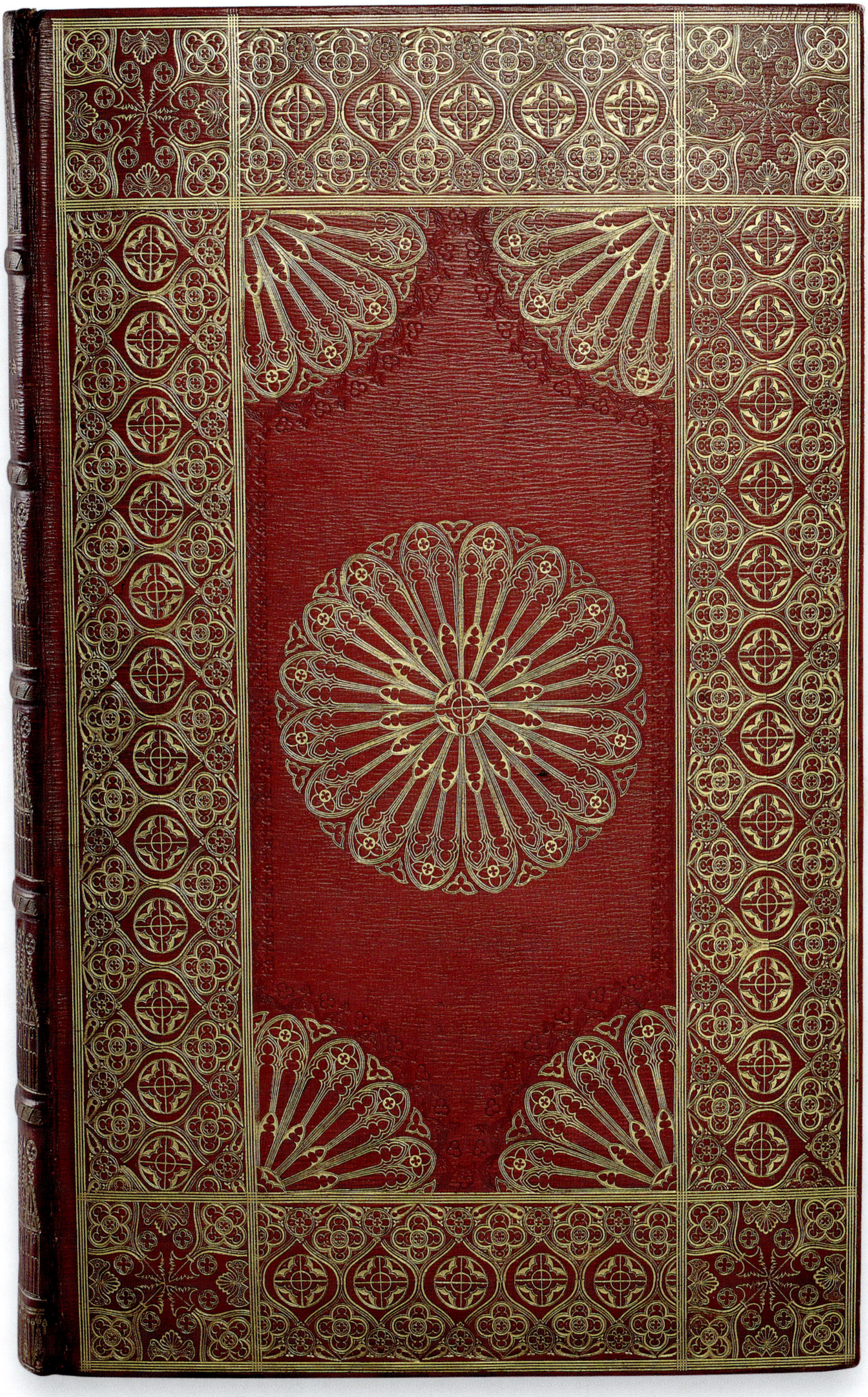

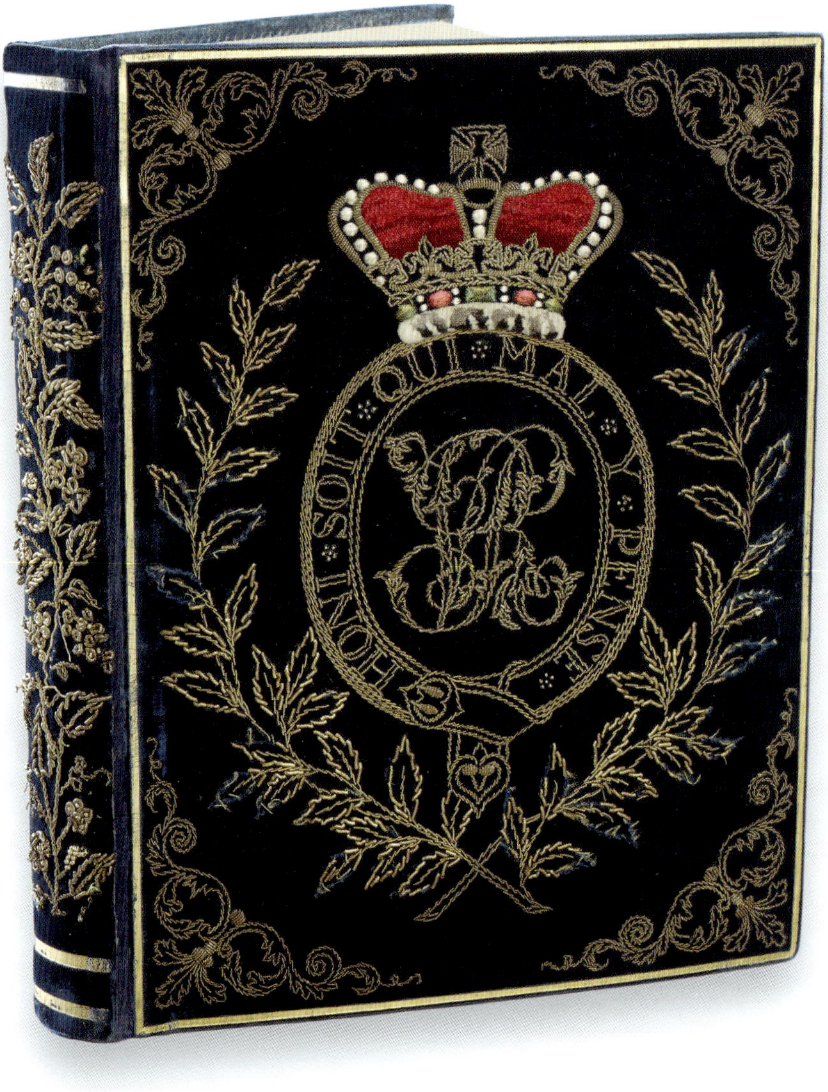

The bookbindings category of the *Great Exhibition* of 1851 showcased advances inspired by the industrial revolution. London binder Joseph Stuart Evans's improved method of blocking in gold and colours, known as 'illuminating', was especially commended by the exhibition jury. The album shown here, bound in blue velvet with the crowned initials of Queen Victoria, contains designs produced by this method. It has been suggested that Evans produced this binding for presentation to the Queen. Evans was first recorded as an account bookbinder in Soho in 1826, but he also bound hand-press books, always striving to achieve a new look. Another of his innovations was a stain that made leather resemble wood. According to the records of St James's Church, Westminster, it seems likely that Evans died in December 1851.

London, mid-nineteenth century
344 x 260 x 48 mm (13.5 x 10.2 x 1.9 inches)
C.188.c.30

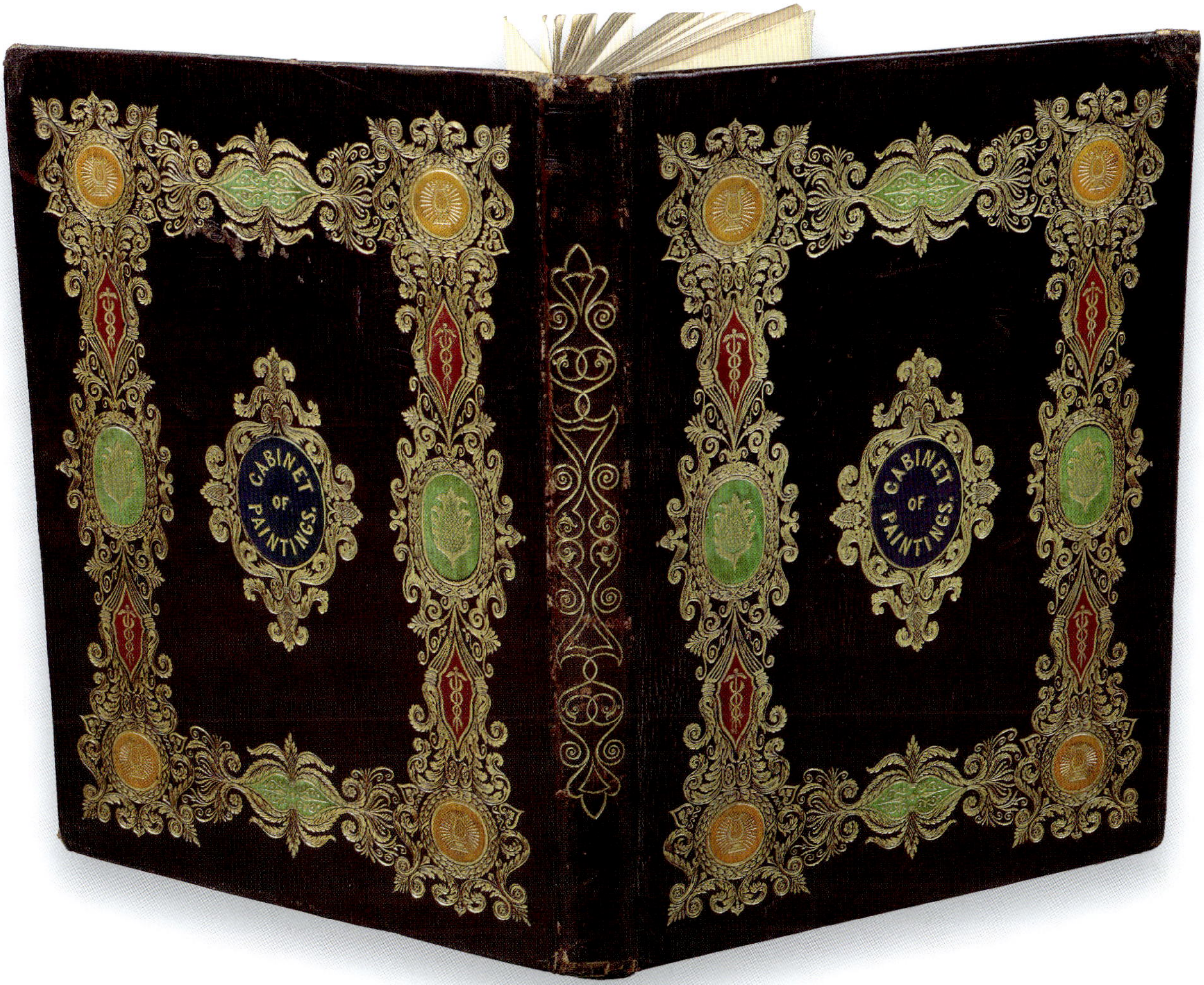

This pictorial album features the wood-engraver George Baxter's new method of illustrating pictures in full colour, a process clearly intended to appeal to a popular audience. The book was bound in an appropriately innovative style in mass-produced, maroon grained leather. Colour is central to its design in the form of jewel-like red, yellow, green and blue onlays, with gilt borders resembling picture frames. A grained surface (achieved by the impressing of specially designed plates developed in England in the early nineteenth century) gave the appearance of expensive straight-grained goatskin by concealing the blemishes of an inferior leather. A variety of surfaces could be applied to cloth bindings in a similar way. The publishers, Chapman and Hall, were quick to profit from the popularity of books featuring new processes, and put out a large number of illustrated editions with cloth bindings in blocked designs, thereby providing a new and lucrative outlet for the artists of the day and paving the way for a golden age in book illustration. Two of the best-known artists, John Leighton and William Harry Rogers, are known to have been employed by Chapman and Hall, but this example is unsigned.

England, *c.*1837
255 x 185 x 25 mm (10 x 7.3 x 1 inches)
C.155.d.8

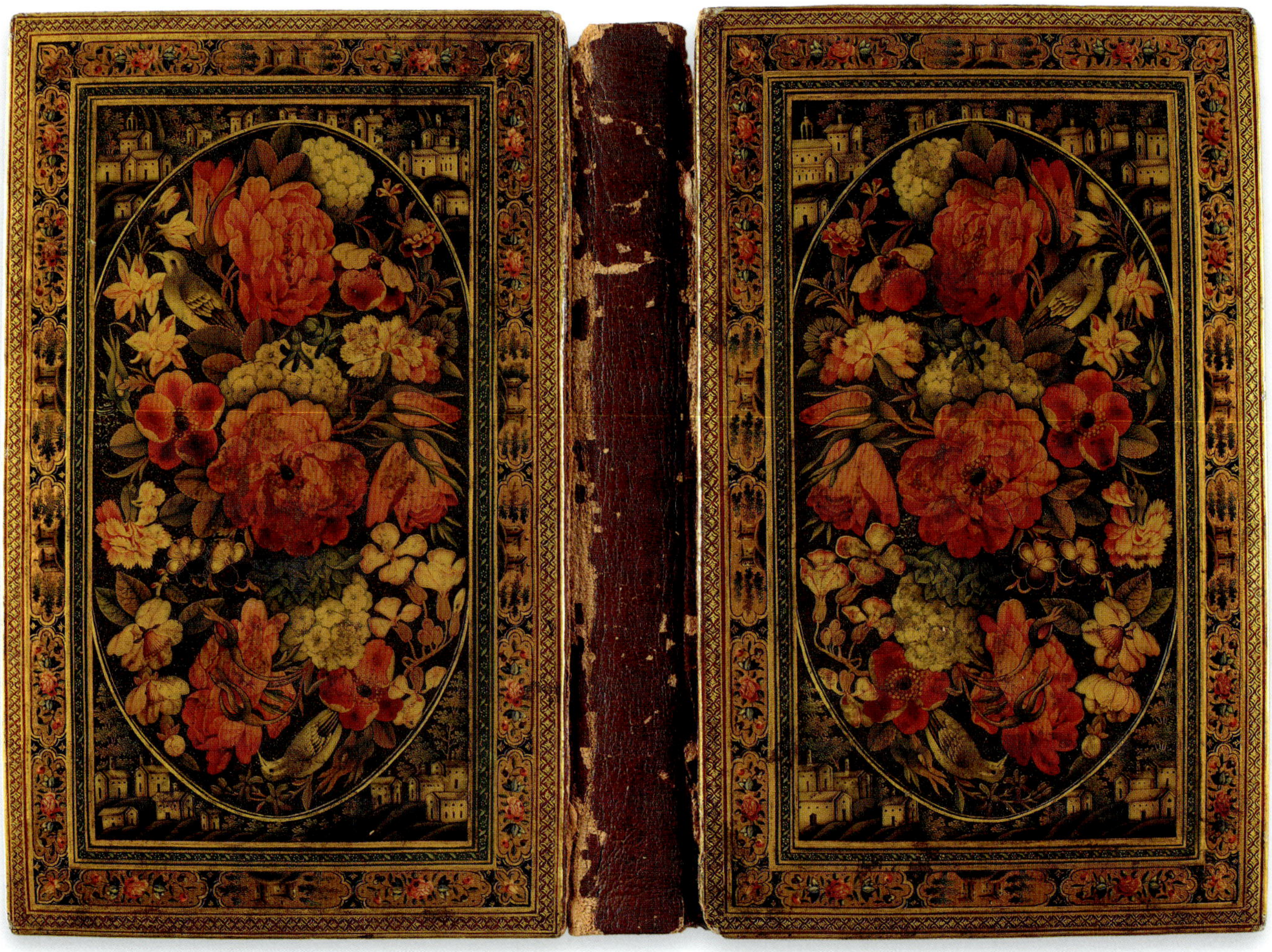

The Qajar dynasty (1779–1924) encouraged the development of a modern technological infrastructure in Persia. However, it was also careful to preserve cherished traditions in cultural and artistic fields. These book covers demonstrate skills used in the production of painted and lacquered items that had been perfected over generations by Persian miniature painters. The rose and nightingale (*gul-o-bul-bul*) decoration in particular was a favourite motif, its use dating back to the seventeenth century. It would have been applied in watercolour to a thin layer of plaster and protected by a thick transparent coating of lacquer (or varnish). The royal court at Shiraz attracted many calligraphers, painters and other artists, and the painter of this set of covers – Loftali – was a significant figure there. The image opposite shows the insides of the boards, which depict a hand clasping a flowering branch and the signature in Arabic of the artist.

Shiraz, Persia, 1861
220 x 139 x 4 mm (9.1 x 5.5 x 0.2 inches)
Davis 653

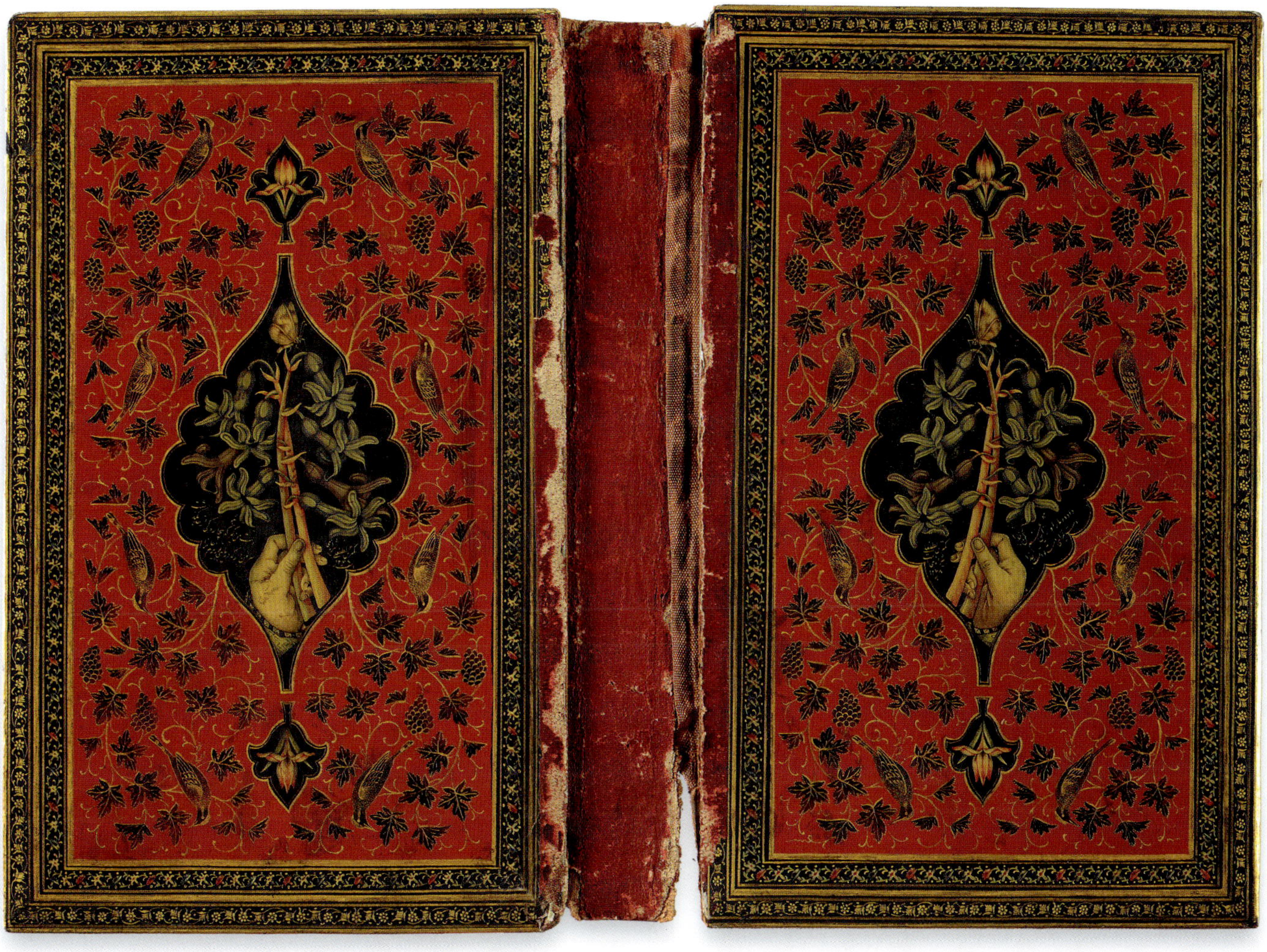

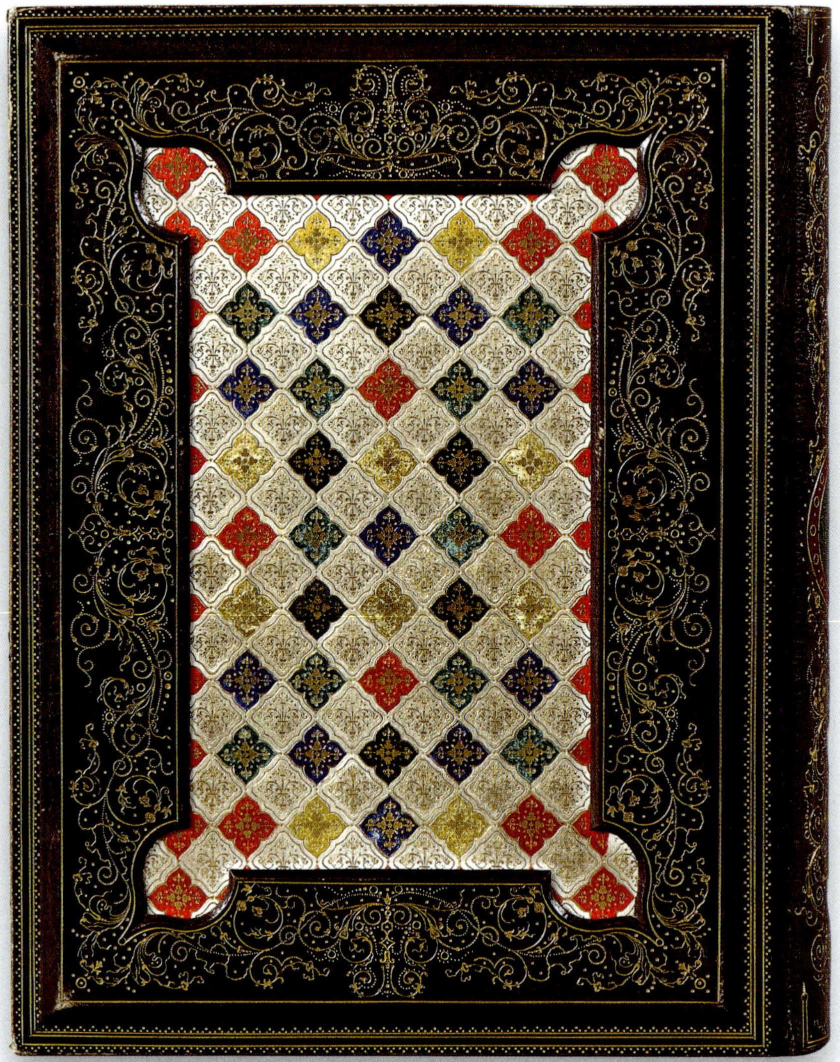

The career of the Hungarian Joseph Zaehnsdorf (1814–1886) demonstrates that bookbinders could readily find employment throughout Europe. Zaehnsdorf himself plied his trade in Austria, Germany, Paris and London, eventually establishing his own business in Covent Garden in 1842. He seems to have been politically active, for at the beginning of his career in London in 1839 he was dismissed for being a union member. Despite this, he later proved to be an unenlightened master, for 19 of his own workers resigned because of his use of low-paid German workmen. Zaehnsdorf's status as a binder was enhanced when examples of his craft were displayed in the 1851 *Great Exhibition*, and the press described his work as 'exquisite in the extreme'. He was receptive to trends in contemporary taste, answering the demand for retrospective bindings with books such as this one, in gold-tooled and onlaid goatskin with a sunken panel. The smooth spine has been cut away to reveal the contrasting leather beneath. The delicate *pointillé* tooling recalls seventeenth-century French work, while the colourful mosaic of the central panel has been influenced by eighteenth-century Parisian styles.

Zaehnsdorf left a shop employing over 100 people to his son Joseph William (1853–1930). The business continued to thrive, and Joseph William promoted the craft through his influential book, *The Art of Bookbinding* (1880).

London, mid-nineteenth century
223 x 160 x 40 mm (8.8 x 6.3 x 1.6 inches)
C.68.i.15

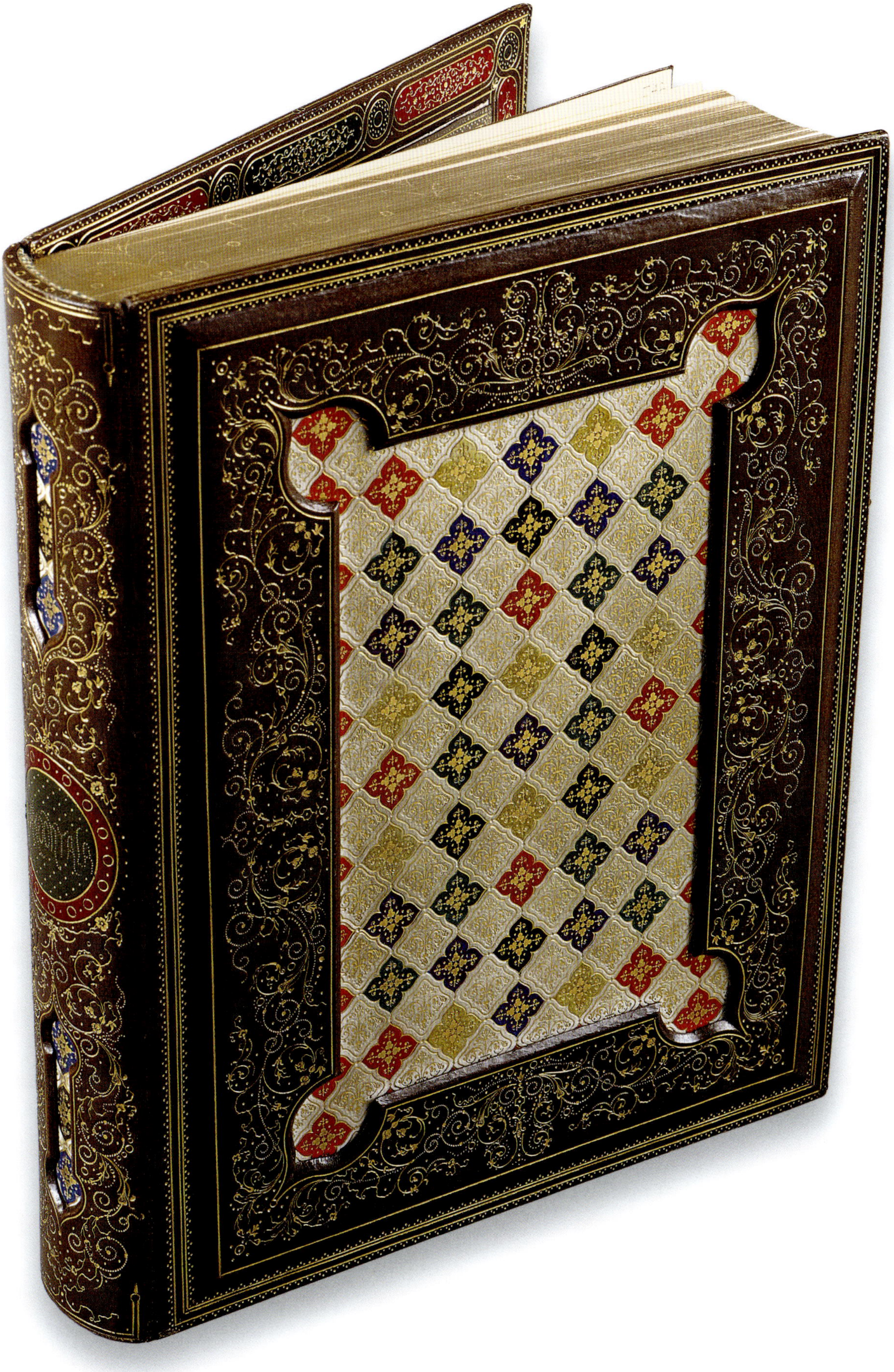

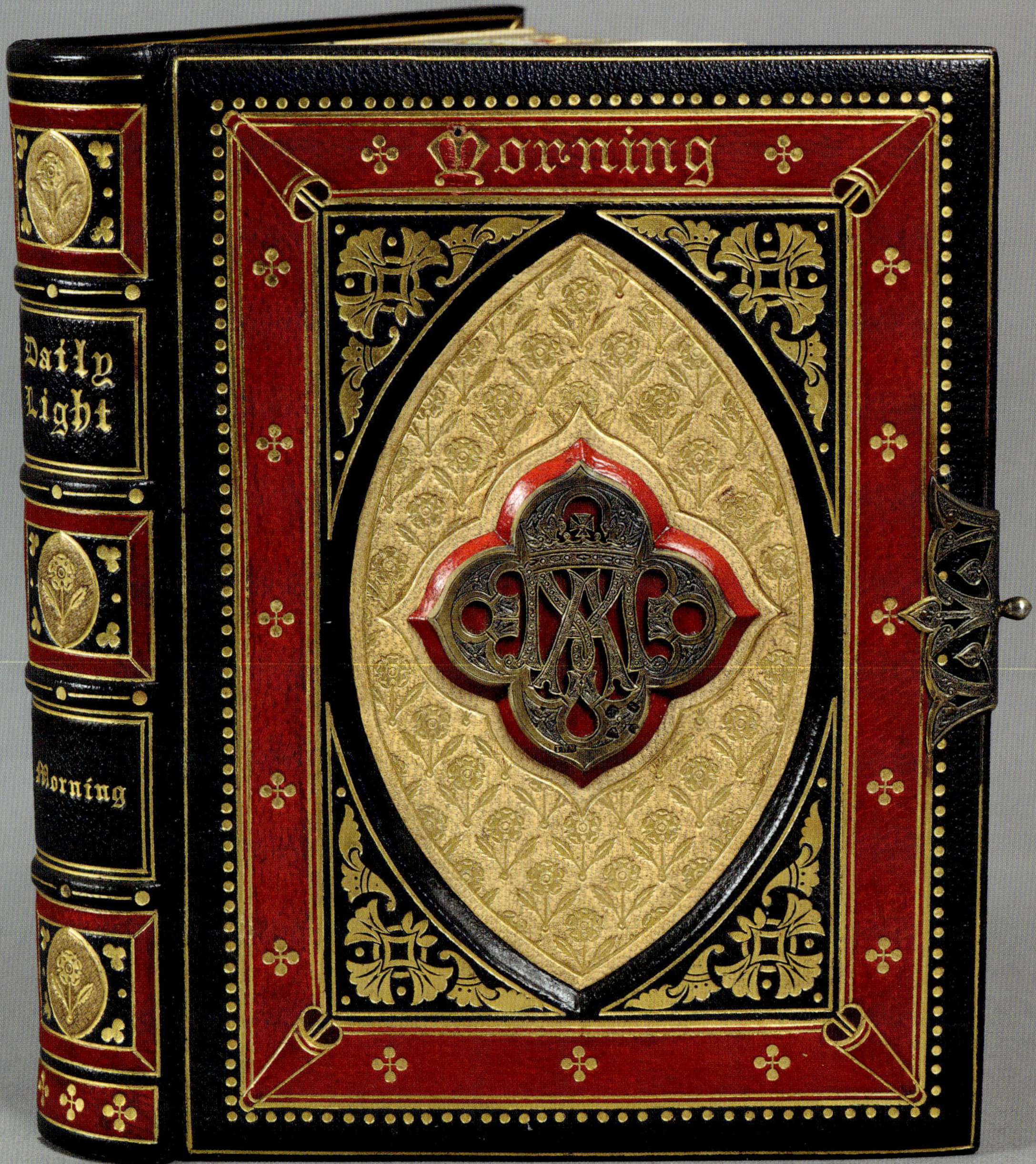
Morning
Daily Light
Morning

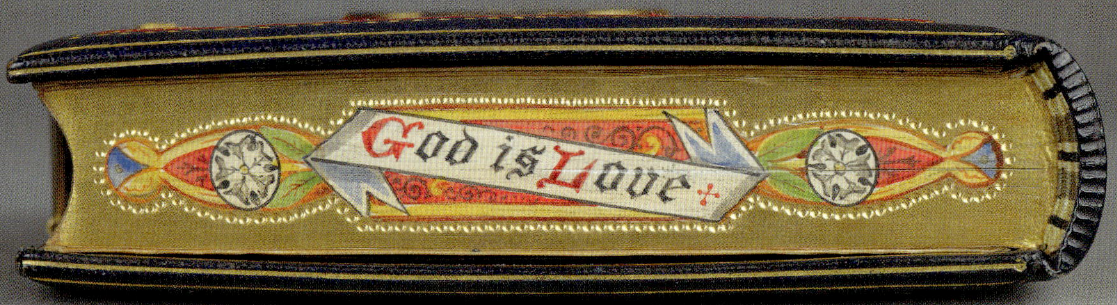
God is Love

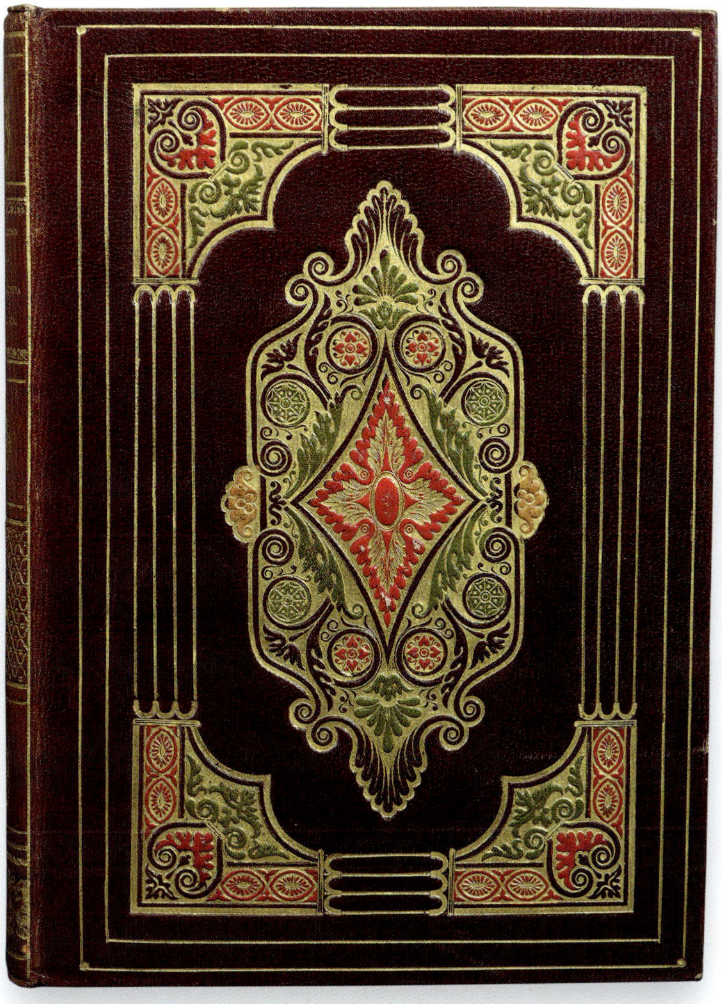

OPPOSITE It was customary for a group called the Maidens of the United Kingdom to present specially bound bibles and devotional works to Victorian royal princesses on the occasion of their weddings. This gold-tooled and onlaid blue goatskin binding is an example of such an offering, and was ordered from the London stationers Houghton & Gunn (a firm which was later taken over by Asprey's). The identity of the binder is not known, but the crowned initials on the upper cover indicate that the recipient was Marie Alexandrovna, daughter of Czar Alexander II, who married Prince Alfred (Queen Victoria's second son) in 1874. The edges have been gilt and painted with the arms of the United Kingdom and Russia, and a scroll lettered 'God is Love'.

London, mid-nineteenth century
144 x 106 x 21 mm (5.7 x 4.1 x 0.8 inches)
C.108.cc.5

ABOVE The printed trade label on the pastedown of this blocked and painted purple goatskin binding reveals it to have been created by Tomas Cobo of Madrid. Cobo was a pupil of the noted royal bookbinder, Pascual Carsí y Vidal, and succeeded him in this position in 1830. Although less well-known than his teacher, Cobo was particularly versatile and could produce bindings in many styles – his colourful works from the Romantic period perhaps being the most regarded.

Madrid, mid-nineteenth century
219 x 159 x 21 mm (8.6 x 6.3 x 0.8 inches)
Davis 661

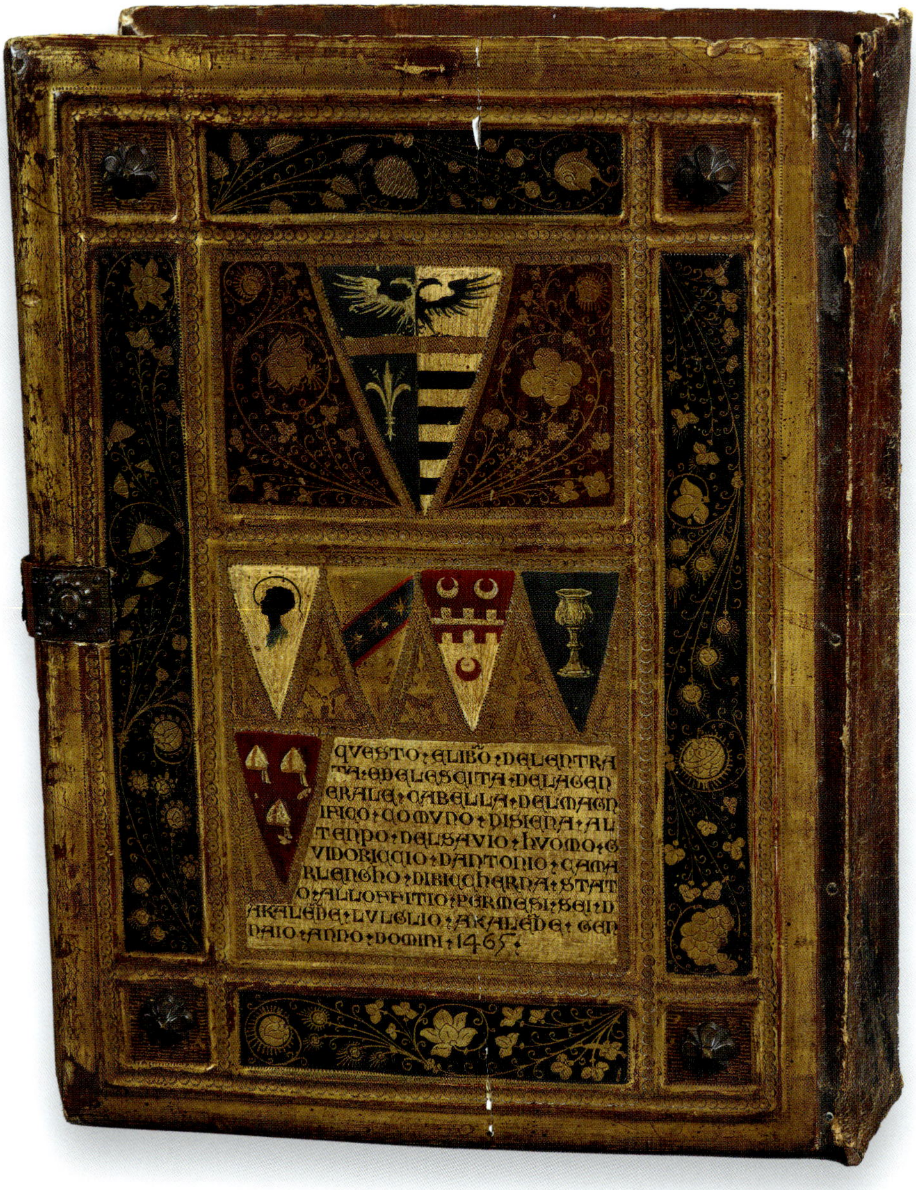

These painted panels (lower cover shown above and upper cover shown opposite) imitate the *tavolette de Biccherna* – wood covers used for the Sienese tax accounts that were produced from the mid-thirteenth century (see p.30 for an illustration of an authentic panel). These examples were made by Icilio Federico Joni (1866–1946), known as the prince of Sienese fakers, who specialized in producing Renaissance and Old Master-style paintings, and whose activities were revealed in his autobiography of 1932. From it, we learn that the panels he produced did not resemble the originals as closely as they should have done because Joni had not bothered to visit the city archives to examine them! Despite this, the *tavolette* were widely traded, even once the forgery was known. Joni was a larger-than-life figure who, as well as being a painter, gilder and restorer, played the mandolin, produced pageants and established a gymnasium in his studio (where he also kept falcons). Like other accomplished forgers, Joni's work is studied and celebrated in its own right in the twenty-first century.

Siena, late nineteenth century
383 x 275 (15.1 x 10.8 inches)
C.188.c.11

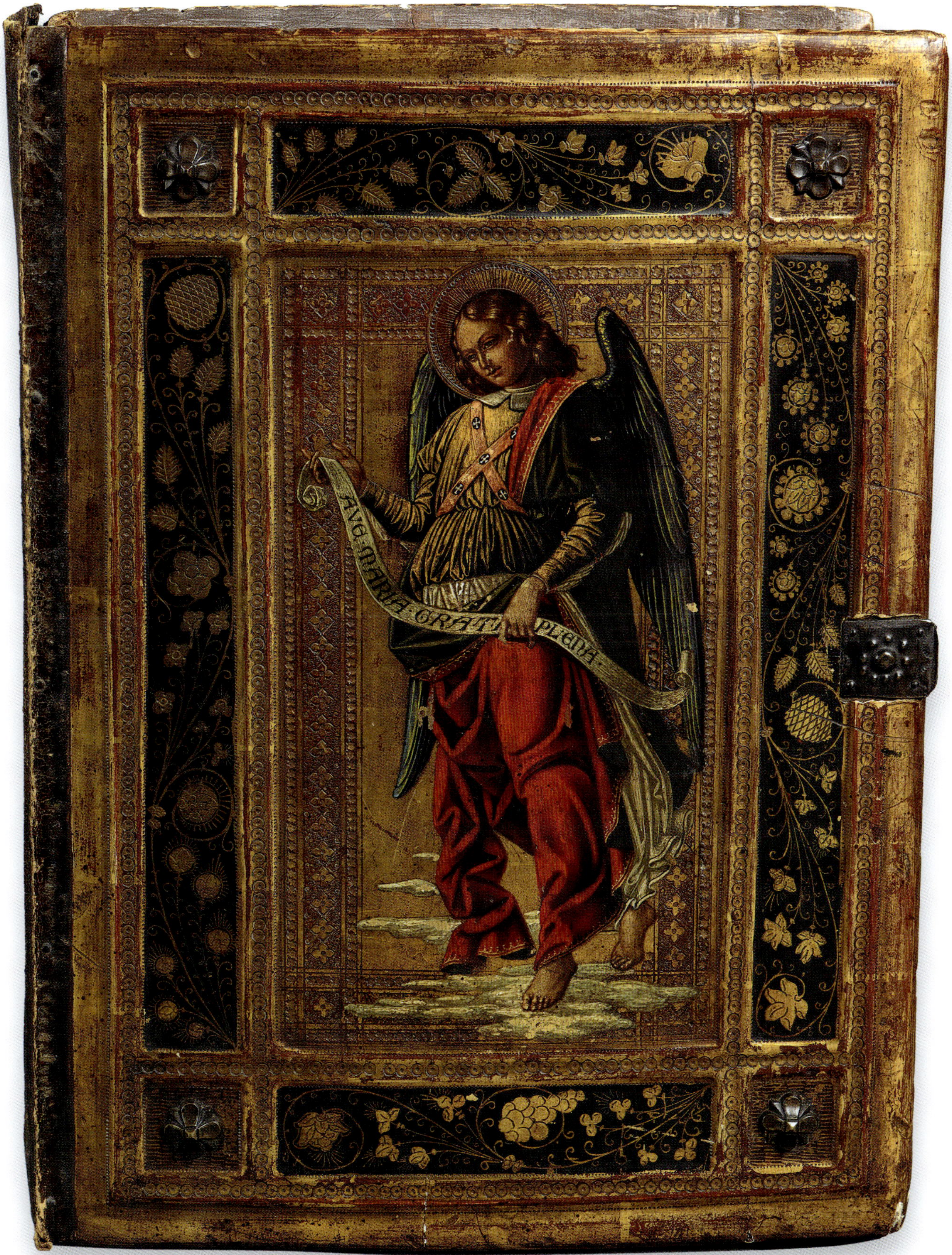
AVE MARIA GRATI PLENA

COBDEN-SANDERSON BINDINGS

Thomas James Cobden-Sanderson (1840–1922), has been described as 'the pre-eminent figure in the more recent history of English bookbinding ... who rescued the craft from half a century of purely imitative work'. He was an enthusiastic supporter of the Arts and Crafts movement, and relinquished work as a lawyer in favour of bookbinding on the suggestion of Mrs William Morris. After training, Cobden-Sanderson worked at first with his wife, Annie (an active campaigner for women's suffrage), but when this arrangement proved impractical he engaged professional craftsmen to work at his famous Doves Bindery, which was established in Hammersmith, London, in 1893. He retained a creative interest in the firm, designing the distinctive finishing tools inspired by blooms and leaves, the same tools being used to decorate the gilt edges of the pages. The bindery, which was run in part on socialist principles, received many commissions and made a small profit, even though the workmen earned above average wages and received generous holidays. Not surprisingly, the established trade binders were rather critical of this new enterprise and questioned aspects of Cobden-Sanderson's work, such as his preference for flat (rather than rounded) spines. In fact, this type of spine made a good background for tooling, as can be seen here, although the early bindings had an adverse tendency to curve inwards with use.

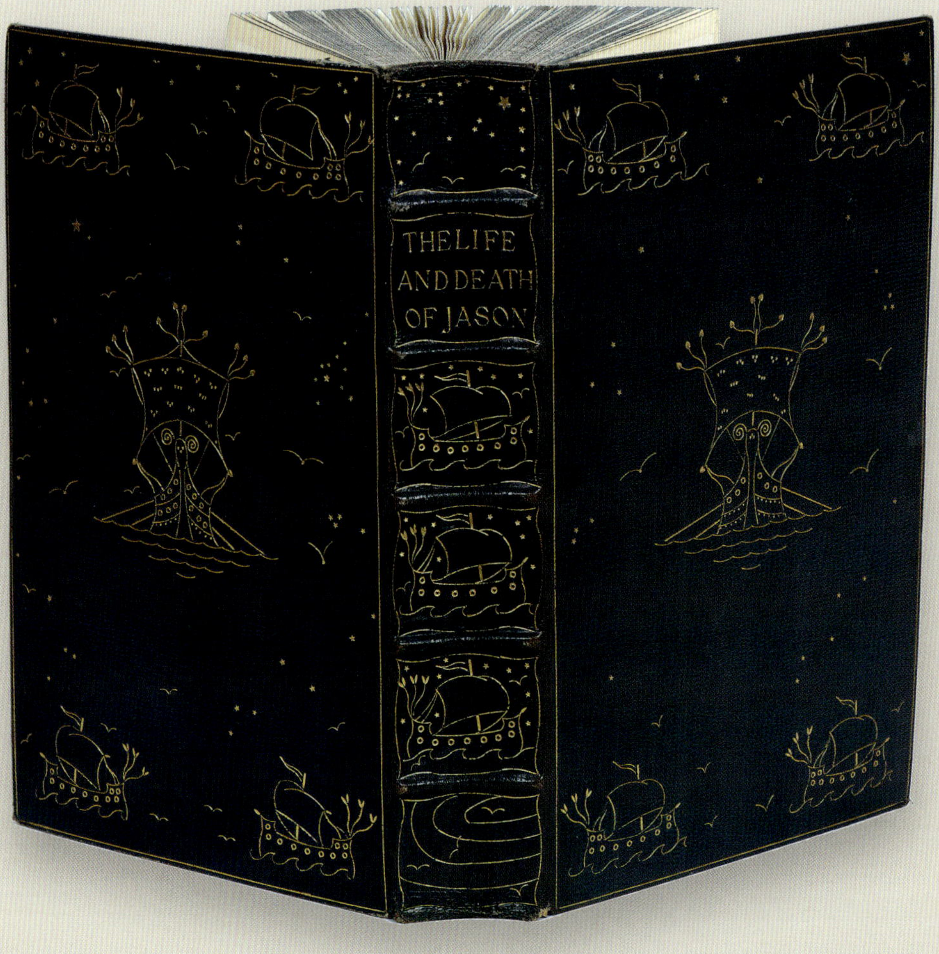

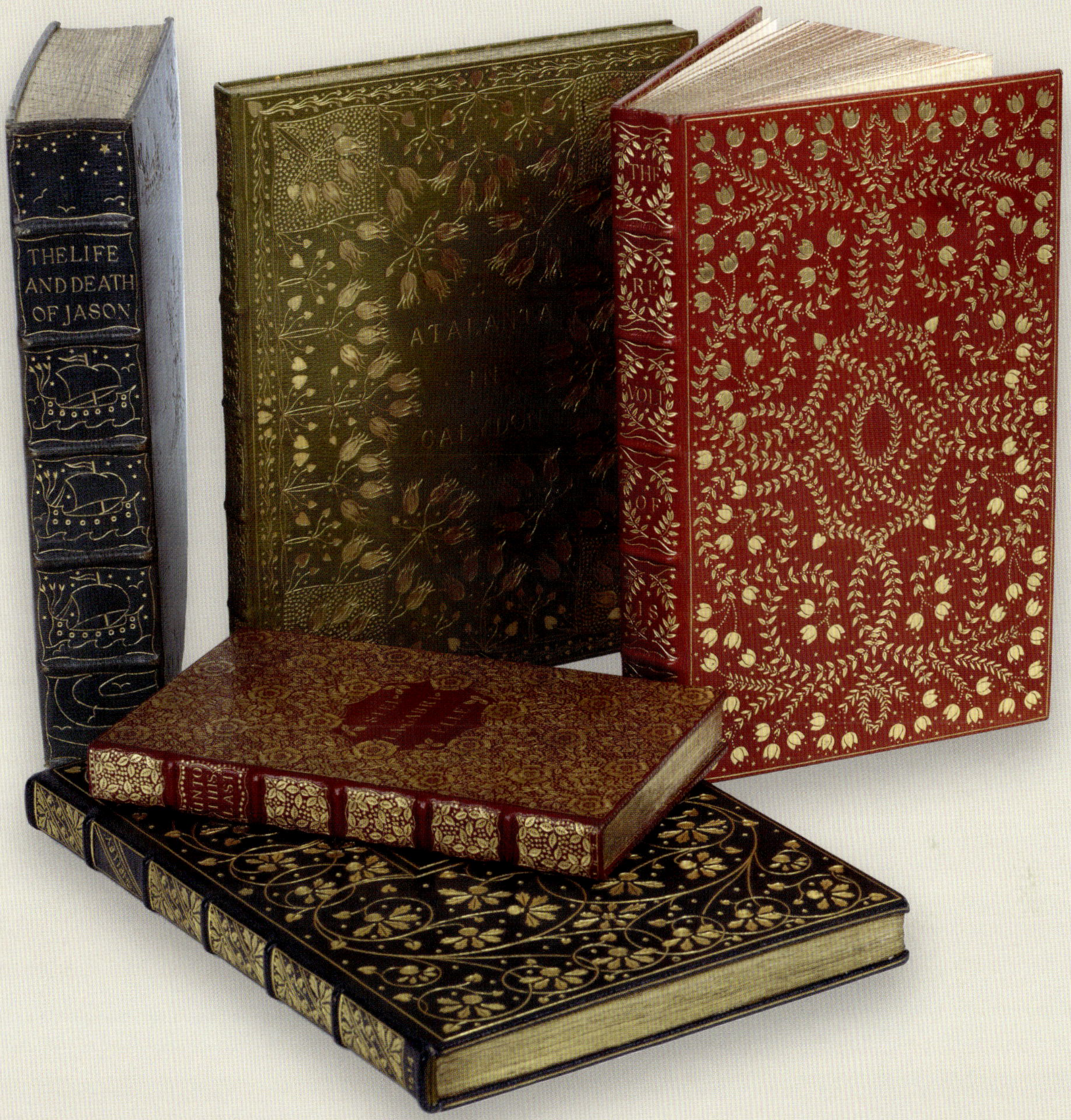

ABOVE Selection of Cobden-Sanderson bindings
London, late nineteenth and early twentieth centuries
Clockwise from left: C.68.i.11; C.68.i.2;
C.68.i.10; C.68.i.4; C.68.i.1

OPPOSITE Bookbinding was more than just a business to Cobden-Sanderson, and this is shown by his designs themselves, which frequently reflect events from his own life and chart his responses to the contemporary world, particularly where art was concerned. The blue-green, straight-grain goatskin binding shown opposite with its stylised ship (based on a Walter Crane design) gives us a flavour of Cobden-Sanderson's knowledge of the sea (he was once apprenticed to a ship builder). The text was signed by its author, Cobden-Sanderson's friend, William Morris. The binding was a new year's gift to Annie Cobden-Sanderson and is inscribed 'to my dear wife... 1 January 1888'.

London, 1888
212 x134 x 41 mm (8.4 x 5.3 x 1.6 inches)
C.68.i.11

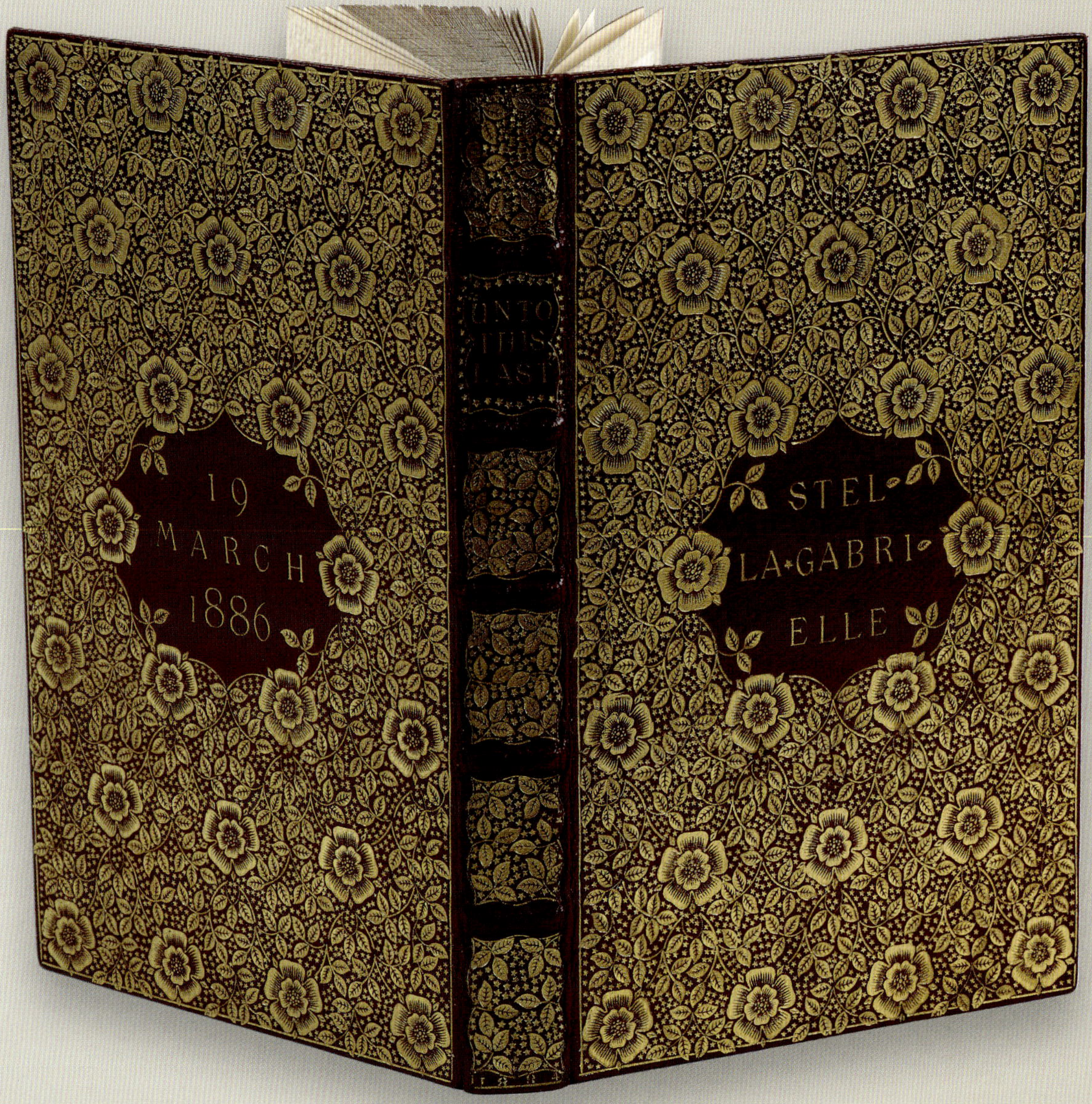

We know from the work book kept by the binder Cobden-Sanderson that this gold-tooled red goatskin binding took just over sixty-five hours to make. An inside inscription indicates that it had been a gift to his daughter, Stella (1886–1979). It reads: 'This book, Stella, I was binding when you were born, and being one of the noblest books I know I covered it with such glory as I could of roses and of stars and set your name in the midst and gave it to you.' A second inscription dated 1910 suggests that Cobden-Sanderson must have retrieved the book at some point. 'This little book, Stella, has been in my possession all these years, from the day that you were born – a brief span! I now hand it over to you on your marriage.' The all-over pattern was achieved using only four tools.

London, 1886
170 x 103 x 18 mm (6.7 x 4.1 x 0.7 inches)
C.68.h.17

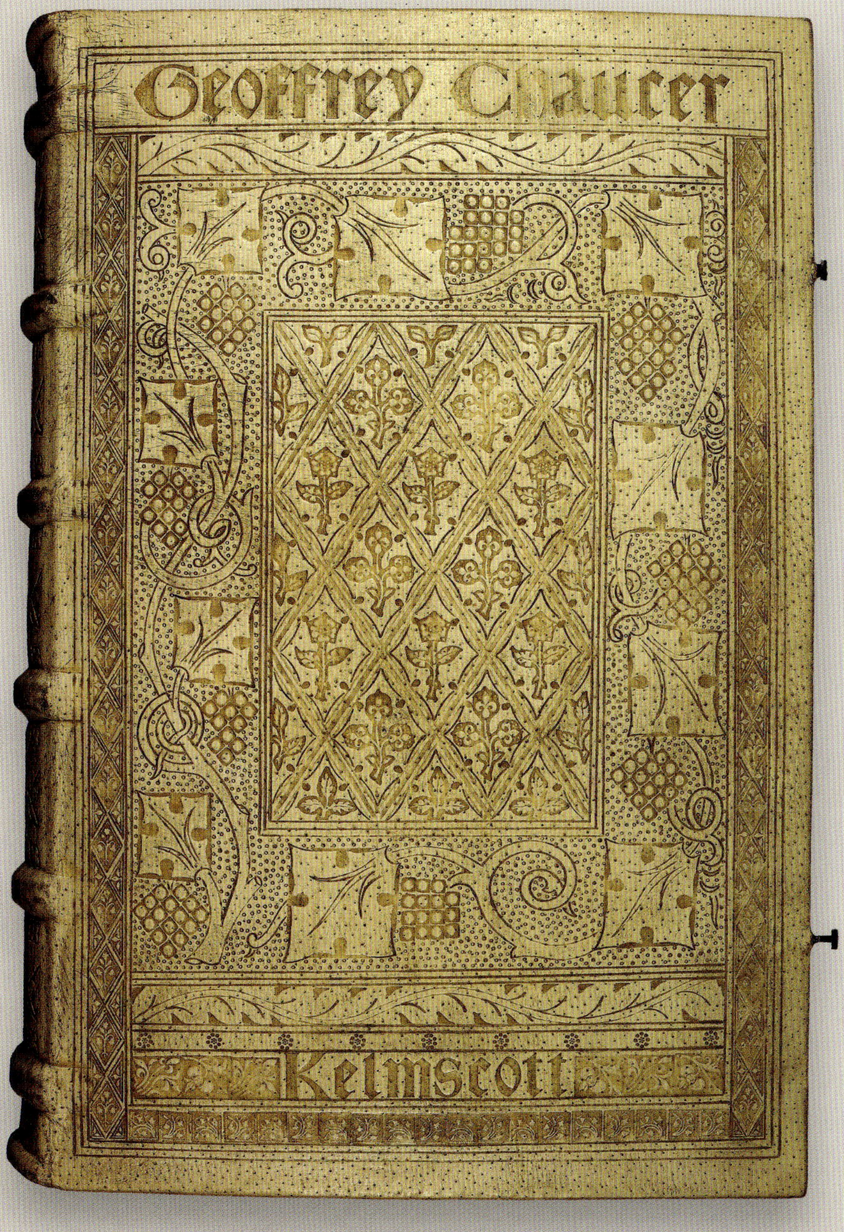

The creation of this blind-tooled alum tawed pigskin binding over oak boards was a long-cherished project of William Morris and his colleagues at the Kelmscott Press in Hammersmith, where the text was printed. The upper cover and the decorative tools used were actually designed by Morris, whereas the lower cover motifs drew inspiration from early German bindings in Morris's own library. It was made at Thomas James Cobden-Sanderson's Doves Bindery, which was situated near the Kelmscott Press. In accord with the Arts and Crafts aesthetic, the binding is strongly influenced by medieval bindings in both style and structure, and reflects the movement's beliefs in the beauty and importance of hand-made items. This copy was specially printed on vellum for the engraver and printer, Emery Walker, who was at that time a business advisor, fellow socialist, friend and neighbour of both Morris and Cobden-Sanderson.

London, 1896
435 x 285 x 86 mm (17.1 x 11.2 x 3.4 inches)
C.42.l.12

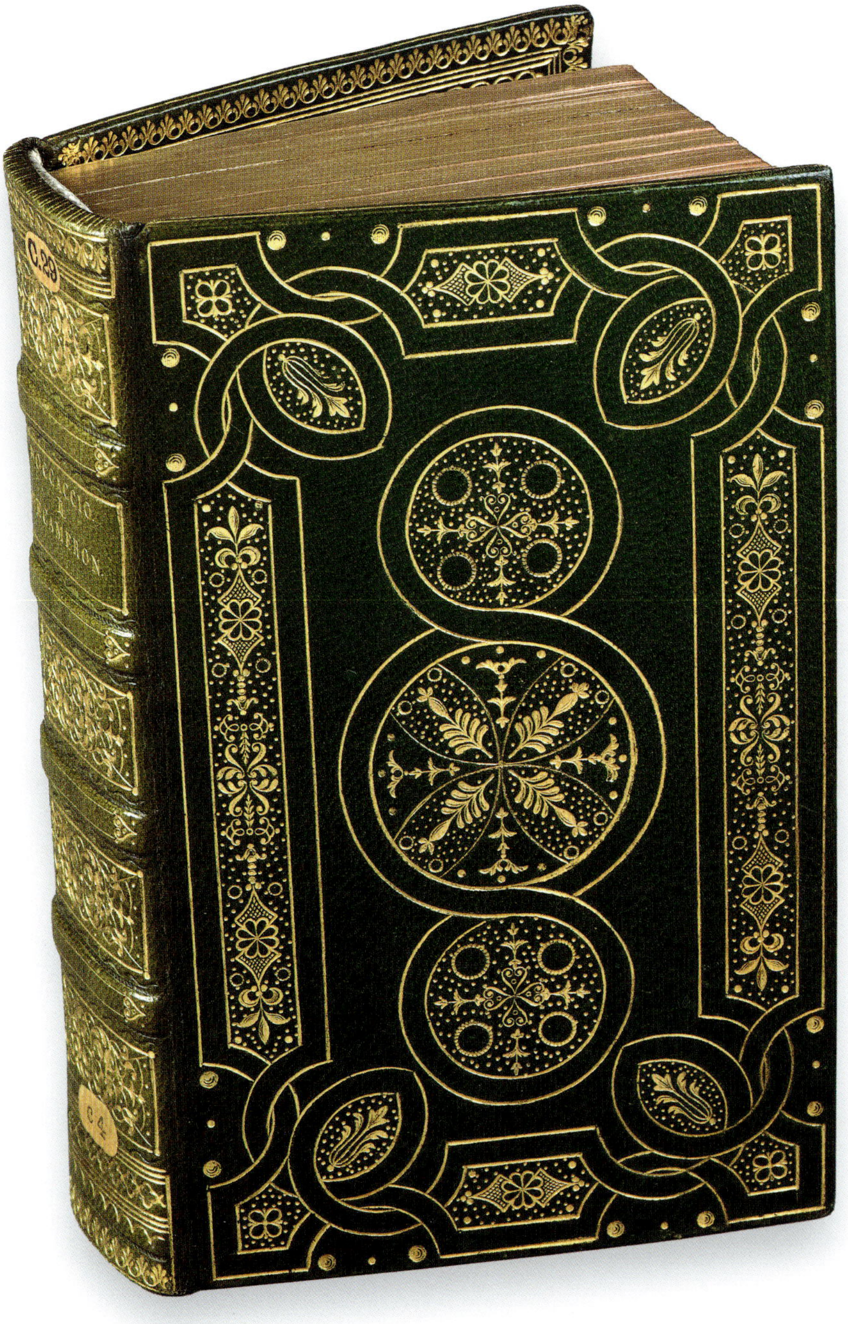

An unusual feature of this nineteenth-century copy of the *Decameron* in three volumes is the fact that it is printed on pink paper. The German binding is of green goatskin and probably dates from the same century. A more common choice for this type of leather is red; other colours, particularly green, tend to fade. The crisp decoration in gold using many individual hand tools, and the fact that the endleaves have been lined in brown silk, indicate that this was a luxury binding, as all of these elements would have made this a costly purchase.

Germany, late nineteenth century
146 x 89 x 34 mm (5.7 x 3.5 x 1.3 inches)
C.29.c.4

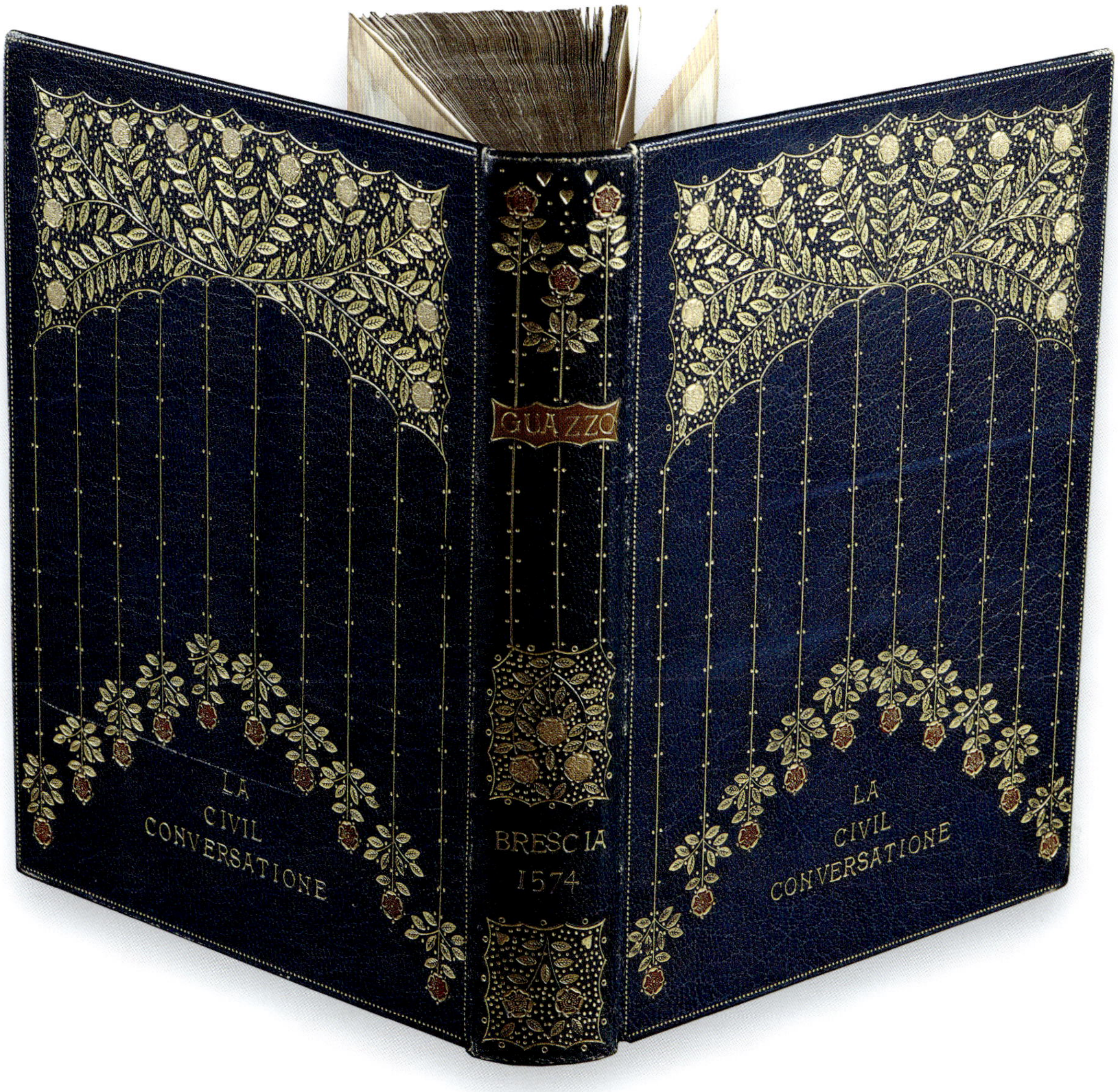

This nineteenth-century gold-tooled and onlaid blue goatskin binding was finished by Sir Edward Sullivan (1852–1928), an Irish barrister and Trustee of the National Library of Ireland. Sullivan did not bind books himself, but his hobby of tooling in gold and his passionate interest in recording historic Irish bindings led to his nickname of 'Bookbinder' amongst friends in the dining and literary society that playfully called itself 'Ye Sette of Odd Volumes'. Sullivan's bindings were signed 'E S Aurifex' (i.e. worker in gold).

Ireland, late nineteenth century
222 x 150 x 35 mm (8.7 x 5.9 x 1.4 inches)
C.68.i.13

TRADE BINDINGS

The nineteenth-century invention of machines and the adoption of the new material (notably book cloths) in the West meant that bindings could be mass-produced cheaply and easily. Hand bookbinders still produced individual commissions for collectors, but the concept of a bookbinding as a unique item began to disappear. Decorative covers were manufactured separately from the text block and the two were attached via the endleaves and spine liners, which were pasted to both parts of the structure.

Innovative techniques such as embossing and blocking allowed publishers to produce lively and eye-catching bindings to tempt the public. Artists and designers began to take part in making design decisions. The painter and printmaker, Sir William Nicholson, specialized in simple yet bold images that expressed the character of a text. A description of the binding for *Her Ladyship's Elephant* (see p.147) in the *Bookbinding Trades Journal* of 1910 noted that Nicholson had successfully 'realized the suitability of broad, flat masses of colour for book-cover decoration'. America, particularly, New York, provided an environment where this new type of book-artist could flourish. Alice C Morse (1863–1961) was remarkably versatile and experimented with historic and modern styles on a wide selection of books, rising to the 'forefront of the first generation of artists to design commercially produced books' (see binding for *Poems of Cabin and Field* on p.147).

Some publishers were to develop a house-style, but initially variety and novelty were paramount. New trends were quickly embraced: for example the Czech colour-blocked covers on parchment below (part of a series of annuals). The selection of bindings shown over the next few pages indicates the variety of formats that trade bindings could take.

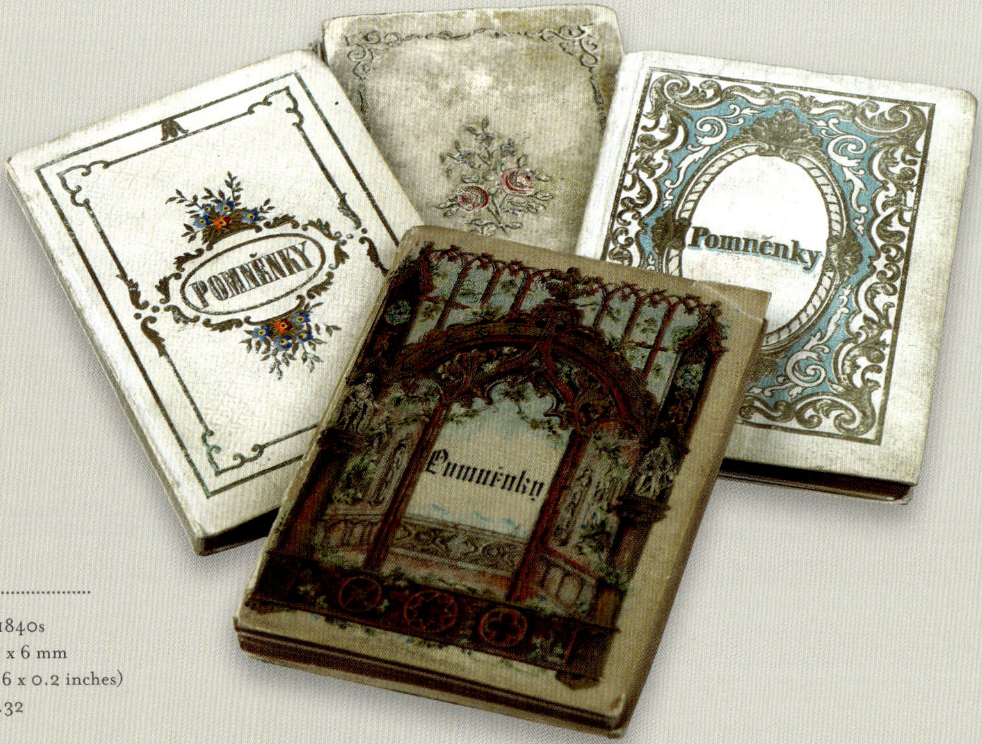

Prague, 1840s
100 x 67 x 6 mm
(3.9 x 2.6 x 0.2 inches)
C.109.e.32

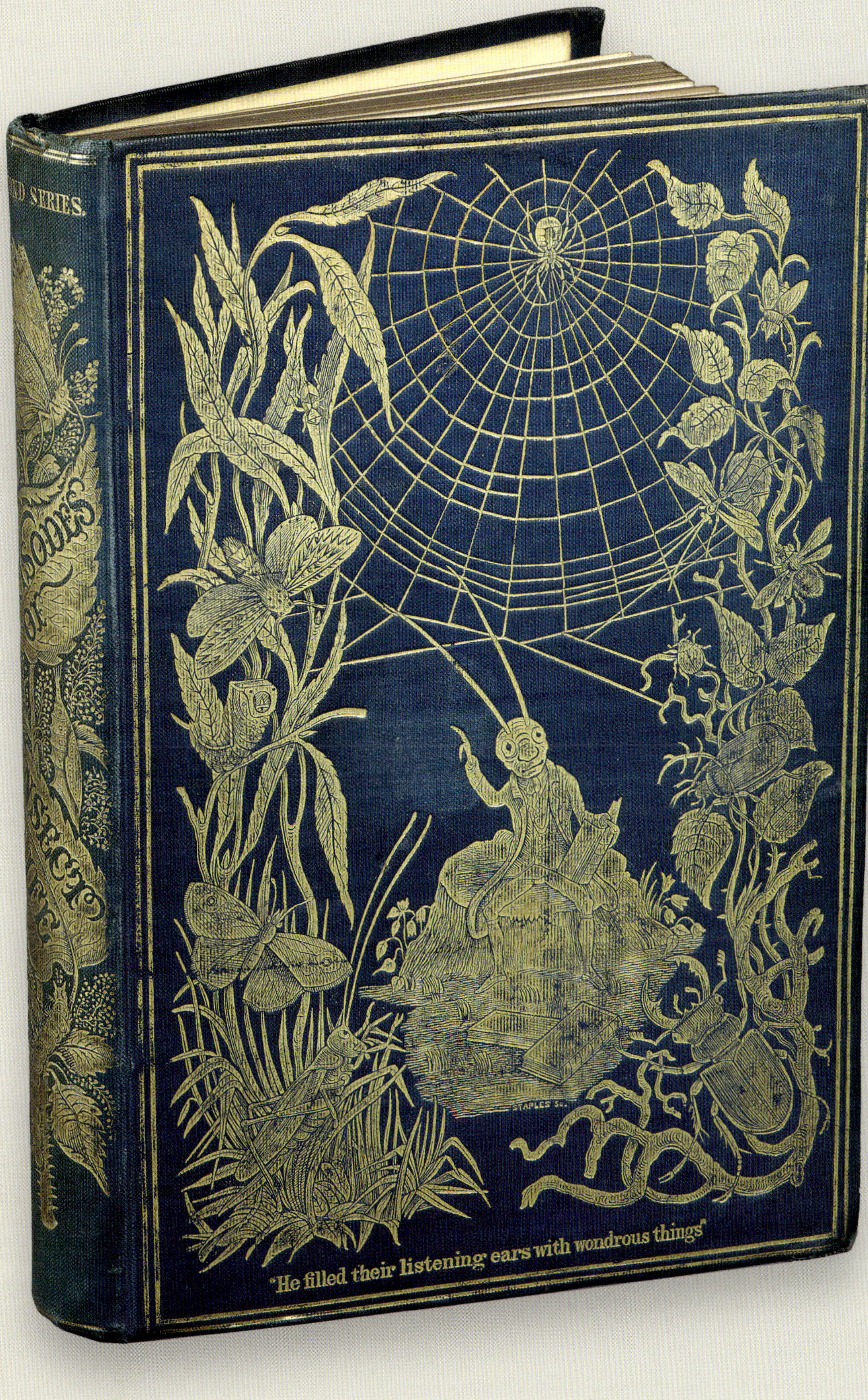

London, mid-nineteenth century
138 x 207 x 32 mm (5.4 x 8.1 x 1.3 inches)

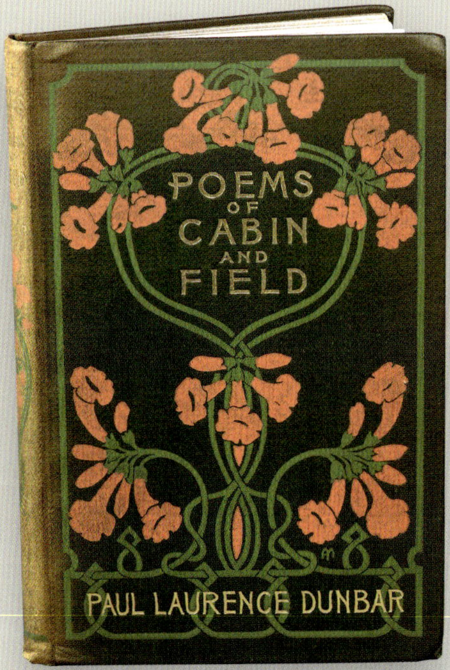

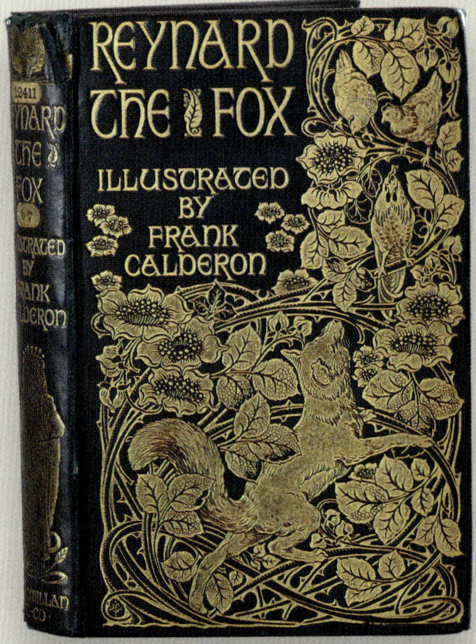

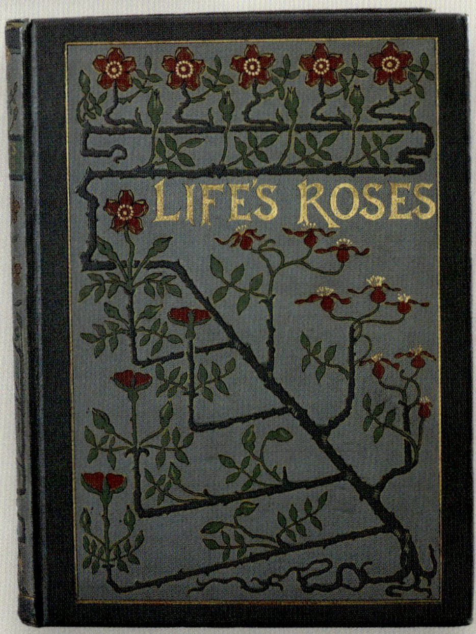

TOP
New York, 1894
225 x 142 x 15 mm (8.9 x 5.6 x 0.6 inches)
X.909/6451.

ABOVE, LEFT
London, 1895
185 x 120 x 25 mm (7.3 x 4.7 x 1 inches)
12411.b.7.

ABOVE, RIGHT
London, 1898
220 x 165 x 20 (8.7 x 6.5 x 0.8 inches)
X.909 6451

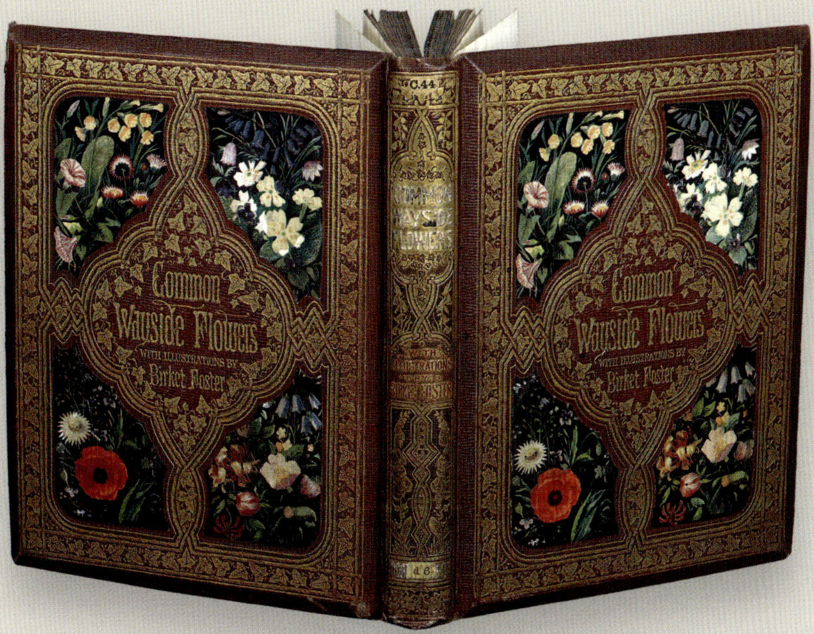

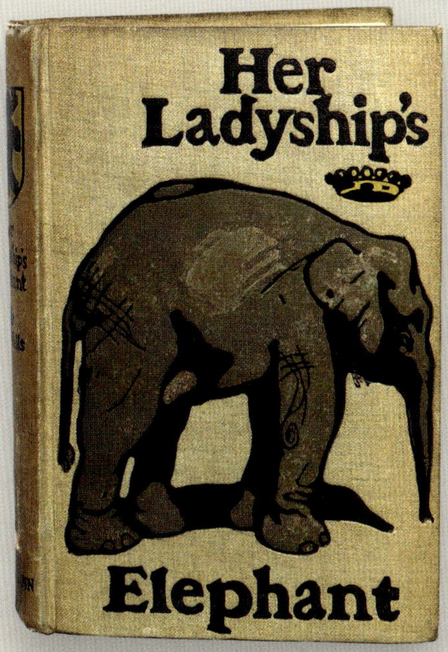

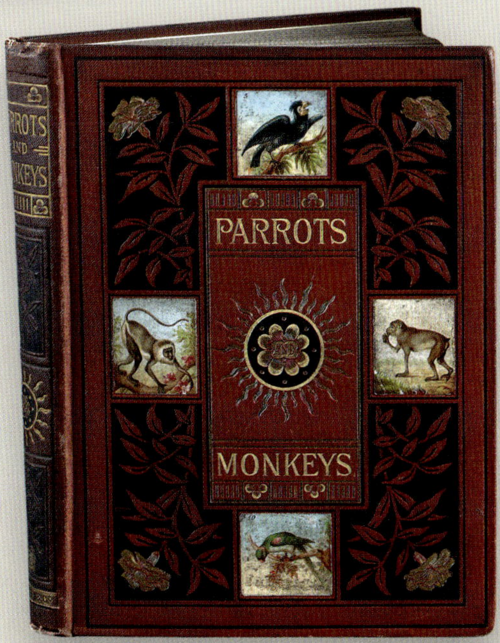

TOP
London, mid-nineteenth century
178 x 227 x 30 mm (7.0 x 8.9 x 1.2 inches)
C.44.d.6

ABOVE, LEFT
London, 1890s
195 x 129 x 29 mm (7.7 x 5.1 x 1.1 inches)
017323i14

ABOVE, RIGHT
London, 1898
193 x 140 x 22 mm (7.6 x 5.5 x 0.9 inches)
12809g2

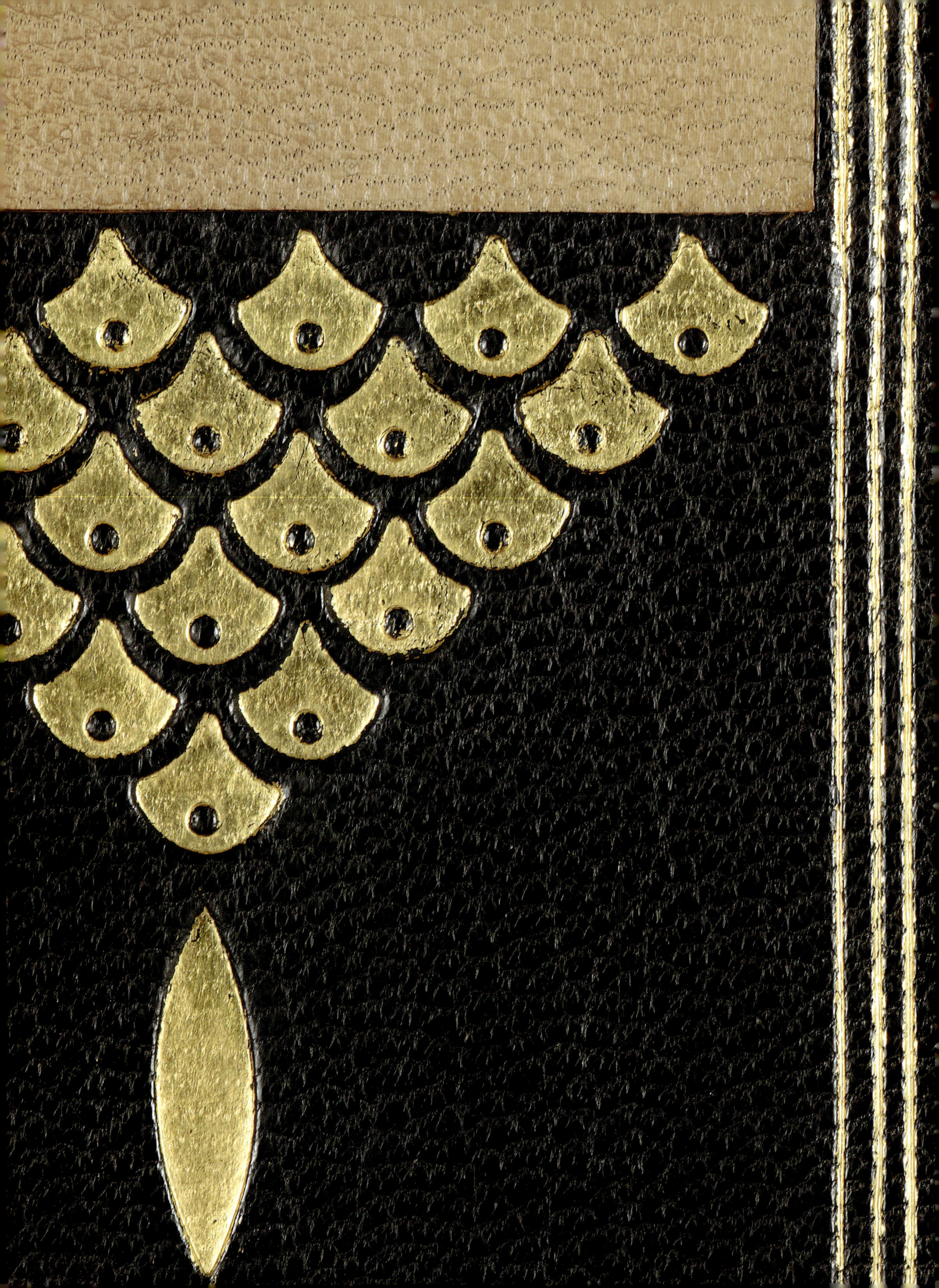

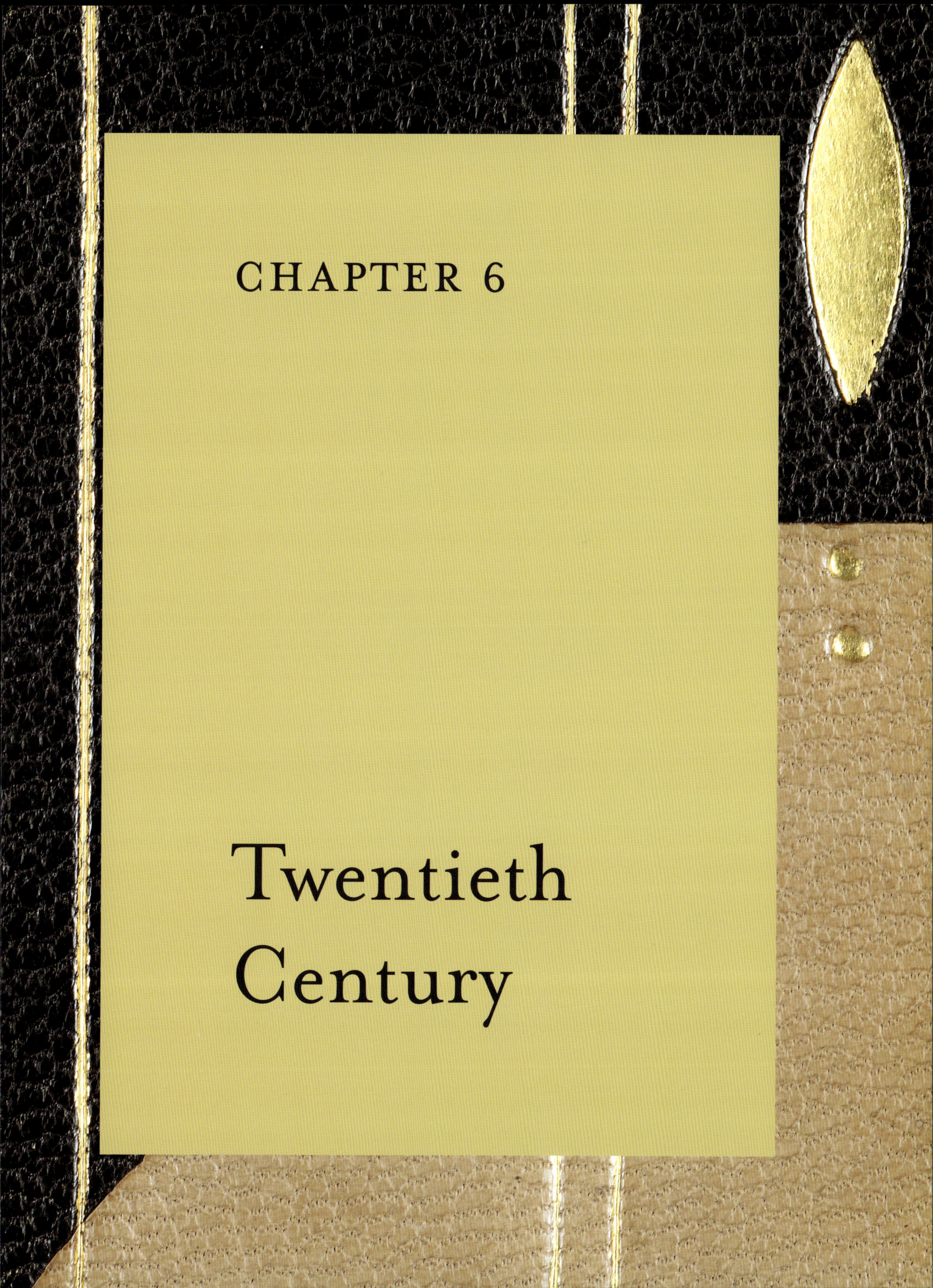

CHAPTER 6

Twentieth Century

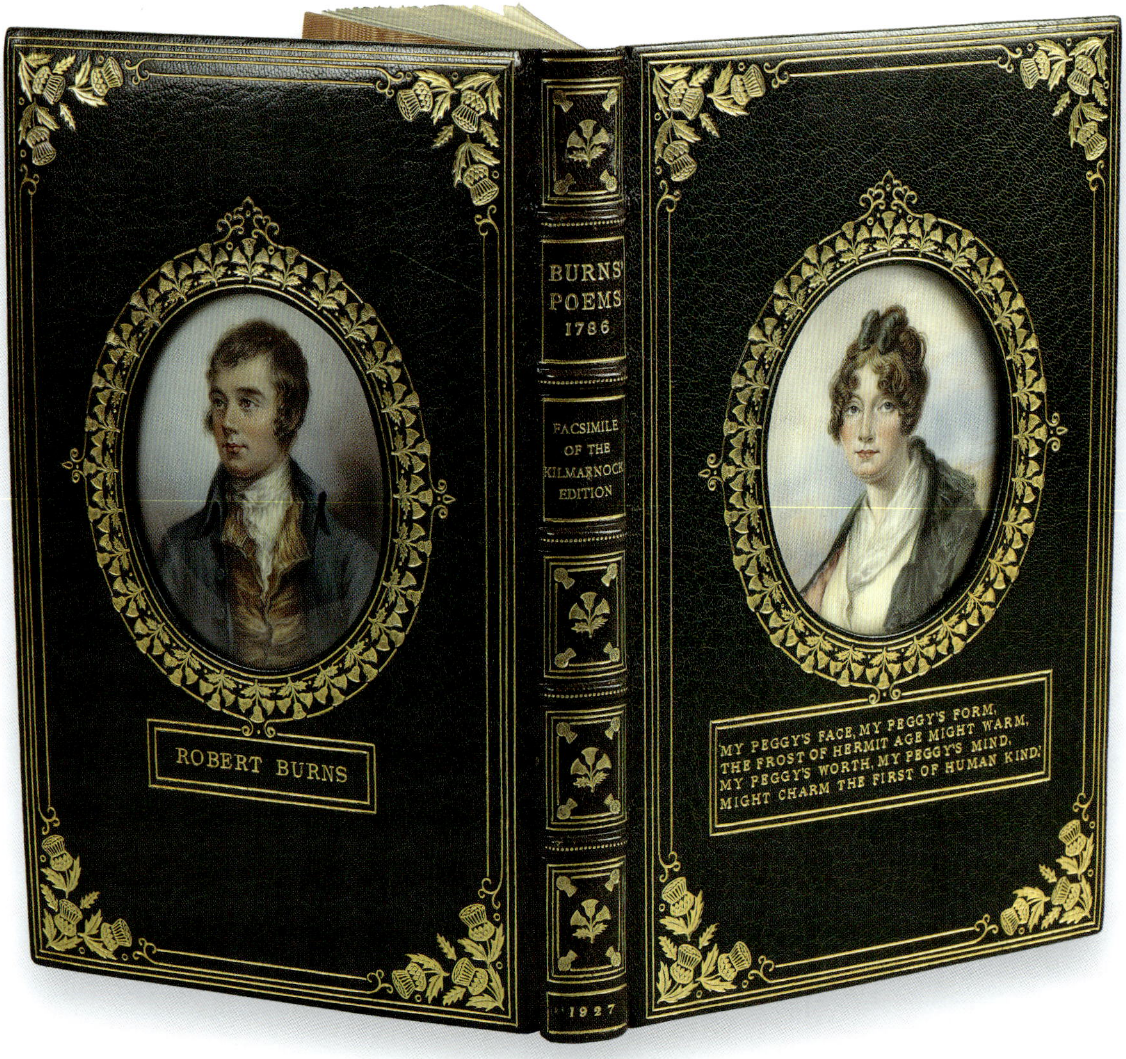

The binding style that incorporated painted portraits was named 'Cosway' by the London bookseller Sotheran's, perhaps after their publication on the miniaturist Richard Cosway. Rivière & Son (fl. 1840s–1939), one of the great names in English bookbinding, made this gold-tooled, green goatskin binding in about 1928. Miss C[aroline] B[illin] Currie was employed as painter, and she also produced fore-edge paintings under gold. The style proved popular, and 900 examples had been commissioned by 1930. The depiction of Robert Burns and his muse Margaret Chalmers demonstrates that the practice of linking binding decoration to contents (in this case Burns's poems) had now been firmly established.

London, *c.*1928
234 x 153 x 24 mm (9.2 x 6 x 0.9 inches)
C.108.e.17

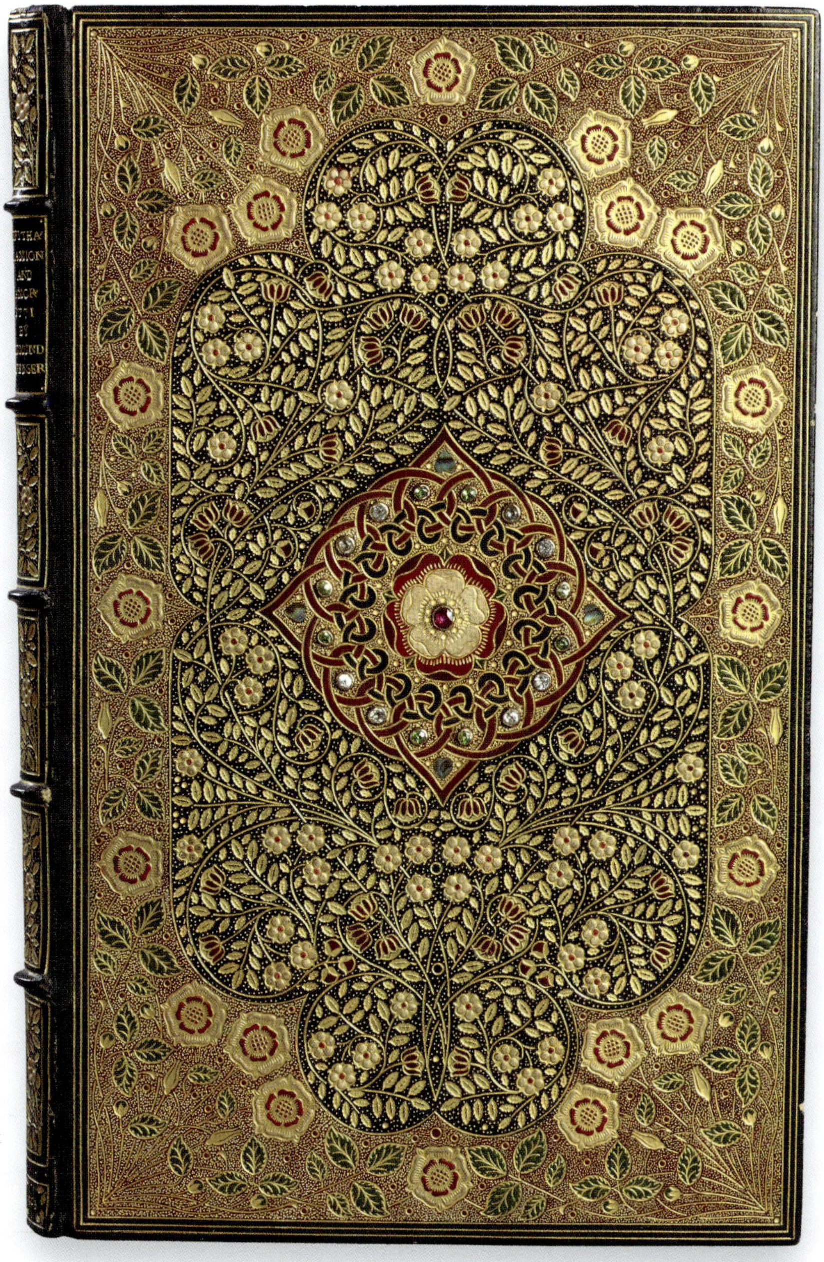

Sangorski & Sutcliffe dominated the twentieth-century London binding trade, although they were in competition with other workshops, notably Zaehnsdorf's and Rivières. Jewelled bindings on a smaller scale were a speciality. An early example is the goatskin binding on this copy of Edmund Spenser's *Epithalamion and Amoretti*, bound in 1905. Designs changed as tastes became simpler, as can be seen in the gold-blocked bindings made by Sangorski and Sutcliffe for the Golden Cockerel Press shown on the following pages.

London, 1905
252 x 154 x 15 mm (9.9 x 6.1 x 0.6 inches)
C.109.p.20

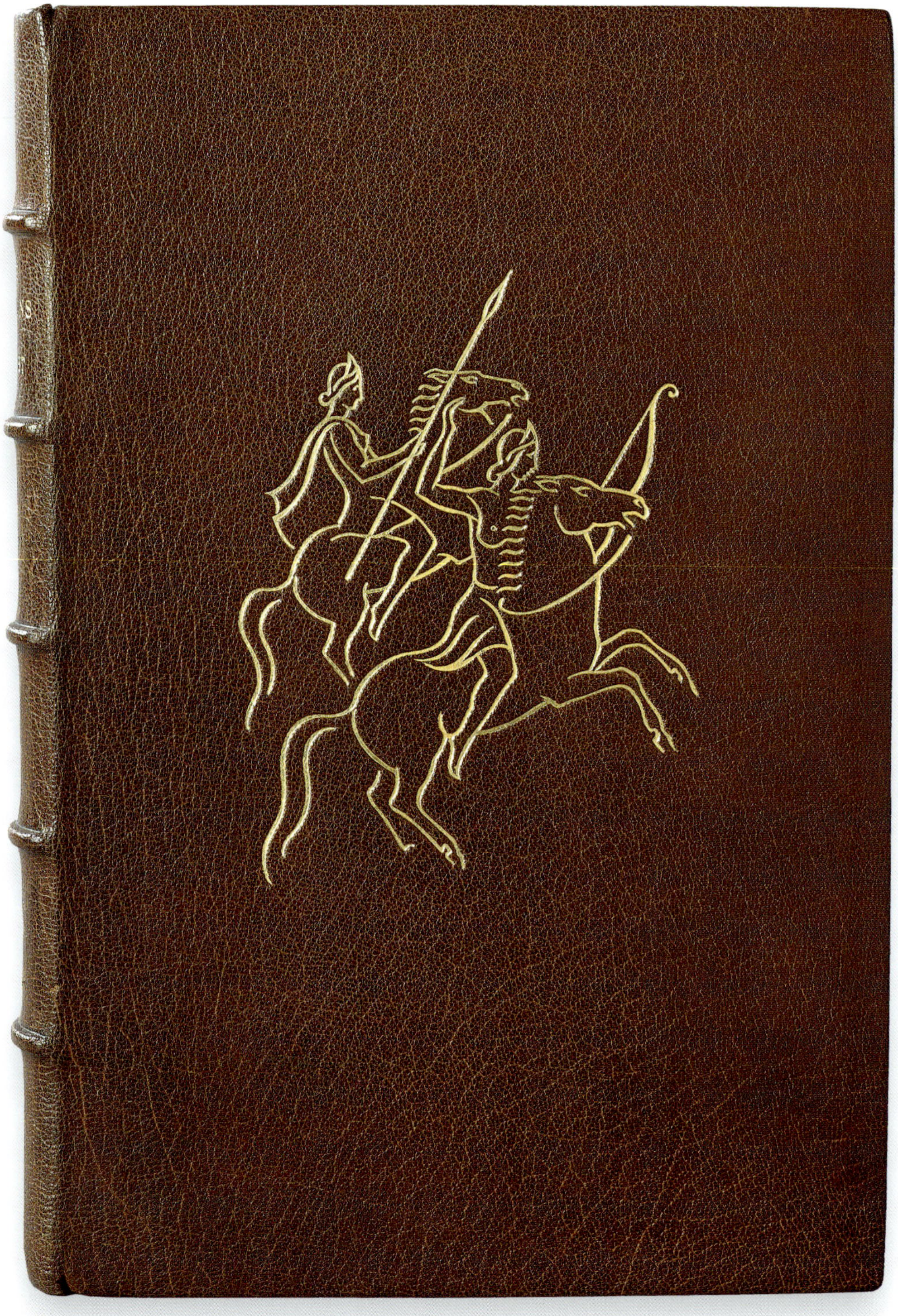

ABOVE
London, 1940s
287 x 190 x 60 mm (11.3 x 7.5 x 2.4 inches)
C.103.g.11

OPPOSITE
London, 1940s
364 x 212 x 35mm (14.3 x 8.4 x 1.4 inches)
C.108.i.6

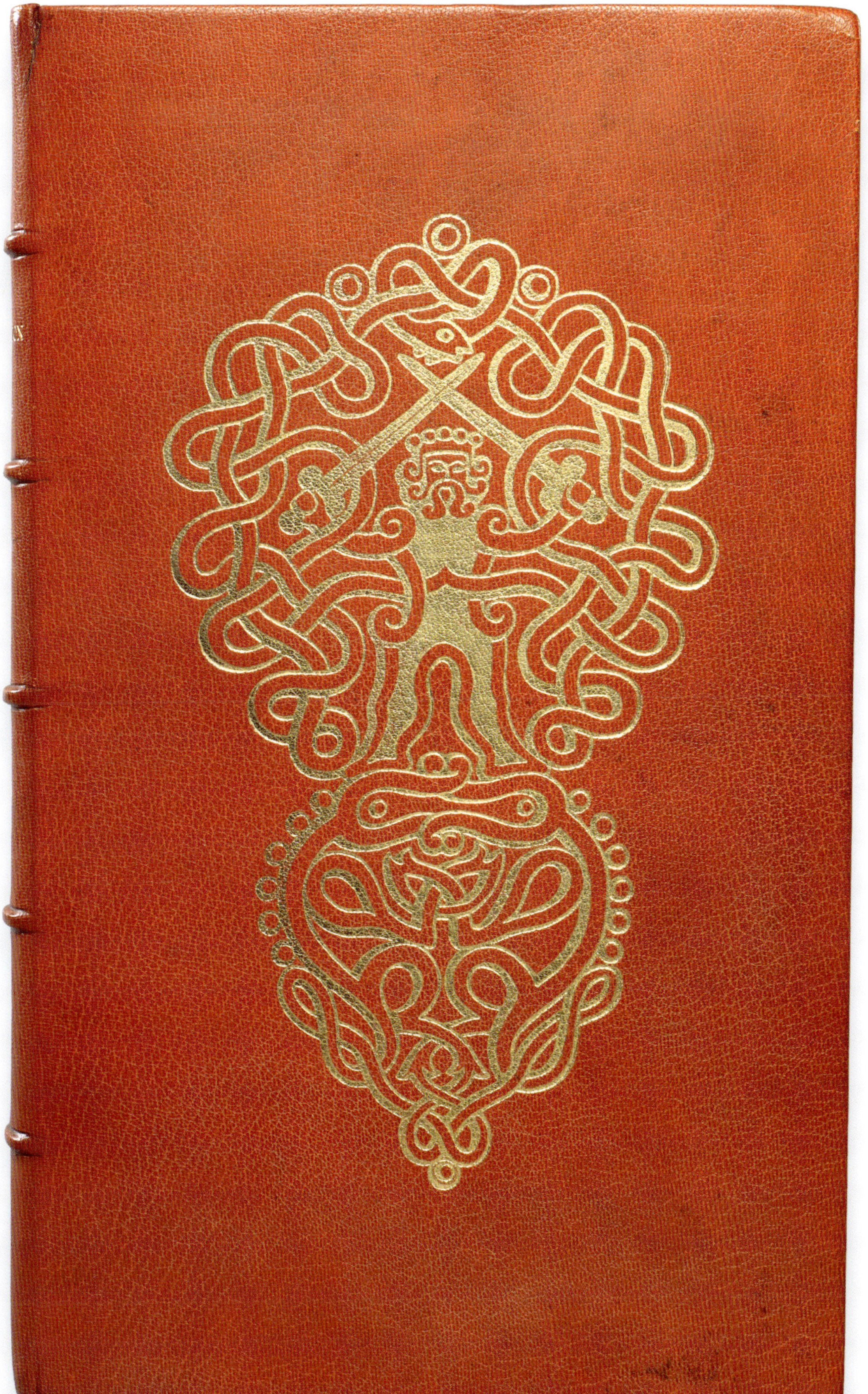

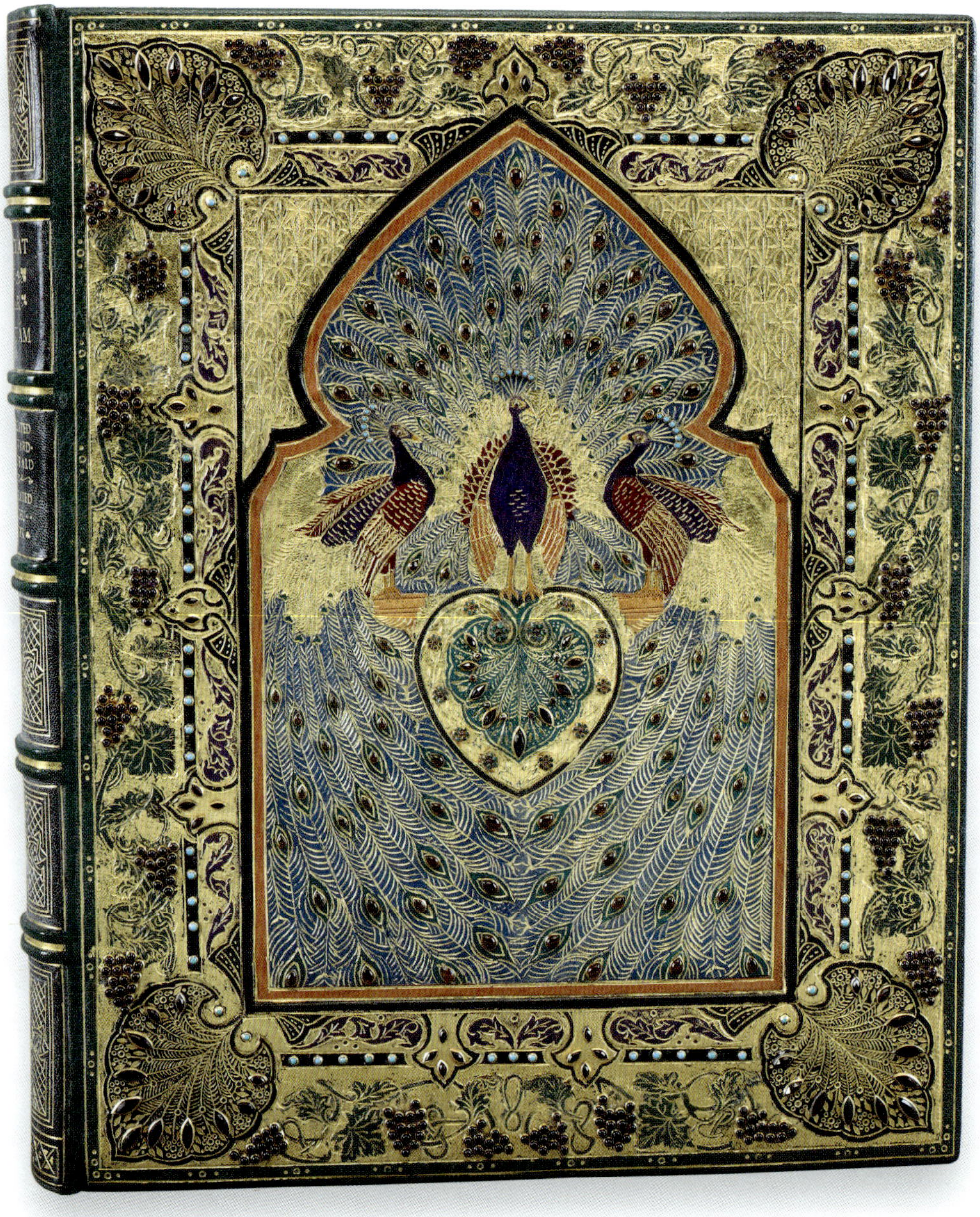

In 1911 Francis Sangorski, of the London firm Sangorski & Sutcliffe, completed a sumptuous jewelled binding on an illustrated copy of the *Rubáiyat of Omar Khayyám*. It was purchased by the American collector, Gabriel Wells, who sent it home on the ill-fated RMS *Titanic*; and, by a strange coincidence, Sangorski himself drowned at sea in the same year. In 1932 Sutcliffe's nephew, Stanley Bray, elected to recreate the binding using the original designs, and on its completion stored it in a bank vault, only for the building to receive a direct hit during the London Blitz. Some of the jewels were salvaged, but the binding was destroyed. Nevertheless, Bray was undaunted and determined to recreate the binding a second time, a task which he completed in his retirement in 1982 when he was 82 years of age. The binding became known as 'the Great Omar III'. The images on the following pages depict the tooled, painted and onlaid doublures of the upper and lower covers.

London, 1982
390 x 310 x 48 mm (15.4 x 12.2 x 1.9 inches)
C.188.c.27

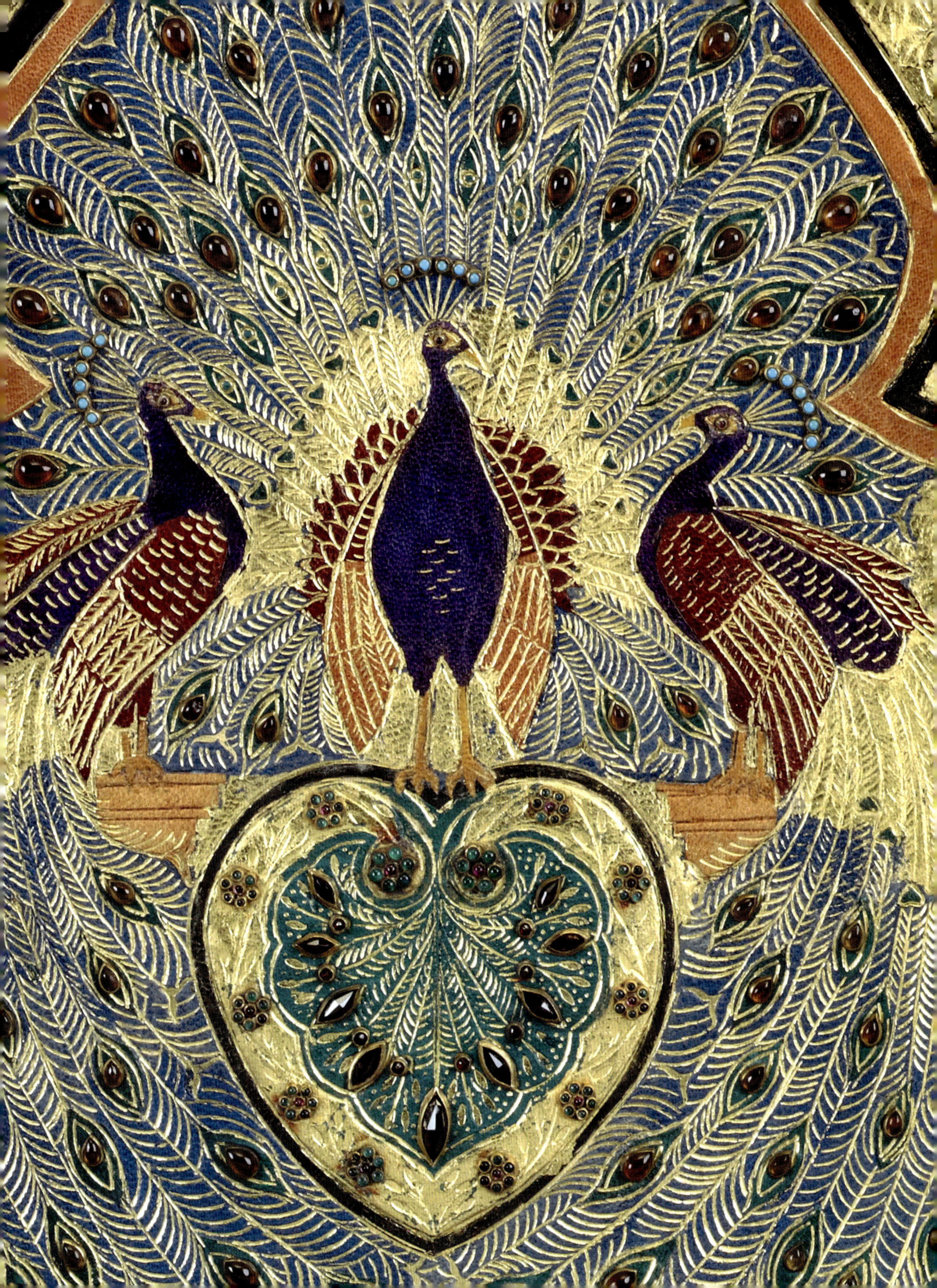

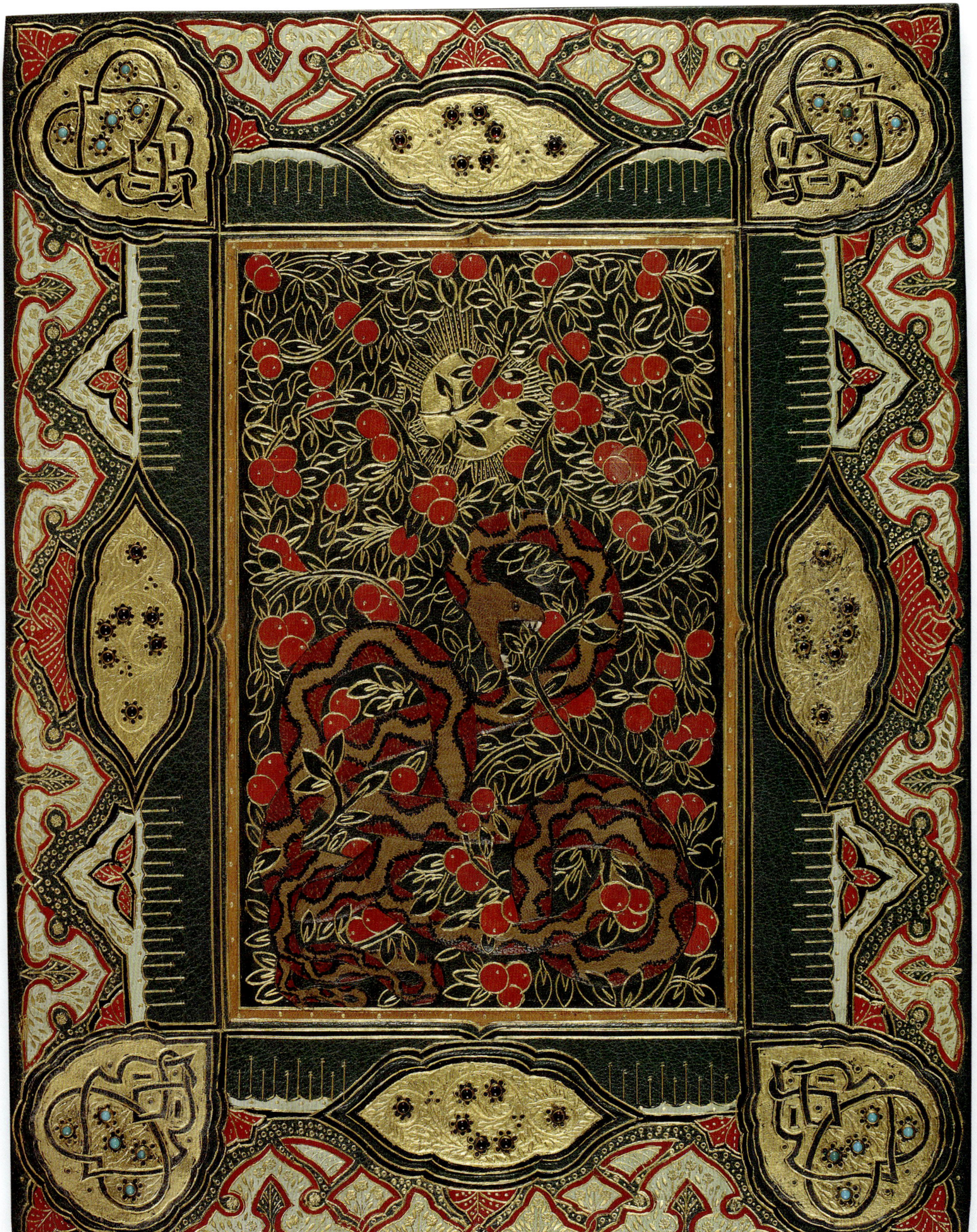

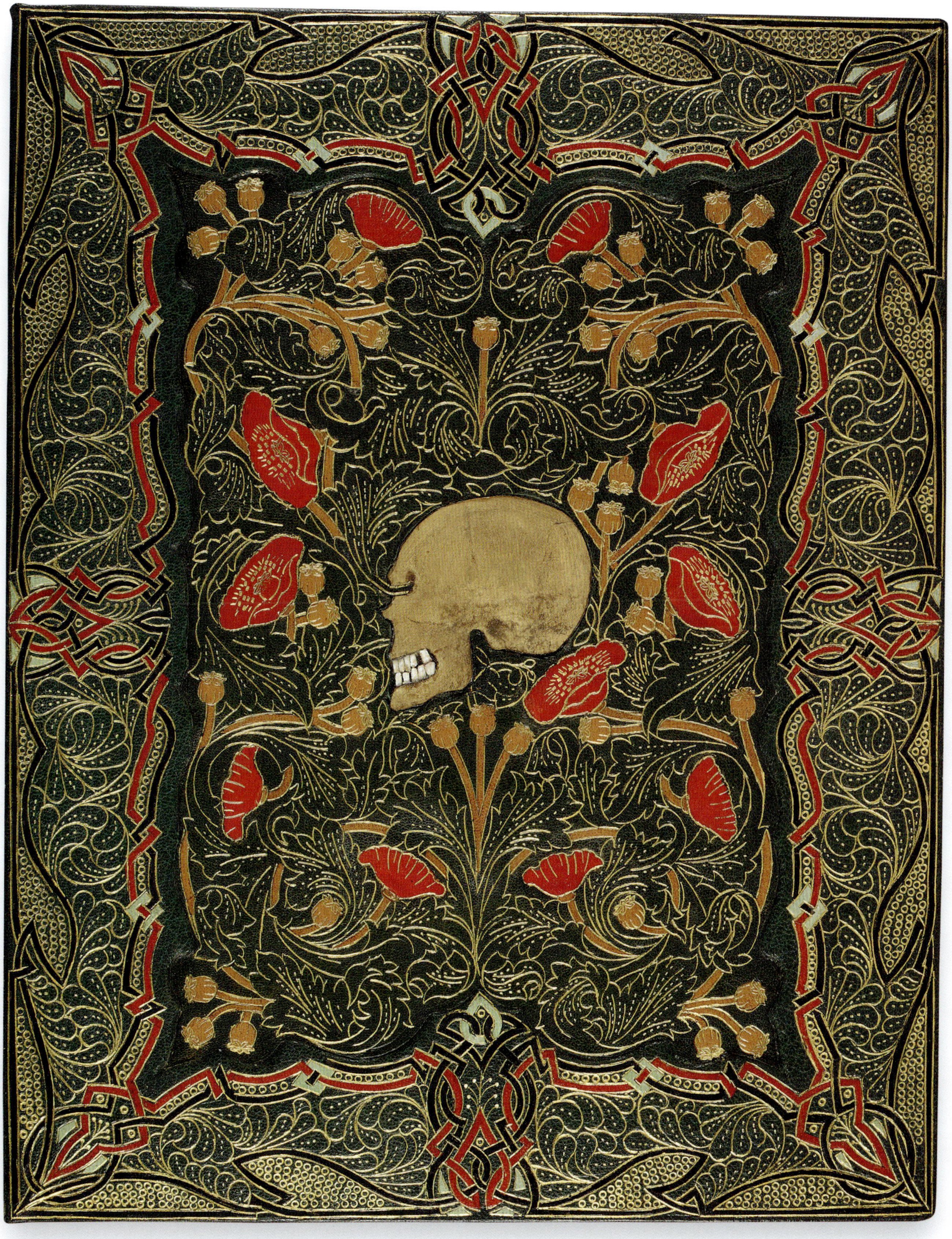

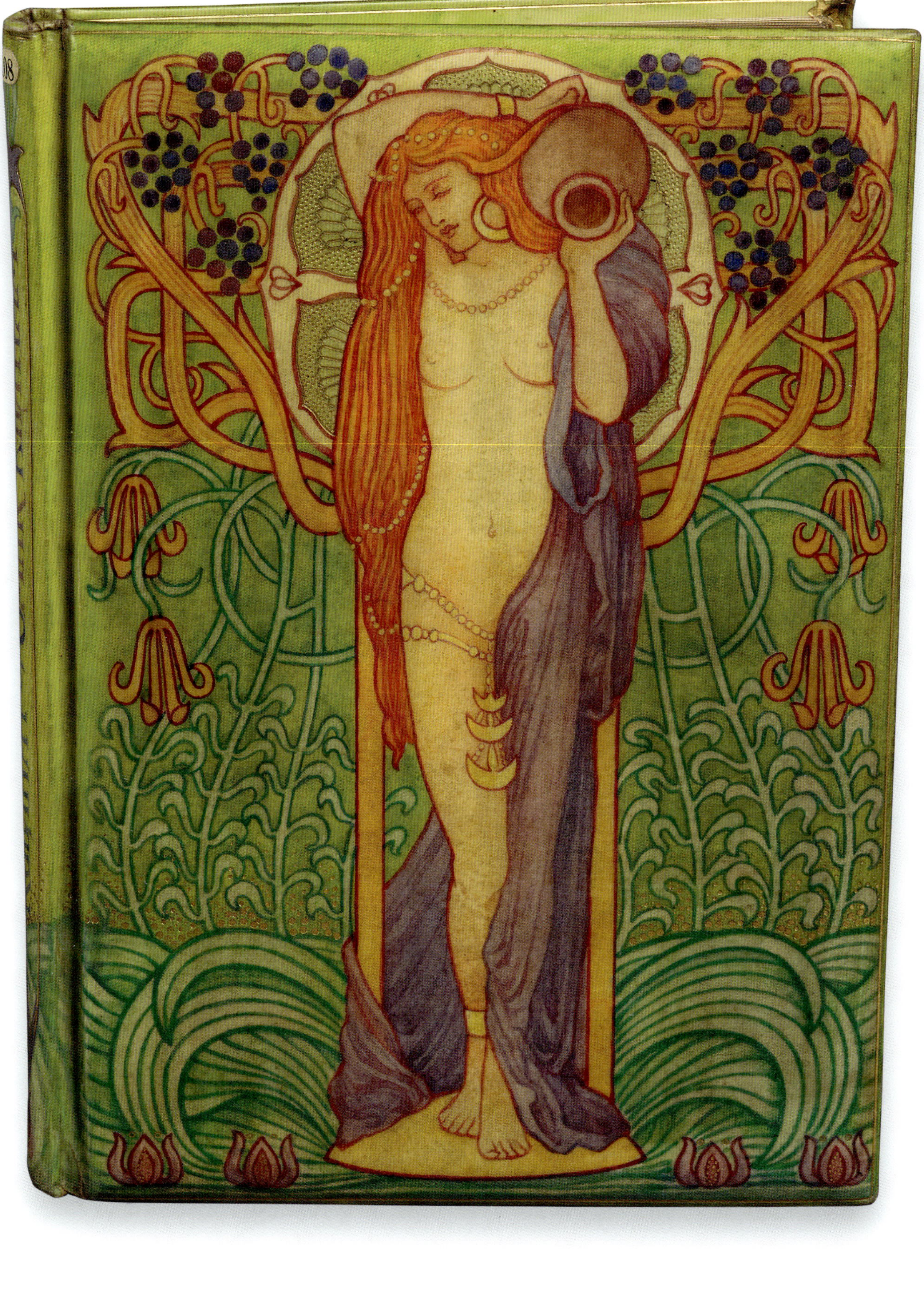

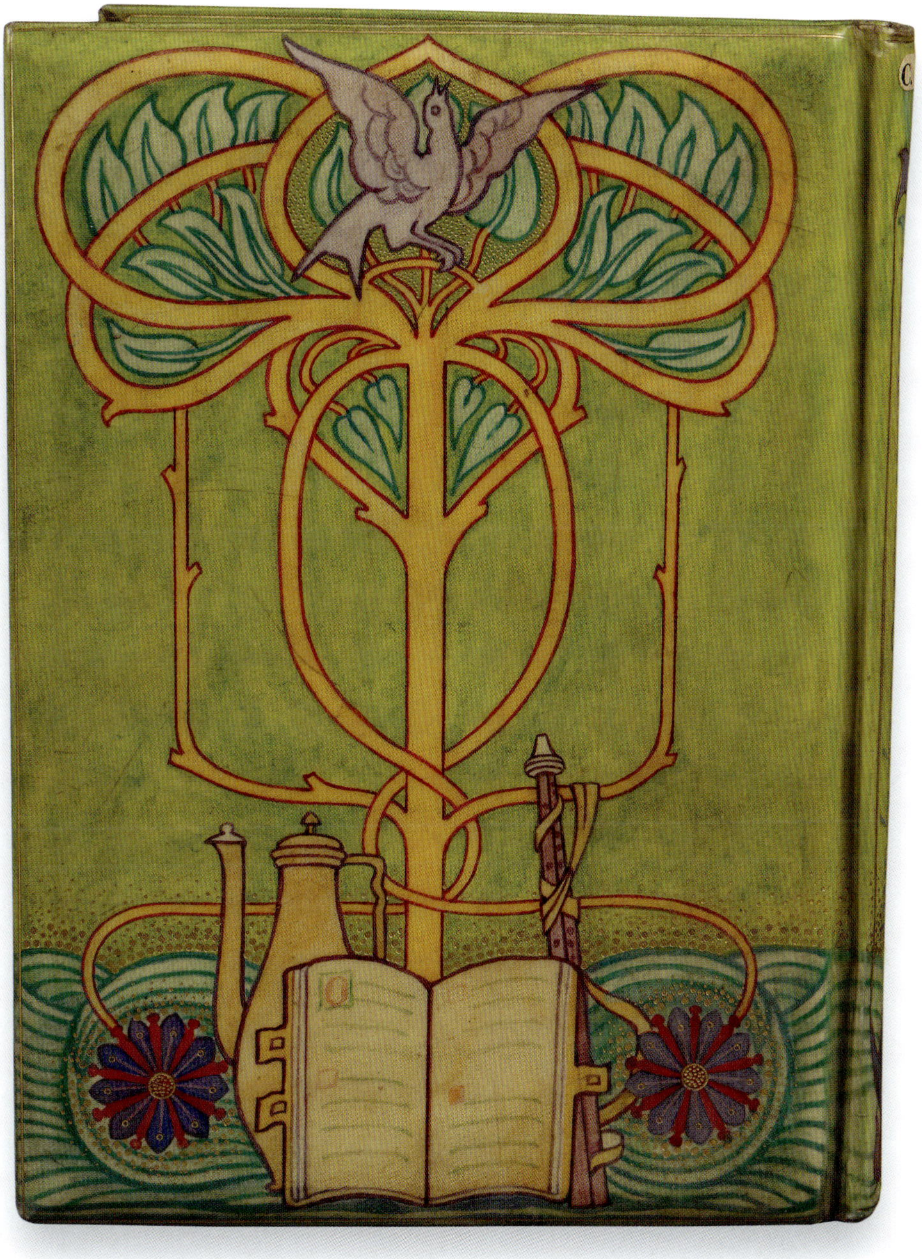

The romantic poem, the *Rubáiyat of Omar Khayyám*, inspired bookbinders and the reading public alike, and is frequently found in ornate bindings. The subject is open to many artistic interpretations; the most famous example in the field of bindings is the jewelled covers made by Sangorski & Sutcliffe (see p.154). Cedric Chivers (d.1929) of Bath devised another unique selling point: vellucent bindings. These resembled the fashionable pictorial bindings produced by the Edwards of Halifax workshop in the eighteenth century (see p.102): transparent vellum revealed colourful hand-painted illustrations on the covers beneath. H Granville Fell was responsible for the Chivers designs and supervised a team of five women painters, whose skill and versatility meant new styles could be adopted quickly. This example shows the influence of Art Nouveau.

Bath, England, early twentieth century
210 x 145 x 15 mm (8.3 x 5.7 x 0.6 inches)
C.108.bbb.3

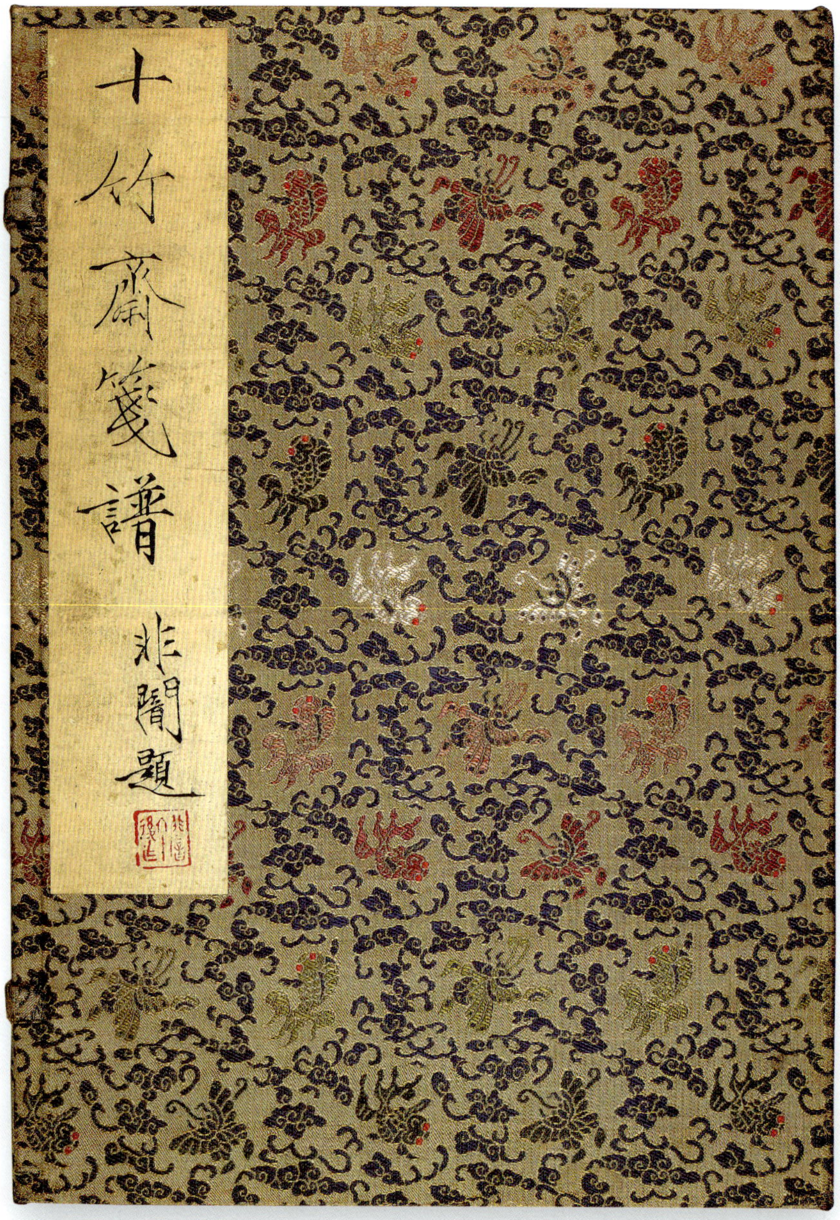

The Chinese silk brocade bindings on these albums may look antique, but they were actually created in the 1950s according to a traditional format. The style chosen was one of several historic styles available to oriental bookbinders: others included the folded-paper concertina style and the butterfly style, in which folded leaves were stitched at the centre. Thread binding as used in this modern binding became the predominant Chinese book format late in the Ming dynasty (1368–1644), although other techniques could be employed to arrive at the desired result: stab stitching through the side, a method later adopted in both Japan and Korea, is one popular example. Post-Ming thread bindings involved the sheet (printed on one side only) being folded and the free ends being sewn in, a significant difference to the Western approach where the stitch passes through the fold. Text blocks were protected by a flap-case (the *tao*), which fastened with toggles of ivory or bone and was covered with blue cotton or, as with the two examples here, silk.

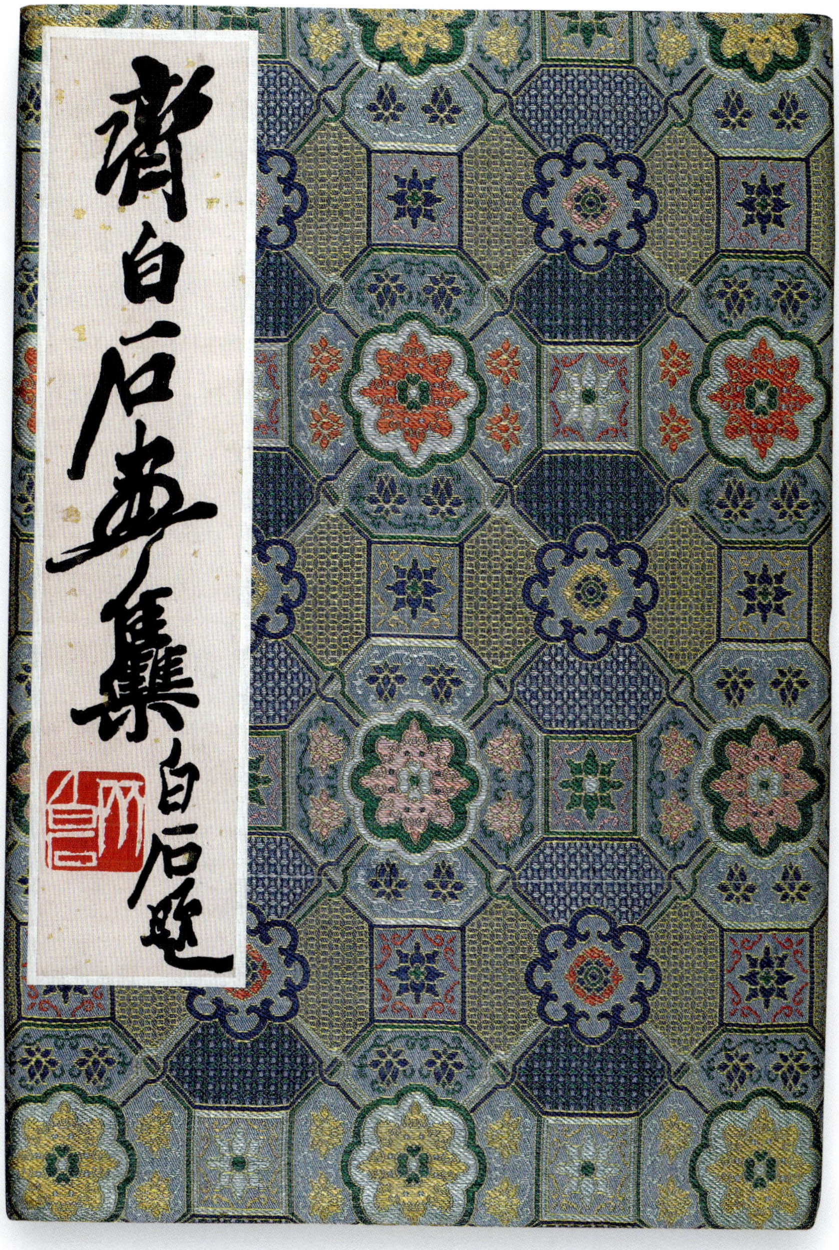

OPPOSITE The title slip here is written by another celebrated twentieth-century Chinese artist, Xu Beihong (1895–1953). The contents of the volume are letter papers (the Chinese wrote on printed or embossed writing paper) and the fabric design (featuring exotic frogs, fish and insects) may have been inspired by seventeenth-century patterns, which contemporaries called 'bizarre silks'.

Rongbaozhai, Beijing, 1952
312 x 220 x 49 mm (12.2 x 8.7 x 1.9 inches)
Or.80.d.9

ABOVE This geometrical patterned Suzhou silk covers a folding album of colour prints by one of the most famous artists of twentieth-century China, Qi Baishi (1864–1957). Silk has been produced in China since ancient times (examples are known from 3,500 BC) and Suzhou has long been an important centre for the trade. The calligraphy on the white title slip was written by the artist himself.

Huaji, Beijing, 1952
315 x 227 x 29 mm (12.4 x 8.9 x 1.1 inches)
Or. 74.d.2

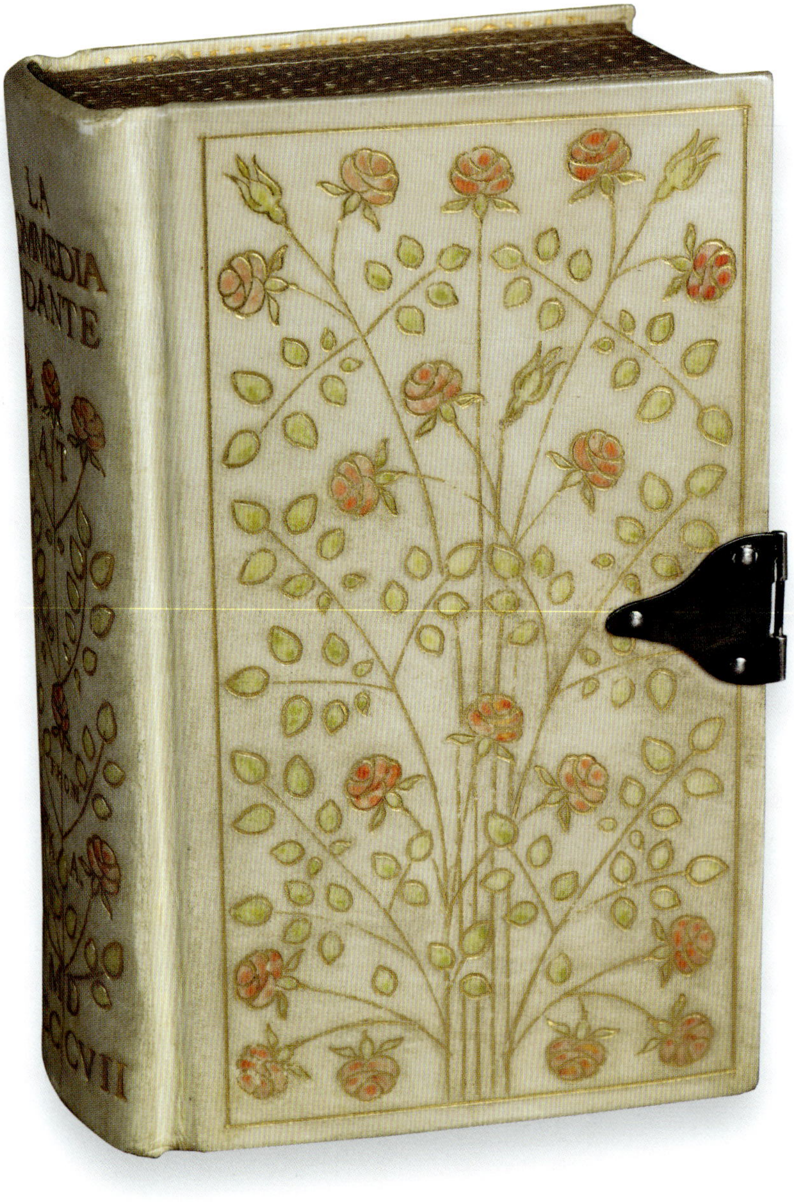

Women had long been involved in the bindings trade on account of their sewing skills, but in England from the late nineteenth century they were able to learn the whole process through courses provided by municipal schools and craft bookbinders. Some women set themselves up as binders in their own right, and Katharine Adams (1862–1952), who bound this example, was one of the most successful. Sarah Treverbian Prideaux (trained by Zaehnsdorf's in London and Gruel in Paris) and Douglas Cockerell (apprenticed at Cobden-Sanderson's workshop) gave Adams lessons and her projects were further encouraged by William Morris and his circle. Her work varied from plain to elaborately tooled bindings, and featured in many Arts and Crafts Exhibition Society displays. Her finishing tools were engraved from her own designs. According to binding historian Howard M Nixon, Adams's work was 'noticeable for a feminine delicacy and the use of small tools'.

England, early twentieth century
104 x 64 x 27 mm (4.10 x 2.5 x 1.1 inches)
Davis 239

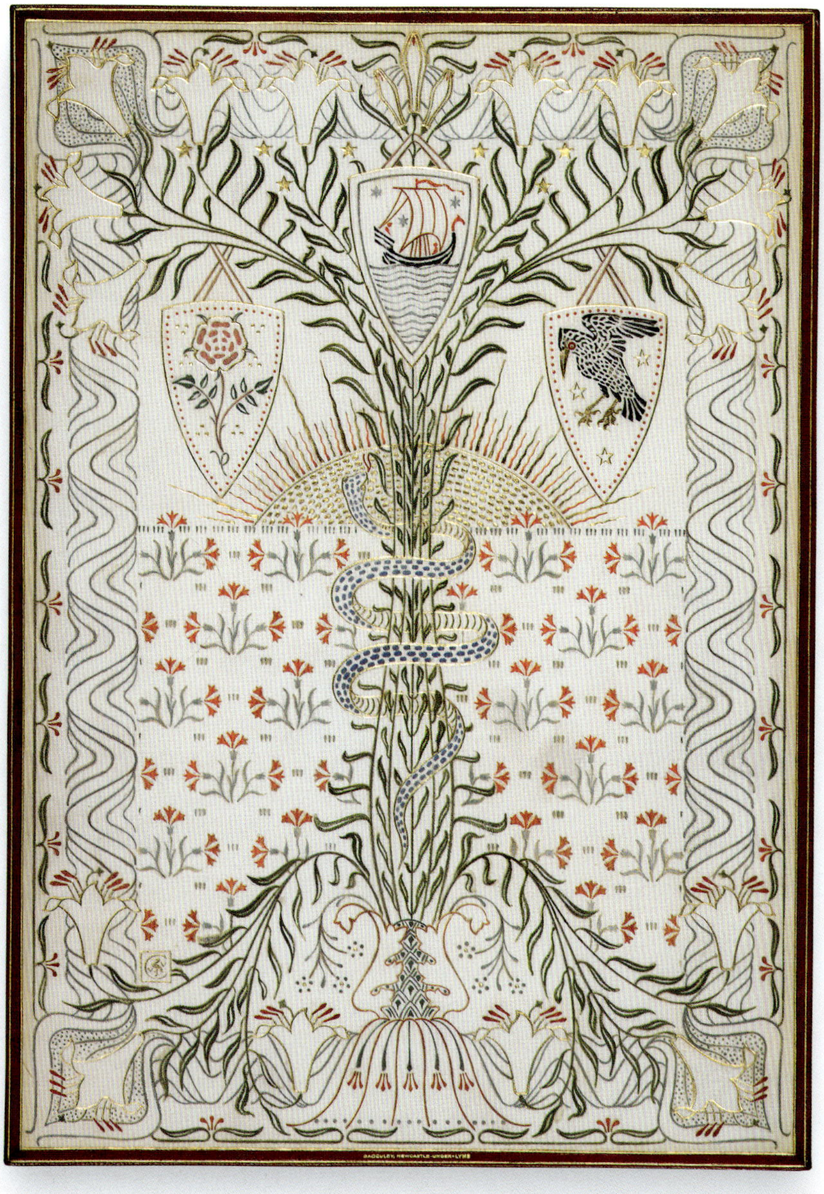

The production of fine bindings was not restricted to London or to the university cities of Oxford and Cambridge: industrial regions could also generate trade in bookbinding. Newcastle under Lyme proved a fruitful location for one successful workshop (fl.1890–1940), which was established by the bookseller George Thomas Bagguley (1860–1950). Bagguley was probably not a trained binder himself, but he did patent a method of tooling in colours. This was called Sutherland decoration, after his patron the Duchess of Sutherland, and was used with great skill by the finishers in his workshop. As shown here, the method was frequently applied to the cream vellum doublures of a book (with plain goatskin covers), providing an effective background for the different colours employed. This 'Sutherland style' quickly became very popular, not least because of a commission given by Queen Victoria.

Newcastle under Lyme, England, early twentieth century
292 x 209 x 20 mm (11.5 x 8.2 x 0.8 inches)
C.69.h.9

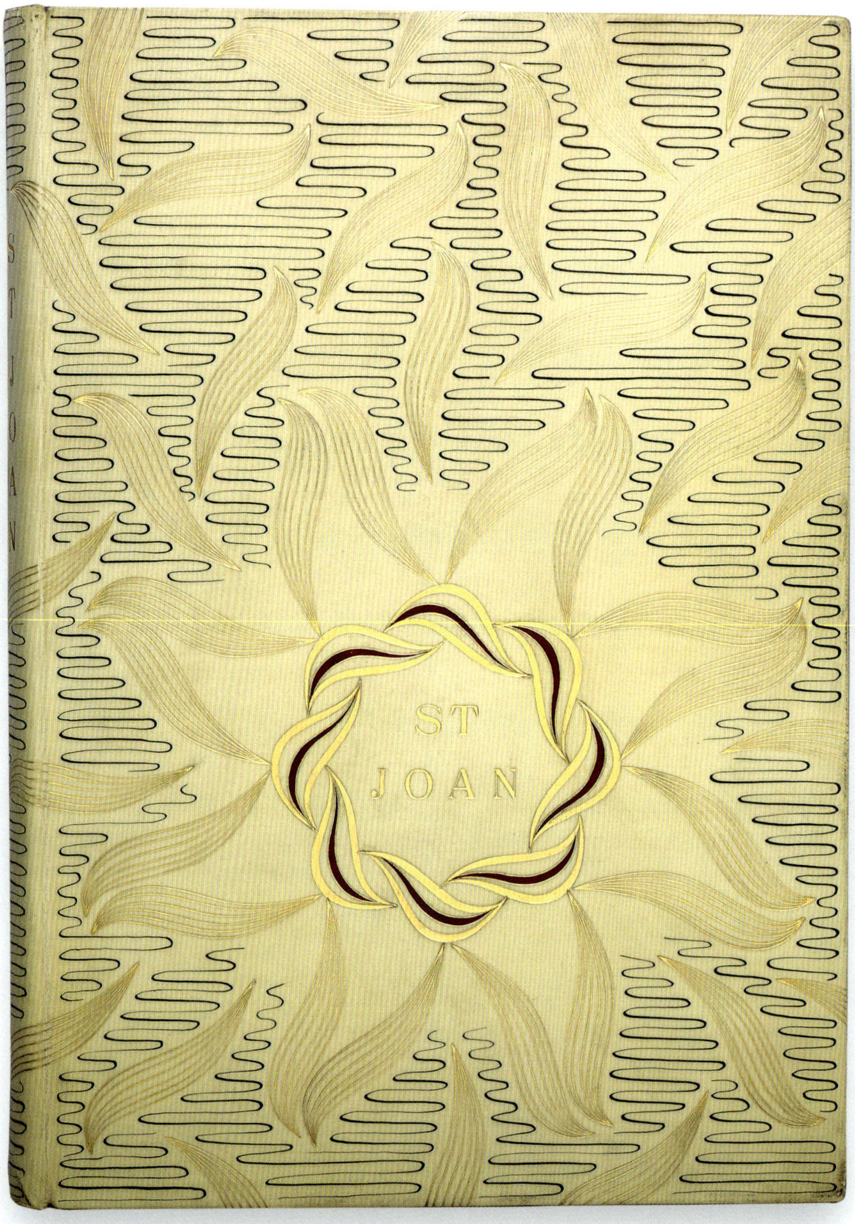

A later product of the Zaehnsdorf firm was this onlaid parchment binding, tooled in gold, black and red and designed by Arthur R Hundleby. The first owner, binding collector and historian Charles Ramsden, noted on the paste-down that it won an award at the 1951 *Festival of Britain* exhibition, but 'it should in my opinion have had the first instead of the second prize'. In the eyes of the binder, Bernard Middleton (see p.184) however, the Festival display did not reflect well on the British craft. Other colleagues (see p.169) shared his view and joined together to form the Guild of Contemporary Bookbinders in an attempt to improve standards and stimulate design.

London, England, twentieth century
420 x 282 x 35 mm (16.5 x 11.1 x 1.4 inches)
C.156.i.9

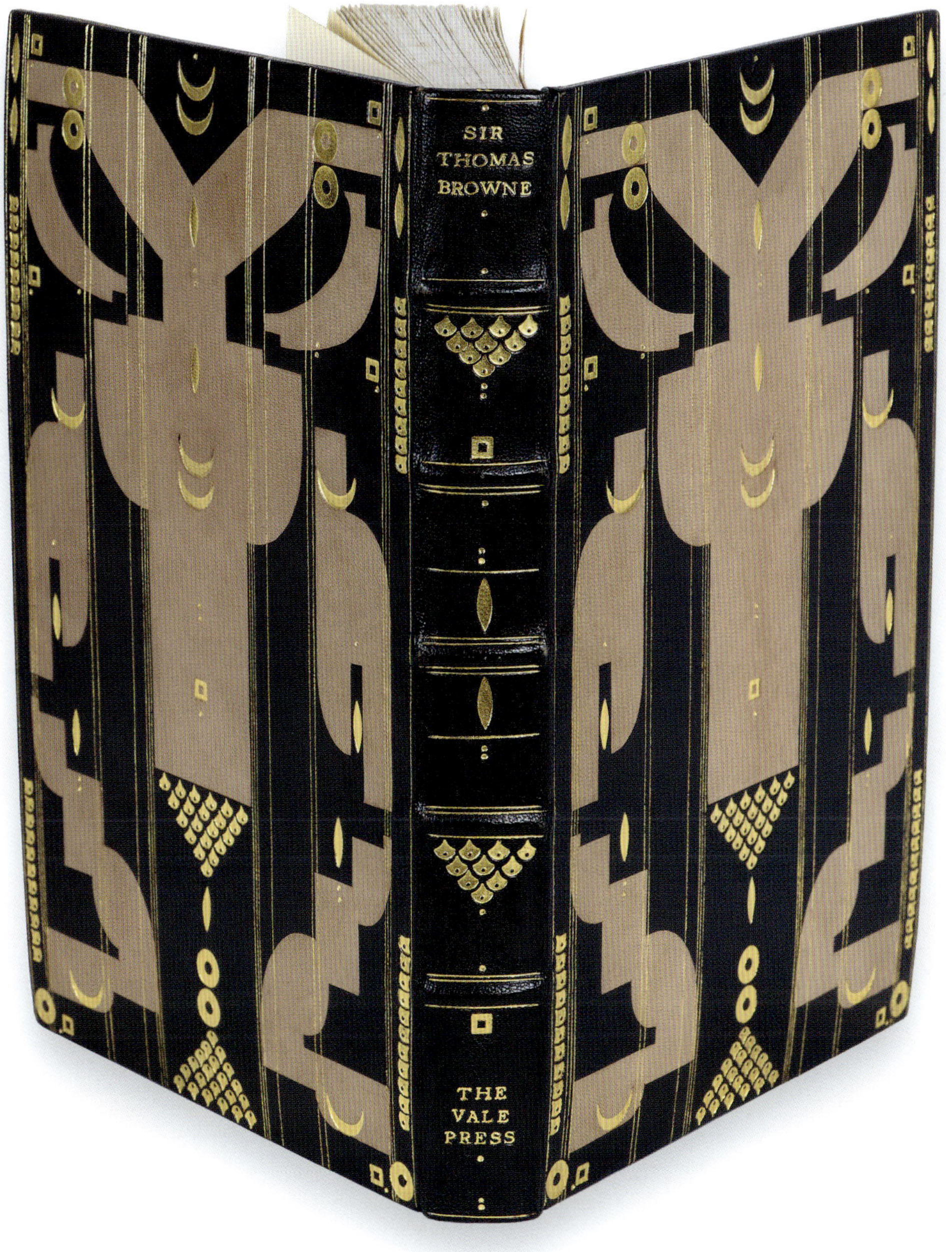

This gold-tooled and inlaid black goatskin binding by Sybil Pye (b.1879) has been described as one of her most sumptuous bindings. It was bound for the British Museum in 1940 and incorporates elements of Art Deco. Pye's bindings are instantly recognizable, despite the fact that she did not consciously adopt a particular style but was inspired by a variety of elements. Pye designed her own finishing tools, as well as making use of some given to her by Charles Ricketts. The fact that Pye was self-taught (using Douglas Cockerell's manual, *Bookbinding and the Care of Books*) did not stop her from adopting the challenging decorative technique of applying leather inlays, a practice with which she became associated. Time has confirmed bindings writer A J A Symons's view of 60 years ago, that 'Miss Pye's best work ... will, a hundred years hence, stand comparison with the classic masterpieces of binding'.

England, *c.*1940
300 x 190 x 35 mm (11.8 x 7.5 x 1.4 inches)
C.108.h.4

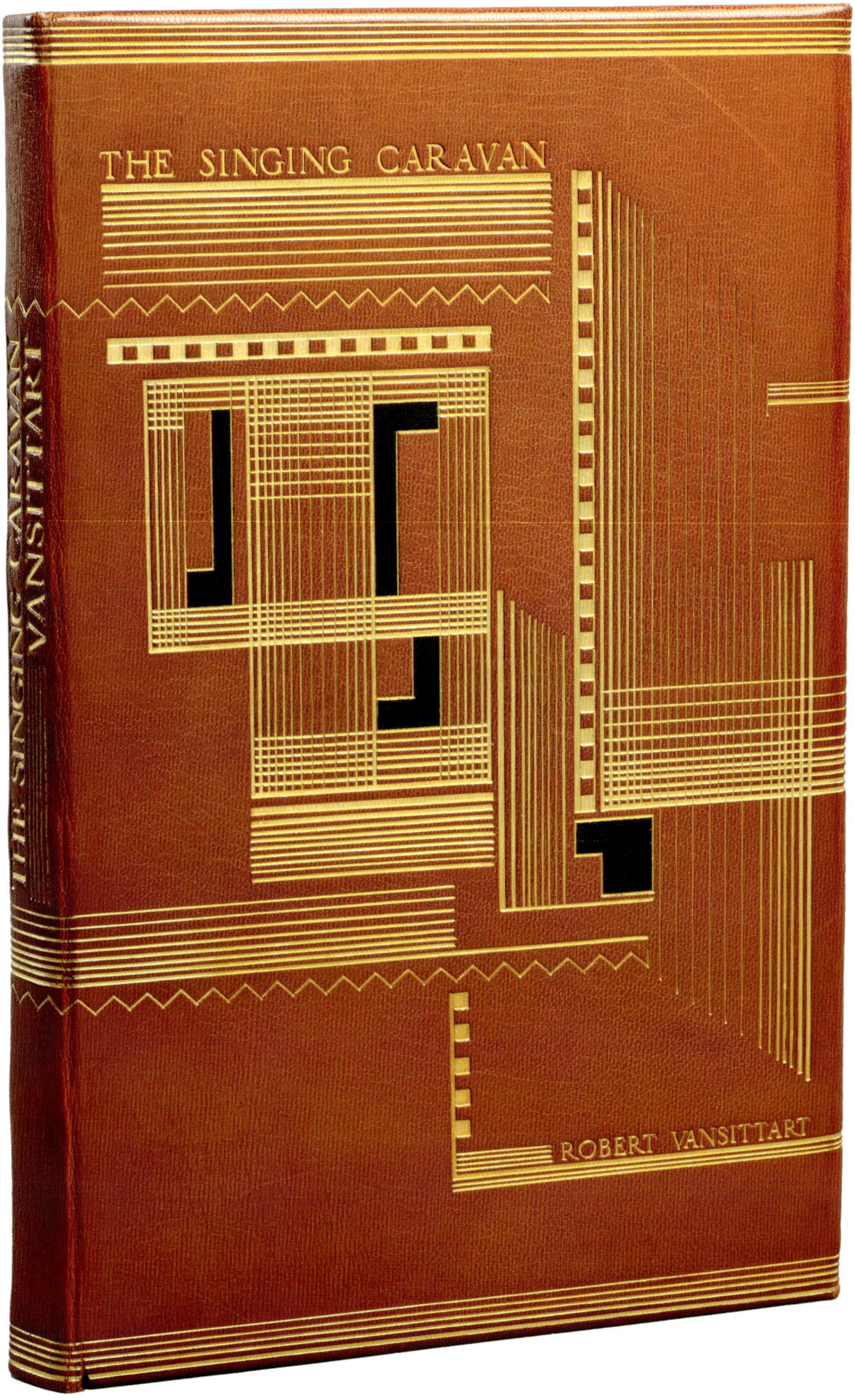
THE SINGING CARAVAN
ROBERT VANSITTART
THE SINGING CARAVAN
VANSITTART

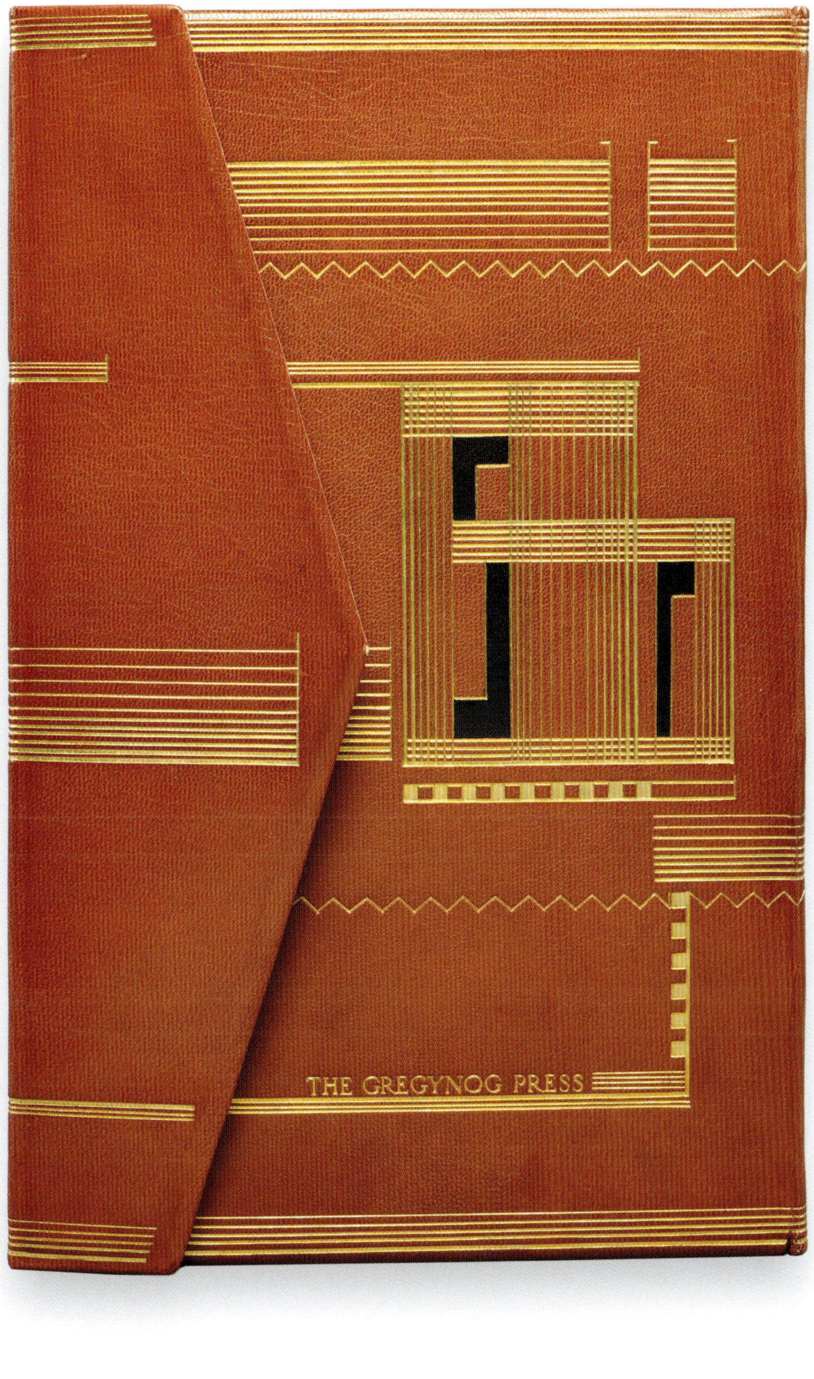

During the twentieth century small presses were established to cater for those who enjoyed collecting finely printed works in limited editions. Binding had a special status at the Gregynog Press, founded in Wales in 1922 by Margaret and Gwendoline Davies. Part of each edition received special bindings and, from 1924, George Fisher (1879–1970) was responsible for this work. This orange goatskin binding with black onlays and a gold-tooled linear design (by William MacCance) was one of 25 special bindings for the edition of 250. It features an Islamic bindings-style fore-edge flap, appropriate to the text, which was subtitled *A Sufi Tale*.

Wales, mid-twentieth century
280 x 280 (including flap) x 22 mm
(11 x 11 (including flap) x 0.9 inches)
C.100.a.3

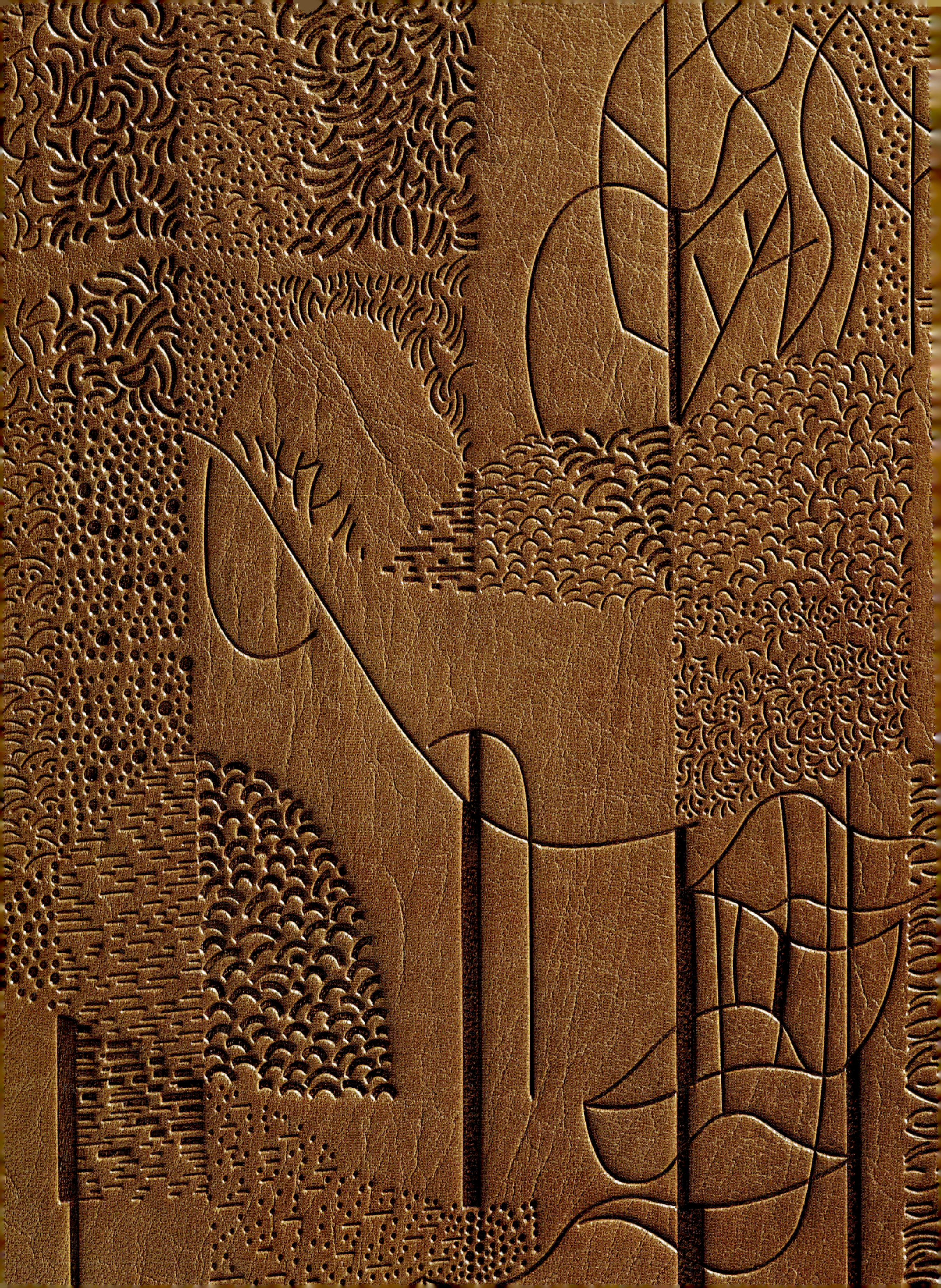

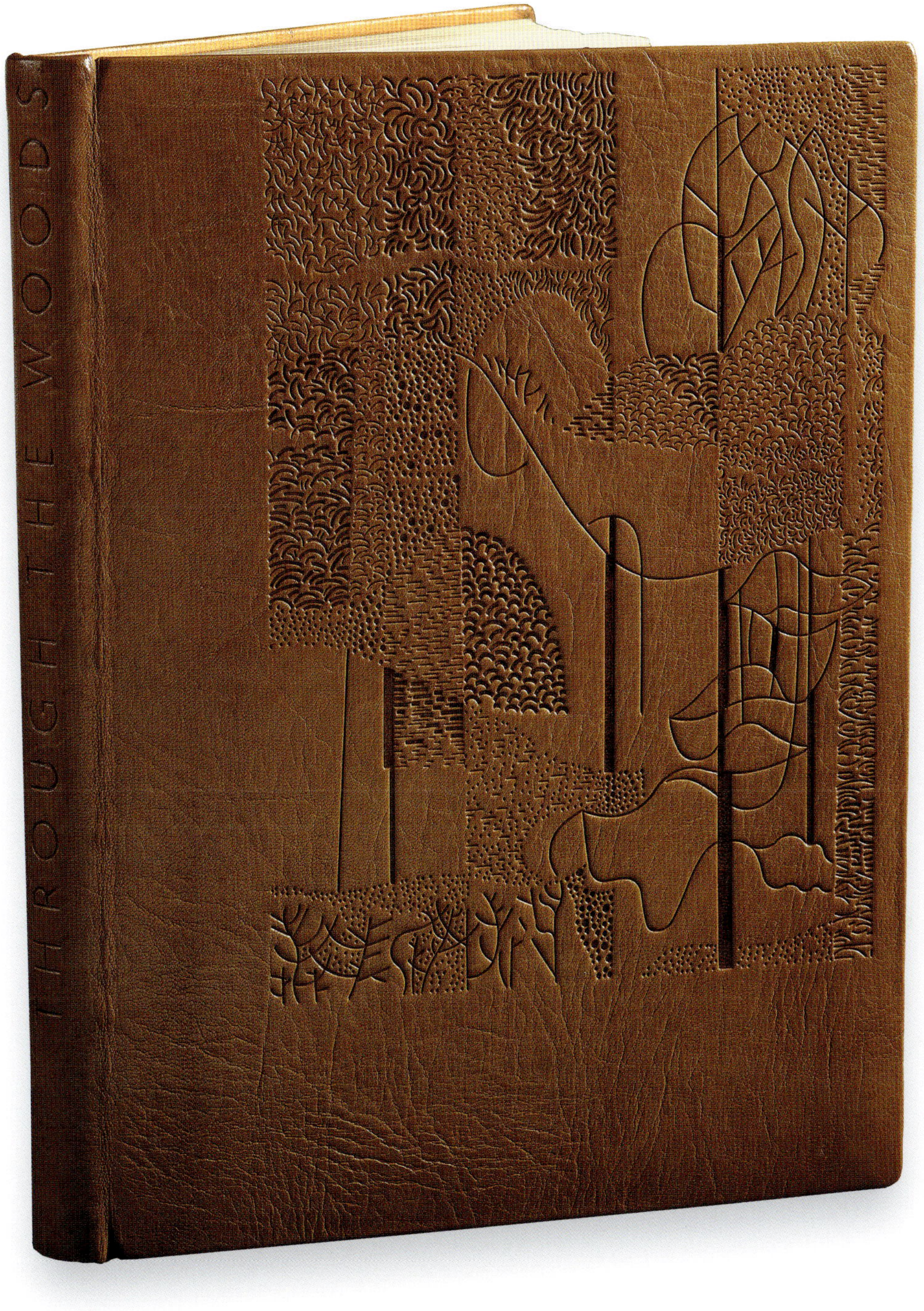

This blind-tooled brown goatskin binding was produced by Edgar Mansfield, bookbinder and sculptor (1907–1996). Mansfield was inspired by contemporary art forms, including Cubism and Surrealism, and his new perspectives underpinning the making of bindings were conveyed to students at the London College of Printing, as well as through his book, *Modern Design in Bookbinding*. 'The nature of the surface of a Mansfield binding and its tactile quality is most important, as befits the work of a sculptor.' Mansfield is considered one of the most influential binders of the twentieth century.

London, mid-twentieth century
265 x 198 x 22 mm (10.4 x 7.8 x 0.9 inches)
C.120.f.10

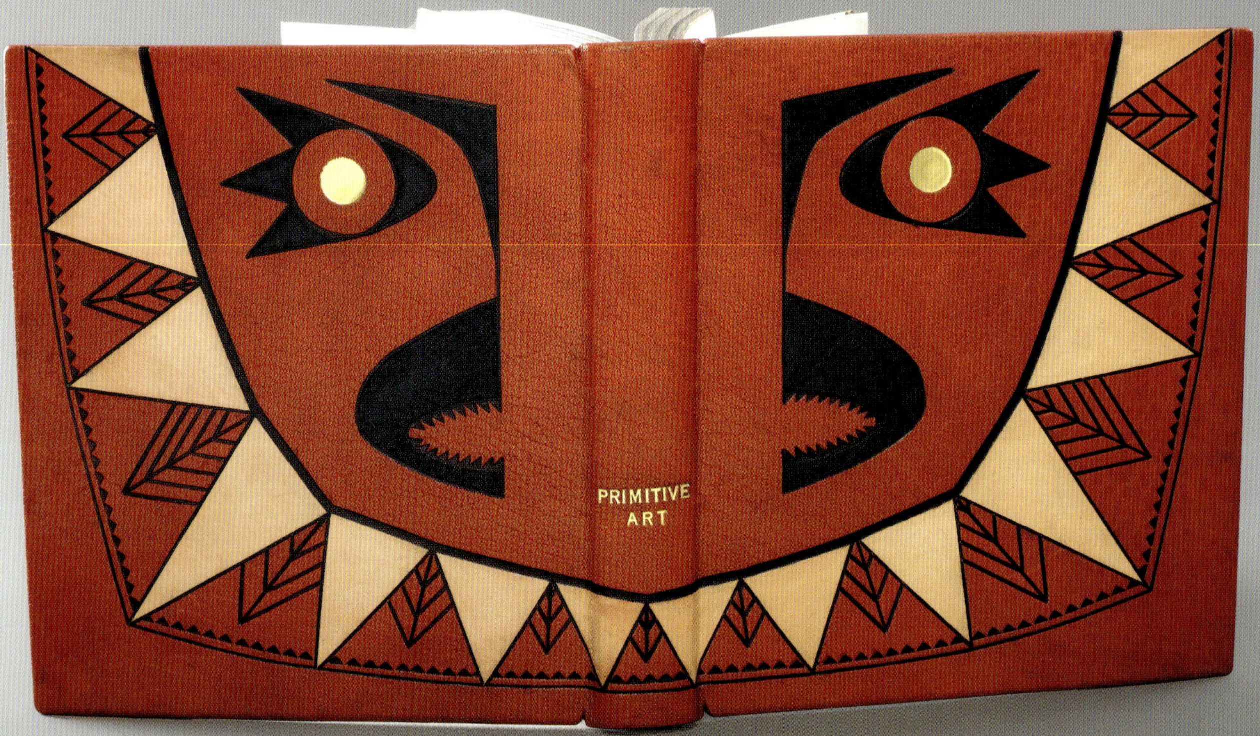

Trevor Jones (b.1931) studied bookbinding with Arthur Johnson at Hornsey College of Art, London. Concerned with the rather stagnant nature of post-1945 British bookbinding, he joined contemporaries in the Guild of Contemporary Bookbinders, formed in 1955, in an effort to revive the craft. This brown goatskin binding uses tooling and onlays to portray a mask, an icon that embraces the subject-matter of the book (primitive art) in a single bold and arresting image. The design is centred on the spine, and can only be viewed in its entirety when both upper and lower covers are visible. According to Jones: 'Each binding can be an adventure in a new direction, though with time we learn that some paths offer more than others. I like to subvert the conventions of bookbinding.'

England, 1958
284 x 253 x 49 mm (11.2 x 10 x 2 inches)
Davis 301

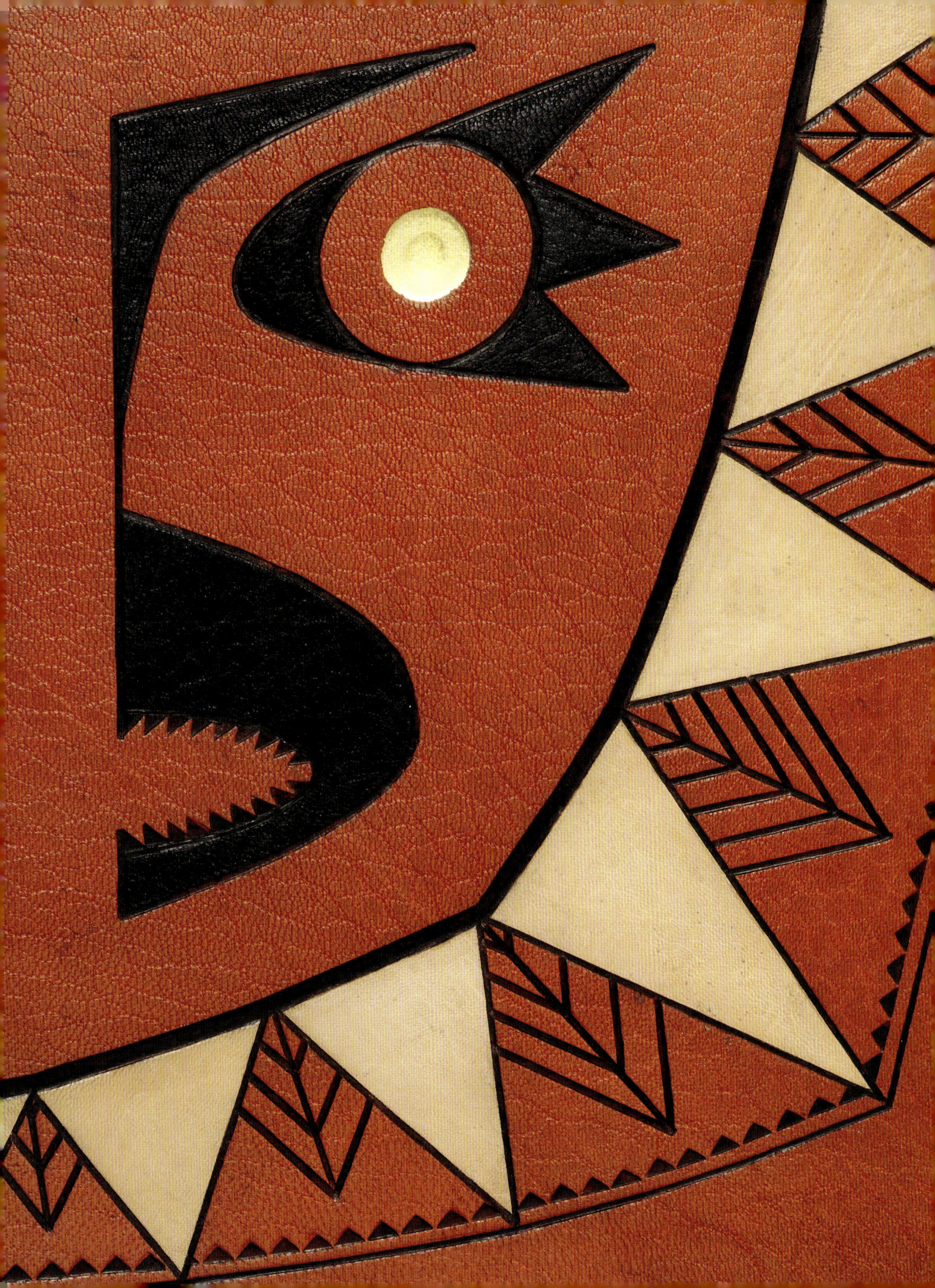

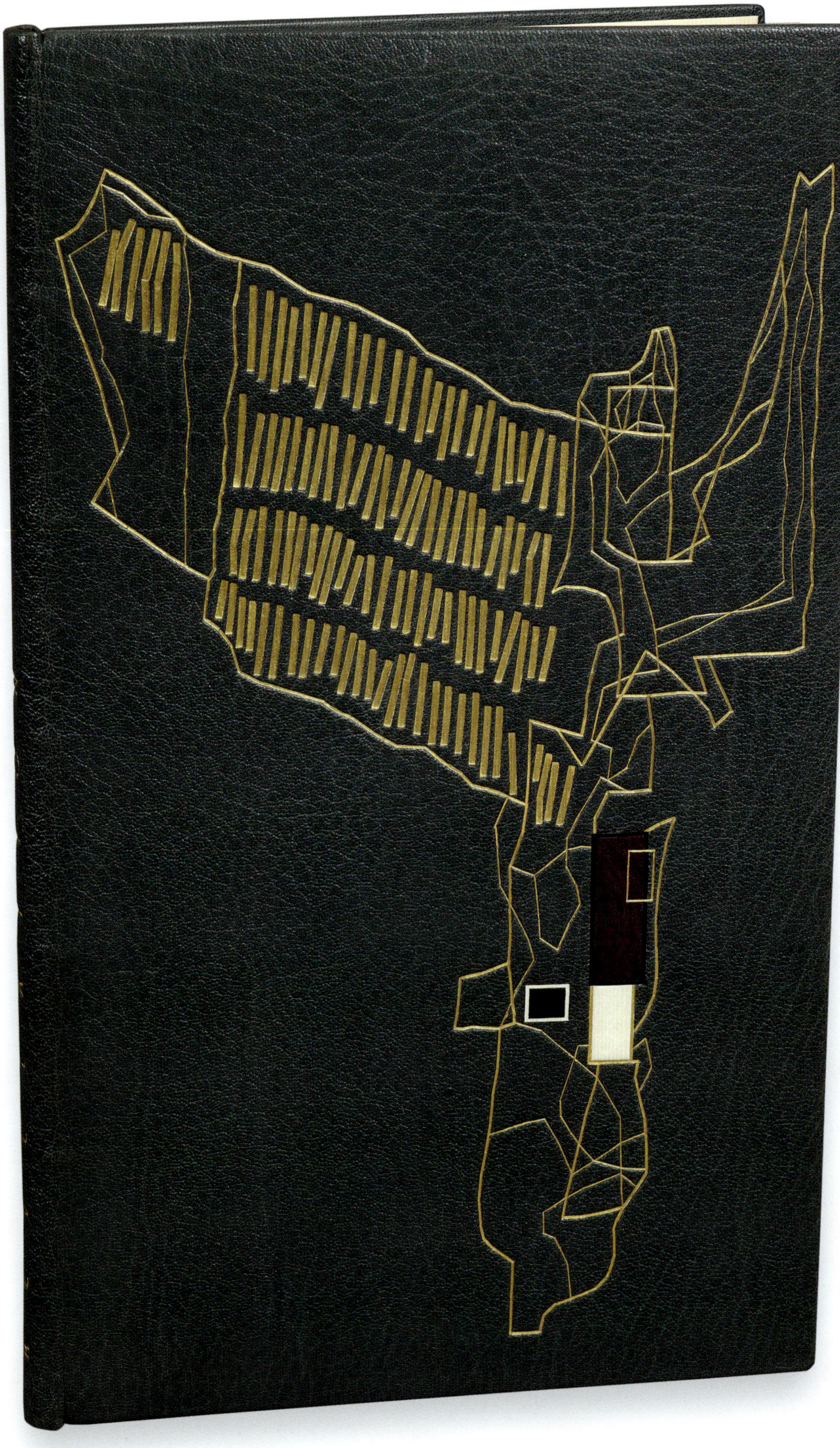

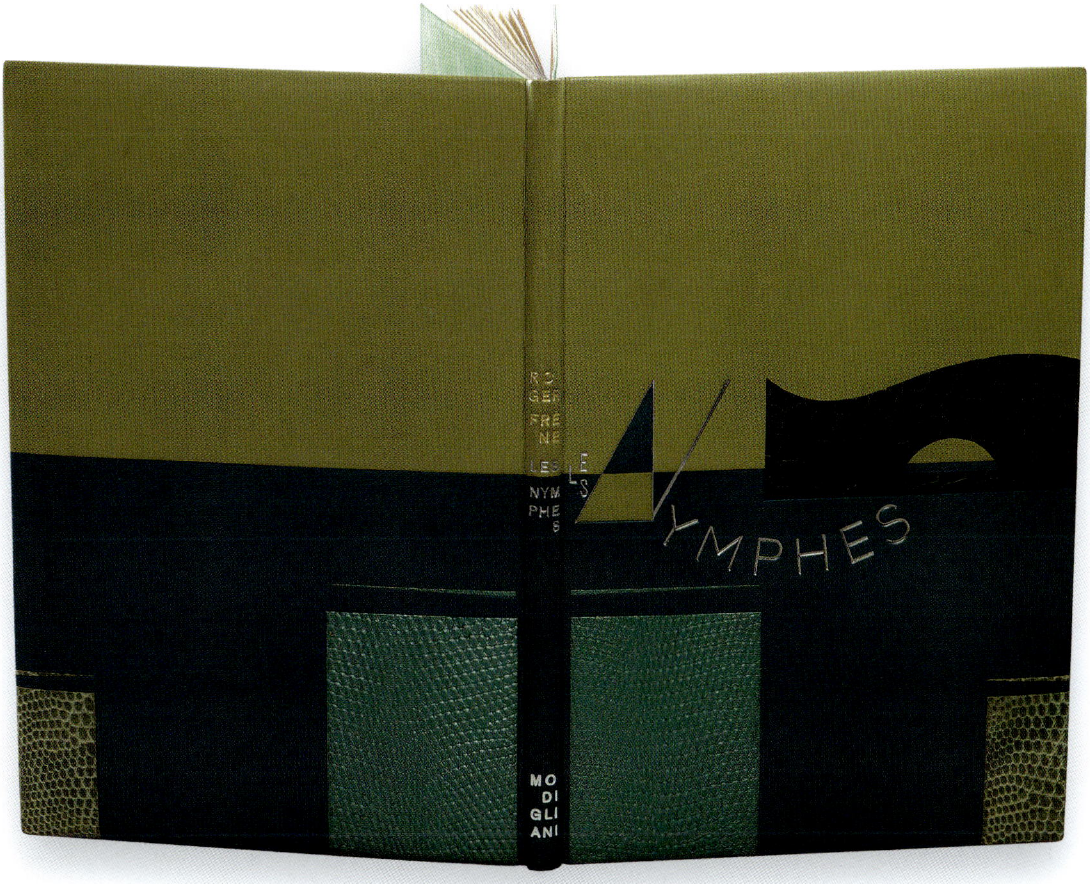

OPPOSITE This onlaid and gold-tooled black goatskin binding is by Ivor Robinson (b.1924). An influential binder, he was a triple medallist in 1971 at the Prix Paul Bonet, the premier binding competition in Switzerland. The skills that were traditionally passed on from master to apprentice are today passed on from teacher to student. Robinson has been part of this continuum, studying at the School of Art in Bournemouth, working in the trade, establishing his own workshop, and in his turn, teaching others at Oxford Brookes University. The myriad of gold-tooled lines is characteristic of Robinson's work; another trait is the application of bold onlays in colour-blocks. The angel of St John seems to emerge from the tooling, although Robinson's vision tends to be essentially abstract. He has said, 'as a binder, I would not consider it my primary task to interpret the text', believing that to be the preserve of the author.

England, mid-twentieth century
350 x 122 x 17 mm (13.8 x 4.8 x 0.7inches)
C.108.w.6

ABOVE Rose Adler (1890–1959) was one of the most remarkable French binders of the twentieth century, and her achievements were recognized when she was awarded the Légion d'honneur in 1951. Adler branched out on her own in the 1920s, following her education at the École des arts décoratifs and a period of study under the French binder, Henri Noulhac. She responded to several influences, notably that of the binder Pierre Legrain. Together, they 'transformed bookbinding into a medium of playful and dazzling experimentation'. As Adler's career progressed her designs became more original, although, in her words, the binding was always 'the servant of the text'. This green and turquoise calfskin binding, with snakeskin onlays and silver letting, is characteristic of her later work, which tended to rely upon more simple and restrained non-figurative forms. André Jeanne, who worked as a finisher for many leading French binders, was responsible for the tooling.

Paris, 1957
205 x 140 x 10 mm (8.1 x 5.5 x 0.4 inches)
Davis 557

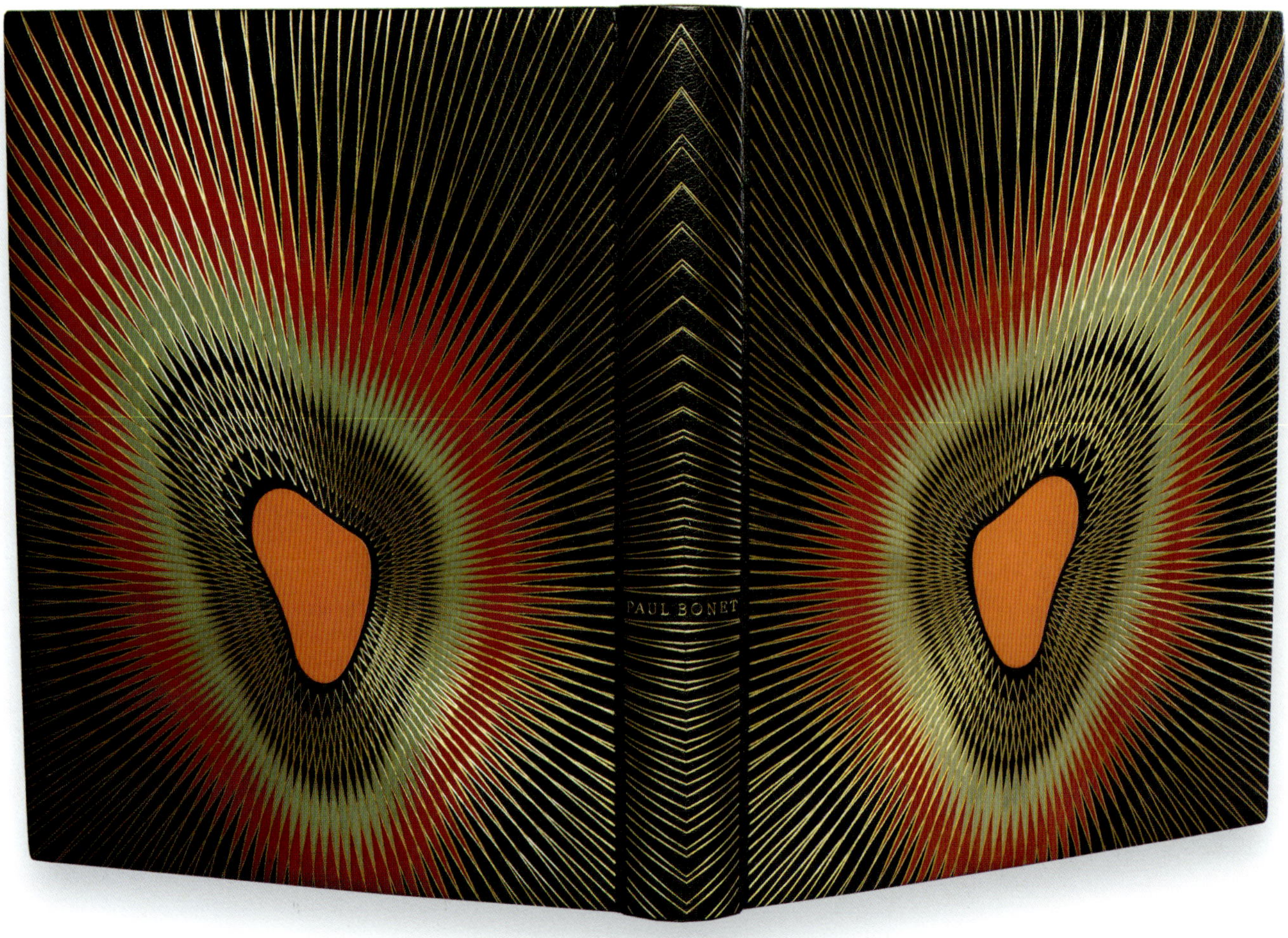

The early career of binder Paul Bonet (1889–1971) was varied, with jobs ranging from working in the family millinery firm to electrician and model-maker. From the 1920s, he began to design bookbindings, influenced initially by his contemporary Pierre Legrain, who had his own workshop. Not only did Bonet study historic binding styles and techniques, he also reacted to modern artistic movements, including Surrealism and Art Deco. This green goatskin binding combines old with new: the onlay style (popular in the eighteenth century) is updated by the gold-tooled sunburst pattern ('rayonnante'), which catches the light and makes the surface shimmer. Although he worked with several forwarders and finishers who interpreted his designs, Bonet stressed the importance of a personal response to a piece of work. He wrote: 'Contemporary binding is perhaps an original creation which reflects the personality of its creator.'

Paris, 1962
331 x 254 x 43 mm (13 x 10 x 1.7 inches)
Davis 415

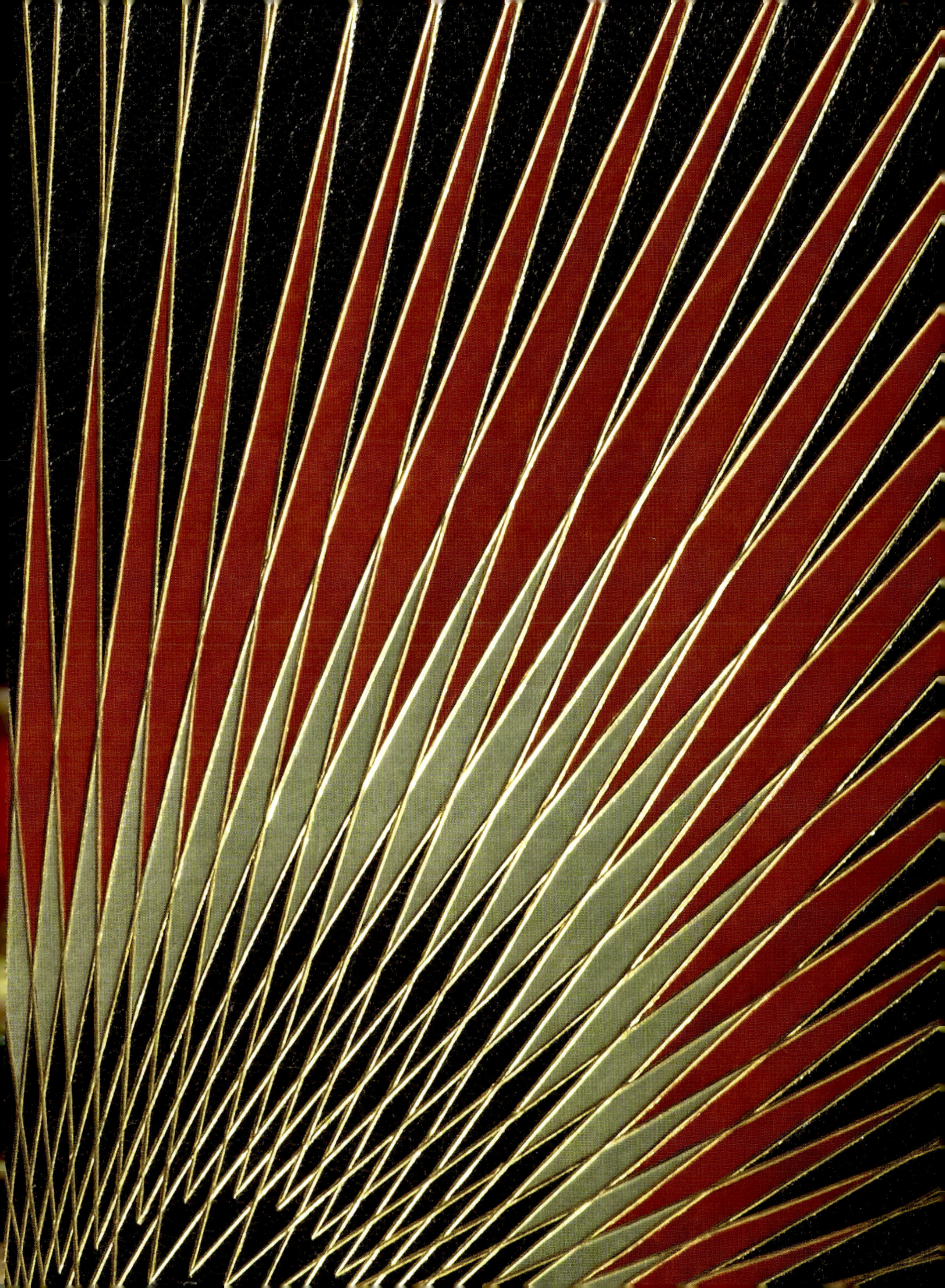

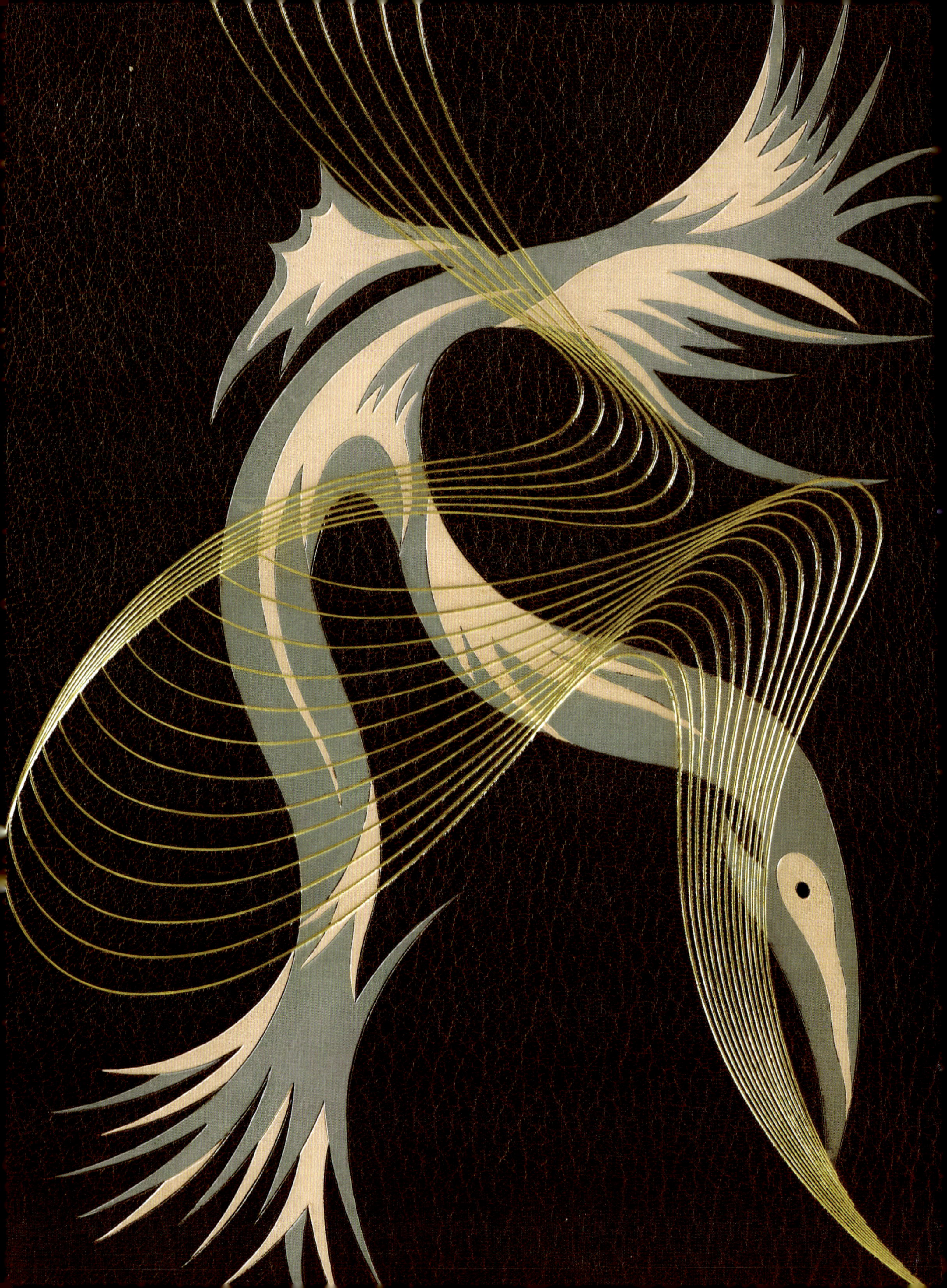

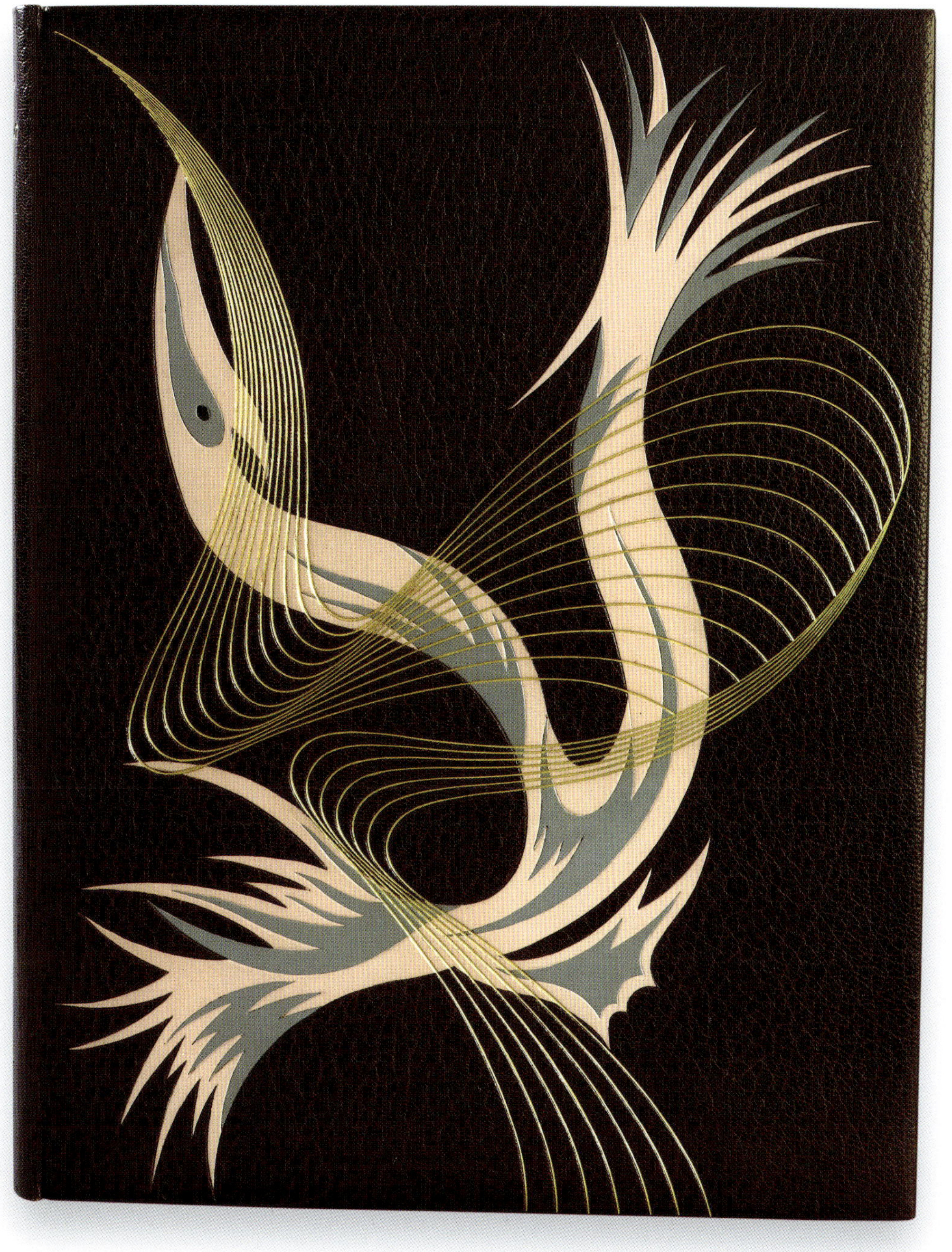

The exuberance and energy of this design shows how far French binding had come from the technically brilliant but staid character of nineteenth-century pastiche styles. Its binder, Thérèse Moncey (fl.1946–65), was a pupil of the influential Paul Bonet, and achieved success in her own right when she was awarded Le Grand Prix of French bookbinding in 1950. Different coloured onlays have been applied to the brown goatskin covers to depict the bird in mid-flight. The virtuoso gold tooling provides an impression of vigour and movement. It was executed by Jules Fache (1901–1972), who worked for many contemporary Parisian binders and also wrote books on decorative technique.

Paris, mid-twentieth century
346 x 266 x 30 mm (13.6 x 10.5 x 1.2 inches)
Davis 413

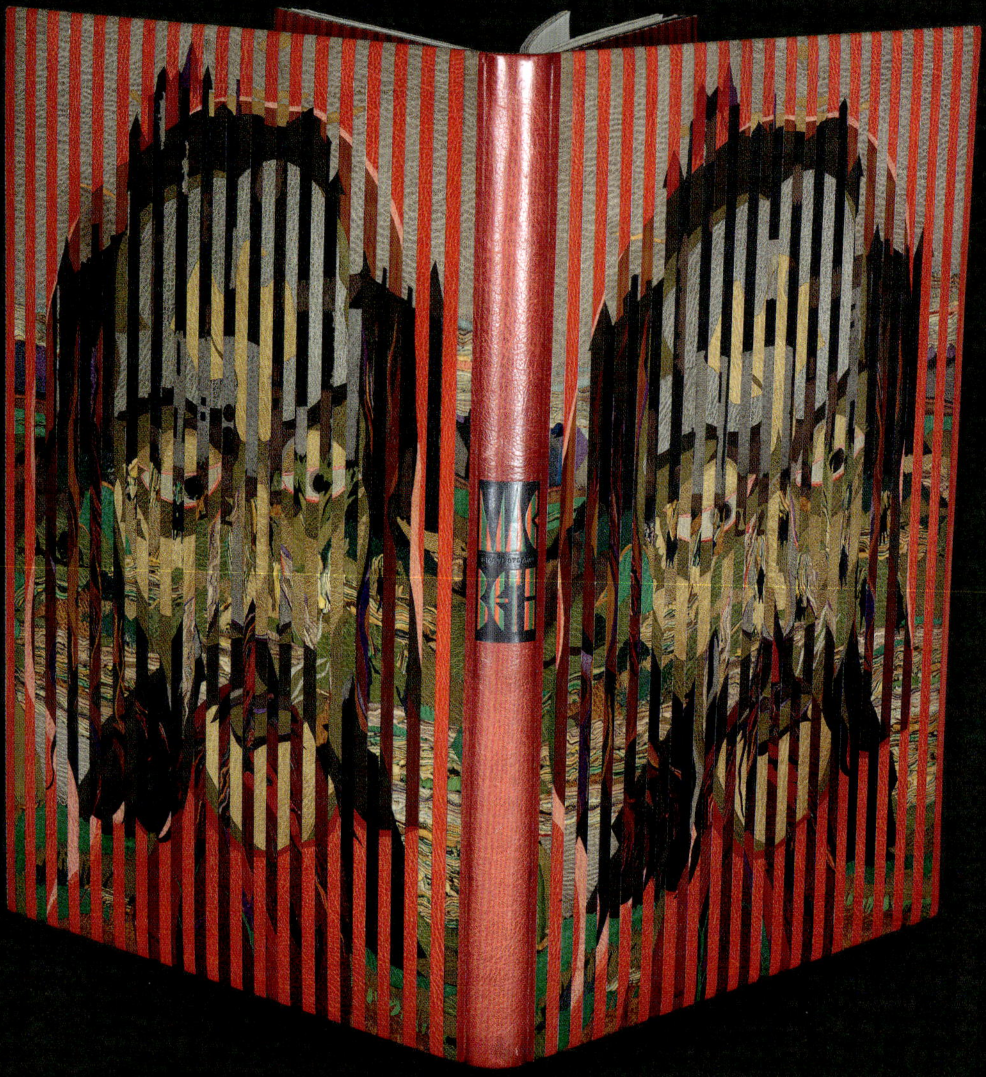

Philip Smith (b.1928) is one of the most famous of contemporary bookbinders. After studying drawing and graphic design at the Royal College of Art, his work with binders Roger Powell and Sydney Cockerell provided him with a solid grounding in the historic roots of bookbinding. From these beginnings, he has been able to extend the boundaries, as he describes in his book *New Approaches in Bookbinding*. This binding for *Macbeth* features one of Smith's techniques: the use of 'maril', a mix of leather fragments and paste which gives a marbled effect when onlaid. In this way, the traditional (the forwarding) and the unconventional (the finishing) are dynamically combined. The strong verticals in the design give the appearance of bars behind which Macbeth is confined, with the maril suggesting inner turmoil. In Smith's words: 'The Macbeth binding was created by alternating strips cut from two images by which Macbeth and his environment are unified.'

England, 1970s
510 x 365 x 29 mm (20.1 x 14.4 x 1.1 inches)
C.188.c.1

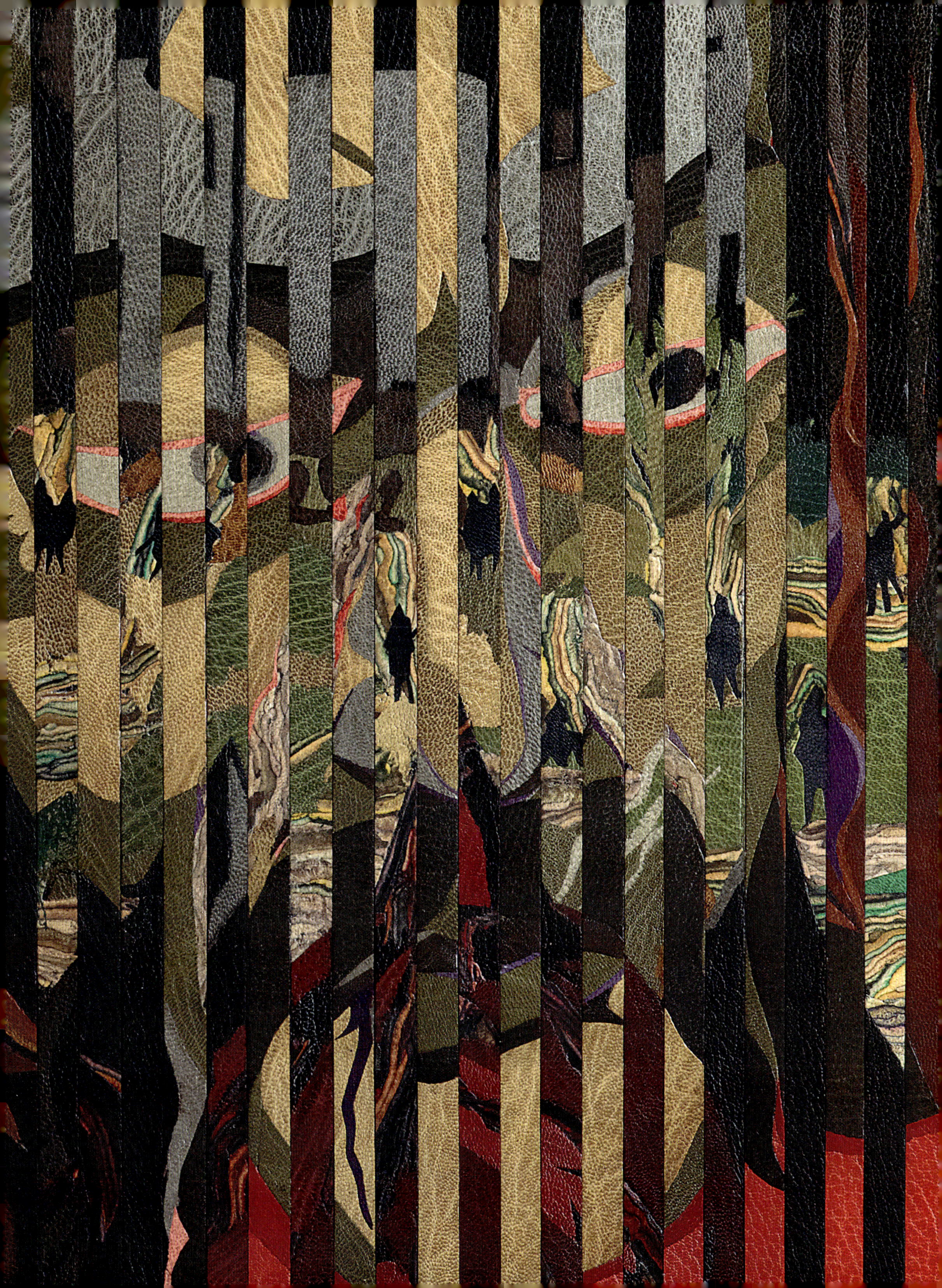

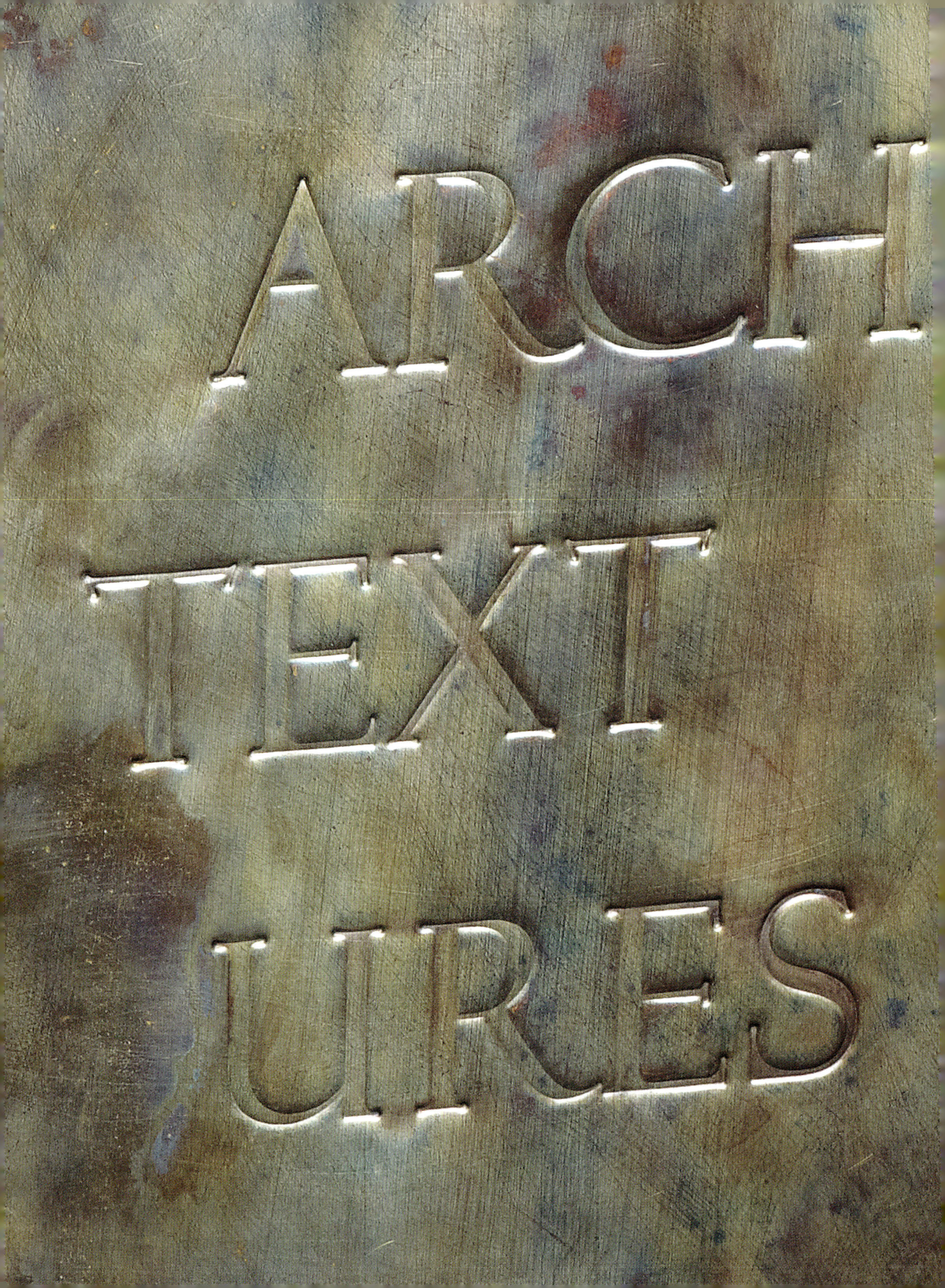
ARCH
TEXT
URES

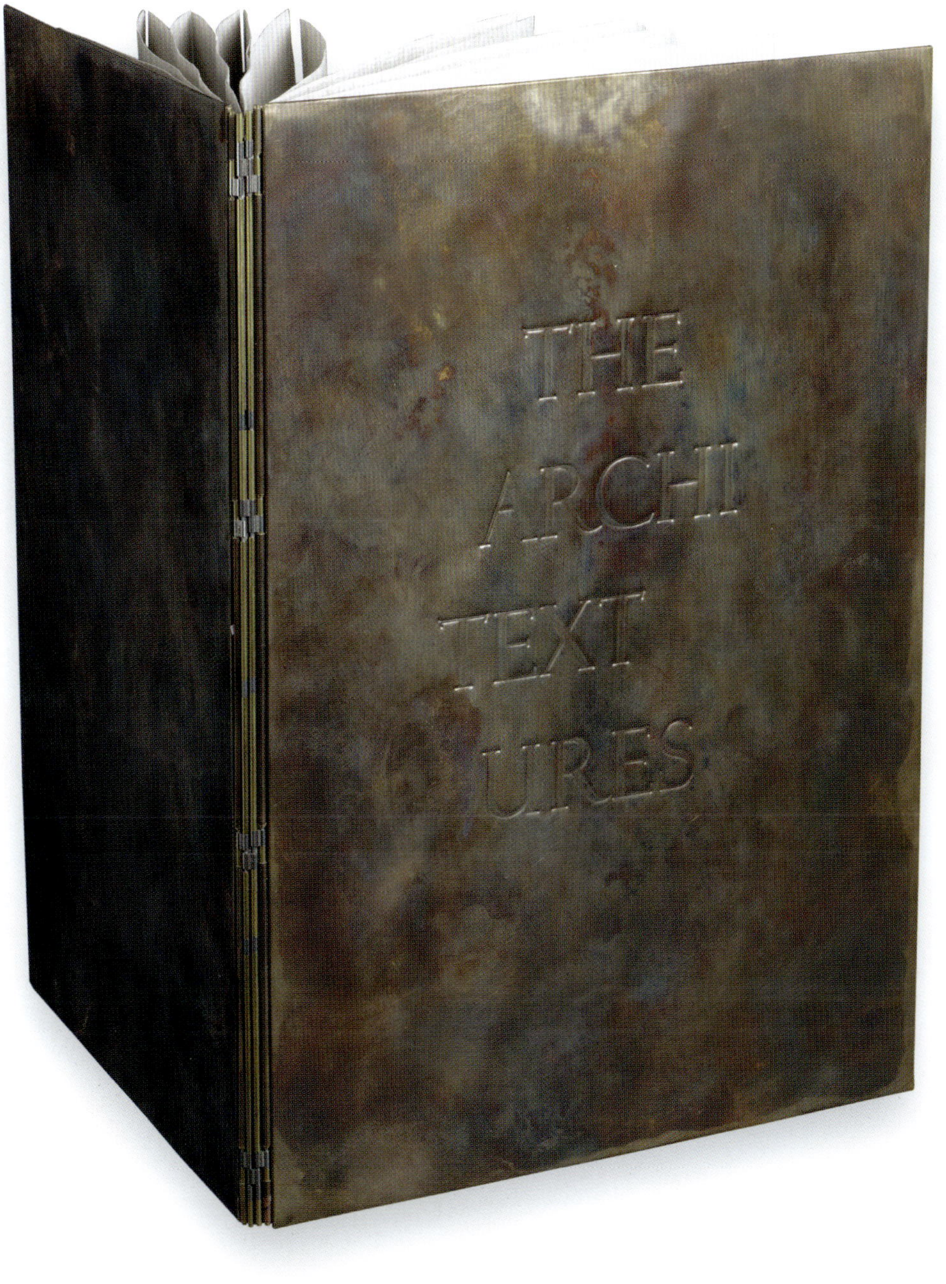

Bindings are successful structures, and although decoration may vary, their basic construction has remained the same for hundreds of years, albeit encompassing many variations. Nevertheless, in recent times craftsmen have begun to reinterpret the traditional components of a binding, looking anew at sculptural and tactile elements. Metal was used extensively on medieval treasure bindings, but the American binder Carolee Campbell has used brass to cover this twentieth-century book of poetry. According to Daniel E Kelm, who was responsible for the attachment of the text via an innovative system of brass rods and stainless steel hinges, 'the deep, expressive qualities of a binding are to be found not just on its surface, but in its form, material and movement. When these integrally support the text and imagery there is a synergistic effect and the impact is potent.'

California, late twentieth century
288 x 210 x 60 mm (11.3 x 8.3 x 2.4 inches)
C.188.b.18

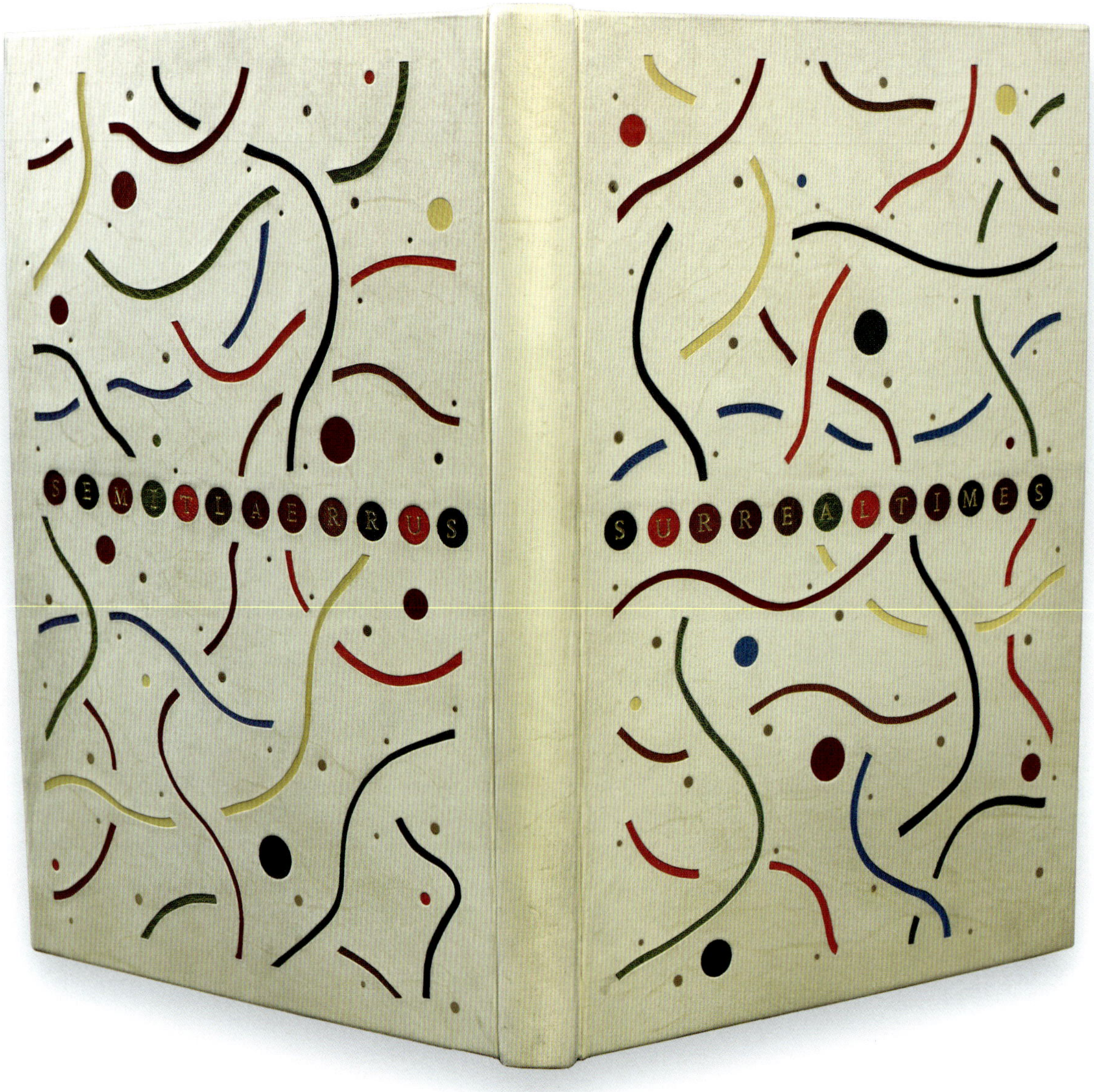

At first glance, this inlaid and onlaid white parchment binding, made in 2008 by Lester Capon (President of the Designer Bookbinders), looks lively but conventional. A closer inspection belies this. Reflecting the text is important to Capon, but he often chooses to do this in an oblique manner. The title letters on the lower cover are reversed, and some of the decorative circles are actually holes that pierce the covers. Capon also works on the restoration of old bindings, as do many binders working today. A recent project has involved the Ethiopian *Garima Gospels* (dated to between 330 to 650 AD), which has been described as the earliest binding still attached to its original contents. Contact with ancient book structures helps craftsmen to bridge the gap between historic method and innovation.

Gloucestershire, England, 2008
330 x 220 x 25 mm (13 x 8.7 x 1 inches)
C.188.c.28

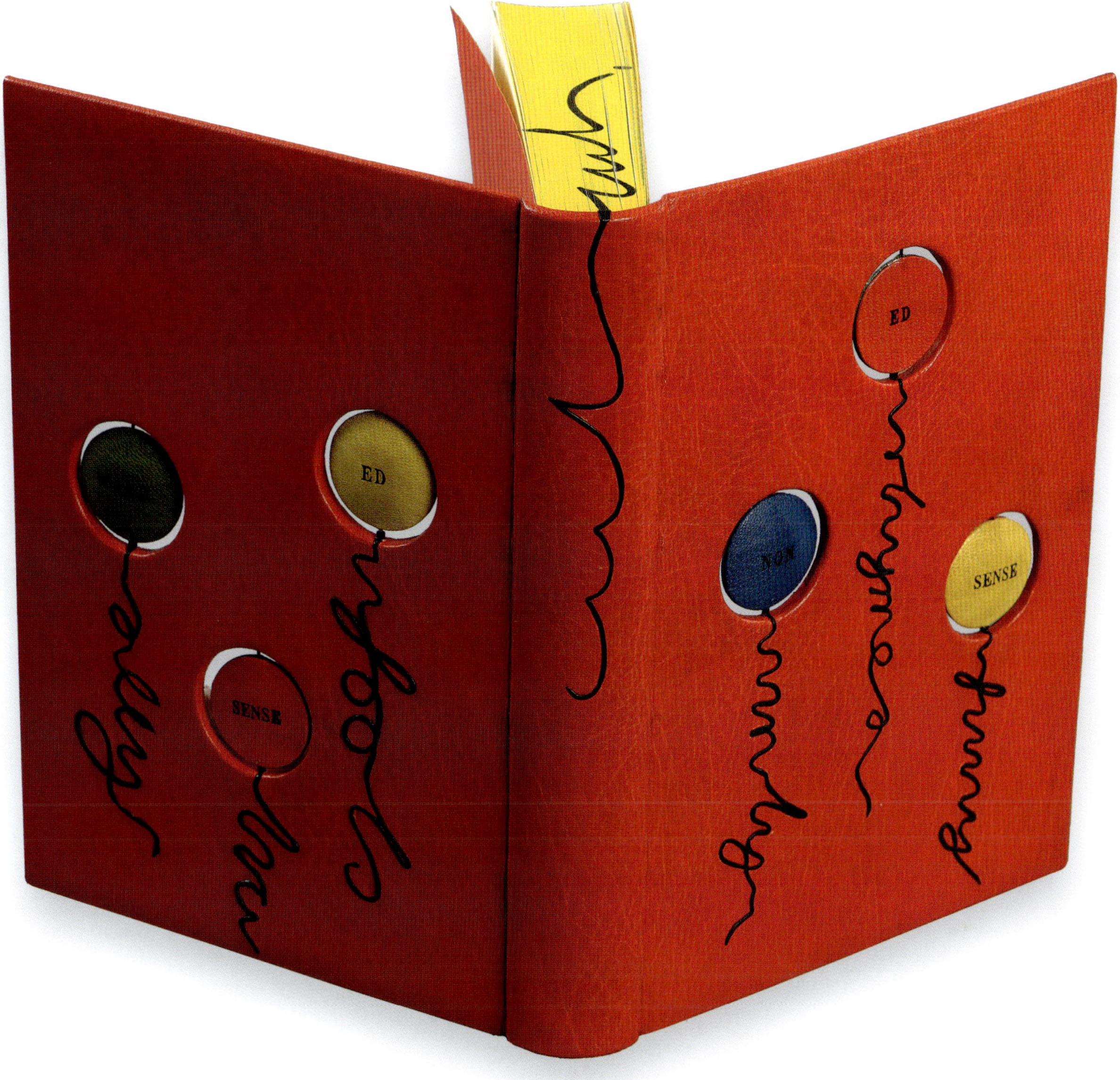

The light-hearted decoration on this twenty-first century English, red goatskin binding by Nesta Davies reflects the charm of the text. Edward Lear's creation, the deluded *Old Man of The Hague*, who 'built a balloon/To examine the moon', may have been one source of inspiration. Davies is keen for her work to have 'an "interactive" element for the reader/viewer, with textures or structures which they feel they want to handle and linger over'. The balloon motifs here are mounted so that they swivel, encouraging the reader to engage with the binding. Matching the covers to the subject-matter of a book is standard practice today, but until the eighteenth century bookbinders had a more utilitarian attitude, tending to use whatever tools would best fit the space.

London, early twenty-first century
237 x 150 x 30 mm (9.3 x 5.9 x 1.2 inches)
C.188.b.22

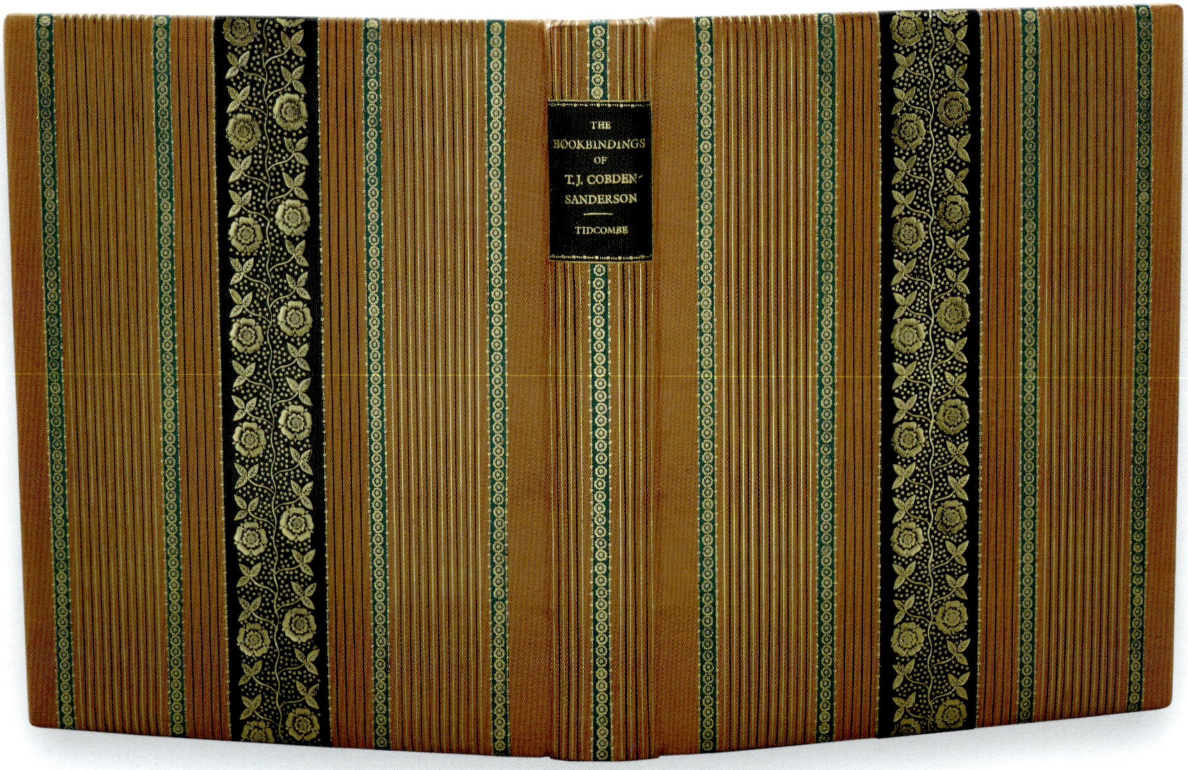

This gold-tooled, inlaid and onlaid brown goatskin binding was made by Bernard Middleton (b.1924), one of the most influential figures in the bookbinding world. His career spans both trade and craft, as he managed the historic London firm Zaehnsdorf's (see pp.132 and 164) before establishing his own workshop. Middleton forms a bridge between old and new. He was born into a bindings family (his father worked for Sangorski & Sutcliffe; see pp.151–4) and research and restoration have played a large part in his professional life. Accounts of his discoveries are recorded in the authoritative *History of English Craft Bookbinding Technique*, as well as other books. Middleton's own bindings, often described in the journal of Designer Bookbinders (of whom he was an early member and later President), reveal that he considers the decoration to be directly inspired by the structure. Binding historian Howard M Nixon has described Middleton as 'essentially a binder who designs, rather than a designer who also binds'. The central strip gold-tooled with blooms recalls the designs of Cobden-Sanderson, the subject of the book (see p.138).

London, early twenty-first century
282 x 220 x 40 mm (11.1 x 8.7 x 1.6 inches)
C.188.b.43

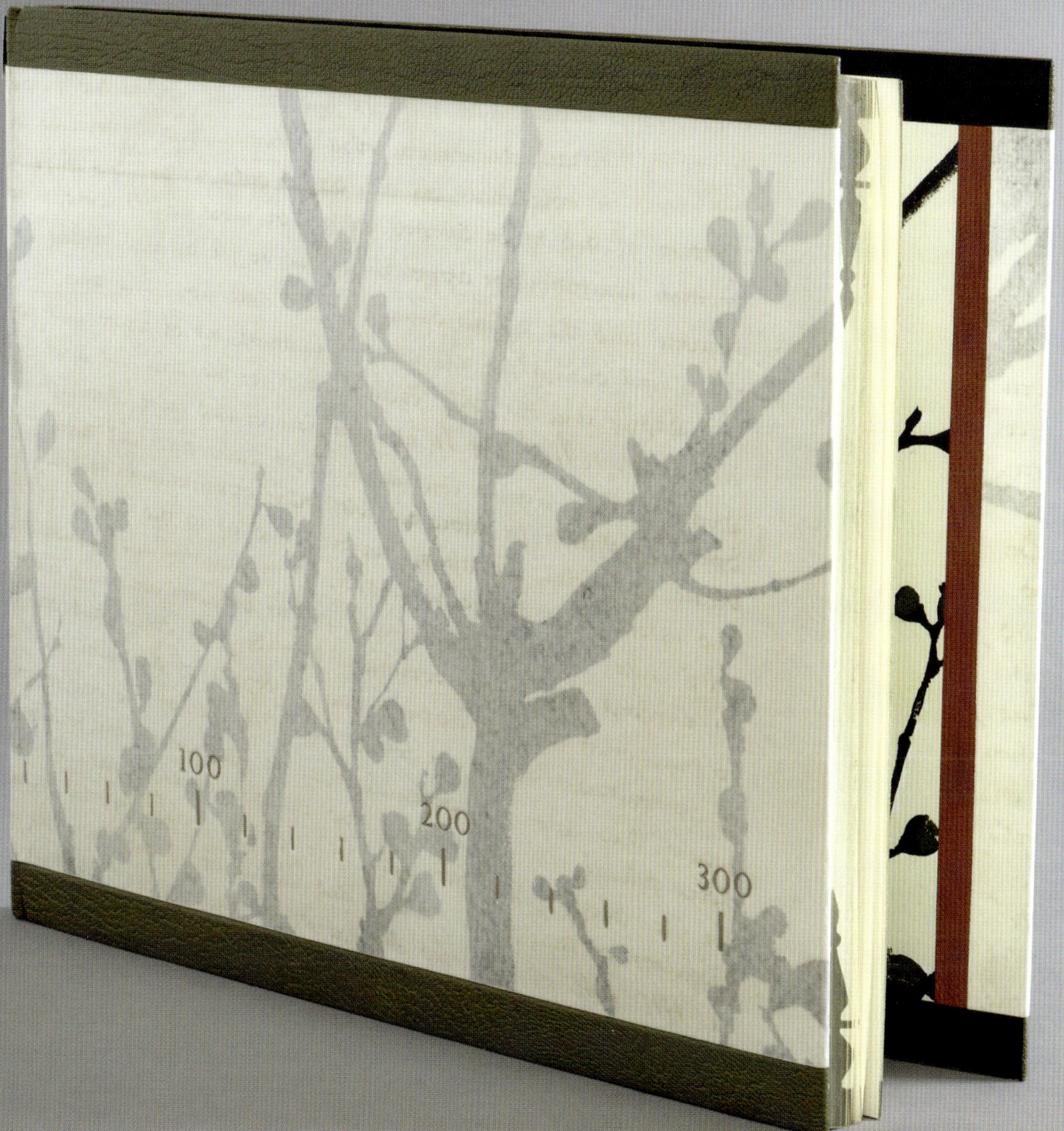

Bookbinding has always been receptive to external influences and continues to be so, an attribute clearly evident in the work of Midori Kunikata-Cockram, a UK-based Japanese binder who draws inspiration from both her home and birth countries. This binding from 2005 features an Oriental-style concertina binding, and makes extensive use of silk, a 'staple' of oriental bookbinders. It also has a protective case, lined in green fabric and held together by two toggles, another traditional Chinese bindings feature, appropriate for the contents: facsimiles of pictures by the Chinese artist Hu Chēng-Yen.

London, 2005
367 x 330 x 70 mm (14.4 x 13 x 2.8 inches)
Taylor 21

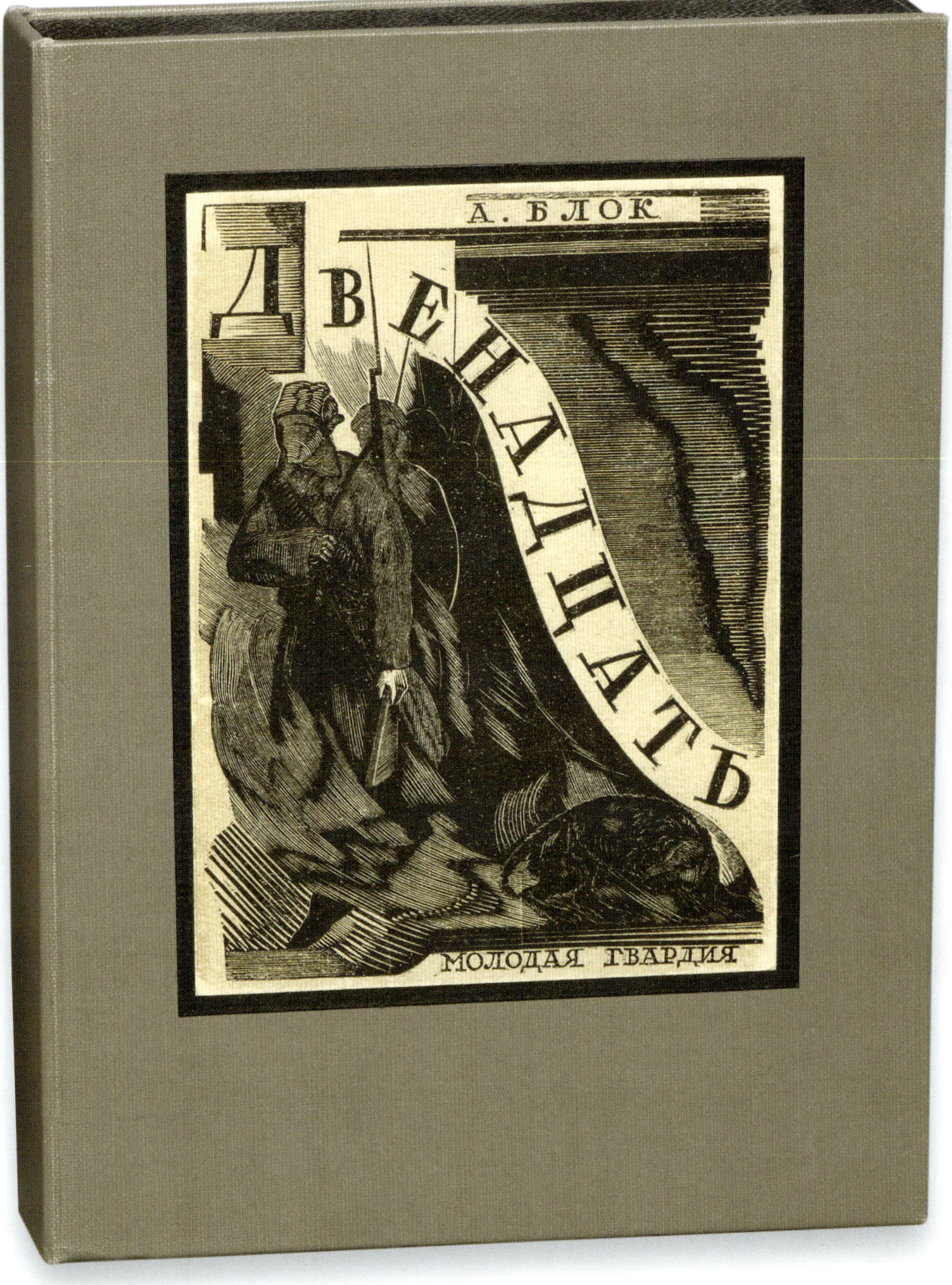
А. БЛОК
ДВЕНАДЦАТЬ
МОЛОДАЯ ГВАРДИЯ

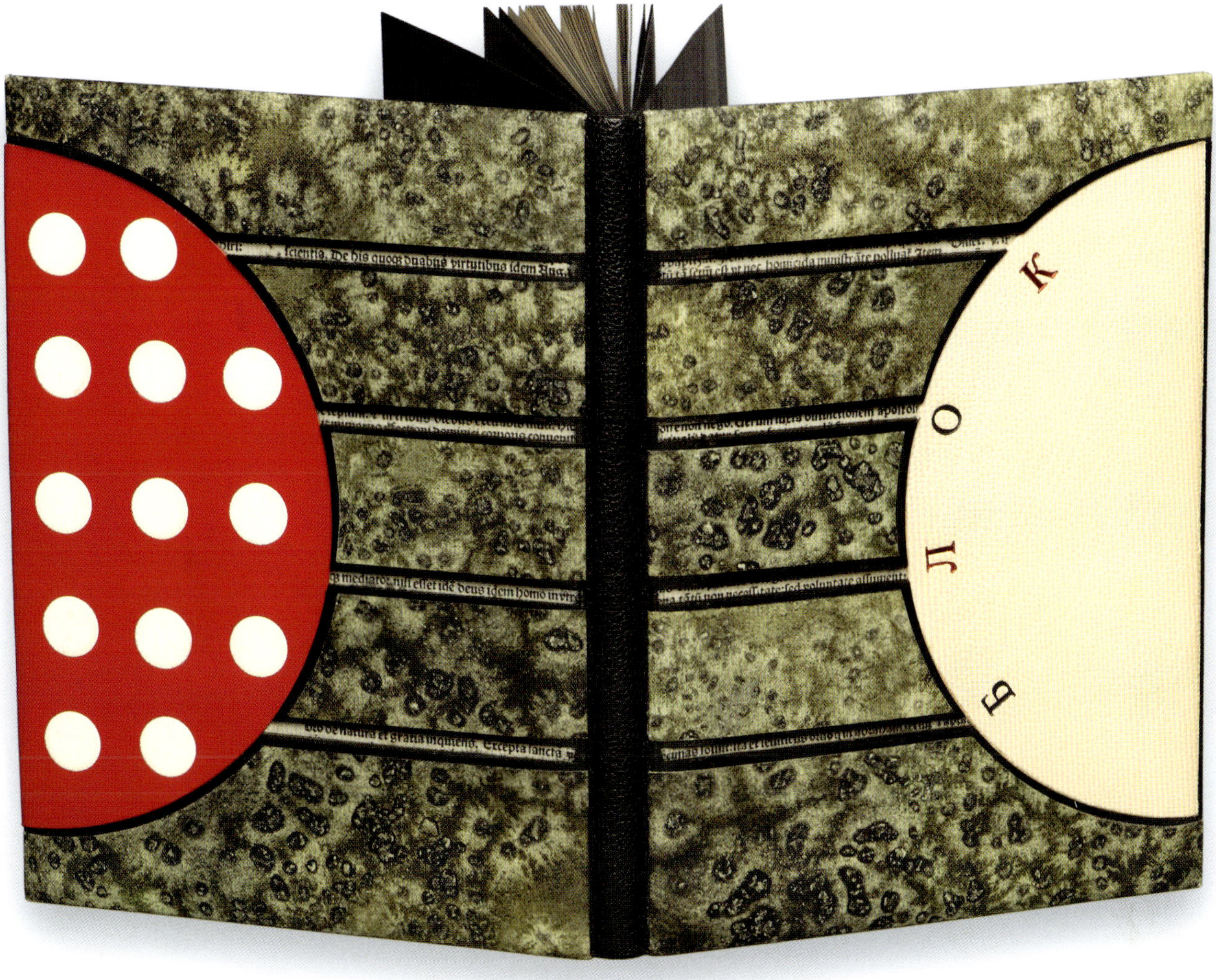

Private commissions make up an important part of the work of contemporary hand bookbinders, and frequently involve collaboration. This binding made in 2001 for the bibliophile Alec Taylor is a case in point. It formed part of a programme of 25 commissions donated to the British Library (see also p.183), which together provided a record of the craft in England at the beginning of the twenty-first century. This item, which consists of a box, left, and a binding, above) is by Stephen Conway (b.1958), whose interest in music made him an ideal choice to bind this second-hand copy of a long and controversial Russian poem by Alexander Blok, which is characterized by polyphonic rhythms and a feeling for sound. Conway writes: 'I try to give my bindings a tactile quality, something I feel to be in keeping with the three-dimensional properties of the book format. Also, to give them an atmosphere, sympathetic to the text, through the use of colour, texture, materials and design.' Blok's poem tells of a journey of 12 Bolshevik soldiers through the streets of Petrograd in a snow storm, and the binder's design presents a variety of tactile experiences with its mixture of colour and materials, including smooth semi-circular leather onlays, sculptured boards, dark mottled paper and text underlays. The contrasts and strong linear feel evoke the sense of dislocation espoused by the Russian avant-garde movement.

England, 2001
Binding 175 x 130 x 15 mm (6.9 x 5.1 x 0.6 inches),
Box 195 x 140 x 30 mm (7.7 x 5.5 x 1.2 inches)
Taylor 19

GLOSSARY

board the material that comprises the upper and lower covers of a book, e.g. wood or pasteboard. The term is also sometimes used to refer to the upper and lower covers in general.

blind tooling impression made with a heated metal tool, without gilding.

oblong-box binding early Islamic binding style practised in tenth-century Yemen, comprising tooled leather over wood with leather thongs and pegs to keep the box closed.

case binding nineteenth-century industrial process whereby the covers and text block of a book are made separately and in bulk.

chemise cloth wrapper added to a bound structure to give an extra protective layer. Associated with the medieval period.

Coptic binding or **sewing** the sewing together of folded pages and upper and lower boards via a linking stitch.

diced a pattern comprising a grid of blind-tooled lines which intersect to form diamond shapes.

doreur craftsman who decorates the binding using gold tooling.

doublur a lining, often made of silk or leather, which can take the place of endleaves.

endbands the collective name given to headbands and tailbands (*see below*).

endleaves protective papers which appear between the first and last pages of the book or manuscript and the covers. Comprises the paste down (pasted to the inside cover) and the fly-leaf, or free endleaf, which lies next to the text block. Sometimes decorated.

fanfare style of decoration originating in France, comprising compartments framed by a double fillet and a single fillet, with the space between either filled with foliage or left empty.

fillet a plain, continuous line used in decoration.

finisher craftsman who decorates the binding.

fly-leaf the free part of the endleaf which lies next to the text block.

forwarder craftsman who makes the binding structure.

gouge metal finishing tool which impresses a curve.

hand-press era period after the invention of printing but before industrialization in the West (roughly mid-fifteenth century to the 1830s).

half-bands horizontal ridges across the spine which are smaller than the raised bands which accommodate the sewing structure. Often used to decorative effect in sixteenth-century Italian bindings.

headband the small core, often made from leather or vellum wrapped with threads, which sits next to the spine and projects slightly beyond the top of the text block. The small core which sits next to the tail of the spine is known as the tailband.

Islamic binding post-seventh-century book or manuscript structure comprising two leather-covered pasteboards joined by a flexible leather spine, to which the chain-stitched paper or parchment sections are affixed. A protective envelope flap is attached to the lower cover and folds over the fore edge.

Mudéjar thirteenth- and fourteenth-century style involving geometric patterns, commonly blind-tooled, deriving from the Moors who emigrated to Spain.

panel stamp rectangular decorative tool, which, when applied to a binding in a press, can decorate the entire upper or lower cover in a single action. In use by the fifteenth century, and perhaps earlier.

pasteboard compressed paper-based laminated sheet which is often used to form the upper and lower cover of a binding. In use since the sixteenth century.

paste down sheet pasted to the inside of the upper and lower covers. Often helps to conceal the ends of the sewing supports.

perfect form of binding whereby pages are attached using an adhesive, not sewing.

plaque metal panel used to effect the rapid transfer of decoration to covers.

plateresque Spanish decorative style involving the scattering of small individual motifs, such as crowns and lions. Derived from silversmiths.

roll hand tool comprising an engraved roll which impresses a design into leather. In use by the late fifteenth century.

sewing supports lengths of cord or strips of leather placed horizontally across the folded sections of Western-style books, around which the sewing thread is wound. The ends are sometimes pasted onto, or laced into, prefabricated holes in the boards.

spine bands raised horizontal ridges, visible on the spine, which accommodate the sewing supports on which the pages are sewn. Common on Western-style bindings but not on Islamic, Coptic and other Oriental styles.

stab sewing or **stitching** (sometimes called **side sewing**) method of securing the leaves of sections of a book with thread near the binding edge, from front to back through the entire thickness of the text block. Creates a strong binding, but one difficult to open flat.

stationery book (sometimes called an account book) a book bound with blank pages.

tacket a reinforcing stitch employed in stationery binding, visible on the outside of the binding.

tail bottom edge of the book.

text block leaves of a volume after they have been sewn together.

treasure binding ornamental case decorated with jewels, enamel, etc, made by a metalworker to accommodate a holy book.

turn-in the area where the covering material of a binding is folded over and fixed to the inside of the upper and lower boards.

NOTES & FURTHER READING

The information given here relates to the contents of the bound printed text or manuscript; details of the actual bindings (which were often made at a later date) are given in the captions. References are given to quotations used in the text of the captions and also to suggestions for further reading.

11 Taken from Joseph Zaehnsdorf, *A Short History of Bookbinding, and a glossary of styles and terms* (London, 1895).

12 Woodcut by Jost Amman, taken from Hans Sachs *Eygentliche Beschreibung Aller Stände auff Erden* (Frankfurt, 1568).

13 Taken from Charles Tomlinson (ed.), *Cyclopaedia of Useful Arts* (London, 1866).

14 Taken from Joseph Zaehnsdorf, *A Short History of Bookbinding, and a glossary of styles and terms* (London, 1895).

20 St Cuthbert Gospel of St John, England, late seventh century. (British Library Loan, owned by Stonyhurst College).

See Howard M Nixon and Mirjam M Foot, *The History of Decorated Bookbinding in England* (Oxford, 1992) pp.1–2.

21 The 'Melisende Psalter' with canticles, prayers, and litany, Jerusalem (?) between 1131 and 1143.

Quote from Mirjam M Foot, *Pictorial Bookbindings* (London, 1986), p.46.

22 Garland Sutra, Korea *c.*1390–1400.

23 Interior/verso of binding boards covering *Pingalattvavyakhya on the Prakrtapaingala*, manuscript on palm leaves; verses on Prakrit prosody attributed to ancient Indian writer Pingala, eastern India, 1491–2.

Quote from J P Losty 'A Pair of Illustrated Binding Boards from Bihar of 1491–2' in *Oriental Art Magazine*, vol. XXIII, no 2, summer 1977, p.199.

24 Qur'an, Marrakesh, *c.*1256.
See A R A Hobson, *Humanists and Bookbinders* (Cambridge, 1989); Mirjam M Foot, *History of Bookbinding as a Mirror of Society: Panizzi Lectures* (London, 1999), p.13, fig.14.

25 Qur'an (part seven), Egypt, 1400.
See K B Gardner 'Oriental Bookbindings at the British Museum' in *Oriental Art*, new series vol. IX, spring 1963, p.137; Mirjam M Foot, *The Henry Davis Gift; A Collection of Bookbindings. Volume III: A Catalogue of South European Bindings* (London, 2009), p.496.

26 *Gospels of St. Luke and St. John*, late twelfth century/early thirteenth century.

See Mirjam M Foot, *Pictorial Bookbindings* (London, 1986), p.53.

27 The Four Gospels in Armenian (Erevan), 1669 written by the scribe Alek'san.

See Vrej Nersessian *Treasures From The Ark* (London, 2001), p.126.

28 **(upper image)** The Four Gospels in Armenian, copied in 1658.

28 **(lower images)** Jean de Bussières, *Flosculi historici delibati nunc delibatiores redditi, sive historia universalis* (Cologne, 1688).

29 The Lindisfarne Gospels, in Latin and Old English. Manuscript probably written on the Holy Island of Lindisfarne, *c.*715–720.

30 A Sienese panel painted for the Biccherna of Siena by Guidoccio Cozzarelli, 1488.

See Mirjam M Foot, *The Henry Davis Gift; A Collection of Bookbindings. Volume III: A Catalogue of South European Bindings* (London, 2009), p.298.

34–5 Indenture made between King Henry VII and John Islippe Abbot of Westminster, London, *c.*1505.

36 Psalms in English verse translated by John Croke, manuscript on parchment, England, sixteenth century.

37 Hours of the Cross and the Holy Spirit, with Penitential Psalms, Litany, and Prayers, manuscript on parchment, France, sixteenth century.

38 *Coustumes du Bailliage de Sens et anciens ressorts d'iceluy* (Sens, 1559).

39 **Left column, top to bottom:**
C.65.d.14, Davis 384, Davis 341
Centre column, top to bottom:
Davis 777, Davis 427, Davis 590
Right column, top to bottom:
Davis 818, Davis 389, C.29.k.8.

40 Aurelius Cornelius Celsus, *De medicina libri VIII* (Venice, 1497)

See Howard M Nixon, *Bookbindings from the library of Jean Grolier* (London, 1965); A R A Hobson, *Renaissance Book Collecting* (Cambridge, 1999).

41 Charles de Bouelles, *Livre singulier et utile... de Geometrie* [and] Vitruvius, *Raison d'architecture antique... traduit d'Espagnol* [by D de Sangredo] (Paris, 1542).

Quote from Marie-Pierre Laffitte, *Reliures royales de la Renaissance: la librairie de Fontainebleau 1544–1570* (Paris, 1999) preface. *See* Mirjam M Foot, *The Henry Davis Gift; A Collection of Bookbindings. Volume III: A Catalogue of South European Bindings* (London, 2009), p.42.

42 Pontanus, *Opera omnia* (Venice, 1518/19).

See A R A Hobson, *Humanists and Bookbinders* (Cambridge, 1989); Mirjam M Foot, *The Henry Davis Gift; A Collection of Bookbindings. Volume III: A Catalogue of South European Bindings* (London, 2009), p.108 and note pp.99–100.

45 *Biblia* (Wittemberg, 1545).

44 Claudius Ptolemaeus, *Almagestum seu magnae constructionis mathemataicae opus* (Venice, 1528).

See Mirjam M Foot, *The Henry Davis Gift; A Collection of Bookbindings. Volume III: A Catalogue of South European Bindings* (London, 2009), p.125.

45 Joannes Tagaultius, *J. Tagaultii de chirurgica institutione libri quinque* (Paris, 1543).

46 Jean Benard, *Account of the Norman Noblemen Who Accompanied William the Conqueror to England in 1066; a treatise on Elizabethan heraldry and genealogy; and an account on the Court of Queen Elizabeth* (Paris, 1569).

47 Translations from the Greek into French made by 'M. Loys Regius' and addressed 'au treshault et trespuissant roy d'Angleterre Edouard vi. de ce nom.' manuscript on parchment, Paris (?) *c.*1550.

48 Marcus Tullius Cicero, *Rhetoric* (Venice, 1546).

50 *Horae in laudem beatissimae virginis Mariae, ad usum Romanum* (Paris, 1549).

See Mirjam M Foot, *The Henry Davis Gift; A Collection of Bookbindings. Volume III: A Catalogue of South European Bindings* (London, 2009), p.88.

52 Girolamo Masher's, *Il Fiore della Retorica in quattro Libri* (Venice, 1560).

53 *Meditationum ac precationum Christianarum libellus* (Geneva, 1552).

See quote from Paul Hentzner, contemporary visitor to London, in Howard M Nixon and Mirjam M Foot, *The History of Decorated Bookbinding in England* (Oxford, 1992) pp.41–2; Mirjam M Foot, *History of Bookbinding as a Mirror of Society;* Panizzi Lectures (London, 1999) fig. 45.

54 Justinian I, *Ius civile manuscriptorum librorum* (Antwerp, 1567).

See Mirjam M Foot, *The Henry Davis Gift: A Collection of Bookbindings Volume II: Catalogue of North European Bindings* (London, 1983), p.401.

55 Plato, *Platonis Convivium* (Paris, 1543).

Quote from Howard M Nixon *Five Centuries of English Bookbinding* (London, 1978), p.44. *See* Mirjam M Foot, *The Henry Davis Gift: Studies in the History of Bookbinding*, vol. I (London, 1978) pp.27–34.

56 Andrea Boiardo, *Libro d'arme e d'amore nomato Philogine* (Venice, 1547).

See Mirjam M Foot, *The Henry Davis Gift; A Collection of Bookbindings. Volume III: A Catalogue of South European Bindings* (London, 2009), p.380.

58 Matthaeus Laymannus *Defensio nobilis causae Honoldinae* (Ingolstadt, 1580).

See Mirjam M Foot, *The Henry Davis Gift: A Collection of Bookbindings. Volume II: A Catalogue of North European Bindings* (London, 1983), p.405.

59 *Officium B. Mariae Virginis* (Antwerp, 1575).

See Mirjam M Foot, *History of Bookbinding as a Mirror of Society;* Panizzi Lectures (London, 1999), p.20.

60–1 The Holy Bible in three volumes (Bath, 1785).

62 Quintus Curtius Rufus, *De rebus gestis Alexandri Magni Regis Macedonum opus* (Basle, 1544).

63 *Der Stat Nürmberg verneute Reformation* (Frankfurt, 1564).

65 Divan in Chaghatay Turkish by Mir Ali-Shir Nava'I, manuscript, *c*.1500.

See K B Gardner, 'Oriental bookbindings at the British Museum' in *Oriental Art*, new series vol. IX, spring 1963 p.139.

66–7 Khamsa by Nizami, manuscript, India, 1595.

Quote from Duncan Haldane, *Islamic Bookbindings* (London, 1983), p.177.

70 Alphonsus Salmeron, *Commentarii in Evangelicam Historiam e in Acta Apostolorum* (Cologne, 1602–4).

71 Alonso Chacon, *Historia utriusque belli dacici a Traiano Cæsare gesti* (Rome, 1616).

See Isabelle de Conihout and Pascal Ract- Madoux, *Reliures françaises du XVIIe siècle: Chefs-d'oeuvre du musée Condé* (Paris, 2002).

72 Book of Common Prayer (London, 1669).

See Howard M Nixon, *English Restoration Bookbindings* (London, 1974), p.17.

73 Thomas Browne, *Certain Miscellany Tracts* (London, 1683).

See Mirjam M Foot, *The Henry Davis Gift: A Collection of Bookbindings Volume II: Catalogue of North European Bindings* (London, 1983), p.146

74 List of all his Majesty's ships employed in 1673.

Quote from Howard M Nixon, *English Restoration Bookbindings* (London, 1974), p.38; *See Catalogue of the Pepys Library at Magdalene College, Cambridge*, vol. VI: Bindings (Woodbridge, 1984); *The British Museum Quarterly*, 1962.

76 *Biblia: Dat is de gantsche H. Schrifture* (Dordrecht, 1739).

77 *Missale romanum* (Antwerp, 1726).

See Mirjam M Foot, *The Henry Davis Gift; Catalogue of North European Bindings. Volume II: A Collection of Bookbindings* (London, 1983), p.367.

78 **(left)** The Holy Bible, bound with Psalms (Cambridge, 1673).

78 **(right)** The Book of Common Prayer (London, 1844).

79 Philipp Kegel, Zwölf geistliche Andachten (Copenhagen, 1674).

80 *Descripcion del real monasterio de S. Lorenzo del Escorial* (Madrid, 1681).

81 *Æsop's Fables* (London, 1687).

See Howard M Nixon and Mirjam M Foot, *The History of Decorated Bookbinding in England* (Oxford, 1992), p.77.

82 Qur'an in Naskhi script, in Persian and Arabic, manuscript, Persia, *c*.1630–50.

Quote from Duncan Haldane, *Islamic Bookbindings* (London, 1983), p.70.

See Mirjam M Foot, *The Henry Davis Gift; A Collection of Bookbindings. Volume III: A Catalogue of South European Bindings* (London, 2009), p.500.

84 A pair of empty Persian book covers, Persia, *c*.1650.

See Mirjam M Foot, *The Henry Davis Gift; A Collection of Bookbindings. Volume III: A Catalogue of South European Bindings* (London, 2009), p.503.

85 Claude Guichard, *Funérailles des Rommains* (Lyons, 1581).

Quote from Isabelle de Conihout and Pascal Ract-Madoux, *Reliures françaises du XVIIe siècle: Chefs-d'oeuvre du musée Condé* (Paris, 2002); *See* Mirjam M Foot, *The Henry Davis Gift; A Collection of Bookbindings. Volume III: A Catalogue of South European Bindings* (London, 2009), p.200.

86 *The Whole Booke of Psalmes* (London, 1633).

87 *The Holy Bible*, two volumes (Cambridge, 1674).

See Cyril Davenport, *English embroidered bindings* (London, 1899), p.78.

89 *The Holy Bible* (London, 1612), bound with John Speed, *The Genealogies recorded in the Sacred Scriptures* (London, 1612[?]).

90 *Missale romanum* (Padua, 1705)

91 *Diario ecclesiastico para o reino de Portugal, principalmente para a cidade de Lisboa* (Lisbon, 1828).

94 *Histoire de l'Académie Royale... avec les mémoires de littérature*, two volumes (Paris, 1717).

See Mirjam M Foot, *The Henry Davis Gift; A Collection of Bookbindings. Volume III: A Catalogue of South European Bindings* (London, 2009), p.221.

95 Andrea Adami da Bolsena, *Osservazioni per ben regolare il coro de i cantori della Cappella Pontificia* (Rome, 1711).

96 Calligraphic exercises of Emperor Ch'ien lung, China, eighteenth century.

See K B Gardner, 'Oriental bookbindings at the British Museum' in *Oriental Art*, new series vol. IX, spring 1963, p.144.

98 *La Sainte Bible du Vieux et du Nouveau Testament*, vol. I (Bern, 1731).

See Mirjam M Foot, *The Henry Davis Gift; A Collection of Bookbindings. Volume III: A Catalogue of South European Bindings* (London, 2009), p.291; Christoph Ernst Prediger, *Der in aller heut zu Tag ublichen Arbeit wohl Anweisendeaccurate Buchbinder und Futteralmacher* [1741–53] vol. 1; Mirjam M Foot, *Bookbinders at Work* (London, 2006), pp.97, 100, figs 41–7.

99 *Heures nouvelles à l'usage de Rome* (Paris, 1749).

Quote from Giles Barber, 'Around the Padeloup and Derome workshops' in *Eloquent Witnesses* (London 2004), p.203.

See Mirjam M Foot, *The Henry Davis Gift; A Collection of Bookbindings. Volume III: A Catalogue of South European Bindings* (London, 2009), p.226.

100 *Vita di Plutarco* (Venice, 1568).

See Mirjam M Foot, *The Henry Davis Gift; A Collection of Bookbindings. Volume III: A Catalogue of South European Bindings* (London, 2009), p.460.

102–3 *The Book of Common Prayer* (Cambridge, 1760).

See Reliquiæ Hearnianæ: the remains of Thomas Hearn (1869), p.243; Howard M Nixon and Mirjam M Foot, *The History of Decorated Bookbinding in England* (Oxford, 1992), p.91.

104 Khavarannama by Muhammad ibn Husam, manuscript, Shiraz, Persia, late fifteenth century.

See K B Gardner, 'Oriental Bookbindings at the British Museum' in *Oriental Art*, new series vol. IX, spring 1963, p.143; J Losty, *Art of the Book in India*, p.133.

106 William Cavendish, *A General System of Horsemanship in all its Branches* (London, 1743).

107 *The Life of Edward, Lord Herbert of Cherbury, Written by Himself* (Strawberry Hill, 1764).

See Howard M Nixon, *Five Centuries of English Bookbinding* (London, 1978), p.162.

108 *Estado military de Espana, Ani de 1783* (Madrid, 1783).

See Mirjam M Foot, *The Henry Davis Gift; A Collection of Bookbindings. Volume III: A Catalogue of South European Bindings* (London, 2009), p.486.

109 **Left:** *Almanach pacifique, ou l'école de la vertu* (Paris, 1793).
Right: *Les Bords rians de la Seine* (Paris,1787).
Lying flat: *Le Petit théâtre de l'univers* (Paris, 1786).

110 *Heures Nouvelles dédiées à la reine* (Paris, 1749).

See Mirjam M Foot, *History of Bookbinding as a Mirror of Society*; Panizzi Lectures (London, 1999), p.18, fig. 28.

111 *La Sainte Bible* (Cologne, 1739).

See Giles Barber, 'Around the Padeloup and Derome Workshops' in *Eloquent Witnesses* (London, 2004) pp.174–205.

112 Constantine Lascaris, *Erotemata* (Venice, 1494–5).

See Mirjam M Foot, *The Henry Davis Gift; A Collection of Bookbindings. Volume I: Studies in the History of Bookbinding* (London, 1978), p.107.

113 St Jean Chrysostome, *Homilies ou sermons*, three volumes (Paris, 1693).

See Mirjam M Foot, *The Henry Davis Gift; A Collection of Bookbindings. Volume III: A Catalogue of South European Bindings* (London, 2009), p.205.

114 Joannes Balthasar Braun, *Historia Augusta, seu Vitae Romanorum Caesarum* (Augsburg and Dillingen, 1698).

See Mirjam M Foot, *The Henry Davis Gift; Catalogue of North European Bindings. Volume II: A Collection of Bookbindings* (London, 1983), p.423.

118 Life of Buddha, illustrated folding manuscript, Burma, mid-nineteenth century.

See Patricia M Herbert, *The Life of the Buddha* (London, 1993).

119 *Osana etoki Bankoku-banashi* [A children's picture book of the world] (Japan, 1860).

120 *Annales romantiques* (Paris, 1830).

See Sophie Malavieille, *Reliures et cartonnages d'éditeur en France au XIXe siècle 1815–1865* (Paris, 1985), p.23 for quote from *Le Bazar Parisien*, (1822).

121 Gilbert White, *Works on Natural History* (London, 1802).

See Howard M Nixon, *Five Centuries of English Bookbinding* (London, 1978), p.194.

123 *Vie de Saint Martin*, (Tours, 1863).

124 Miguel de Cervantes Saavedra, *El ingenisoso hidalgo Don Quijote de la Mancha* (Paris, 1827).

See Mirjam M Foot, *The Henry Davis Gift; A Collection of Bookbindings. Volume III: A Catalogue of South European Bindings* (London, 2009), p.249.

125 **Left:** Jacques Charles Brunet, *Manuel du libraire et de l'amateur de livres* (Paris, 1814).

Quote from Thomas Frognall Dibdin, *Bibliomania, or Book Madness* (1842), p.127.

See The History of Decorated Bookbinding in England (Oxford, 1992), p.99.

Right: Terence, *Terentii Afri Comoediæ sex ex M. Antonii Mureti exemplari* (Lyon, 1586).

See Mirjam M Foot, *The Henry Davis Gift; A Collection of Bookbindings. Volume III: A Catalogue of South European Bindings* (London, 2009), p.164.

126 Tacitus, *Opera*, vol. I (Parma, 1795)

See Mirjam M Foot, *The Henry Davis Gift; A Collection of Bookbindings. Volume III: A Catalogue of South European Bindings* (London, 2009), p.493.

127 *Reports from the Commissioners appointed by His Majesty to execute the measures recommended in an address of the House of Commons respecting the public records of Ireland* (Dublin, 1815).

128 An album of gilt and illuminated blocks and original artwork produced by Joseph Stuart Evans (London, *c.*1845).

See George Bayntun, *EBC Catalogue 15* (Bath, 2007), no.66.

129 *The Pictorial Album* (London, 1837).

130–1 Empty book covers painted by Lotfali, Shiraz, Persia, 1861.

See Mirjam M Foot, *The Henry Davis Gift; A Collection of Bookbindings. Volume III: A Catalogue of South European Bindings* (London, 2009), p.505.

132 *Sakoontala*, or *The Lost Ring*, translated into English prose and verse from Sanskrit by Monier Williams, (Hertford, 1855.)

Quote from The Belfast News-Letter (Belfast, Ireland) Monday 26 June 1865. *See* Howard M Nixon and Mirjam M Foot, *The History of Decorated Bookbinding in England* (Oxford, 1992), p.104.

134 *Daily Light on the Daily Path*, vol. II (London, 1862[?]).

135 Don Celestino del Piélago, *Introduccion al estudio de la arquitectura hidráaulica* (Madrid, 1841).

See Mirjam M Foot, *The Henry Davis Gift; A Collection of Bookbindings. Volume III: A Catalogue of South European Bindings* (London, 2009), p.487.

136–7 Empty wooden covers painted by Ilicio Federico Joni, Italy, late nineteenth century.

See Icilio Federico Joni, *Affairs of a Painter* (London, 1936).

138 William Morris, *The Life and Death of Jason* (London, 1882)

Quote from Marianne Tidcombe, *The Bookbindings of T J Cobden-Sanderson* (London, 1984) p.190.

139 **Clockwise from left:**
William Morris, *The Life and Death of Jason* (London, 1882).
Algeron Charles Swinburne, *Atlanta in Calydon* (London, 1865).
Percy Shelley, *The Revolt of Islam* (London, 1818).
Percy Shelly, *Shelley*, (Hammersmith, 1914).
John Ruskin, *Unto This Last* (Orpington, 1884).

140 John Ruskin, *Unto This Last* (Orpington, 1884).

See Marianne Tidcombe, *The Bookbindings of T J Cobden-Sanderson* (London,1984), p.122.

141 Geoffrey Chaucer *The Works of Geoffrey Chaucer Now Newly Imprinted*, (Hammersmith, 1896).

See Marianne Tidcombe, *The Doves Bindery* (London, 1991), pp.46–61.

142 Giovanni Boccaccio, *Il Decameron* (Berlin, 1829).

143 Stefano Guazzo, *La Civil Conversatione del Sig* (Brescia, 1574).

144 *Pomněnky na rok* (Prague, 1842, 1844, 1845 and 1846)

145 'Acheta Domestica' [pseudonym for L M Budgen], *Episodes of Insect Life* (London, 1849).

146 **Top:** Paul Laurence Dunbar *Poems of Cabin and Field* (New York, 1894). Binding designed by Alice C Morse.
Lower left: *The Most Delectable History of Reynard the Fox* (London, 1895). Binding designed by A A Turbayne.
Lower right: *Life's Roses: a volume of selected poems* (London, 1898). Binding designed by Alice C Morse.

147 **Top:** Thomas Miller, *Common Wayside Flowers* (London, 1860). Binding designed by Albert Warren.
Lower left: David Dwight Wells *Her Ladyship's Elephant* (London, 1898). Binding designed by William Nicholson.
Lower right: *Monkeys and Parrots* (London, 1898).

For all Trade Bindings *see* Mindell Dubansky, *The Proper Decoration of Book Covers: the life and work of Alice C Morse* (New York, 2008), p.9; Edmund M B King *Victorian Trade Bindings* (London, 2003).

150 Robert Burns, *Poems, Chiefly in the Scottish Dialect* (Glasgow, 1927).

See Howard M Nixon, *Five Centuries of English Bookbinding* (London, 1978), p.222.

151 Edmund Spenser, *Epithalamion and Amoretti* (London, 1903).

152 Ivor Bannet, *The Amazon* (London, 1948).

153 *The Golden Cockerel Mabinogion* (London, 1948).

154–7 *Rubaiyat of Omar Khayyám, the astronomer-poet of Persia, rendered into English verse by Edward Fitzgerald, with an accompaniment of drawings by Elihu Vedder* (Boston, 1884).

158–9 *Rubaiyat of Omar Khayyám, the astronomer-poet of Persia, rendered into English verse by Edward Fitzgerald, with an accompaniment of drawings by Elihu Vedder* (London and New York, 1903).

160 Zhengyan Hu *Shi zhu zhai jianpu*, (Beijing, 1952).

161 'Qi Baishi huaji', (Beijing, 1952).

162 Dante, *La Divina Commedia* (Florence, 1907).

See Mirjam M Foot, *The Henry Davis Gift; Catalogue of North European Bindings. Volume II: A Collection of Bookbindings* (London, 1983), p.276.

163 William Morris, *The Story of the Glittering Plain* (Hammersmith, 1894).

See Howard M Nixon, *British Bookbindings Presented by Kenneth H Oldaker to the Chapter Library of Westminster Abbey* (London, 1982), p.126.

164 George Bernard Shaw, *Saint Joan: a Chronicle Play in Six Scenes and an Epilogue* (London, 1924).

Quote from Bernard C Middleton, *A History of English Craft Bookbinding Technique* (London, 1996), p.300.

165 Thomas Browne, *Religio Medici Urn Burial, Christian Morals, and Other Essays* (London, 1902).

See Marianne Tidcombe, *Women Bookbinders* (London, 1996), p.155.

166–7 Robert Vansittart, *The Singing Caravan* (Newtown, 1932).

See Anthony Dowd *The Special Bindings of Gwasg Gregynog* (2004).

169 H E Bates, *Through the Woods* (London, 1936).

Quote from obituary of Trevor Mansfield by Trevor Jones in *The Independent*, 15 August 1996.

170 Erwin O Christensen, *Primitive Art* (New York, 1955).

See exhibition catalogue *Designer Bookbinders in North America* (London, 2000), p.55; Mirjam M Foot, *The Henry Davis Gift; Catalogue of North European Bindings. Volume II: A Collection of Bookbindings* (London, 1983), p.281.

172 *The Revelation of Saint John the Divine* (Newtown, 1932.).

173 Roger Frène, *Les Nymphes* (Paris, 1921).

Quote from Tracey Rowledge, 'I Walk the Line' in *The New Bookbinder*, 1996, p.38

See Yves Peyré and H George Fletcher, *Art Deco Bookbindings: the Work of Pierre Legrain and Rose Adler* (Paris, 2004); Mirjam M Foot, *The Henry Davis Gift; A Collection of Bookbindings. Volume III: A Catalogue of South European Bindings* (London, 2009), p.270.

174 Paul Valéry, Paul Eluard, R Moutard-Uldry, G Blaizot, L-M Michon, *Paul Bonet* (Paris, 1945).

Quote from Julien Flety, *Dictionnaire des relieurs français ayant exercé de 1800 à nos jours* (1988), p.27.

See Mirjam M Foot, *The Henry Davis Gift; A Collection of Bookbindings. Volume III: A Catalogue of South European Bindings* (London, 2009), p.274.

177 Jean Lurçat, *Géographie animale* (Geneva, 1948).

See Mirjam M Foot, *The Henry Davis Gift; A Collection of Bookbindings. Volume III: A Catalogue of South European Bindings* (London, 2009), p.269; Julien Flety, *Dictionnaire des reliures francais ayant exerce de 1800 a nos jours*, 1988 p.131.

178 William Shakespeare, *Macbeth* [with silk screen images by Ronald King] (Guildford, 1970).

See Philip Smith, 'Awareness, the Creator of Everything' in *The New Bookbinder*, vol. XXIV, 2004, p.87.

181 Nathaniel Tarn, *The Architextures 1–7* (California, 1999).

Quote from Daniel E Kelm, *Poetic Science; Bookworks*, leaflet accompanying exhibition at Smith College Museum of Art, Massachusetts, 2008.

182 John Buckland Wright, *Surreal Times* (Denby Dale, 2000).

See exhibition catalogue *Designer Bookbinders in North America* (London, 2000), p.51.

183 Edward Lear, *The Complete Nonsense of Edward Lear* (London, *c*.1996).

184 Marianne Tidcombe, *The Bookbindings of T J Cobden-Sanderson* (London, 1984).

See Bernard C Middleton, *Recollections. A Life in Bookbinding* (London, 2000), foreword by Marianne Tidcombe.

185 Jan Tschichold, *Early Chinese Colour Prints* (London, 1951).

See 'The Alec Taylor Collection of Commissioned Bindings' in *The New Bookbinder*, vol. XXIV, 2004.

186–7 Alexander Blok, *The Twelve* (Novgorod, 1929).

Quote from http://home.clara.net/kbooks/bookbindsc.htm. Retrieved September 2010.

See 'The Alec Taylor Collection of Commissioned Bindings' in *The New Bookbinder*, vol XXIV, 2004.

ACKNOWLEDGEMENTS

I would like to acknowledge the help given by British Library staff, notably Gill Ridgley, whose suggestions considerably enlivened the content. John Goldfinch has pointed out omissions, made corrections and provided valuable management support. Teresa Harrington has supplied encouragement and good advice.

Thanks, as always, are due to Mirjam Foot, for her teaching and, on this occasion, for checking the text and recommending changes.

The advice of Library specialists including Colin Baker, San San May, Hamish Todd, Muhammad Isa Waley and Frances Wood has been invaluable with regard to the Asian and Oriental bindings. Thanks are also due to Karen Limper-Herz and Wan Lan Sng.

The Library publishing team of Lara Speicher, Jenny Lawson and Sally Nicholls, who selected many bindings for inclusion, have been a source of unfailing encouragement and have frequently gone that extra mile.

This book relies on its images, many taken by Elizabeth Hunter, who has faced the challenge of capturing the vitality of a three-dimensional binding with great patience and care. I would also like to thank designer Kate Slotover whose use of image details has presented bindings in a totally different way.

Patricia Bettis, Oliver Bettis, Peter Bettis, Nick and Susie Marks and Roger Marks deserve my gratitude for their constant encouragement.

I am grateful to Anne Barrett, Archivist & Corporate Records Manager of Imperial College for her 'shoring up' interventions. Thanks to Angela Forester for her unfailing support and to Sharon Eckman, Kady Milne, Max Veiga-Pires and Clive Manley.

The study of bindings requires careful scholarship, and fortunately there are specialists outside the British Library who are happy to share their knowledge. I would like therefore to thank Edward Baynton-Coward who cares for bindings; Robert Harding for his generosity; Nicholas Poole-Wilson who can be relied upon to find a solution to a tricky problem; Jeff Weber for tracking down so many fore-edge paintings and Philip Oldfield who has stayed cheerful in the face of innumerable British armorial queries.

Bookbinding is a subject where non-professionals can and do contribute a great deal. The enthusiasm of those who research bindings in their spare time is exceptional. In this regard, I would like to mention Steve Mandelblatt, and also Lawrence A Miller, who has pioneered new techniques in the digital magnification of images of bookbinding tools.

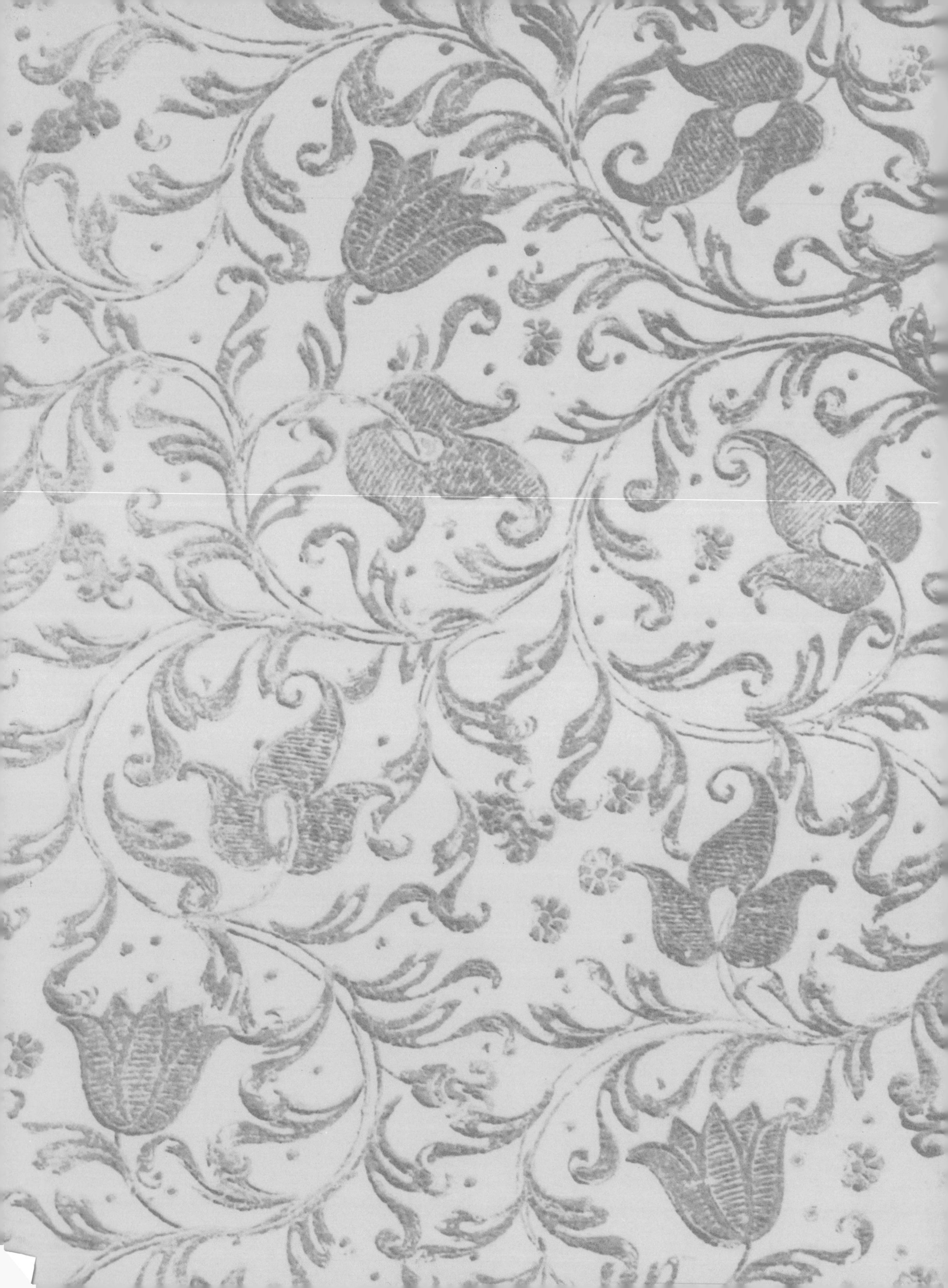